The Orthodox Corruption o

The Orthodox Corruption of Scripture

The Effect of Early
Christological Controversies on
the Text of the New Testament

BART D. EHRMAN

New York   Oxford
OXFORD UNIVERSITY PRESS
1993

Oxford University Press

Oxford   New York   Toronto
Delhi   Bombay   Calcutta   Madras   Karachi
Kuala Lumpur   Singapore   Hong Kong   Tokyo
Nairobi   Dar es Salaam   Cape Town
Melbourne   Auckland   Madrid

and associated companies in
Berlin   Ibadan

Copyright © 1993 by Bart D. Ehrman

Published by Oxford University Press, Inc.,
200 Madison Avenue, New York, New York 10016

Oxford is a registered trademark of Oxford University Press

Translations of the New Testament and the Apostolic Fathers are the author's own. Translations
of the patristic writers—including Justin, Irenaeus, Hippolytus, and Tertullian—are from the
Ante-Nicene Fathers (eds. Alexander Roberts and James Donaldson; Edinburgh; T & T Clark
American Reprint Edition; Grand Rapids: Eerdmans, 1971), unless otherwise indicated. Quotations from Eusebius are drawn from G. A. Williamson, *Eusebius: The History of the Church
from Christ to Constantine* (rev. and ed. Andrew Louth; London: Penguin, 1989). These various
translations have been occasionally modified in order to make them more inclusive.
The *JBL* style sheet has been used for all abbreviations.
Portions of the book incorporate material, slightly revised, from several of the author's earlier
articles, all used here with the permission of the publishers, gratefully acknowledged: "1 John 4.3
and the Orthodox Corruption of Scripture," *ZNW* 79 (1988) 221–43; "The Cup, the Bread, and
the Salvific Effect of Jesus' Death in Luke–Acts," *SBLSP* (1991) 576–91; "The Text of Mark in
the Hands of the Orthodox," *Biblical Hermeneutics in Historical Perspective* (eds. Mark Burrows
and Paul Rorem; Philadelphia: Fortress, 1991) 19–31, found also in *LQ* 5 (1991) 143–56.

Library of Congress Cataloging-in-Publiction Data
Ehrman, Bart D.
The Orthodox corruption of scripture: the effect of early
Christological controversies on the text of the New Testament /
Bart D. Ehrman.
p. cm.   Includes bibliographical references and index.
ISBN 0–19–508078–5
1. Bible. N.T.—Criticism, Textual. 2. Jesus Christ—History of
doctrines—Early church, ca. 30–600. 3. Heresies, Christian—
History—Early church, ca. 30–600. I. Title.
BS2325.E47 1993   225'06—dc20   92–28607

1 3 5 7 9 8 6 4 2

Printed in the United States of America
on acid-free paper

Richard L. Ehrman
in memoriam

Acknowledgments

My personal and institutional debts have grown dramatically with the writing of this work, and here I would like to make a grateful, if partial, acknowledgment. The University of North Carolina at Chapel Hill has been supportive on all levels: the Faculty Research Council generously provided funding through a Faculty Development Grant in 1989, and the Institute for Arts and Humanities, under the direction of Ruel Tyson, awarded me faculty fellowships for the summer of 1989 and the spring of 1992, easing my teaching burden and providing a forum for intellectual discourse with scholars in other fields—a surprisingly rare treat in modern academia. I am also obliged to my graduate research assistants, C. W. Thompson and Kim Haines Eitzen, who proved assiduous in gathering, checking, and evaluating bibliographical items, and, above all, to my colleagues in the Department of Religious Studies, who have tendered their moral and material support every step along the way.

I am especially grateful to my wife, Cindy, whose understanding and good humor grew with the length of the manuscript, and to my daughter, Kelly, and son, Derek, whose capacity for fun and zest for life have always provided a healthy antidote for the long hours that Dad was shut up in his study or lost on another planet.

I would like to extend my special thanks to friends and teachers who have read parts of the manuscript: my two perspicacious colleagues, Peter Kaufman and Laurie Maffly-Kipp, extraordinary for their recognition of inelegance; Elizabeth Clark and Bruce Metzger, whose seasoned judgments have always been graciously extended and gratefully received; and especially Joel Marcus, now of the University of Glasgow, and Dale Martin, of Duke, two exceptional New Testament scholars with mighty red pens, who carefully pored over every word of the manuscript, saving me from numerous egregious errors and infelicities of expression. Those that remain can be chalked up to my willful disposition in refusing (in good heretical fashion) to take their sage advice.

I have dedicated this work to the memory of my father, who did not live to see the completion of the project, but whose intangible presence can be felt throughout. Above all, he taught me that hard work can be rewarding, that humor always has a place, and that some convictions are worthy of a good fight.

Chapel Hill, North Carolina   B.D.E.
February 1993

Contents

Introduction

This is a book about texts and their transmission, about the words of the emerging New Testament and how they came to be changed by scribes of the early Christian centuries. My thesis can be stated simply: scribes occasionally altered the words of their sacred texts to make them more patently orthodox and to prevent their misuse by Christians who espoused aberrant views.

Textual critics are commonly charged—not always unfairly and often from among their own ranks—with disregarding research done in other fields. Narrowly focusing on the manuscripts of the New Testament, they often neglect the *realia* of ecclesiastical and social history that can elucidate features of the text. And restricting their theoretical field of vision to methods espoused by philology and Biblical higher criticism, they bypass important foundational questions, such as what it might mean to refer to the "corruption" of a text that is offhandedly called the "original."

If these charges are leveled against the present study, it will have failed in one of its principal designs. To some extent, the study is meant to dispel the notion that New Testament textual criticism is at best an arcane, if rudimentarily necessary, discipline, of little interest to the enterprises of exegesis, the history of theology, and the social history of early Christianity—let alone to broader interests of scholars in the humanities, such as the history of late antiquity, the use of literature in religious polemics, and the construal of texts.

To be sure, the explicit goal of the study is itself traditional. I am interested in seeing how scribes modified the words of Scripture they inherited. The methods I use to attain this goal are also traditional: they are the critical procedures customarily used to establish any text, classical or biblical. But I am less concerned with interpreting the words of the New Testament as they came from the pens of its authors than with seeing how these words came to be altered in the course of their transcription. Moreover, my understanding of this process of transmission, that is, the way I conceptualize scribal alterations of a text, derives less from traditional categories of philology than from recent developments in the field of literary theory.

In Chapter 1 I sketch the socio-historical context for the phenomenon I will call, and justify calling, the "orthodox corruption of Scripture." Here I deal with the theological debates of the second and third Christian centuries, a period of intense rivalry among various groups of Christians who advo-cated divergent ways of understanding their religion. By the fourth century, one of these groups had routed the opposition, co-opting for itself the desig-nation "orthodoxy" and effectively marginalizing the rival parties as "here-sies." Proponents of fourth-century orthodoxy insisted on the antiquity of their views and embraced certain authors of the preceding generations as their own theological forebears. My study focuses on these earlier Chris-tians—the representatives of an "incipient orthodoxy"—because most scribal alterations of the New Testament text originated during the time of their disputes, that is, in the ante-Nicene age.

In particular, this chapter explores the ways proto-orthodox Christians used literature in their early struggles for dominance, as they produced po-lemical treatises, forged supporting documents under the names of earlier authorities, collected apostolic works into an authoritative canon, and in-sisted on certain hermeneutical principles for the interpretation of these works. The documents of this new canon could be circulated, of course, only to the extent that they were copied. And they were copied by warm-blooded scribes who were intimately familiar with the debates over doctrine that made their scribal labors a desideratum. It was within this milieu of controversy that scribes sometimes changed their scriptural texts to make them *say* what they were already known to *mean*. In the technical parlance of textual criticism—which I retain for its significant ironies—these scribes "corrupted" their texts for theological reasons. Chapter 1 concludes with a proposed theoretical framework for understanding this kind of scribal activity.

The bulk of the study examines the textual tradition of the New Testa-ment for variant readings that appear to have been generated within the con-text of orthodox polemics, specifically in the area of Christology. Using ru-brics provided by the orthodox heresiologists themselves, I devote each of three chapters to a different christological "heresy" of the period: adoption-ism, the view that Christ was a man, but not God; docetism, the view that he was God, but not a man; and separationism, the view that the divine Christ and the human Jesus were distinct beings. Each chapter describes the heresy in question (at least as understood by its orthodox opponents), before discussing textual variants that appear to have been created out of opposition to it. In some instances this requires extensive text-critical argumentation to distinguish the earliest form of the text from modifications effected during the course of its transmission. I have provided a proportionately greater treat-ment to variants of special interest to New Testament exegesis, the develop-ment of Christian doctrine, and the history of interpretation. A much briefer fifth chapter considers textual variants that appear to have arisen in opposi-tion to the patripassianist Christologies of the late second and early third centuries. Chapter 6 summarizes my methodological and material conclu-sions, and proffers some suggestions concerning the significance of the study for understanding the debates between heresy and orthodoxy in early Chris-tianity.

Because this book is intended not only for textual scholars but also for a variety of persons who might find the issues it raises of some relevance to their own academic interests, I suggest two different strategies of reading. For those who are not specialists in the text or interpretation of the New Testament, who are primarily interested in such things as the history of early Christianity, the development of religious polemics, or the effects of texts on readers, I suggest reading Chapter 1, the introductory and concluding sections of each of the main chapters, and the conclusion (Chapter 6). These portions of the book are relatively free from technical jargon; together they set the theoretical framework and historical context of the study, explain in greater detail my overarching thesis, describe the kinds of data I have used to establish this thesis, summarize the conclusions that I think we can draw from these data, and reflect on the broader significance of these conclusions for textual critics, exegetes, theologians, and historians of late antiquity. On the other hand, textual scholars and exegetes who are interested in examining the evidence and evaluating the arguments I have adduced will want to read the detailed exposition of each chapter. It is here that I address a number of textual and exegetical issues that have intrigued scholars throughout the modern era, and demonstrate on a case by case basis how proto-orthodox scribes of the second and third centuries modified their texts of Scripture to make them conform more closely with their own christological beliefs, effecting thereby the "orthodox corruption of Scripture."

The Orthodox Corruption of Scripture

1

The Text of Scripture in an Age of Dissent: Early Christian Struggles for Orthodoxy

Christianity in the second and third centuries was in a remarkable state of flux. To be sure, at no point in its history has the religion constituted a monolith. But the diverse manifestations of its first three hundred years—whether in terms of social structures, religious practices, or ideologies—have never been replicated.

Nowhere is this seen more clearly than in the realm of theology. In the second and third centuries there were, of course, Christians who believed in only one God; others, however, claimed that there were two Gods; yet others subscribed to 30, or 365, or more. Some Christians accepted the Hebrew Scriptures as a revelation of the one true God, the sacred possession of all believers; others claimed that the Scriptures had been inspired by an evil deity. Some Christians believed that God had created the world and was soon going to redeem it; others said that God neither had created the world nor had ever had any dealings with it. Some Christians believed that Christ was somehow both a man and God; others said that he was a man, but not God; others claimed that he was God, but not a man; others insisted that he was a man who had been temporarily inhabited by God. Some Christians believed that Christ's death had brought about the salvation of the world; others claimed that his death had no bearing on salvation; yet others alleged that he had never even died.

Few of these variant theologies went uncontested, and the controversies that ensued impacted the surviving literature on virtually every level. The one level I will be concerned with in the present study involves the manuscripts of the evolving Christian Scriptures—what would eventually be called the New Testament. The New Testament manuscripts were not produced impersonally by machines capable of flawless reproduction. They were copied by hand, by living, breathing human beings who were deeply rooted in the conditions and controversies of their day. Did the scribes' polemical contexts influence the way they transcribed their sacred Scriptures? The burden of the present study is that they did, that theological disputes, specifically disputes

3

over Christology, prompted Christian scribes to alter the words of Scripture in order to make them more serviceable for the polemical task. Scribes modified their manuscripts to make them more patently "orthodox" and less susceptible to "abuse" by the opponents of orthodoxy.

I cannot begin to detail the evidence of this kind of scribal activity without first establishing its socio-historical context. The present chapter inaugurates the study by isolating the kinds of issues that were at stake in the theological controversies of the second and third centuries and by showing how these controversies were generally carried out in the literary realm. Once this polemical milieu is established, I can turn in the chapters that follow to the important, if widely neglected, aspect of these struggles that serves as the object of my primary concern, the "orthodox corruption of Scripture."

Orthodoxy and Heresy: The Classical View

For many students of late antiquity, the disparate forms of early Christian belief suggest a paradigm for understanding the development of the religion. During its first two and a half centuries, Christianity comprised a number of competing theologies, or better, a number of competing Christian groups advocating a variety of theologies. There was as yet no established "orthodoxy," that is, no basic theological system acknowledged by the majority of church leaders and laity. Different local churches supported different understandings of the religion, while different understandings of the religion were present even within the same local church. Evidence for this view has been steadily mounting throughout the present century: we know of the widespread diversity of early Christianity from both primary and secondary accounts, and can sometimes pinpoint this diversity with considerable accuracy.

This is not to say, however, that historians of early Christianity have always shared this perspective. To the contrary, it represents a distinctive shift in thinking, effected only in relatively recent times. Prior to the beginning of this century, virtually all investigators were held, more or less consciously, under the sway of the histories of early Christianity produced during the period itself. Particularly influential was the *Ecclesiastical History* of Eusebius, the fourth-century bishop of Caesarea and so-called "father of church history," whose work set the tone for Christian historiography for ages to come.[1]

Eusebius had a providential view of history that allowed him to paint a rather sanguine picture of Christianity's first three hundred years, a picture somewhat remarkable in view of the external hardships and internal tensions that the religion actually endured. But Eusebius could detect the hand of God behind the scenes at every stage, directing the church's mission and destiny. Believers controlled and sustained by God's spirit faced persecution with boldness, so that the church grew despite opposition, and "heresy" was quickly and effectively overcome by the original and apostolic teaching of the church's vast majority, a teaching that was by definition "orthodox" (in that it was "right").[2]

Eusebius, of course, did not load this term with the technical baggage of a later age. Writing before the Council of Nicea in 325 C.E. in which the Arian controversy found an initial resolution, and well in advance of the Council of Chalcedon (451 C.E.), best known for its highly nuanced, if paradoxical, statement of Christology,[3] Eusebius meant something relatively basic by "orthodox" Christianity: it is that kind of belief preached by the apostles and their followers from the beginning, as opposed to major deviations that came subsequent to it, deviations that deny such indispensible Christian doctrines as the goodness of the creation, or the deity of Christ, or the unity of the Godhead. Heresies, then, are secondary incursions into the community of true believers, inspired—as is all evil for Eusebius[4]—by the devil and his wicked demons, who move willful persons to corrupt the faith proclaimed by the apostles of Jesus (e.g., *Hist. Eccl.* II, 14, 1–3; III, 26–27; IV, 7, 1–3).

Eusebius's treatment of Simon Magus, portrayed as the first heretic and father of them all, exemplifies his views. Quoting the apologist and heresiologist Justin, Eusebius claims that the demonically inspired Simon appeared in the course of the apostolic mission, performing black magic and misleading others to believe that he was himself divine. Not only did Simon advocate blasphemous and false doctrines, he also lived a profligate life, openly consorting with a public prostitute named Helen and engaging in secret and vile rituals. Those whom he misled accepted his heretical teachings and similarly indulged in scandalous practices: "For whatever could be imagined more disgusting than the foulest crime known has been outstripped by the utterly revolting heresy of these men, who make sport of wretched women, burdened indeed with vices of every kind" (*Hist. Eccl.* II, 13, 8).[5]

According to Eusebius, God raised up the Apostle Peter to refute this ignominious heretic in Judea,

> extinguishing the flames of the Evil One before they could spread. . . .
> Consequently neither Simon nor any of his contemporaries managed to form
> an organized body in those apostolic days, for every attempt was defeated
> and overpowered by the light of the truth and by the divine Word Himself
> who had so recently shone from God on humans, active in the world and
> immanent in His own apostles (*Hist. Eccl.* II, 14, 2–3).

Having been defeated in Judea, Simon fled to Rome, where he achieved no little success—away from an apostolic presence—until Peter again appeared and once and for all dispensed with this henchman of Satan through a radiant and powerful proclamation of truth (*Hist. Eccl.* II, 14, 5–6).

There is more vitriol than substance in Eusebius's treatment of Simon. The account nonetheless attests a schematic understanding of the nature of Christian heresy, and it is this basic conceptualization that proved so influential for the traditional assessment of the development of Christian doctrine. The "classical" view of orthodoxy and heresy formalizes this basic understanding.[6] For this view, "orthodoxy" (literally meaning "right opinion") represents the teachings advocated by Jesus and his apostles, spread throughout the world by Christians of the first generation, and attested by the vast majority of believers in all periods.[7] Those who claim to be Christian but who deny any point of this teaching, or who modify it in any significant way, represent "heresy" (literally meaning "choice"), because they have willfully chosen to misrepresent or deny the truth. Heresy, then, is always secondary to the truth and derived from it by a kind of corruption or perversion. For Christian polemicists, such perversions are the minority opinion of depraved individuals; for scholars of the period less interested in these evaluative categories, but nonetheless under the influence of their schematic underpinnings, the resultant heresies are at least derivative in nature. In either case, heresy represents a contamination of the original teachings of Christianity by ideas drawn from the outside, either from Jewish circles or from the teachings of pagan philosophers.

Although Eusebius was certainly responsible for popularizing these views, he by no means invented them. To the contrary, he self-consciously placed himself within a stream of tradition that runs back through a series of earlier writers that he and his orthodox associates embraced as their own theological forebears, writers such as Origen, Hippolytus, Tertullian, Irenaeus, and Justin.[8] Interestingly, the basic understanding of orthodoxy and heresy found among these progenitors of orthodoxy can be traced all the way back to the first century, to the oldest surviving account of Christianity's early years, the New Testament book of Acts.[9]

To be sure, Acts is concerned less with the relationship of theological divergences within early Christianity than with the dissemination of the religion itself. The term "orthodoxy" does not occur here, and "heresy" lacks any pejorative sense, meaning simply "sect."[10] But undergirding Acts' narrative are notions that proved particularly amenable to the classical understanding of orthodoxy and heresy. Here the true faith is based on the eyewitness accounts of the apostles, who execute their mission to spread this faith under the guidance of the Holy Spirit. The apostolic churches stand in complete harmony with one another—even latecomers such as Paul agree with Jesus' original followers on every important point of doctrine and practice. It is true that even here difficulties arise within the Christian communities. But these derive from the greed and avarice of their individual members (5:1–11), or from the thirst for power of those who come to infiltrate their midst (8:4–25). The vast majority of converts remain true to the apostolic message, and theological issues are readily resolved by an appeal to apostolic authority, which in every case—even after serious debate and reflection—reveals the most remarkable of all unities (15:1–29). Disunities can be attributed to "false teachings," that is, to deviations from the theological views of Jesus' own apostles. Such deviations are the perverse doings of degenerate individuals, wolves who infiltrate the flock of sheep to do great damage, but who cannot, ultimately, overcome a church unified behind the original apostolic teaching (10:28–31).

This is the apostolic Christianity to which later ages could appeal. Small wonder, given this canonical precedent, that the views embraced by Eusebius and his peers should receive such a wide hearing, should indeed become the normative way of understanding the development of Christian theology down to the modern age.[11]

The Challenge: Walter Bauer

The classical understanding of the relationship of orthodoxy and heresy met a devastating challenge in 1934 with the publication of Walter Bauer's *Rechtgläubigkeit und Ketzerei im ältesten Christentum*,[12] possibly the most significant book on early Christianity written in modern times. Bauer argued that the early Christian church in fact did not comprise a single orthodoxy from which emerged a variety of competing heretical minorities. Instead, early Christianity embodied a number of divergent forms, no one of which represented the clear and powerful majority of believers against all others. In some regions, what was later to be termed "heresy" was in fact the original and only form of Christianity. In other regions, views later deemed heretical co-existed with views that would come to be embraced by the church as a whole, with most believers not drawing hard and fast lines of demarcation between the competing views. To this extent, "orthodoxy," in the sense of a unified group advocating an apostolic doctrine accepted by the majority of Christians everywhere, did not exist in the second and third centuries. Nor was "heresy" secondarily derived from an original teaching through an infusion of Jewish ideas or pagan philosophy. Beliefs that were, at later times, embraced as orthodoxy and condemned as heresy were in fact competing interpretations of Christianity, one of which eventually (but not initially) acquired domination because of singular historical and social forces. Only when one social group had exerted itself sufficiently over the rest of Christendom did a "majority" opinion emerge; only then did the "right belief" represent the view of the Christian church at large.

As can be seen by this thumbnail sketch, one of the goals implicit in Bauer's reconstruction of orthodoxy and heresy was the deconstruction of the terms of the debate.[13] His discussion clearly assumes, and for most subsequent scholars, clearly demonstrates, that orthodoxy and heresy can no longer be taken to mean either what their etymologies suggest or what they traditionally have implied. Bauer does not assume that orthodoxy refers to "right beliefs" and heresy to "willful misbeliefs." He uses the terms descriptively to refer to social groups, namely, the party that eventually established dominance over the rest of Christendom (orthodoxy) and the individuals and groups that expressed alternative theological views (heresies). In doing so, he implies no value judgment (one group was right, the others were wrong), and does not embrace the traditional notion that one of the groups (orthodoxy) could claim historical priority and numerical superiority over the others.[14]

To establish his claims, Bauer chose certain geographical regions of early Christendom for which we have some evidence—particularly Edessa, Egypt, Antioch, Asia Minor, Macedonia, and Rome—subjected the ancient sources for the Christianity of these regions to the closest scrutiny, and demonstrated that contrary to the reports of Eusebius, the earliest and/or predominant forms of Christianity in most of these areas were heretical (i.e., forms subsequently condemned by the victorious party). To be sure, Christians advocating views later embraced by fourth-century orthodoxy could be found scattered throughout these regions, but in most cases they represented a minority position. Bauer recognized, of course, that most of the writings surviving the conflict attest this later understanding. But this is not at all due to the fact (no longer seen as a fact) that they are broadly representative of nascent Christian opinion. It is rather due to the "accident" of their preservation. It is the winners who write the history: later proponents of orthodoxy (i.e., the victors) preserved the writings of their theological forebears and insisted that they represented the opinion of the majority of Christians from apostolic times.

How, though, did this one form of Christianity—the form that came to influence all major branches of Christendom down to the present day, the form responsible for the Apostles' and Nicene creeds, for Roman Catholicism, Eastern Orthodoxy, and Protestantism—attain a level of dominance? For Bauer this was the kind of Christianity found predominantly in the church of Rome, a church that had always used its superior administrative prowess and its vast material resources to influence other Christian communities.[15] Among other things, the Roman church urged a hierarchical structure on other churches—the monarchial episcopate—which, given the right bishop, could persuade the majority of church members to adopt certain perspectives. And to some degree the Roman influence was purely economic: the manumission of slaves and the purchase of prisoners brought large numbers into their fold, while the judicious use of gifts and alms effected a generally sympathetic hearing of their views.

Specific details of Bauer's demonstration were immediately seen as problematic by a number of his reviewers, and recent times have seen detractors come increasingly to the fore.[16] Many of the arguments have focused on methodology: Bauer has been charged, for good reason, with attacking orthodox sources with inquisitorial zeal and with exploiting the argument from silence.[17] In terms of the substantive issues, virtually all of the regions that Bauer examined have been subjected to further scrutiny, rarely to the advantage of his specific conclusions. The regnant view now is that Bauer probably overestimated the influence of the Roman church[18] and underestimated the extent of orthodoxy throughout the Mediterranean.[19] It would be a mistake, however, to think that the repudiation of Bauer's specific findings has freed scholars to return to the classical formulation of the problem inherited from the early orthodox writers themselves. Quite to the contrary, the *opinio communis* that has emerged is that despite the clear shortcomings of his study, Bauer's intuitions were right *in nuce*: if anything, early Christianity was even less tidy and more diversified than he realized,[20] and contrary to his opinion, we do not need to wait for the second century to begin painting this picture.[21] What later came to be known as orthodoxy was simply *one* among a number of competing interpretations of Christianity in the early period. It was neither a self-evident interpretation nor an original apostolic view.[22] Indeed, as far back as New Testament times, Christianity was remarkably varied in its theological expressions, with the diversity of the New Testament becoming manifest yet more clearly in the diversity of the second and third centuries,[23] when competing groups embraced a wide range of conflicting theologies, and fixed lines of demarcation were in scarce supply.

The Regnant *Opinio Communis:* Orthodoxy and Heresy in Early Christianity

I have not yet provided any evidence for the *opinio communis* that has emerged in Bauer's wake. Given the purpose of the present study—to build on this consensus rather than to establish it—it will be enough simply to cite evidence that has proved generally convincing and that relates in some measure to my own concerns, namely, the ways these early controversies affected the scribes who transmitted the text of the New Testament.

The existence of wildly diverse expressions of Christianity is abundantly attested in our early sources, many of which bemoan the fact as a sorry state of affairs.[24] Thus, the Apostle Paul, our earliest Christian author, defends his understanding of the faith against various "aberrations," for example, Judaizing opponents in Galatia and the enthusiasts of Corinth. Warnings against "heterodox" views permeate the pages of the books later canonized as the New Testament, both from circles that were associated with Paul,[25] and those that were not.[26] So too, the writings of the so-called "church fathers" (i.e., the early writers later embraced by orthodox authors of the fourth century and later) are dominated by anti-heretical concerns, from the occasional epistles of Ignatius in the second century, who on his way to martyrdom warns the churches of Asia Minor against Judaizing and docetic kinds of Christians,[27] through a range of such heresiologists as Justin, Irenaeus, Tertullian, and Hippolytus, who devote prodigious amounts of energy to refuting individuals and groups that propound unpalatable ideas. The point is not that these familiar authors evidence the predominance of the orthodox view. It is rather that they demonstrate the existence of rival groups at every turn, in virtually every region of Christendom of which they, and we, have knowledge.

The spectacular discoveries of heretical writings during the present century have confirmed the existence of such groups and clarified some of their theological characteristics. One would naturally not expect the victors of the struggle to reproduce the literature of their opponents. And indeed they by and large did not, except in excerpts that they quoted simply for purposes of refutation. This means that prior to such fortuitous findings as the library of Gnostic writings uncovered near Nag Hammadi, Egypt, in 1945, our understanding of heterodox Christianity was necessarily one-sided.[28] But with this discovery we now have firsthand information about the beliefs and, to a lesser extent, the practices of one or more variant forms of Christianity.[29] Not the least interesting thing about the Nag Hammadi tractates is that some of them engage in polemics against heretical tendencies of other groups, including the group that eventually acquired dominance—that is, the "orthodox" Christians themselves.[30] Thus, the common notion that heresy was always on the run, always assuming a defensive posture, has now had to be revised. Groups later labeled heretical saw themselves as orthodox (holding the "right beliefs") and sometimes attacked groups that held views they themselves considered aberrant.[31]

It may appear somewhat incongruous that a world of such intense polemic produced few lines of demarcation to differentiate the positions of the various groups. This is nonetheless another clearly attested feature of the period. This is not to say that battle lines were *never* drawn. Polemical confrontations by their very nature require some evaluation of the differences between oneself and one's opponents. In particular, specific differences of opinion emerged in the area of Christology, the area of our most immediate concern. At the same time, the sources clearly show that prior to the establishment of a rigid orthodoxy, with its highly nuanced understanding of the faith, there was a broad tract of unnavigated territory, or to switch the metaphor, a murky penumbra between theological positions that to us might appear quite disparate.[32] In some measure, the absence of clear boundary lines explains Irenaeus's famous lament that Gnostic Christians proved so difficult to uproot from the church because they were far from easy to locate and differentiate from simple believers.[33] To a large degree, of course, the problem of detection resulted from a peculiarity of Gnostic Christians: as we shall see, they had no qualms about professing beliefs espoused by other Christians, while assigning to them a deeper meaning that, to the literally minded Irenaeus and his constituency, proved tantamount to denying them. But on another level the Gnostics could not readily be detected because many of the things they believed had not yet been pronounced as aberrant by any generally recognized authority. Irenaeus was, in a sense, breaking new ground.[34]

The general absence of theological precision in the period can help explain why writers who were later embraced as forerunners of orthodoxy espoused views that look remarkably heretical: both Clement of Alexandria and Origen, for example, acknowledged that Jesus' body could readily change appearance at will—a decidedly docetic notion—with Clement claiming that Jesus ingested food not for nourishment but simply to convince his followers that he actually had a body.[35] Such views were difficult to construe as either orthodox or heretical in the late second century, as the requisite boundary lines had not in every case been clearly drawn. When, at a later time, they *were* drawn, even such "champions of orthodoxy" as Tertullian and, especially, Origen, fell under the strictures of the party they had helped establish.[36] The more nebulous context of their own day also explains why Christians of radically different theological persuasions could be actively involved in the life and worship of the same church. I have already mentioned Irenaeus's general complaints about the Gnostic Christians. We can also speak of specific instances: Valentinus, Ptolemy, and Justin were apparently all accepted as faithful members of the congregation in Rome, at approximately the same time.[37]

Nowhere are the blurred lines separating "acceptable" and "aberrant" beliefs more evident than in the "popular" Christian literature of the second and third centuries, literature, that is, that was written for and read by general audiences not overly concerned with theological niceties. This is especially true of the apocryphal Acts, fictional accounts of the activities of apostles such as Peter, John, and Thomas. These works have always proved puzzling for historians of doctrine, because they represent theological views that at times appear orthodox and at times heretical.[38] This is due both to their nature ("Romances" for popular consumption) and to the time of their writing, when such distinctions cannot have been clearly made. But the blurred lines can also be seen in ostensibly polemical literature, that is, in documents that purportedly work to *resolve* theological issues. This is why christological affirmations made by second- and third-century Christians interested in theological "correctness" can appear so primitive by fourth- or fifth-century standards on the one hand, yet seem to be headed towards orthodoxy, with its paradoxical affirmations, on the other. Ignatius evidently considered his creed sufficiently nuanced to disallow the conceivable aberrations:

> There is one physician
> both fleshly and spiritual
> begotten and unbegotten,
> come in flesh, God,
> in death, true life,
> both of Mary and of God,
> first passible and then impassible,
> Jesus Christ, our Lord (Ign. *Eph.* 7, 2).[39]

Orthodox theologians of a later age would have viewed such a creed as hopelessly vague.

Theological Polemics and the Problem of Nomenclature

I have already intimated that, contrary to what one might expect, the indistinct lines separating theological positions of early Christians do not at all suggest a generally tolerant attitude among the disparate groups. To be sure, some groups may have been tolerant, and many Christians no doubt were indifferent. But the surviving sources are permeated with just the opposite disposition—a kind of spirited intolerance of contrary views, matched only by that shown to nonbelieving Jews and pagans. Before the conversion of the Roman emperor to Christianity and the legal proscription of heresy, even before the earliest councils that were called to adjudicate among theological claims and to depose heretics from positions of authority, as far back in fact as our earliest sources go, we find Christians castigating others who similarly claim the name but differently interpret the religion. Furthermore, all of the intolerant parties appear certain of their own interpretations, which means among other things that every group understood itself to be orthodox (i.e., to subscribe to the "right beliefs") and every other group to be heretical. Such a state of affairs is, of course, natural: when do persons of strong conviction ever believe themselves to be wrong?

Intellectual historians may be able to adjudicate some of the historical claims of the various Christian groups—their claims, that is, to stand in basic continuity with earlier forms of Christian belief.[40] But by their very nature the historical disciplines do not allow for judgments in any ultimate sense concerning who was "right" and who was "wrong." As a result, historians who choose descriptive categories must remain content to assess the surviving data without subjecting them to their own prescriptive norms. Among other things, this means that it is not the historian's task to privilege the claims of one group over another.

We are driven, then, to the problematic character of our labels, the problem that confronted Bauer.[41] *Are* the labels orthodoxy and heresy appropriate for describing early Christian movements? Most scholars recognize that they cannot be used in their traditional sense, namely, to designate the true or original faith on the one hand and secondary aberrations from it on the other. At the same time—in essential agreement with Bauer against some of his detractors—the labels *can* retain their usefulness as descriptions of social and political realities, quite apart from their theological connotations. That is to say, they can serve as adequate descriptions of the group that eventually attained a level of dominance within the Christian tradition, and the multiplicity of groups that it overcame. For it is a historical fact that, owing to a variety of reasons, one group within early Christianity achieved social dominance and enforced its views on other groups that had supported divergent opinions. Looked at in sociohistorical terms, orthodoxy and heresy are concerned as much with struggles over power as with debates over ideas.

Is it appropriate, though, to apply these labels to the competing groups before one of them had attained a level of dominance? Is it sensible to speak of Christian orthodoxy and heresy before the fourth century? In one sense, of course, it is not. If the term orthodoxy means the dominant form of Christianity, then prior to its domination, the views of this group are scarcely orthodox. But even before the decisive events of the fourth century there were individual Christians who espoused views very similar to those that came to dominate, and these writers of the second and third centuries were embraced by the later champions of orthodoxy as their own theological forebears. These forebears came to be quoted as authoritative sources for deciding theological issues, and were presented as true heirs of the apostolic tradition, as reliable tradents who passed along the doctrines of the faith from apostolic to Nicene times.[42] Chief among these were such figures as Ignatius of Antioch, Polycarp, Justin, Irenaeus, Tertullian, Hippolytus, and even Clement of Alexandria and Origen—the writers whose works were preserved by the victorious party and who continue today to influence students concerning "the" nature of Christianity after the New Testament period.

Given this state of affairs, how should these progenitors of the dominant party be labeled? We may be somewhat loath to call them "orthodox," because, on the one hand, their positions had not yet attained a level of dominance, and, on the other, they themselves had not yet defined these positions with the degree of clarity that was later obtained. For this reason, we might best describe them as "proto-orthodox," or say that they represent a kind of "incipient orthodoxy."[43] While these labels do indeed appear more accurate, they are after all merely labels—artificially constructed signifiers—and have the disadvantage of being somewhat cumbersome. I have chosen therefore to use the term orthodox interchangably with these more accurate descriptions to denote the views that later came to a position of dominance in Christianity, and to apply the term heresy to positions adopted by competing parties. I do so fully cognizant of the caveats required by our discussion: these labels are not meant to denote either a theological approbation of the various positions or a historical assessment of the relative numerical superiority of their adherents.

Moreover, by grouping together these early representatives of orthodoxy, these proto-orthodox Christians, I do not mean to say that they attest either a monolithic theology among themselves or a perfect theological continuity with the representatives of fourth-century orthodoxy.[44] I have already noted both the ambiguity of Ignatius's theology and the final condemnation of Origen's. At the same time, there are certain points of continuity among these thinkers and clear lines of development that move toward the fourth century.

It is striking that the lines of continuity are sometimes seen more clearly in what these writers *reject* than in what they *affirm*. Nowhere is this more conspicuous than in their discussions of Christology. All of the proto-orthodox authors appear to have embraced a paradoxical view of Christ, as seen, for example, in the somewhat ambiguous statement of Ignatius already quoted.[45] For them as a group, Christ was in some sense both human and divine. But neither the relationship of Christ's two "natures" nor his relationship to God were yet defined with the kind of nuance one finds in the later christological formulations. The paradoxical affirmations were nonetheless strongly characteristic of these forerunners of orthodoxy, and it was precisely such affirmations that later came to be crystallized in the orthodox creeds.

In no small measure, the christological paradoxes were forced upon these second- and third-century thinkers by their polemical contexts, in which Christians who espoused opposing views denied one or another aspect of the Christian tradition that they themselves found important to affirm, the perplexing results notwithstanding. This is to say, these proto-orthodox Christians opposed anyone who claimed that Christ was a man but not God, and anyone who claimed that he was God but not a man, and anyone who claimed that he was two distinct beings, one divine and one human. It appears to have been the opposition to variant claims that compelled the orthodox of a later generation to espouse such highly paradoxical Christologies as emerge in their creeds.

There is considerable evidence for the existence during the second and third centuries of a variety of Christian groups that made one or another of these "aberrant" claims, and I will be discussing their views at greater length in the chapters that follow, assessing how opposition to them led orthodox scribes to modify their texts of Scripture. Those groups I will describe as adoptionists believed that Christ was a full flesh and blood human being, who was neither pre-existent nor (for most adoptionists) born of a virgin. He was born and he lived as all other humans. But at some point of his existence, usually his baptism, Christ was adopted by God to stand in a special relationship with himself and to mediate his will on earth. Only in this sense was he the "Son of God": Christ was not divine by nature, but was human in every sense of the term. Orthodox Christians opposed such Christologies because, for them, Christ had to be more than a "mere man" for his work of salvation to be effectual. He must himself have been divine.[46]

Other Christians agreed with the adoptionists that Jesus was a full flesh and blood human and that something significant had happened to him at his baptism. For them, however, it was not that he was adopted to be God's Son; instead, at his baptism Jesus came to be indwelt by God. It was then that an emissary from the divine realm, one of the deities of the Godhead, named "Christ," entered into Jesus to empower him for his ministry. Again, at some time prior to his crucifixion, the divine Christ departed from Jesus to return to the Pleroma, the divine realm, leaving him to suffer his fate alone. This is a Christology that I will label separationist, because it posits a division between the man Jesus and the divine Christ. As we will see, it is a view that was prevalent among second-century Gnostics, one that the orthodox found objectionable on a number of grounds.[47]

Other Christians, both among the Gnostics and outside of their ranks (e.g., Marcion), went in another direction, claiming that Jesus Christ was one unified being who was in fact completely divine. Christ was God himself, come to earth for the redemption of his people. But because he was God, he could scarcely have experienced the restrictions and finitude of humanity. And so Jesus was not really human; he only "seemed" or "appeared" to be. Such Christians have been traditionally called docetists (from the Greek word δοκεῖν, meaning to seem or appear).[48] They were opposed by the orthodox, who insisted that Christ's appearance was no deception: he had actually been a real human being, the Word of God made real flesh.

There were other christological views that came to be rejected by the representatives of incipient orthodoxy, views that, for a number of reasons to be spelled out in the course of our discussion, are neither as prominent in the sources nor as germane to this project.[49] Indeed, the picture overall was far more complex than orthodox sources make it out to be. But, as I will repeatedly point out, my concerns for the present study are less with heresy as it actually was than with heresy as it was perceived–perceived, that is, by the forerunners of the party that eventually attained a level of dominance. For it was the perception of their opposition that led scribes of the proto-orthodox party to change the sacred texts that they transmitted. These Christians understood their opponents as denying one or another of the central theses of the faith. For the representatives of incipient orthodoxy, Christ was divine. He was also human. Yet, he was not two beings, but one. The orthodox Christology of the fourth and fifth centuries, that is, the Christology that came to be the dominant position within Christianity, represents a careful working out of the consequences of these paradoxical affirmations.

The Use of Literature in Orthodox Polemics

If it is true that the proto-orthodox writers of the second and third centuries can be understood better by what they rejected than by what they affirmed, we would do well before proceeding much further to consider the character of their opposition to views they considered erroneous.

For the purposes of this sketch I will not concern myself with nonliterary forms of opposition, such as social ostracism, economic pressures, and political machinations. Of course, these measures were sometimes used and often proved effective, and an accounting of them makes for an interesting story. To no small extent, Bauer's own work was concerned with such matters. But the concerns here are more directly related to the literature produced and transmitted by the orthodox party, for it is within the context of their literary endeavors that I can situate the phenomenon of my particular interest, namely, the ways scribes modified their texts of Scripture in light of the polemical contexts within which they worked, altering the manuscripts they reproduced to make them more orthodox on the one hand and less susceptible to heretical misuse on the other.

Polemical Tractates and Popular Literature

The polemical literature of the second and third centuries comprises both tractates aimed directly at exposing and refuting heretical opinion (e.g., the lost works of Justin and Hegessipus, and the more familiar writings of Irenaeus, Hippolytus, and Tertullian[50]) and literary works ostensibly devoted to other ends that happen to take up the polemical task midstream (e.g., the writings of Clement of Alexandria and Origen). As a rule, these writings anticipate Eusebius in their predilection for vitriol, and it is not certain in every case whether the heresiologists correctly understood the positions they attacked, or even, when they did, whether they presented them accurately. In any case, their reports were anything but disinterested. To some extent, the question of accuracy is raised by the accounts themselves, as they occasionally stand at odds with one another.[51] But the question has become particularly perplexing since the discovery of the Nag Hammadi library, where Gnostics appear in some respects quite different from how they were depicted by their orthodox opponents.[52]

The attacks leveled by the orthodox against opposing viewpoints became stereotyped fairly quickly:[53] Heretics are nearly everywhere accused of being self-contradictory, patently absurd, and mutually divergent. In contrast, orthodox Christians are described as consistent, sensible, and unified. Heretics invent doctrines that evidence no clear connection to the apostolic tradition they claim to represent. The orthodox, on the other hand, faithfully transmit the teachings of Jesus and his apostles, as these have been known from the very beginning. Heretics disavow the clear teachings of Scripture, perverting scriptural doctrines with ideas drawn from Judaism or pagan philosophy.[54] The orthodox preserve the teachings of Scripture unsullied, setting forth their original meaning apart from external influences.

Most of these pronouncements are, of course, emotionally charged, and prove less useful for understanding the actual teachings of the heretical groups than for seeing the values of the orthodox: for them truth is unified, coherent, clear, ancient, and apostolic. The heat of the debate is evident in other respects as well, for instance, in the stereotyped charges of moral impropriety leveled with surprising frequency against heretical opponents. Eusebius's claim that Simon and his followers engage in activities "more disgusting than the foulest crime known" is fairly typical.[55] Particularly unsavory are the detailed allegations of vile religious practices: For instance, Irenaeus, whose *Against the Heresies* is the earliest heresiological work to have survived, claims that the Valentinians instruct those who possess the divine seed to give their spirit to spiritual things and their flesh to fleshly things, making indiscriminate copulation not only permissable but a *desideratum* for the *pneumatikoi* (*Adv. Haer.* I, 6, 3–4); that the Carpocratians practice indiscriminate sex, indeed that their theology compels them to violate every conceivable moral law and ethical norm so as to avoid being reincarnated *ad infinitum* (*Adv. Haer.* I, 25, 4); and that the heretic Marcus excites attractive women by inspiring them to speak in tongues, after which they become putty in his lascivious hands (*Adv. Haer.* I, 13, 3).[56] Whether these charges are Irenaeus's own or those of his sources is in many instances nearly impossible to decide. In any case, this kind of Christian polemic scarcely originated with controversies at the end of the second century. Quite to the contrary, Irenaeus was simply applying proven techniques attested as early as the New Testament period itself. Thus, Frederik Wisse has demonstrated that the portrayal of one's enemies as promiscuous reprobates was firmly entrenched in Christian circles by the time of the writing of the letter of Jude.[57] The deviant Christians that Jude opposes are licentious (v. 4); indulge in unnatural lust (v. 7) and corrupt the flesh (v. 8); they carouse together (v. 12) and follow their ungodly passions (v. 18). As Wisse points out, it is hard to imagine such wild folk catching any congregation unawares (v. 4), making it appear that Jude himself is falling back on traditional rhetoric to polemicize against his opponents.[58] Moreover, it is surely significant for recognizing the stereotypical character of these slurs that the Gnostic writings themselves paint an altogether different picture, consistently urging an ascetic life-style for their followers.[59]

The heinous behavior alleged of the heretics stands in sharp relief with the flawless purity of the orthodox. Starting quite early in our period we find stories circulating concerning the refusal of orthodox leaders to commit any immoral act, regardless of the punishment.[60] The most popular form of such stories is the Christian martyrology, a tale that demonstrates the absolute moral rectitude of the faithful, even in the throes of torture and death. The earliest surviving example is the famous *Martyrdom of Polycarp*, the story of an orthodox saint who refuses to compromise his convictions, even when confronted with public scorn and execution. The fictitious elements of the account are significant precisely because the bulk of the report appears to have been derived from an eyewitness.[61] The story in its published form heightens the miraculous character of this great orthodox saint, to whom God bore witness in the hour of his greatest torment. There is some question, in fact, as to whether Polycarp actually suffers any pain when burned at the stake, for the author suggests that God performed a miracle in not allowing the fire to touch the martyr's body, while the sweet smell of incense, instead of the reek of sizzling flesh, filled the air. Even more remarkable—and fully indicative of this champion of orthodoxy's right standing before God—when a soldier pierces Polycarp's side, such a quantity of blood issues forth as to douse the entire conflagration. A later pious redactor has gone even further to portray a dove flying forth from the gash in Polycarp's side, perhaps signifying his yielding up of the (holy) spirit.

Here, then, is a saint whose God thwarts his opponents' plots against him, even in death. The embellishments of the account serve a clear purpose in magnifying a well-known leader of the orthodox movement. It is no accident, in this connection, that it was the orthodox party in particular that stressed the glories of martyrdom and the need to remain faithful even in the face of death. Accounts of such glorious martyrdoms help buttress this characteristically orthodox view, both for the fortification of the martyrs and for the confutation of other Christian groups, notably certain Gnostics, who allegedly spurned the necessity of such stalwart adherence to the faith.[62] In any event, after the circulation of Polycarp's martyrdom, other martyrologies began to make their appearance. In these as well, the martyrs retain their purity before God, refusing to engage in activity of any kind that might compromise their faith. In return, God sustains the orthodox faithful in their time of trial, enabling them to remain courageous and faithful in torture and death—hard proof of the divine approval of their understanding of the faith.[63]

The Canon of Scripture

As I have shown, implicit in the allegations against the heretics of heinous behavior on the one hand and in the accounts of the supreme piety of the orthodox on the other are unexpressed assumptions about the nature of "truth"—for example, that it is related to moral rectitude and sincerity, whereas its opposite, "falsehood," is associated with vile practices and duplicity. For most of the participants in these early Christian debates, "truth" was also closely related to "authority." Just as the early theological debates were in part over power and who was able to wield it, so too they were concerned with authority and who was able to claim it. It is this issue of authority that relates most closely to another use of literature in this polemical context. Not only did different parties produce literature designed to confute the positions of others while establishing the validity of their own, several groups also argued that certain writings from earlier days were endowed with sacred authority, and could be employed to authorize a correct understanding of the religion. This is the movement toward a canon of Scripture, a movement that eventuated in the formation of a "New" Testament, a collection of authoritative books that the orthodox used to arbitrate theological claims. Because the overarching concern of this study is with the alteration of these books in the course of their transcription, we do well to consider the theological importance of this canon for Christians of the early centuries.

The history of the development of the canon is complex, and we are fortunate to have full and competent treatments readily available.[64] Although numerous details concerning the process remain in dispute, certain points of significance for the present discussion appear relatively secure. The earliest Christians already possessed a group of books that they considered authoritative, namely, the Jewish Scriptures—or at least a large portion of them, for this canon had itself not been finalized by the first century.[65] Early within the Christian movement, as early as the New Testament period, some of Jesus' followers began to regard his own teachings as having an authority equal to that of Scripture. The words of Jesus were used to resolve theological and practical issues within early Christian communities and were occasionally qualified as Scripture before the end of the first century.[66] So too the writings of the Apostle Paul were accorded an authoritative status in some circles, where they were similarly ranked among the Scriptures (2 Pet. 3:16). Thus, even within the period of the New Testament, some Christians had begun to adopt a new set of authorities—Jesus and his apostles—to be placed on an equal footing with the Old Testament. It is no accident that the New Testament eventually incorporated Gospels (Jesus) and apostolic writings (Paul and others).

We may never know precisely what role the controversies between orthodoxy and heresy played in the development of the New Testament canon. But this much is certain: one of the salient criteria applied to determine whether a writing could be considered canonical was whether it was "apostolic," meaning, at the very least, that it could reasonably be attributed to Jesus' apostles or their close allies.[67] This does not mean that a mere claim of apostolic authorship guaranteed a book's inclusion among the Scriptures. The orthodox bishop Serapion, who had initially permitted the reading of the *Gospel of Peter* in his congregations, rescinded his decision as soon as he read the book for himself and saw in it a heretical Christology.[68] His decision was followed by the church at large, which also construed the book's contents as nonapostolic. For him, and for them, this meant that decisions concerning "apostolicity" were ultimately based not on claims of authorship per se, but on a book's essential conformity to the *regula fidei,* that is, to the "apostolic" doctrine that orthodox Christians claimed as their own unique possession.

Implicit in such judgments is the entire notion of the "apostolic succession," to which the orthodox made endless appeal in their efforts to ground their teachings in the time-honored truths conveyed by Jesus to his followers and through them to the orthodox churches.[69] These churches were thought to have been established by the apostles, who had appointed their leaders, endowed them with authority, and bequeathed to them their own writings. So, for a heresiologist like Tertullian, the arguments for apostolic succession and Scriptural authority go hand in hand. In his *Prescription of Heretics* he can maintain that orthodox Christians need not even engage heretics in debate over the meaning of Scriptures, the fountain of all truth. The Scriptures belong to the heirs of the apostles, and to them alone. Heretics have no claim to these sacred texts, and so their interpretations of them are automatically ruled out of court.

This is by no means to say that a book's orthodoxy was the only criterion that mattered to church leaders concerned with determining the scope of Scripture. Clearly, the actual antiquity of a writing proved important: the Muratorian canon excludes the *Shepherd* of Hermas, for instance, in part because it was penned "recently."[70] So, too, the judgment of the (orthodox) church at large always proved significant: reluctant Christians of the West ultimately accepted the Epistle to the Hebrews as canonical, in part because it was so widely used by the orthodox of the East. This fate was mirrored by the Book of Revelation, whose widespread usage in the West led to its reluctant acceptance in the East.[71] At the least, we can say that books which could not make credible claims of antiquity or of catholicity were not, for the most part, considered as canonical, however orthodox they might be. At the same time, regardless of its claims to authorship or antiquity, no book that lacked an orthodox appeal would be admitted into the canon. Conformity to the orthodox *regula fidei* was a sine qua non.

In discussions of the canon, the question of criteria is normally kept distinct from the issue of "motivation." The distinction is artificial, however, as some of the issues that motivated the formation of the canon supplied the criteria by which canonical decisions were made. This is seen most clearly with respect to the theological agenda of the party that finalized the grouping of today's twenty-seven book collection. The orthodox rule of faith was the salient criterion for determining a book's canonicity, but it was precisely the struggle to authorize an orthodox system of theology that motivated the movement toward canon in the first place. It is no mere coincidence that whereas there is no hard evidence of a solidified (or solidifying) canon of Scripture before Marcion (e.g., in the Apostolic Fathers), soon thereafter the lines begin quickly to harden. In the middle of the second century, Justin at least knows of the Gospels (which he more frequently calls the "Memoirs of the Apostles") and refers to their usage in the churches.[72] He is remarkably noncommittal, however, concerning which of these "Memoirs" he finds authoritative: he never calls any of them by name and never insists that these and only these comprise Scripture. But the heretic Marcion, his contemporary, began to advocate a well-defined canon of Scripture that conformed closely to his own theological agenda. As we shall see, Marcion's theology was rooted in a kind of radical Paulinism that was divested of any trace of Judaism. His canon comprised the ten Pauline epistles he knew, purged of all Jewish traits (e.g., Old Testament quotations), and one Gospel, evidently a form of Luke, similarly purged. He accepted none of the books of the Old

Testament. Such a canon not only attested his understanding of Christianity (or so he claimed), it also served to justify it.[73]

It comes as no surprise to see orthodox Christians after Marcion strongly urging their own versions of the Christian Bible. Irenaeus, for instance, a self-conscious ally of Justin, but writing some thirty years later, embraces the Old Testament and insists with some vehemence that four Gospels belong to the sacred Scriptures—Matthew, Mark, Luke, and John—and that this number is fixed by nature, because there are, after all, four winds, and four corners of the earth over which Christianity had spread, and therefore necessarily [!] four pillars, the Gospels, upon which it is built (*Adv. Haer.* III, 11, 7–8). Moreover, Irenaeus explicitly attacks a variety of heretics, both for creating Gospels of their own (i.e., nonapostolic books that are therefore to be rejected) and/or for accepting only one of the canonical four. The Ebionites wrongly appeal only to Matthew, those who separate Jesus from the Christ (apparently some kind of Gnostic) only to Mark, Marcion only to Luke, and the Valentinians only to John (*Adv. Haer.* III, 11, 7). For Irenaeus it is the fourfold apostolic Gospel that in its totality preserves the truth of God: anything more or anything less leads to heresy. It scarcely appears to be accidental that between the noncommittal Justin and the emphatic Irenaeus looms the spreading church of the Marcionites, with their established canon of Scripture.

Much more could be observed about the role heresy played in the debates over the canon, but enough has been said to illustrate my point.[74] The new canon might have begun to develop already by the end of the first century, but the conflict among various Christian groups was what led one of them—the one that was later embraced by the champions of the conflict—to argue for the authority and, therefore, the canonicity, of certain writings thought to be apostolic, that is, thought to contain the teachings of Jesus' earliest followers. The rise of the Christian canon thus represents one of the weapons of the orthodox arsenal, used to establish the orthodox version of Christianity to the exclusion of all competing views.

The Hermeneutical Debate

The canonization of textual authorities was not in itself, however, a sufficient weapon for the orthodox party. *Having* a text is not the same thing as *understanding* a text, and, as orthodox Christians knew too well, interpreters can understand texts any way they choose, given adequate ingenuity and a sufficiently flexible hermeneutic. I cannot go into all the complexities of the early hermeneutical debates here, but I can point out that one of the foci of the intra-Christian conflicts in the period was precisely the matter of how one determines the meaning of a text. The issues raised have not yet subsided, as even in our own day literary critics continue to debate whether texts have meanings that are inherent and self-evident. For orthodox church fathers, they do. And it is these self-evident meanings, the clear teachings of Scripture that can be unpacked through accepted methods of grammatical, lexical, and historical exegesis—that is, by what they called "literal" exegesis—that form the center of the apostolic teachings, and consequently, of the orthodox theology.

It is not that the orthodox opposed the use of figurative or allegorical interpretation per se.[75] Even those fathers who insisted most strenuously on construing texts "literally" practiced allegorical exegesis when it suited their purposes, making texts refer to persons, events, or doctrines that in fact appeared unrelated to their literal meanings.[76] But the orthodox did oppose the use of allegory when it imposed meanings on the text that the Scriptures, when literally construed, explicitly rejected. This "misuse" of the method was attacked even among the orthodox for whom allegory was the hermeneutical method of choice: Origen of Alexandria, the most avid advocate of allegory among the orthodox, actually argued for the primacy of the literal sense of Scripture, refusing to acknowledge the force of a literal interpretation only when it proved to be impossible, absurd, or blasphemous.[77] In establishing the primacy of the literal sense, whenever such a sense was possible, Origen explicitly set himself against his Gnostic opponent Heracleon, whose allegorical commentary on the Fourth Gospel was the immediate occasion for his own.

It was in fact the Gnostics that the orthodox found particularly disconcerting when it came to the interpretation of Scripture. As is repeatedly affirmed in the heresiological reports, Gnostic Christians evidenced an uncanny ability to find the details of their own doctrinal systems in texts that appeared at first glance (following the canons of literal exegesis) to discuss nothing of the sort.[78] And so, as shown by examples drawn from Irenaeus, Gnostic interpreters read their belief in a divine realm consisting of thirty aeons in Luke's statement that Jesus was thirty years of age when he began his ministry; they found their notion that the final set of divinities within this thirty-fold Pleroma comprised a duodecad in Luke's reference to Jesus as a twelve-year-old in the temple; and they saw evidence of their doctrine that the twelfth aeon of the duodecad, Sophia, had fallen from the divine realm (the cosmic catastrophe that led to the creation of the material world) in the New Testament story of Judas, one of the twelve who betrayed Jesus.[79] None of these interpretations could be accepted by Irenaeus, who not only found them absurdly unrelated to the literal meanings of the texts themselves, but also directly contradicted by the "clear and plain" (i.e., clear and plain to Irenaeus, not to the Gnostics) teachings of Scripture—that there is only one God, who is the good creator of a good creation, marred not by the fall of a divine being but by the sin of a human. In a harsh but effective image, Irenaeus likened the capricious use of Scripture among the Gnostics to a person who, observing a beautiful mosaic of a king, decides to dismantle the precious stones and reassemble them in the likeness of a mongrel dog, claiming that this was what the artist intended all along (*Adv. Haer.* I, 8).[80]

I do not intend to take sides in this debate. Indeed, for modern interpreters, some of the exegetical leaps that Irenaeus, Tertullian, and their orthodox colleagues made in order to find their own doctrines in Scripture appear no less farfetched than those made by the Gnostics.[81] The point is that regardless of the validity of the argument and regardless of its effectiveness (the Gnostics, at least, did not buy it), orthodox church writers insisted not only that there was an authoritative canon of Scripture filled with apostolic teaching, but that they themselves knew what that teaching was and that it was readily unpacked by means of a literal, that is, historico-grammatical mode of exegesis.

It would be a mistake to think, however, that the Gnostics saw themselves as advocating arbitrary and groundless speculations for texts that in fact had nothing to do with them. In point of fact, the Gnostics claimed authorization for their views by appealing to the apostles, and through them to Jesus, as the guarantors of their doctrines. After his resurrection, Christ had allegedly revealed the secrets of true religion to his apostles, who in turn transmitted them orally to those they deemed worthy. This secret knowledge comprised both the mystical doctrines of the (Christian-) Gnostic religion and the hermeneutical keys needed to find these teachings in the sacred texts, texts that the majority of church people errantly insisted on construing literally. Interestingly enough, the Gnostic Christians could make plausible claims for the apostolicity of their views. Clement of Alexandria reports in his *Stromateis* that Valentinus was a disciple of Theudas, allegedly a follower of Paul, and that Basilides studied under Glaukia, a supposed disciple of Peter (*Strom.* 7, 17, 106).[82] On the surface of it, these genealogical links are no more or less credible than those found in the bishop lists of the orthodox historian Eusebius, who ties the regnant leadership of the major Christian sees to the apostles, largely through otherwise unknown intermediaries.[83]

Nor did Gnostic Christians need to rely exclusively on secret oral traditions to establish their claims to represent the apostolic religion. For they, along with other Christian groups vying for converts, possessed literary works published in the names of the apostles that could be used—even if read literally—to support their interpretations. Orthodox writers claimed that these books had been forged, a claim that, as far as it goes, is absolutely credible. Indeed, our evidence suggests that the practice of forgery was remarkably widespread, and that all sides (the early representatives of orthodoxy included) were occasionally liable to the charge.

The Use of Forgery

The creation and dissemination of ancient forgeries makes for a fascinating area of study, one that has been rigorously pursued in modern scholarship.[84] That Christians were engaged in such activities comes as no shock to scholars of the period: accusations of forgery rifled back and forth, and there is at least one instance of a forger—he happens to have belonged to an orthodox church—confessing to the deed.[85] Unlike the modern Christian world, which by and large knows only twenty-seven books from the early Christian period, this was a world that saw "apostolic" gospels, acts, epistles, and apocalypses by the dozens, most of them pseudonymous, nearly all of them late—from the second century and beyond.[86]

The frequent occurrence of forgery in this period does not suggest a basic tolerance of the practice. In actuality, it was widely and strongly condemned, sometimes even within documents that are themselves patently forged.[87] This latter ploy serves, of course, to throw the scent off one's own deceit. One of its striking occurrences is in the orthodox *Apostolic Constitutions,* a book of ecclesiastical instructions, ostensibly written in the name of Jesus' apostles, which warns its readers to avoid books falsely written in the name of Jesus' apostles (VI, 16). One cannot help thinking of 2 Thessalonians, which cautions against letters falsely penned in Paul's name (2:1–2); many New Testament scholars believe that 2 Thessalonians is itself non-Pauline.

We have seen that Irenaeus accuses various heretical groups of producing and distributing forged documents. We are fortunate to have some of these documents now in our possession, in part due to the remarkable discoveries of the present century. As already seen, however, heretics were not alone in producing such works. The *Apostolic Constitutions* is in fact an orthodox production, as is 3 Corinthians, forged by the presbyter of Asia Minor whom Tertullian condemns. So far as can be determined, in neither case was the deceit meant for ill: the deposed presbyter claimed that he did it "out of love for Paul," meaning, we might suppose, that his use of Paul's pen to condemn a docetic Christology was meant to honor the apostle's memory as one who strove for orthodoxy even from beyond the grave. Similar motivations—that is, the grounding of one's views in the writings of the apostles—occurred quite early in the Christian tradition, as the questionable authorship of many of the canonical writings themselves attest. Along with 2 Thessalonians, for which the jury is still out, we can mention the two other deutero-Pauline Epistles of Colossians and Ephesians, whose authorship remain seriously disputed after decades of intensive research. And notwithstanding attempts to reopen the debate, the Pastoral Epistles are almost universally regarded as pseudonymous, as is 2 Peter. The authorship of 1 Peter, on the other hand, remains an open question.[88]

It would be anachronistic to claim these New Testament specimens as orthodox forgeries. If we cannot really speak of orthodoxy per se in the second and third centuries, we can scarcely speak of it during the New Testament period itself. What is clear, however, is that these pseudepigraphs proved useful to the incipient orthodoxy of our period in its struggles with various forms of heresy. It is also clear that incentives for forgery did not expire when the urgency of assembling a Christian canon had passed away. Quite to the contrary, the evidence suggests that with the passing of time there came an increased rate of production of forgeries from all sides. It is especially intriguing to note that in the fourth century and later, as the proto-orthodox writers themselves came to be valued as theological authorities by their orthodox descendants, documents came to be forged in *their* names to provide early instances of theological precision otherwise unattested in writings of the ante-

Nicene age. Most of these forgeries—for example, those in the names of Ignatius and Dionysius—were not exposed until modern times.[89]

Even within our period one finds forged documents that similarly serve theological ends in justifying the ideas of proto-orthodoxy by putting them on the lips of the apostles. Rather than becoming sidetracked into a lengthy account, I will simply mention two prominent examples. The *Epistula Apostolorum* is a letter allegedly written by Jesus' eleven remaining disciples after his resurrection from the dead. A number of doctrinal themes recur throughout the work, which in part mimics the revelation discourses so cherished by the Gnostics. Chief among these themes, interestingly, are two that represent an orthodox response to Gnostic teachings particularly associated with these revelation discourses: the doctrines of the resurrection of the flesh and its christological corollary, the real fleshliness of Jesus. Here the eleven closest followers of Jesus, and through them Jesus himself, assure their readers that the Gnostics err in rejecting these doctrines, for Jesus actually did take on real flesh in his incarnation, and those who believe in him will themselves be raised in the flesh.[90]

A document that proved far more significant for the actual development of Christian theology was the second- or third-century *Protevangelium Jacobi*.[91] Here is recorded, in greater detail than in any New Testament Gospel, the events leading up to Jesus' birth. Beginning with the miraculous birth of Mary, the author (allegedly James, the brother of the Lord) goes to great lengths to show that Jesus really was born of a woman, who was nonetheless a pure vessel for the Son of God in that she herself had been born miraculously and remained a virgin. Both of these points allowed this forged account to serve an important instructional purpose for orthodox believers, especially as they confronted groups of Ebionite Christians who denied the notion of Jesus' miraculous birth altogether. More than anything else, however, the work came to advance the church's developing Mariology, a matter that relates only tangentally to the discussion at hand.

Summary: The Literary Struggle for Orthodoxy

I have discussed the polemical relationships of various groups of second- and third-century Christians in order to set the context for my study of the "orthodox corruption of Scripture." This was an age of competing interpretations of Christianity. The competition cannot be conceived as a purely ideational struggle, however, since it consisted of more or less well-defined social groups, each of which pressed for its understanding of the religion, but only one of which proved successful. The members of the victorious party had all along claimed their interpretations to be ancient and apostolic, and argued that their competitors espoused corrupted versions of the primitive faith. They pressed home these claims to such an extent that their views became normative for Christianity in their own day and determinative of the course of Christianity for time to come.

The Christians who represented these views in the second and third centuries were not, strictly speaking, orthodox in either the traditional or modern understandings of the term. They did not understand the faith with the nuance and sophistication later required of orthodox thinkers, nor did they yet (apparently) comprise an absolute majority. But as ideational ancestors of the party that was destined to prevail—speaking metaphorically rather than theologically—these Christians did represent a kind of incipient orthodoxy, and can well be labeled proto-orthodox.

Although these Christians could not know that their views would eventually predominate, they fought diligently toward that end. One significant arena of their engagement was literary. The literary assault included detailed descriptions and castigations of heretical positions, fabricated accounts of the heinous behavior of their opponents and of the moral rectitude of their own leaders, and concocted writings allegedly written by the original followers of Jesus, in which their own positions were advanced and those of their opponents were attacked. There was as yet no "New Testament" per se, although there was certainly a movement afoot to create one, to collect a group of "apostolic" authorities that attested the orthodox understanding of the faith. At the same time, the proto-orthodox group began to insist that the textual authorities of this canon be interpreted in certain (literal) ways. This was a rearguard move to prevent the "misuse" of the texts in the hands of heretics who proved adept at finding their own aberrant doctrines wherever they chose to look for them.

Despite the growing sense among proto-orthodox Christians that the apostolic writings were authoritative bearers of tradition, these documents were not themselves inviolable in any real, material sense.[92] As we move beyond the context of our study into the study itself, this is the one point we must constantly bear in mind. The texts of the books that were later to comprise the New Testament were neither fixed in stone nor flawlessly reproduced by machines capable of guaranteeing the exactitude of their replication. They were copied by hand—one manuscript serving as the exemplar of the next, copied by errant human beings of differing degrees of ability, temperament, and vigilance. The earliest scribes were by and large private individuals, not paid professionals, and in many instances their copies were not double-checked for accuracy.[93] As we now know so well, mistakes—scores of them—were made.

Were any of these "mistakes" intentional alterations? The copyists were warm-blooded Christians, living in a world of wide-ranging theological debates; most scribes were surely cognizant of these debates, and many were surely participants. Did their polemical contexts affect the way these Christians copied the texts they construed as Scripture? I will argue that they did, that scribes of the second and third centuries in fact altered their texts of Scripture at significant points in order to make them more orthodox on the one hand and less susceptible to heretical construal on the other.

Orthodox Modifications of the Text of Scripture

It is somewhat surprising that scribal changes of the text of Scripture have rarely been examined in connection with the polemical debates of the second and third centuries, either by historians of the conflict or by specialists in the text.[94] Of course the basic idea that Christian scribes would alter their texts of Scripture in order to make them "say" what they were already thought to "mean" is itself nothing new. From the earliest of times we know that Christians were concerned about the falsification of texts—including, sometimes, their own. The fear is expressed by the first-century prophet John, who uses a standardized curse formula to protect the text of his Apocalypse from malevolent tampering (22:18–19).[95] Somewhat later the proto-orthodox authors Irenaeus and Dionysius of Corinth evidence similar concerns,[96] whereas Origen explicitly attacks an opponent, the Valentinian Candidus, for falsifying the transcript of their public debate.[97] The falsification of Origen's own writings subsequently became fashionable, as they alternately inspired and horrified the orthodox of a later age.[98] But who would dare to falsify Scripture? According to Dionysius, the heretics would: "It is therefore no wonder that some have attempted even to falsify the Scriptures of the Lord, when they have done the same in writings that are not at all their equal" (Eusebius, *Hist. Eccl.* IV, 23).[99]

Dionysius was not alone in making such accusations. In fact they became a standard feature of the polemics of the period.[100] While a variety of Christian groups may well have made the charge, we know it best from the pens of the orthodox, a fact not altogether surprising, as theirs are the works that have survived. Above all, the heresiologists found Marcion culpable on these grounds, since, as we have seen, they uniformly believed he had surgically removed unpalatable portions of both the Pauline epistles and Luke—passages that undermined his claims that Christ was alien to the God of the Old Testament, his creation, and his Scriptures, that Christ was in fact the Stranger-God himself on earth, come only in the "appearance" but not the reality of human flesh.[101] Interestingly, heretical groups with just the *opposite* theological proclivities were charged with precisely the *same* scribal activities. The orthodox historian Eusebius found the Roman adoptionists guilty on this score. These second- and third-century heretics were followers of Theodotus the Cobbler, who asserted that Christ was a "mere man" and not at all divine. Eusebius cited with approval an anonymous source that claimed the Theodotians had interpolated this notion into their texts of Scripture, offering as proof the fact that copies produced by the group were still available, and could be compared with one another to reveal their tendentious character.[102] Nor were the Gnostics exempt from such charges, even though, as we have observed, orthodox heresiologists considered them somewhat exceptional in their abilities to find their doctrines in just about any text, regardless of its wording.[103] Nonetheless, they too were accused of altering Scripture in accordance with their own notions, as when Tertullian accused them of modifying the prologue to the Fourth Gospel so as to eliminate the idea of Jesus' miraculous birth ("who was born not of blood nor of the will of the flesh nor of the will of man, but of God"; 1:13), and to introduce the notion of *their own* ("who *were* born . . .").[104]

What is revealing about this final instance is that Tertullian was clearly wrong. It was not the Valentinian Gnostics who modified the passage, but, as we shall see, Tertullian (or more likely, an orthodox scribe before him).[105] There is no Greek manuscript that attests Tertullian's form of the text, and only a solitary witness of the Old Latin. This leads to the striking observation that despite the frequency of the charge that heretics corrupted their texts of Scripture, very few traces of their having done so have survived antiquity.[106] In part this may simply show that the winners not only write the history, they also reproduce the texts. Orthodox Christians would not be likely to preserve, let alone replicate, texts of Scripture that evidence clear heretical biases. Did they, however, produce copies of Scripture that support their own biases? I will try to amass evidence that they did, but first we must deal with preliminary questions that make this evidence credible, that is, with certain kinds of textual *realia* presupposed by my study.

First, a word about the extent of textual variation among the surviving manuscripts. Although the proto-orthodox Christians of the second and third centuries began to ascribe canonical standing to the writings that later became the New Testament and simultaneously to urge the literal interpretation of their words, they regrettably did not preserve any of the autographs. To be sure, they may not have been able to do so. The autographs may well have perished before the second century. In any event, none of them now survive. What do survive are copies made over the course of centuries, or more accurately, copies of the copies of the copies, some 5,366 of them in the Greek language alone, that date from the second century down to the sixteenth.[107] Strikingly, with the exception of the smallest fragments, no two of these copies are exactly alike in all their particulars. No one knows how many differences, or variant readings, occur among the surviving witnesses, but they must number in the hundreds of thousands.[108]

Not all textual variants, however, are created equal. By far the vast majority are purely "accidental," readily explained as resulting from scribal ineptitude, carelessness, or fatigue. Haphazard scribal blunders include such things as misspelled words, the inadvertent omission of a word or line, and its obverse, the meaningless repetition of a word or line. The reality is that scribes, especially in the early centuries before the production of manuscripts became the domain of the professional, were not as scrupulous in their transcriptions as one might have hoped or expected.[109] And even the most conscientious were not free from error.

My interest in the present study, however, is not with accidental changes but with those that appear to have been made intentionally. It is not easy to draw a clean line between the two. Even a misspelled word may have been generated deliberately, for example, by a scribe who wrongly assumed that his predecessor had made an error. Nonetheless, there are some kinds of textual changes for which it is difficult to account apart from the deliberate activity of a transcriber. When a scribe appended an additional twelve verses to the end of the Gospel of Mark, this can scarcely be attributed to mere oversight.

This is not to say that scholars can speak glibly of scribal "intentions," if we mean by that an assessment of an individual scribe's personal motivations:[110] we do not have access to scribes' intentions, only to their transcriptions. For this reason it is easier—and theoretically less problematic—to speak metaphorically of the intentions of scribal *changes* rather than the intentions of *scribes*, conceiving of the category in strictly functional terms. Some changes of the text function to harmonize it with parallel passages. Others function to eliminate possible grammatical inconcinnities or exegetical ambiguities or embarassments. Still others function to heighten clarity or rhetorical force. And a significant number of others, I will argue, function to establish the orthodox character of the text, either by promoting more fully an orthodox understanding of Christ or by circumventing the heretical use of a text in support of an aberrant teaching.[111]

How many such "intentionally orthodox" modifications actually derive from the period of my concern? It proves to be a key question for this study, for although I am interested in changes of the text generated during the christological debates of the second and third centuries, most of the New Testament manuscripts actually date from the fourth century and beyond. With such sparse evidence from the early period, it is not always possible to locate a particular variant reading in a manuscript of the time. The problem is more apparent than real, however, as most scholars are convinced that this scant attestation is purely a result of the haphazard and fragmentary character of the surviving witnesses. The majority of textual variants that are preserved in the surviving documents, even the documents produced in a later age, originated during the first three Christian centuries.[112]

This conviction is not based on idle speculation. In contrast to the relative stability of the New Testament text in later times, our oldest witnesses display a remarkable degree of variation. The evidence suggests that during the earliest period of its transmission the New Testament text was in a state of flux, that it came to be more or less standardized in some regions by the fourth century, and subject to fairly rigid control (by comparison) only in the Byzantine period.[113] As a result, the period of relative creativity was early, that of strict reproduction late. Variants found in later witnesses are thus less likely to have been generated then than to have been reproduced from earlier exemplars. Additional evidence for this view derives from the fact that although our earliest witnesses are widely divergent both among themselves and in relation to the later types of text, they scarcely ever attest individual textual variants that do not also appear in one or another later source.[114] Thanks to the discovery of early papyri during the present century, readings that may have appeared unusual when we had only later witnesses are now known to have occurred early. What, then, does this indicate about unusual readings of later sources that do not happen to be attested in the fragmentary remains of the ante-Nicene age? Although the merits of the claim need to be assessed on a case-by-case basis—as will happen in the course of this study—most scholars agree that even such "late" readings are by and large best understood as deriving from documents of the first three centuries, documents that simply have not chanced to survive the ravages of time.[115]

It may be useful to summarize the textual *realia* discussed so far. The vast majority of all textual variants originated during the period of our concern, the second and third centuries.[116] This was also a period in which various Christian groups were actively engaged in internecine conflicts, particularly over Christology. A number of variant readings reflect these conflicts, and appear to have been generated "intentionally." Scribes sometimes changed their manuscripts to render them more patently orthodox, either by importing their Christology into a text that otherwise lacked it or by modifying a text that could be taken to support contrary views.

Textual Changes as Textual Corruptions

Before commencing the study of such variant readings, however, I must justify my designation of them as orthodox corruptions of Scripture. The term "corruption" derives from traditional text-critical discourse, in which the "original" text (i.e., as it was actually penned by an author) is the dominant concern, with changes of that text—whether accidental or intentional—representing contaminations of that original.[117] Not everyone, however, assigns a pejorative sense to the term. For some scholars, corruption refers neutrally to any scribal change of a text. This neutral usage is found particularly among critics who recognize the problem of privileging the original text over forms of the text created during the course of transmission. To be sure, the idea of establishing a text as it came from the pen of its author may prove useful for exegesis (i.e., for exploring what an author might have meant, for which, presumably, we need to have access to his or her words), but in itself it overlooks the possibilities of using subsequent forms of the text for understanding the history of exegesis and, consequently, for contributing to our knowledge of the history of Christianity.

This takes me now to a different theoretical understanding of the significance of textual variation in the New Testament manuscripts, an understanding that derives less from traditional categories of originals and corruptions than from modern literary theories that call these categories into question.[118] Because scribes occasionally changed their texts in "meaningful" ways, it is possible to conceptualize their activities as a kind of hermeneutical process. Reproducing a text is in some ways analogous to interpreting it.[119] In construing this analogue, it is useful to reflect on the conventional wisdom of biblical scholarship, that exegesis (interpretation) without presuppositions is impossible, that one's presuppositions—indeed, all of one's dispositions, ideologies, and convictions, not only about the text but about life and meaning itself—cannot possibly be discarded, removed like so much excessive clothing, when coming to a text. In fact, there is a kind of symbiotic relationship between texts and interpretations: it is not simply a one-way street in which texts yield their meaning, but a two-way street in which the meaning that one brings to a text in part determines how the text is read and understood. Some literary theorists have gone even farther, arguing that the basic assumptions, values, and desires (both conscious and unconscious) that readers bring to a text actually determine its meaning.[120] In this view, the meanings of texts are never self-generating, but are necessarily forged by living and breathing human interpreters who are bound to an intricate network of social, cultural, historical, and intellectual contexts, contexts that affect both who a person is and how he or she will "see" the world at large, including the texts within it. According to these theorists, this nexus of factors does more than *influence* the way texts are interpreted; it actually *produces* interpretations.[121]

To be sure, few readers realize that they are *generating* meanings from a text, that is, that they are employing culturally conditioned interpretive strategies to make sense of the words on a page. Interpretive strategies, according to the common assumption, are necessary only for ideologically slanted (i.e., biased) interpretations, not for understanding a text's "common-sensical" or "obvious" meaning. But in point of fact, even common sense requires (by definition) a community of like-minded readers, a group of interpreters who share basic assumptions both about the world and about the process of understanding. This is why, given a different world and a different set of assumptions, any text—say, the parable of the Good Samaritan—can mean radically different, even exclusive, things, for example, to an allegorizing Alexandrian of the fourth century, an Anglican parson of the nineteenth, or a Marxist academic of the twentieth. None of these interpreters need believe he or she is seeing something in the text that is not really there; none is necessarily duplicitous in his or her construals. Their different, sometimes unrelated, understandings are rooted as much in who they are and how they perceive their world as in the words printed on the page.[122]

What, though, has this to do with our study of scribes and their transcriptions? On the practical level, very little. As I have already indicated, this study pursues a traditional line of historical inquiry (determining the earliest available form of a text and the changes made subsequent to it) and does so according to recognized canons of criticism, long applied by classicists and biblical scholars for establishing their texts. Anyone with a different set of hermeneutical assumptions—for example, most historical critics who may be interested in the study—will find nothing offensive in either the questions it asks or the methods it applies. But the theoretical question of interpretation does have a bearing on the *significance* of the study. Its significance, at least as I see it, lies in showing what scribes were actually *doing* when they copied and modified their texts. As I have suggested, these scribal activities are analogous to every act of reading and interpretation. All of us interpret our texts and ascribe meaning to them, and in that sense we "rewrite" them (i.e., we explain them to ourselves "in our own words"). The scribes, somewhat more literally, actually *did* rewrite them. And not infrequently it was precisely their understanding of these texts that led them to rewrite them—not only in their own minds, which all of us do, but actually on the page. When we rewrite a text in our minds so as to construe its meaning, we interpret the text; when a scribe rewrites a text on the page (i.e., modifies its words to help fix its meaning) he physically alters the text. On the one hand, then, this scribal activity is very much like what all of us do every time we read a text; on the other hand, by taking this business of rewriting a text to its logical end, scribes have done something very different from what we do. For from the standpoint of posterity, they have actually transformed the text, so that the text henceforth read is quite literally a different text. Only from this historical perspective can one apply the standard text-critical nomenclature to this scribal activity and call it the corruption of a text.

I am therefore consciously employing irony in my denotation of the orthodox corruptions of Scripture. On the one hand, I am using the term in its technical text-critical sense of "alterations of a text"; at the same time, I am using it to refer to the effect of rereading or rewriting of texts in the history of their transmission, claiming not that scribes misunderstood their texts and perverted them (as if corruption were necessarily pejorative), but that in their transmissions of the text they engaged in much the same process of interpretation and interaction that we all engage in, rereading and therefore rewriting our texts at every turn.

About the Study

Each of the following chapters begins with a sketch of a major christological heresy, its leading spokespersons, and salient beliefs. The bulk of each chapter analyzes textual variations that can plausibly be attributed to the orthodox opposition to these beliefs. In terms of method, the analysis proceeds along customary lines. At every point of variation I work to establish the earliest form of the text, employing standard kinds of text-critical argumentation (evaluating, that is, the strength of each reading's external attestation and such things as intrinsic and transcriptional probabilities). Once I have established—or at least contended for—one form of the text as antecedent to the others, I evaluate the variant readings in relation to the christological debates of the second and third centuries. Given my concern to see how these debates affected the manuscript tradition itself, I will consider only those textual variants that appear in the manuscripts. Among other things, this means that I will not evaluate readings that are found only in patristic sources; this kind of data may indicate how the text was quoted by the church fathers, but not, necessarily, how it was transcribed. Nor will I take into account variant modes of punctuation that prove christologically significant, as these cannot be traced back to the period of our concern, when most manuscripts were not punctuated.[123]

Other methodological issues will be discussed in the course of the study itself. It *is* necessary, however, to make a final disclaimer. I do not intend to note every instance of christologically motivated variation that has survived antiquity. To do so would require access to comprehensive collations of every surviving witness, collations that do not yet exist and possibly never will. I *can* claim to have found a large number of such variants, perhaps most of the ones that ultimately prove significant for the history of the text and for exegesis. But I almost certainly have not uncovered them all. The following enumeration and discussion, then, is extensive and, I trust, representative; it is not exhaustive. The truth of the matter is that we may never recognize the full extent of the orthodox corruption of Scripture.[124]

Notes

1. For recent treatments, see Robert M. Grant, *Eusebius as Church Historian*, and Glenn F. Chesnut, *The First Christian Histories*. For a brief discussion, Kirsopp Lake's introduction in the Loeb Classical Library is still quite useful *(Eusebius: The Ecclesiastical History)*.

2. See Glenn F. Chesnut, "Radicalism and Orthodoxy: The Unresolved Problem of the First Christian Histories," and his convenient discussion in *First Christian Histories*, 127–30.

3. "[O]ur Lord Jesus Christ [is] at once complete in Godhead and complete in manhood, truly God and truly man, consisting also of a reasonable soul and body; of one substance *[homoousias]* with the Father as regards his manhood; like us in all respects, apart from sin; . . . one and the same Christ, Son, Lord, Only-begotten, recognized in two natures, without confusion, without change, without division, without separation; the distinction of natures being in no way annulled by the union, but rather the characteristics of each nature being preserved and coming together to form one person and subsistence *[hypostasis]*, not as parted or separated into two persons, but one and the same Son and Only-begotten God the Word, Lord Jesus Christ" (translated in Henry Bettenson, *Documents of the Christian Church*).

4. *Hist. Eccl.* V, pref., 3–4; VI, 39, 5; X, 8, 2. See further Chesnut, *First Christian Histories*, 79–80. In this Eusebius is simply following the lead of his theological forebears, such as the apologist Justin Martyr (e.g., I *Apol.* 14, 26, 54–58; II *Apol.* 5).

5. Here and throughout, unless otherwise indicated, I will use the translation of Eusebius found in G. A. Williamson, *Eusebius: The History of the Church from Christ to Constantine.*

6. See especially H. E. W. Turner, *The Pattern of Christian Truth*, 3–35.

7. This teaching comprised the so-called *regula fidei* (or *regula veritatis*), the rule of faith understood as a kind of sine qua non for believers. See, for example, Irenaeus, *Epideixis* 6; *Adv. Haer.* I, 22, 1; III, 11, 1; IV, 35, 4; Tertullian, *Prescription* 13, Origen, *de Princ.* I, preface. Included in the *regula fidei* were such things as the belief that the one true God is the creator of heaven and earth, and that He sent his only Son Jesus Christ to be born of the Virgin Mary and to become fully human; Christ lived a completely human life, and died on the cross for the sins of the world, in fulfillment of the divinely inspired Scriptures (the Old Testament). He was then raised bodily from the dead and exalted to heaven, whence he will come in judgment at the end of the age. For useful discussions of the *regula*, see L. William Countryman, "Tertullian and the Regula Fidei"; A. Benoit, *Saint Irénée, Introduction à l'étude de sa théologie;* and Eric Osborn, "Reason and the Rule of Faith in the Second Century A.D."

8. Thus Origen's oft-quoted remark "All heretics are at first believers; then later they swerve from the rule of faith" (*Commentary on the Song of Songs*, 3; compare Clement of Alexandria, *Strom.* 7.17.). See also Tertullian's argument in *Prescription*, 29: "[Were there] heresies before true doctrine? Not so; for in all cases truth precedes its copy, the likeness succeeds the reality. Absurd enough, however, is it, that heresy should be deemed to have preceded its own prior doctrine, even on this account, because it is that (doctrine) itself which foretold that there should be heresies against which [people] would have to guard!"

9. Much of Book II of Eusebius's ecclesiastical history consists of a summary of the narrative of Acts, with details and anecdotes supplied from other sources (see *Hist. Eccl.* II, pref., 2).

10. Acts 5:27; 15:5; 24:5, 14; 26:5. See Marcel Simon, "From Greek Haeresis to Christian Heresy."

11. The precedent is not limited to Acts: the Pastoral epistles and 2 Peter—pseudonymous writings within the canon (see p. 23)—show "Paul" and "Peter" warding off aberrations of the truth that the apostles had themselves conferred upon their followers (e.g., 1 Tim 6:20; Tit 1:9; and 2 Pet 3:2). See the discussion of Wolfgang A. Bienert, "Das Apostelbild in der altchristlichen Überlieferung," in Wilhelm Schneemelcher and Edgar Hennecke, *Neutestamentliche Apokryphen*. So too, Frederik Wisse has convincingly demonstrated that the letter of Jude employs a traditional understanding of the relationship of heresy and orthodoxy. See his study, "The Epistle of Jude in the History of Heresiology." None of this is to say that Eusebius's views held sway *simply* because they found canonical precedent. The orthodox party found them to be useful on their own merits as well.

12. *Beiträge zur historischen Theologie.* All page references will be to the English translation of the second edition.

13. Bauer has sometimes been attacked for retaining the terms orthodoxy to refer to the form of Christianity that *eventually* became dominant and heresy to refer to everything else. But the attack can scarcely be justified: Bauer was quite right that changing the terms would only create confusion (they are, after all, only ciphers). The only rationale for doing so would be to designate which group actually *was* in the majority position; but these positions are relative, shifting in different places over time (pp. xxii–xxiii).

14. Nor, because he is concerned about the social and political characteristics of early Christian controversies, does he construe the debate in strictly theological terms. He has occasionally been taken to task for this by scholars who continue to insist on essentialist understandings of Christianity and who, as a consequence, see as one of their primary tasks determining the "appropriateness" of the various developments in the early history of the religion (appropriateness, that is, as gauged by extrinsic theological norms). This is the case even for several scholars who affirm Bauer's basic position with regard to early Christian diversity. See, for example, Hans Dieter Betz, "Orthodoxy and Heresy in Primitive Christianity," and Helmut Koester, "Gnomai Diaphoroi." Others have wanted to address the theological question because they have seen yet more clearly than Bauer—though to be sure as a direct result of his own researches—the close relationship between struggles for power and issues of ideology. See for example, Elaine Pagels, *The Gnostic Gospels.*

15. Bauer can trace this Roman influence back to the first-century letter of 1 Clement, which he subjects to a careful and illuminating analysis (*Orthodoxy and Heresy*, 95–129).

16. A useful discussion of its initial reception is provided in Georg Strecker's

essay on "Die Aufnahme des Buches," pp. 288–306 of the second German addition. This essay was expanded and revised in the English translation by Robert Kraft, "The Reception of the Book," Appendix 2, pp. 286–316. The discussion was updated by Daniel Harrington, "The Reception of Walter Bauer's Orthodoxy and Heresy in Earliest Christianity During the Last Decade." Recent studies that directly challenge one or more aspects of Bauer's program include the following: Hans-Dietrich Altendorf, "Zum Stichwort: Rechtgläubigkeit und Ketzerei im ältesten Christentum"; Gary T. Burke, "Walter Bauer and Celsus"; Han Drijvers, "Rechtgläubigkeit und Ketzerei im ältesten syrischen Christentum"; A. I. C. Heron, "The Interpretation of 1 Clement in Walter Bauer's *Rechtgläubigkeit und Ketzerei im ältesten Christentum*"; James McCue, "Orthodoxy and Heresy: Walter Bauer and the Valentinians"; id., "Bauer's *Rechtgläubigkeit und Ketzerei im ältesten Christentum*"; Frederick W. Norris, "Ignatius, Polycarp, and 1 Clement"; id., "Asia Minor Before Ignatius"; and C. H. Roberts, *Manuscript, Society and Belief in Early Christian Egypt*. The two full-length critiques of Bauer's thesis, Turner's *The Pattern of Christian Truth* (see note 6) and Thomas Robinson, *The Bauer Thesis Examined*, both argue, at the end of the day, for a view much closer to the classical understanding.

I should stress that although it has become somewhat fashionable to cast aspersions on Bauer's reconstruction, it was not simply built on idle speculation, but was grounded in an exhaustive acquaintance with, and synthetic grasp of, the primary sources of second-century Christendom. Overall, the treatment still retains the power to persuade. Bauer's influence, evident in virtually all recent studies of the period, can be particularly seen in general and schematic sketches of orthodoxy and heresy, such as Helmut Koester, "Häretiker im Urchristentum"; Martin Elze, "Häresie und Einheit der Kirche im 2.Jahrhundert"; Josef Blank, "Zum Problem 'Häresie und Orthodoxie' im Urchristentum"; and Norbert Brox, "Häresie."

17. For example, Thessalonica must have had a majority of "heretics" in the early second century, because neither Ignatius nor Polycarp—so far as we know—wrote them a letter! Bauer, *Orthodoxy and Heresy*, 74–75.

18. See, for example, the brief but insightful comments of Robert M. Grant, *Jesus After the Gospels*, 84–95. On the one hand, it appears that the early Roman church was in fact not particularly interested in theological matters: neither Paul's letter to the Romans nor *1 Clement* mentions heresy, whereas the *Shepherd* of Hermas states only in passing that belief in one God, the Creator, is a sine qua non (introductory comment of the *Mandates*). Furthermore, as has long been known, Cerdo, Marcion, Valentinus, and Ptolemy were all active in Rome in the mid-second century, and there is no reliable evidence to indicate that the church at large differentiated closely between their teaching ministries (see note 37). Moreover, none of the Roman bishops prior to the end of the second century was known to be a theologian—except, interestingly, the anti-pope Hippolytus—and there is no record of any of them taking an active role in theological disputes.

At the same time, it should be noted that Marcion *was* excommunicated from the Roman church, apparently in the mid-140s, that the heresiologist Justin was active there, and that Irenaeus locates the center of theological orthodoxy there (*Adv. Haer.* III, 3, 2). Furthermore, bishops did excommunicate the adoptionists by the end of the century, and in the third century Origen defended his orthodoxy to Fabian of Rome, who was also involved with such matters in Carthage, Alexandria, and Antioch. Moreover, the Roman emperor Aurelian decided the issue of Paul of Samosata on the basis of which party in Antioch stood in agreement with the bishops of Italy and Rome (Eusebius, *Hist. Eccl.* VII, 30).

It appears then, that the authority of Roman theology developed during the last half of the second century and the beginning of the third, perhaps out of the necessity afforded by the presence of so many diversified forms of Christian faith there and under the impetus of the such popular figures as Justin and Irenaeus.

19. See especially the works of Drijvers, Harrington, Heron, McCue, Norris, Roberts, and Robinson cited in note 16.

20. A point emphasized, for example, by Han Drijvers for early Syriac Christianity. See his various essays collected in *East of Antioch,* especially "East of Antioch: Forces and Structures in the Development of Early Syriac Theology," 1–27; "Rechtgläubigkeit und Ketzerei im ältesten syrischen Christentum," 291–308; and "Quq and the Quqites: An Unknown Sect in Edessa in the Second Century A.D." 104–29.

21. Bauer, of course, cannot be faulted for overlooking earlier evidence of Christianity in regions (such as Edessa) that find no attestation in the New Testament. Moreover, it should be noted that many of the subsequent studies of the diversity of New Testament Christianity, which have by now become commonplace, are directly dependent upon his own research into the later period. See, for example, Koester and Robinson, *Trajectories,* and the more schematic treatment of James Dunn, *Unity and Diversity in the New Testament.*

22. No apostle, for example, described Jesus in Nicean terms as "begotten of the Father before all worlds, God of God, light of light, very God of very God, begotten not made, being of one substance with the Father . . . who for us and for our salvation came down from heaven and was incarnate from the virgin Mary."

23. See, for example, Koester and Robinson, *Trajectories;* Dunn, *Unity and Diversity.*

24. A number of recent scholars have argued that it is inappropriate to construe the early internecine conflicts as theological controversies *per se,* because Christian leaders were concerned primarily with issues of self-definition, that is, with determining acceptable parameters and with establishing rules of exclusion and inclusion (ways of deciding "who was in" and "who was outside" the church), not with specific points of doctrine. In this view, the anachronistic understanding of early debates in terms of heresy and orthodoxy has been inherited from the heresiologists of the fourth century, who saw all conflicts in these doctrinal terms. From a variety of perspectives, see Elze, "Häresie und Einheit"; Alain le Boulluec, *Le notion d'hérésie dans la littérature grecque IIe–IIIe siècles;* R. A. Marcus, "The Problem of Self-Definition: From Sect to Church"; and Frederik Wisse, "The Use of Early Christian Literature as Evidence for Inner Diversity and Conflict."

In one sense this assessment results from the recognition of the uneasy terms of differentiation between heresy and orthodoxy in the early period—about which I will be speaking presently. But at the same time, it is important to insist that even if the issue is "who is within and who is without" rather than "who is right and who is wrong," it is nonetheless resolved in large part, already in the early period, on the theological principle of "which views are true and which are in error." From the earliest sources—at least those associated with proto-orthodoxy (the group with which I am primarily concerned here)—persons are "excluded" from the true church not on explicitly political, ethnic, geographical, or gender-related grounds, but on theological ones, and the polemics against offending parties were almost always carried out in some measure on this level, whether by Paul, Ignatius, or Justin. This is simply another way of emphasizing that debates over theology are not necessarily restricted to the ideational plane, but relate to—or better, are infused by—socio-political concerns as well.

25. For example, 2 Thessalonians 2:2; Colossians 2:8, 16–19; Ephesians 4:14; 5:6, 1 Timothy 1:3–7, 19–20; 4:1–5; 6:3–5; 2 Timothy 2:16–18; 3:6–9; 4:3–4; Titus 1:9, 13–16; 3:9–11.

26. For example, Matthew 24:11, 23 (pars.); 1 John 2:18–22; 4:1–6; 2 John 7–11; Jude 4, 10–19; Revelations 2:2, 14–15, 20.

27. On the relation of these kinds of heresies in Ignatius, see Chapter 4, note 12.

28. As I will observe later, these tractates demonstrate that the "sects" to which the heresiologists assigned various Gnostics represent the schematizations of outsiders. In many respects, the Gnostics we now know about from primary sources are quite different from those described in theological terms by the orthodox fathers. See further pp. 15–16 and Chapter 3, n. 8. Here I should emphasize that throughout this discussion, I am concerned only with *Christian* Gnosticism. As a result, as I will explain more fully in Chapter 3, I am not directly concerned with the issue of the origin of Gnosticism or with its non-Christian manifestations.

29. The Nag Hammadi library is itself no monolith, but contains a wide variety of literature of mixed provenance. Translations and brief introductions can be found in James M. Robinson, ed. *The Nag Hammadi Library in English,* and (together with other primary sources of Gnosticism) Bentley Layton, *The Gnostic Scriptures.* The latter also provides useful bibliographical information. An exhaustive bibliography can be found in David M. Scholer, *Nag Hammadi Bibliography 1948–1969;* this is updated annually by D. Scholer in "Bibliographia Gnostica: Supplementum," in *NovT.* Two of the masterful treatments of Gnosticism for general readers are Hans Jonas, *The Gnostic Religion,* and Kurt Rudolph, *Gnosis: The Nature and History of Gnosticism.* For an instructive overview of the state of research as of 1983, see R. van den Broek, "The Present State of Gnostic Studies."

30. See especially Klaus Koschorke, *Die Polemik der Gnostiker gegen des kirchliche Christendum,* and Birger Pearson, "Anti-Heretical Warnings in Codex IX from Nag Hammadi," in M. Krause, ed., *Essays on the Nag Hammadi Texts in Honour of Pahor Labib,* revised and republished in Birger Pearson, *Gnosticism, Judaism, and Egyptian Christianity.* References to this latter work will be made to the revised edition.

31. Also included among the culprits attacked in the writings at Nag Hammadi, interestingly, are docetists—a group castigated by orthodox writers in other contexts. See the discussion of the tractate *Melchizedek* in Pearson, "Anti-Heretical Writings," 184–88.

32. The latter image comes from Turner, *Pattern of Christian Truth,* 81.

33. For example, *Adv. Haer.* III, 16, 8; 17, 4; IV, 33, 3. See especially Koschorke, *Die Polemik der Gnostiker.*

34. This is not to say that he lacked predecessors, as my discussion of Ignatius and Justin, for example, clearly shows. But Irenaeus himself laments the failure of his predecessors to uproot the Gnostics from the church, claiming that they were unable to do so precisely because they did not understand adequately the systems they opposed (*Adv. Haer.* IV, pref., 2).

35. Clement, *Strom.* VI, 9; Origen, *SerMt* 100. The notion is expressed most clearly in the docetic accounts of the *Acts of John,* 89–93. See the discussion of John A. McGuckin, "The Changing Forms of Jesus." See further the discussion of Chapter 4, note 21.

36. Tertullian's decision to align himself with the Montanists was later seen as a fall from the true faith; Origen, a staunch advocate of orthodoxy in his day and probably the single most influential theologian between Paul and Augustine, came to

be violently opposed by the fourth-century heresiologist Epiphanius (*Panarion* 64), who saw in him the archheretic responsible for spawning the dangerous aberration of Arius. See especially Jon Dechow, *Dogma and Mysticism in Early Christianity.*

37. See the persuasive discussion of Gerd Lüdemann, "Zur Geschichte des ältesten Christentums in Rom. I. Valentin und Marcion; II. Ptolemäus und Justin."

38. See the comments of Wilhelm Schneemelcher, "Apostelgeschichten des 2. und 3. Jahrhunderts," Hennecke-Schneemelcher, *Neutestamentliche Apokryphen.* The English translation by R. McL. Wilson, *The New Testament Apocrypha,* is of an earlier edition, which, for many articles, including the one cited here, has been left essentially unchanged.

39. The translation is from William R. Schoedel, *Ignatius of Antioch,* 59. See his discussion of the passage, pp. 59–62. Compare Ignatius's other christological statements as well (e.g., Ign. *Pol.* 3, 2; *Smyrn.* 3, 2–3; *Trall.* 9, 1–2; *Eph.* 18, 2), and Schoedel's comments *ad loc.*

40. Most historians, of course, can trace their own lineage back through a tradition that claims the triumph of Christian orthodoxy as one of its historical roots. And so it is scarcely surprising to see that many historians find this form of Christianity essentially compatible with the teaching of Jesus and his followers. We should not allow this consensus to blind our eyes to the impossibility of disinterested evaluation in the hands of contextually situated investigators; the postmodern world has seen in this modernist quest for objectivity a myth of its own. (This applies, of course, to *all* investigators: even those who repudiate the consensus.) Moreover, I would be amiss not to observe that, speaking historically, the Apostle Paul leads just as certainly to Marcion and Valentinus as he does to Irenaeus and Origen.

41. Although it is not altogether clear that even he saw the problem of labeling the victorious group orthodox, as though its representatives attested a monolithic theology. On this, see Turner, *Pattern of Christian Truth,* chaps. 1–2.

42. See especially Robert M. Grant, "The Use of the Early Fathers, from Irenaeus to John of Damascus."

43. As should be clear from the discussion, I do not mean to imply any sense of historical determinism by these labels. It is not that the proto-orthodox Christians represented views that were inevitably going to attain a level of dominance. They can be labeled orthodox in any sense, therefore, only in retrospect.

44. See note 24. Elze ("Häresie und Einheit," 407–08) in particular castigates modern scholars for falling prey to Irenaeus's notion of the internal unity of orthodox Christianity (as well as of the basic coherence of various forms of heterodoxy).

45. See Ign. *Eph.* 7:2, cited on p. 11 above.

46. See the fuller discussion of pp. 47–54 below.

47. See further pp. 119–24 below.

48. See further pp. 181–87 below.

49. Most notably the view known as Patripassianism (also called Sabellianism and modalistic monarchianism)—the view that Christ was actually God the Father in the flesh. See Chapter 5.

50. And somewhat later, for example, those of Ephraem and Epiphanius. For a basic discussion of the polemical tacts taken by some of the prominent heresiologists, see Gérard Vallée, *A Study in Anti-Gnostic Polemics.* A fuller and more carefully nuanced investigation is now available in the two-volume work of Le Boulluec, *Notion d'hérésie.* Left out of Le Boulluec's study (intentionally) is an analysis of Hippolytus of Rome, of whom Klaus Koschorke has provided a particularly incisive study: *Hippolyt's Ketzerbekämpfung und Polemik gegen die Gnostiker.* Of the burgeoning

periodical literature, see especially, Barbara Aland, "Gnosis und Kirchenväter," and the literature she cites there. On the controversies in general, a good deal of valuable information is still readily available in Adolf von Harnack, *History of Dogma,* especially volumes 2 and 3. For a popular treatment by a weighty authority, see Robert M. Grant, *Jesus After the Gospels,* especially Chapters 4–7 (on the Apostolic Fathers, Justin, Theophilus, and Irenaeus). Many of the earlier studies consisted of detailed, and often erudite, investigations of the literary relations of the various heresiologists, both to one another and to the works of others (e.g., Hegessipus and Justin), which have not survived. See especially Adolf Hilgenfeld, *Die Ketzergeschichte des Urchristentums.*

51. For example, the contradictory descriptions of the Gnostic Christian Basilides in Irenaeus (*Adv. Haer.* I, 24, 3–7) and Hippolytus (*Refutation* 7, 10–15).

52. See especially Frederick Wisse, "The Nag Hammadi Library and the Heresiologists"; Rowan Greer, "The Dog and the Mushrooms"; and Koschorke, *Hippolyt's Ketzerbekämpfung.*

53. In addition to the works cited in note 50, see Frederik Wisse, "The Epistle of Jude." The charges I sketch here can be found, for example, in Irenaeus, *Adv. Haer.*, Hippolytus, *Refutation,* and Tertullian, *Prescription, passim.*

54. This charge in particular forms the basis of Hippolytus's *Refutation.* See especially Koschorke, *Hippolyt's Ketzerbekämpfung.*

55. See above, p. 5. The "polemics of profligacy" is a widely studied phenomenon. See Robert M. Grant, "Charges of Immorality Against Various Religious Groups in Antiquity"; Burton L. Visotzky, "Overturning the Lamp"; Albert Henrichs, "Pagan Ritual and the Alleged Crimes of the Early Christians"; Wolfgang Speyer, "Zu den Vorwürfen der Heiden gegen die Christen"; Stephen Gero, "With Walter Bauer on the Tigris"; Jurgen Dümmer, "Die Angaben über die Gnostische Literatur bei Epiphanius, Pan. Haer. 26"; and Klaus Koschorke, *Die Polemik der Gnostiker,* 123–24. On a more popular level, see Robert L. Wilken, *The Christians as the Romans Saw Them,* and Stephen Benko, "The Libertine Gnostic Sect of the Phibionites."

56. It should be noted that Irenaeus claimed to have firsthand knowledge of the shameless behavior of Marcus from some of the women he had reportedly seduced (*Adv. Haer.* I, 8, 3–6). It may be that he assumed that other heretics behaved similarly. For these other groups, there is nothing to suggest that Irenaeus had himself actually witnessed the alleged immoralities or had before him reliable sources that had. In any event, it is certainly one thing to claim that a member of a sect engaged in immoral activities, and quite another to claim that such activities were sanctioned by the group. For other orthodox slurs against Gnostic morality, see Clement of Alexandria's charges against the Carpocratians (*Strom.,* III, 2, 10–16) and Justin, I *Apology* 26, 7.

57. "The Epistle of Jude in the History of Heresiology."

58. Even our earliest Christian author, the Apostle Paul, maligns his opponents as gluttonous reprobates: "whose God is their belly, whose glory is in their shame, and who set their minds on earthly things" (Phil 3:19). Those outside the Christian community fare no better. Perhaps following standard Jewish polemic, Paul castigates without differentiation the profligate behavior of all pagans: "Their hearts are given up to impurity, to the dishonoring of their bodies amongst themselves. . . . Their women exchanged natural relations for unnatural, and the men likewise gave up natural relations with women and were consumed with passion for one another; men committing shameless deeds with men, receiving in their own persons the due penalty for their error" (Rom 1:24–27). This polemical thrust was perpetuated in the Pauline

tradition as far as it can be traced. Thus, the author of Ephesians warns his readers against deceivers in their midst, who sanction filthiness, illicit fornication, and all manner of impurity (Eph 5:1–7), while the author of 2 Timothy warns of those who are lovers of self, of money, and of pleasure, who ensnare weak women through seductive teachings that counterfeit the truth (2 Tim 3:1–9).

59. See especially Frederik Wisse, "Die Sextus-Sprüche und das Probleme der gnostischen Ethik." Gero ("With Walter Bauer on the Tigris") argues that the (Egyptian) Nag Hammadi tractates cannot be used to establish ascetic tendencies among Gnostics elsewhere, especially a Syro-Mesopotamian group like the Phibionites—a curious claim, given the fact that Epiphanius locates the group precisely in Egypt.

60. Compare the claims made by orthodox apologists such as Justin regarding the refusal of Christians (meaning, that is, Christians of his persuasion) to engage in immoral activities (I *Apol.* 16–18; II *Apol.* 2), despite their constant abuse by the civil authorities, in contrast to heretics such as the Marcionites, who are both flagrantly immoral and honored by the state (I *Apol.* 26).

61. A convenient edition with brief introduction can be found in Cyril Richardson, *Early Christian Fathers.* For an analysis of tradition and redaction, see Hans von Campenhausen, "Bearbeitungen und Interpolationen des Polykarpmartyriums," especially 39–41, and the reaction of Timothy D. Barnes, "Pre-Decian *Acta Martyrum,*" reprinted in *Early Christianity and the Roman Empire.*

62. Irenaeus, *Adv. Haer.* IV, 33, 9–10; and Tertullian, "Scorpiace." For discussion, see especially Elaine Pagels, "Gnostic and Orthodox Views of Christ's Passion."

63. As other scattered examples, see Tertullian, *Prescription* 36 (John is plunged into boiling oil and emerges unharmed); the "Acts of Paul and Thecla" (Hennecke-Schneemelcher, *New Testament Apocrypha* I. 359, 362: Thecla is miraculously delivered from certain death); Eusebius, *Hist. Eccl.* V, 1 (God enpowers and sustains the martyrs of Lyons and Vienne). See the various accounts translated in H. Musurillo, ed., *The Acts of the Christian Martyrs.*

64. A thorough treatment of the historical development of the New Testament canon can be found in Bruce M. Metzger, *The Canon of the New Testament.* For an authoritative account of the rise of the Christian Bible during the first three centuries, see Hans von Campenhausen, *The Formation of the Christian Bible.* More concise accounts are provided by Harry Gamble, *The New Testament Canon: Its Making and Meaning;* F. F. Bruce, *The Canon of Scripture;* and Wilhelm Schneemelcher, "Zur Geschichte des neutestamentlichen Kanons," in Hennecke-Schneemelcher, *Neutestamentliche Apokryphen,* I. 7–40.

65. For recent discussion, see the essays collected in Jean-Daniel Kaestli and Otto Wermelinger, eds., *Le canon de l'Ancien Testament. Sa formation et son histoire.* Here I do well to note that the early Christians themselves occasionally quoted authorities that never made it into the final Hebrew canon (cf. Jude 9), and by and large accepted the books of the so-called Old Testament Apocrypha as authoritative.

66. Already in our earliest author, the Apostle Paul, Jesus' words are used to settle matters of doctrine and practice (1 Thess 4:15 [?]; 1 Cor 7:10, 9:14, 11:23–26). Staying within the Pauline tradition, near the end of the first century Jesus' words are cited in 1 Timothy 5:18, along with Deuteronomy 25:4, and designated as "Scripture" (ἡ γραφή). Cf. also the agraphon of Acts 20:35. In different circles somewhat later, depending on when one decides to date the Coptic *Gospel of Thomas,* Jesus' words were understood even more extraordinarily as the very means of salvation: "Whoever finds the explanation of these words will not taste death" (*Gos. Thom.* 1; cf. John 5:24).

67. See, for example, the discussions of apostolic authorship of the New Testament writings in Origen, as preserved in Eusebius, *Hist. Eccl.* VI, 25, 3–14, and in Eusebius himself in *Hist. Eccl.* III, 25, 1–7. The latter also disputes the claims of some heretics for the apostolic authorship of the Gospels of Peter, Thomas, and Matthew [Pseudo-Matthew!] and of the Acts of Andrew and John.

68. Eusebius, *Hist. Eccl.* VI, 12, 1–6. In the letter that Eusebius extracts, Serapion emphasizes that "We . . . receive Peter and all the apostles as we receive Christ, but the writings falsely attributed to them we are experienced enough to reject." He then narrates the events leading up to his rejection of the *Gospel of Peter*.

69. See, for example, Irenaeus, *Adv. Haer.* III, 2–4; IV, 26, and the discussion of Bienert, "Das Apostelbild," in Hennecke-Schneemelcher, *Neutestamentliche Apocryphen*, II. 25–26.

70. But also because the author was known to be the brother of Bishop Pius of Rome. This is usually taken to mean that the book is not among the Scriptures because it cannot claim apostolic authorship.

71. See, for example, Ep Jer cxxix (to Claudienus Postumus Dardanus), quoted in Metzger, *Canon*, 236, and the full discussion of "Defining the Limits of the New Testament Canon," chap. 6 of Hans von Campenhausen, *Formation of the Christian Bible*, 210–68.

72. See especially the discussion in Metzger, *Canon*, 143–48. Justin refers to the "Memoirs of the Apostles" on eight occasions (e.g., I *Apol.* 66, 3 [where the books are further identified as "Gospels"]; 67, 3; and *Dial.* 103, 6), and to the "Memoirs" on four other. His references to these texts demonstrate a fair knowledge of the Synoptics, but his acquaintance with and view of the Fourth Gospel is disputed. The apparent quotation of John 3:3–4 in I *Apol.* 61 is sometimes dismissed, in view of the lack of other evidence, as deriving from common tradition rather than a literary source. For discussion of Justin's Gospel references, see Arthur J. Bellinzoni, *The Sayings of Jesus in the Writings of Justin Martyr*, and William Petersen, "Textual Evidence of Tatian's Dependence upon Justin's 'ΑΠΟΜΝΗΜΟΝΕΥΜΑΤΑ."

73. A great deal has been written on Marcion's life and thought, for which his views of the canon proved to be of central importance. See the works cited in note 22, Chapter 4. For his role in the formation of the orthodox canon, see especially Metzger, *Canon*, 90–99, and the literature he cites there. Von Campenhausen (*Formation of the Christian Bible*, 148–64) in particular sees Marcion's paramount significance: "The idea and the reality of a Christian Bible were the work of Marcion, and the Church which rejected his work, so far from being ahead of him in this field, from a formal point of view simply followed his example," (p. 148).

74. See especially von Campenhausen, *Formation of the Christian Bible*, 210–68; and Metzger, *Canon*, 75–106.

75. For a full discussions of the use of such methods, see Jean Pepin, *Myth et allégorie*; id., *La tradition de l'allégorie*; and now especially, David Dawson, *Allegorical Readers and Cultural Revision in Ancient Alexandria*.

One of the most influential articles in this field has been J. Tate, "Plato and Allegorical Interpretation." On the use of allegorical methods in the early church, a standard work is still R. P. C. Hanson, *Allegory and Event*. For concise overviews, see Robert M. Grant and David Tracy, *A Short History of the Interpretation of the Bible*, and the collection of texts in Karlfried Froehlich, *Biblical Interpretation in the Early Church*. Specifically on the conflict between heresy and orthodoxy on this issue, see Le Boulluec, *Notion d'hérésie*, 189–244, and more briefly, id., "La Bible chez les marginaux de l'orthodoxie."

76. Compare Irenaeus's interpretation of the "clean and unclean" foods of Leviticus 11:2, Deuteronomy 14:3, etc. (*Adv. Haer.* V, 8, 4): animals that have cloven hoofs are clean, representing people who steadily advance towards God and his Son through faith; animals who chew the cud but do not have cloven hoofs are unclean, representing the Jews who have the words of Scripture in their mouths but do not move steadily toward the knowledge of God. Tertullian (*Adv. Marc.* III, 7) argues that the two goats presented on the Day of Atonement (Lev 16) refer to the two advents of Christ, comparable in appearance but different in effect! See the discussion of J. H. Waszink, "Tertullian's Principles and Methods of Exegesis."

77. *De Principiis* IV, 2–3. A good deal has been written on Origen's methods of exegesis. For general studies, see the recent overviews of Henri Crouzel *(Origen)*, and Joseph W. Trigg *(Origen: The Bible and Philosophy in the Third-Century Church)*. The latter is self-consciously dependent upon the detailed investigation of Pierre Nautin, *Origène: sa vie et son oeuvre*. Of the studies devoted specifically to Origen's allegorical method, the following have been found to be particularly useful: R. P. C. Hanson, *Allegory and Event;* M. F. Wiles, "Origen as Biblical Scholar," in *The Cambridge History of the Bible;* Bernard Neuschäfer, *Origenes als Philologe;* and Karen Torjesen, *Hermeneutical Procedure and Theological Method in Origen's Exegesis.*

78. Gnostic exegeses of specific New Testament texts are conveniently collected and discussed by Elaine Pagels, *The Johannine Gospel in Valentinian Exegesis,* and id., *The Gnostic Paul.* On the orthodox reaction to gnostic exegesis, see, for example, Norbert Brox, *Offenbarung, Gnosis, und gnostischen Mythos bei Irenäus von Lyon,* and Waszink, "Tertullian's Principles and Methods of Exegesis." See further, Chapter 3, note 25.

79. See his discussion in *Adv. Haer.* II, 20–26, one of his finest uses of irony.

80. Compare also his striking illustration of the Homeric cento, on which see Robert Wilken, "The Homeric Cento in Adversus Haereses I, 9, 4."

81. See note 76.

82. Compare also Ptolemy's Letter to Flora, quoted in Epiphanius, *Pan.* 33, 6, 6, where Paul is claimed as the source of the Valentinian doctrine.

83. See Bauer's famous dismissal of Eusebius's list of Alexandrian bishops: "The first ten names (after Mark, the companion of the apostles) are and remain for us a mere echo and a puff of smoke; and they scarcely could ever have been anything but that," *Orthodoxy and Heresy,* 45.

84. See especially the exhaustive study of Wolfgang Speyer, *Die literarische Fälschung im heidnischen und christlichen Altertum.* He gives a briefer account in his "Religiose Pseudepigraphie und literarische Fälschung im Altertum." Other significant studies include Norbert Brox, *Die falsche Verfasserangaben,* and David Meade, *Pseudepigrapha and Canon.* A concise statement concerning the apparent motivations of ancient literary forgers can be found in Bruce M. Metzger, "Literary Forgeries and Canonical Pseudepigrapha."

85. The author of the *Acts of Paul,* who, according to Tertullian (*de baptismo,* 17), was a presbyter of a church in Asia Minor. See the discussion and translation of the text by William Schneemelcher in Hennecke-Schneemelcher, *New Testament Apocrypha,* II. 663–83.

86. Many of the texts are conveniently discussed and translated (in whole or in part) in Hennecke-Schneemelcher, *New Testament Apocrypha;* the 5th (6th) German edition (1989/90) incorporates yet more material, including many of the texts from Nag Hammadi. For still more complete collections of solely Gnostic materials, see Robinson, *The Nag Hammadi Library,* and Layton, *The Gnostic Scriptures.* For an

extensive bibliography, see James Charlesworth, *The New Testament Apocrypha and Pseudepigrapha.*

87. Extensively documented in Speyer, *Die literarische Fälschung,* and Brox, *Die falsche Verfasserangabe,* 71–80.

88. The letters of Jude and James and the book of Revelation are probably homonymous rather than pseudonymous: nothing in them suggests an intentional deceit so much as the simple use of a common name, mistakenly taken later to be that of an earthly companion of Jesus. The Gospels and Acts are, of course, simply anonymous.

89. See especially R. M. Grant, "Use of the Early Fathers."

90. See the updated discussion and translation of C. Detlef and G. Müller in Hennecke-Schneemelcher, *Neutestamentliche Apocryphen,* I. 205–33.

91. See the discussion and translation of Oscar Cullmann in Hennecke-Schneemelcher, *Neutestamentliche Apocryphen,* I. 334–49.

92. The fluidity of the textual tradition in the early period of transmission, about which I will have more to say presently, has long been recognized within the field. In addition to the works cited in note 94, see F. C. Grant, "Where Form Criticism and Textual Criticism Overlap"; Manfred Karnetzki, "Textgeschichte als Überlieferungsgeschichte"; Helmut Koester, *Synoptische Überlieferung bei den apostolischen Vätern;* and especially the intriguing analysis of François Bovon, "The Synoptic Gospels and the Non-Canonical Acts of the Apostles," especially 32–36.

93. See the reflections in Chapter 6.

94. This is not to say that isolated instances of such variants have never been detected. See, for example, the insightful studies of K. W. Clark, F. C. Conybeare, Adolf von Harnack ("Zwei alte dogmatische Korrekturen"; "Zur Textkritik und Christologie"), J. Rendel Harris, Wilbert F. Howard, Kirsopp Lake, Daniel Plooij, Donald Riddle, Heinrich Vogels, C.S.C. Williams, Leon E. Wright, and especially Eric Fascher, cited in the bibliography. More recent investigations, including my own analyses of specific units of variation, will be cited throughout the study. The most extensive treatment of the subject occurs in one of those truly great works of a previous generation that is scarcely read today, Walter Bauer's *Das Leben Jesu im Zeitalter der neutestamentlichen Apocryphen.* Bauer's discussion focuses on the portrayals of Jesus in the second- and third-century apocrypha, and shows how extensively these portrayals came to be reflected in the manuscript tradition of the New Testament. A particularly fruitful study of a different sort is Eldon J. Epp, *The Theological Tendency of Codex Bezae Cantabrigiensis in Acts.* Rather than isolating doctrinally motivated variants across a broad spectrum of witnesses (which will be my tack), Epp concentrates on one significant manuscript and works to ascertain the theological proclivities that may account for its variant readings. Unfortunately, Epp's lead, while widely acclaimed, has been little followed (see, though, the unpublished dissertations of George Rice and Michael Holmes, cited in Chapter 5, note 4).

All of these works represent a direct challenge to the views of other textual scholars who deny the significance of theologically motivated variations among the New Testament manuscripts altogether. Compare the classical statement of the nineteenth-century critic F.J.A. Hort, in his otherwise brilliant *Introduction* to *The New Testament in the Original Greek:* "It will not be out of place to add here a distinct expression of our belief that even among the numerous unquestionably spurious readings of the New Testament there are no signs of deliberate falsification of the text for dogmatic purposes" (New York: Harper and Brothers, 1882; 2.282). Hort goes on to say that instances of variation that appear to be doctrinally motivated are due to scribal carelessness or laxity, not to malicious intent. Comparable views have been expressed in the twentieth century as well; see, for example, Leon Vaganay, *An Introduction to the Textual Criticism of the New Testament*, 12.

95. Compare the curse pronounced on anyone who would modify the text of the LXX, as found in the *Letter of Aristeas*, 310–11.

96. Eusebius, *Hist. Eccl.* IV, 23, 12; V, 20, 2.

97. In a letter quoted by Rufinus, in his "On the Falsifying of the Books of Origen," 7.

98. Leading, for example, to the debates between Rufinus and Jerome concerning Origen's orthodoxy. See Elizabeth Clark, *The Origenist Controversy*.

99. My own translation. See the discussion in Bauer, *Orthodoxy and Heresy*, 160–69. Among the other writings so "falsified" are some of the Apostolic Fathers, most clearly, the letters of Ignatius. Here again, however, it appears that at least in the witnesses that have survived, it was precisely the orthodox Christians who changed the text. See Schoedel, *Ignatius*, 5.

100. See A. Bludau, *Die Schriftfälschungen der Häretiker*. Bludau catalogs *in extenso* the accusations of tampering, discusses each individually, and concludes that they by and large constitute charges of tampering with the *sense* of Scripture, rather than the actual *words;* accusations of actual tampering with the wording of the text, according to Bludau, can for the most part be discounted as groundless polemic. In my judgment, Bludau was overly skeptical of the charges and overly confident that the debates over the text of Scripture themselves worked to guarantee its integrity. In point of fact, there was no mechanism by which orthodox and heretic alike *could* serve as the "watchdogs" over the text that Bludau envisages.

101. See Irenaeus, *Adv. Haer.* I, 27, 2; Tertullian, *Prescription* 38; *Adv. Marc.* Books IV and V, *passim*; Epiphanius, *Pan* 42, 11–16.

102. *Hist. Eccl.* V, 28. See my article, "The Theodotians as Corruptors of Scripture."

103. See further Pagels, *The Gnostic Paul*, 163–64, and Frederik Wisse, "The Nature and Purpose of Redactional Changes in Early Christian Texts."

104. *de carne Christi*, 19.

105. See p. 59.

106. See especially Bludau, *Die Schriftfälschungen*. On several possible traces, see J. Rendel Harris, "New Points of View in Textual Criticism," and, for example, my discussion of Matthew 1:16 (pp. 54–55).

107. I have taken the number from the most up-to-date statement of Kurt and Barbara Aland (who maintain the numbering system of newly discovered manuscripts at the Institute for New Testament Textual Research in Münster), *The Text of the New Testament*. In addition, of course, are the thousands of manuscripts of the early versions (over eight thousand of the Latin Vulgate alone) and the thousands of citations of the New Testament in the Greek and Latin ecclesiastical writers of the early centuries, two other sources for establishing the New Testament text. These sources further complicate an already complex situtation.

108. The first serious critical apparatus of the Greek New Testament was published by John Mill in 1707. Although he had access only to 100 or so Greek manuscripts, to the Latin translations of several early versions in Walton's Polyglot Bible, and to uncritical editions of patristic sources, he nonetheless uncovered some 30,000 variant readings. As manuscripts came to be discovered and carefully studied over the

years, this number increased exponentially—by a factor of five over the next hundred years. See further Bart D. Ehrman, "Methodological Developments in the Analysis and Classification of New Testament Documentary Evidence."

109. On the absence of professional scriptoria for the production of manuscripts prior to about 200 C.E., see Aland and Aland, *Text of the New Testament*, 55, 70. Before that time, professional scribes may have worked on their own; it is likely that a high number of the earliest transcriptions were made simply by literate individuals who wanted a copy for themselves or for their congregations. See Chapter 6, note 1.

110. Indeed, it has become problematic to speak of the "intentions" even of authors of whom we have extensive personal knowledge and from whom we have quantities of literary productions. It is not that authors (or scribes) did not actually *have* intentions, so much as that intentions are not always conscious, that they are rarely unambiguous or pure, and that, for the most part, they cannot be known by outsiders. Authors produce texts, not intentions. Nonetheless, I have retained the category of "intentional" modifications of texts, not to build a literary interpretation or a historical reconstruction on speculated intentions—a dubious undertaking—but to differentiate between "senseless" changes and "sensible" ones. The category of "intentional" changes, as opposed to "accidental," can thus serve a useful heuristic purpose by highlighting certain functional characteristics of scribal modifications, even when we refuse to speculate about the psychological states and hidden volitions of individual scribes.

111. For a discussion of my use of the term "significant," see Chapter 6.

112. This view is shared by a wide-range of eminent textual specialists who are otherwise not known for embracing compatible views. See the arguments adduced by E. C. Colwell, "The Origin of the Text Types of the New Testament," 138; George Kilpatrick, "Atticism and the Text of the Greek New Testament"; Eldon J. Epp, "The Significance of the Papyri for Determining the Nature of the New Testament Text in the Second Century," especially 101–103; and Barbara Aland, "Die Münsteraner Arbeit am Text des Neuen Testaments und ihr Beitrag für die frühe Überlieferung des 2. Jahrhunderts."

113. Again, a view embraced by a wide range of scholars. See Epp, "Significance of the Papyri," and Aland and Aland, *Text of the New Testament*, 48–71. This is not to say that scribes would have been absolutely prevented from modifying their texts at a later date. In fact, we know not only that scribal errors occurred even into the high Middle Ages, but that the texts were "intentionally" changed even then, and sometimes for doctrinal reasons. (See, e.g., Ernest W. Saunders, "Studies in Doctrinal Influences on the Byzantine Text of the Gospels.") But these instances are by all counts exceptional; the bulk of the evidence suggests that scribes of later times by and large exercised considerable restraint in reproducing their texts. On the vicissitudes of the text in the earliest period, that is, before 150 C.E., see especially Barbara Aland, "Die Rezeption des neutestamentlichen Textes in den ersten Jahrhunderten."

114. See the articles by Epp and B. Aland cited in note 112 (both from *Gospel Traditions in the Second Century*).

115. In addition to the works cited in note 112 (especially Kilpatrick) see Günther Zuntz, *The Text of the Epistles*, who demonstrates that the Byzantine editors *chose* rather than *created* their distinctive readings. The reasons for scribes applying "looser" standards (looser, that is, from our point of view) in earlier times than later are not hard to locate, given what has already been seen concerning early developments within the Christian religion. It was not until near the end of the second century that Christians began attributing canonical status to the Gospels and apostolic writings and

insisting on their literal interpretation—sometimes called a "word for word" (Greek: πρὸς ῥῆμα) interpretation. The characterization of certain writings as sacred Scripture and the insistence on the importance of their actual words would themselves suggest the need for greater care in their transcription. Not surprisingly, it is precisely during the second half of the second century that accusations begin to arise that heretics have tampered with the words of the text. For these reasons, one might suppose that later scribes of the fourth, fifth, and even later centuries were less inclined to create variant readings than to reproduce them. This view happens to coincide with what we know from other evidence, namely, that even into the middle of the second century the texts of the Gospels were heavily influenced by the oral tradition—another indication that they had not yet been widely regarded as "fixed," let alone "scriptural," at this stage. See especially Koester, *Synoptische Überlieferung bei den apostolischen Vätern.*

116. I emphasize that not *all* of them did, not even all of the theologically interesting ones. As a striking example, I have felt constrained to leave out of my study a discussion of the so-called *Comma Johanneum* (1 John 5:7–8), even though this represents the most obvious instance of a theologically motivated corruption in the entire manuscript tradition of the New Testament. Nonetheless, in my judgment, the comma's appearance in the tradition can scarcely be dated prior to the trinitarian controversies that arose after the period under examination. In this I am in full agreement with the instructive discussion of Raymond E. Brown, *The Epistles of John,* 775–87.

117. Throughout this discussion I understand the term "text" in an empirical sense to mean any concatenation of words or symbols that can be sensibly construed.

118. The observations that follow are most closely related to various literary theories that are loosely labeled "reader response." Unlike some of its predecessors in the field, such as new criticism and structuralism, the kind of reader-response criticism I have in view is not narrowly concerned with the text per se, that is, with a document as some kind of "objective" entity from which meanings can be culled like so many grapes from a vine. It is instead interested in the process of interpretation. Reader-response critics, of course, proffer a number of approaches to the task—some emphasizing the actual effects of actual texts on actual readers; others considering the linear-spatial character of written texts and their significance for understanding (i.e., as words are read sequentially on the page); others pursuing the question of how texts can structure meaning through "givens" and "indeterminacies"; yet others exploring the philosophical underpinnings of these other (and all) theories of how texts "work," that is, of how meaning can be or is construed during the process of reading. Two anthologies may serve as a useful entrée into the field: Susan R. Suleiman and Inge Crosman, eds., *The Reader in the Text,* and Jane Thompkins, ed., *Reader-Response Criticism.*

119. This is to say, although transcribing a text is a conservative process, it is not an innocent one. To be sure, a transcription preserves the text for posterity, but in doing so it also implies a value judgment (the text is worth preserving at some cost). Furthermore, when changes are made in the process of transmission, other kinds of judgment are at work (e.g., that the text should say what it is supposed to mean). For a brief sketch of these issues, in which some of the data of the present study are incorporated, see Bart D. Ehrman, "The Text of Mark in the Hands of the Orthodox."

120. The most controversial spokesperson for this view is Stanley Fish. See his two collections of essays, *Is There a Text in This Class?* and *Doing What Comes Naturally.* I should emphasize that one does not have to embrace Fish's views in full

to see in them a forceful challenge to the modernist assumptions of the possibility of an "objective" stance towards a text.

121. This reader-response view represents a direct and conscientious challenge to one of the founding principles of the so-called New Criticism, as laid out by W. K. Wimsatt and M. Beardsley some forty years ago in their seminal essay, "The Affective Fallacy." Wimsatt and Beardsley insisted that a text's meaning is independent of its effect, psychological or otherwise, on the reader. For them, meaning resides within the text, and it is the task of the critic to discover that meaning by applying objective interpretive criteria in the process of analysis. Reader-response critics like Fish object to this "myth of objectivity," and argue to the contrary that meaning does not and cannot exist independently of readers who construe texts. This is shown by the fact that the same words can mean radically different things in different contexts, and by the related fact that readers with different assumptions typically assign different meanings to the same text. Even the same reader will frequently understand a text differently at different times. Thus, every time a text is read its meaning is construed; every time it is reread it is reconstrued, and reconstrued more or less differently. In this sense, reading—the process of construing a text—does not differ substantially from writing, so that every time we read a text, whether we know it or not, we recreate or rewrite the text.

122. This applies even to those who take pride in their ability to transcend themselves to attain an "objective" interpretation of a text, since this very endeavor itself derives from a modern (i.e., time-bound) consciousness that is rooted in a host of ideological assumptions unthinkable before the Enlightenment. For challenging and entertaining discussions, see especially Stanley Fish, "Normal Circumstances and Other Special Cases," "Is There a Text in This Class?" "How To Recognize a Poem When You See One," "What Makes an Interpretation Acceptable?" and "Demonstration vs. Persuasion: Two Models of Critical Activity," all in *Is There a Text in This Class?*

123. Significant passages that I am therefore obliged to overlook are John 1:3–4 and Romans 9:5, passages that proved important for debates over Jesus' divinity. On both problems, see Bruce M. Metzger, *A Textual Commentary on the Greek New Testament*, 195–96, 520–23.

124. Needless to say, I do not think that such changes form the majority of "intentional" modifications of the New Testament text. Harmonizations, for example, are made with far greater frequency. This is not surprising: numerous passages of the New Testament have parallels elsewhere (e.g., nearly the entire Gospel of Mark!); by comparison, relatively few passages figured prominently for the christological debates. Changes motivated by such debates can scarcely be expected to have occurred in passages that are unrelated to Christology (which includes most of the passages of the New Testament). I am therefore speaking of dozens of changes, perhaps hundreds, but not thousands. At the same time, these dozens of changes occur in significant portions of the New Testament books, in passages, that is, that historically proved to be important in christological developments. See further, the reflections in Chapter 6.

2

Anti-Adoptionistic Corruptions of Scripture

Introduction: Adoptionism in Early Christianity

While Christians of the first three centuries agreed that Christ was the Son of God, they disagreed over what this sonship might entail. For most believers, it entailed a different level of existence from the rest of humankind. For them, Christ was himself divine.

Other Christians, however, rejected this claim and argued that Christ was a flesh and blood human being without remainder, a man who had been adopted by God to be his Son and to bring about the salvation of the world. To be sure, these representatives of adoptionism constituted no monolith; they differed among themselves, for example, concerning the moment at which Jesus' adoption had taken place. But by the second century, most believed that it had occurred at his baptism, when the Spirit of God descended upon him and a voice called out from heaven, "You are my Son, today I have begotten you."

For the vast majority of believers, whether heretical or orthodox, this form of Christology represented an error of the most egregious kind.[1] For if Christ were a "mere man" ($\psi\iota\lambda\grave{o}\varsigma$ $\check{\alpha}\nu\theta\rho\omega\pi\sigma\varsigma$), then the salvific efficacy of his work could be radically called into question. Irenaeus appears to have been genuinely perplexed, his rhetoric notwithstanding: "How can they be saved unless it was God who wrought out their salvation upon earth? Or how shall a human pass into God, unless God has first passed into a human?" (*Adv. Haer.* IV, 33, 4).[2]

As we have seen, such controversies over Christology were linked by the combatants themselves to questions concerning the text of the New Testament. I have already considered the proto-orthodox pamphlet cited by Eusebius, a pamphlet that accuses the Roman adoptionists Theodotus, Asclepiades, and Hermophilus of tampering with the manuscripts of the New Testament in order to secure their own theology within them (*Hist. Eccl.* V, 28).[3] Whether the charge was justified can no longer be determined: the anonymous author cites as evidence the variant exemplars produced by the group, and these are no longer extant. Furthermore, few other traces of this kind of activity among the heretics have survived antiquity.[4] What have survived are the scriptural texts produced by scribes who held to the author's own theological persuasion. Interestingly enough, some of these "orthodox" texts do evidence tampering—precisely in passages that might have otherwise proved useful as proof texts for the adoptionists. The alterations, that is, do not lean toward the heretical point of view, but toward the orthodox.

Before we can consider specific instances of such corruptions, however, it is necessary to understand more fully who the early adoptionists were and why their christological opinions proved so offensive to the ancestors of orthodoxy.

The Earliest Adoptionists

Christians of the second and third centuries generally—regardless of theological persuasion—claimed to espouse the views of Jesus' earliest followers.[5] With regard at least to the adoptionists, modern scholarship has by and large conceded the claim. These Christians did not originate their views of Christ; adoptionistic Christologies can be traced to sources that predate the books of the New Testament.

The business of reconstructing the preliterary sources of the New Testament is a highly complex affair, and a discussion of the attendant difficulties lies beyond the purview of the present investigation. It is enough to observe that form-critical analyses of the New Testament creedal, hymnic, and sermonic materials have consistently demonstrated earlier strata of tradition that were theologically modified when incorporated into their present literary contexts.[6] Many of these preliterary traditions evidence adoptionistic views.

One of the earliest examples derives from the opening verses of Paul's letter to the Romans, in which he appears to be quoting a bipartite christological creed: "[Christ Jesus . . .] who came from the seed of David according to the flesh, who was appointed Son of God in power according to the Spirit of holiness by his resurrection from the dead" (Rom 1:3–4). That the text embodies a pre-Pauline creed is evident on both linguistic and ideational grounds:[7] terms such as ὁρισθέντος ("appointed") and πνεῦμα ἀγιωσύνης ("Spirit of holiness") occur nowhere else in Paul, nor does the notion of Jesus' Davidic descent.[8] In particular, the idea that Jesus received a divine appointment to be God's Son at his resurrection is not at all Pauline. What has struck a number of scholars in this connection is that the highly balanced structure that one normally finds in such creedal fragments[9] is here broken by a phrase that *is* distinctively Pauline, "ἐν δυνάμει."[10] Once this Pauline feature is removed, a balanced structure is restored, and one is left with a christological confession that appears to pre-date the writings of our earliest Christian author, or at least his letter to the Romans (dated usually in the late 50s C.E.), a confession that acknowledges that Christ attained his status of divine sonship only at his resurrection.[11]

Interestingly, the same christological notion occurs in other preliterary sources embedded in the New Testament. Thus, a form-critical analysis of

Paul's speech in Acts 13 reveals traditional material that has been incorporated in a surprisingly unedited form.[12] Here Paul makes the following pronouncement: "What God promised to the [Jewish] fathers he has fulfilled to us their children, by raising Jesus from the dead—as it is written in the second Psalm, 'You are my Son, today I have begotten you'" (vv. 32–33). The force of the final clause should not be minimized: it is on the day of his resurrection that Jesus receives his sonship.[13] This corresponds closely with other preliterary traditions of the book of Acts. In his sermon on the day of Pentecost, Peter proclaims that Jesus' unjust treatment at the hands of his executioners was reversed by his glorious vindication when God raised him from the dead and exalted him to his right hand: "Let all the house of Israel know that God made him both Lord and Christ, this Jesus whom you crucified" (2:36); later, when addressing Cornelius's household, Peter speaks of Jesus as "the one who has been appointed (ἐστιν ὁ ὡρισμένος, cf. Rom 1:4) by God to be the judge of the living and the dead" (10:42). Paul also, in his speech on the Areopagus, speaks of God having appointed (ὥρισεν) Jesus in connection with his resurrection (17:31). The adoptionistic thrust of these passages is not mitigated by a minor change of wording, as happened in Romans 1:3–4, but by their incorporation into the wider context of Luke–Acts, where Jesus is the Son of God already at his birth (Luke 1:35).[14]

As I have already stated, most of the later adoptionists that we can actually identify—the Ebionites, Theodotus, Artemon—located the time of Jesus' adoption not at his resurrection, but at his baptism. One would naturally expect that unless they invented this notion themselves, traces of it should be found in earlier traditions. Such traces do in fact exist, and most of them, as we shall see, were changed in one way or another by various scribes during the history of their transmission. Adoptionists could read the Gospel of Mark itself as one indication that Jesus was made the Son of God at his baptism. There is no birth narrative here, no mention of Jesus at all until he is an adult; his first public appearance comes at his baptism, when the Spirit of God comes upon him and the divine voice proclaims him to be his Son. Whether Mark "intended" an adoptionistic Christology is difficult to say. What is clear is that this, our earliest Gospel, makes absolutely no reference to Jesus' virginal conception, nor to his pre-existence or deity.[15]

With respect to other New Testament traditions concerning Jesus' baptism, the earliest textual witnesses of the Gospel according to Luke preserve a conspicuously adoptionistic formula in the voice from heaven, "You are my Son, today I have begotten you" (Luke 3:22). I will argue that this text is, in fact, original to Luke and that it coincides perfectly with his portrayal of Jesus' baptism elsewhere in his two-volume work. Here it is enough to observe that an adoptionistic construal of the scene appears to be as primitive as our oldest textual witnesses to the Gospel.

Other potentially adoptionistic texts within the New Testament will be discussed throughout the course of this chapter, as we see how they were invariably changed by one or another orthodox scribe. This introductory sketch is sufficient to show that the adoptionists of the second and third centuries stood in a long line of christological tradition and could therefore appeal to this earlier tradition in support of their views.[16]

The Ebionites

Whether seen from a social or theological point of view, Jewish Christianity in the early centuries was a remarkably diversified phenomenon.[17] This has become increasingly clear to scholars conversant with the wide range of New Testament materials: Matthew and Paul are both in the canon, as are Hebrews, James, and Jude; many of Paul's opponents were clearly Jewish Christians, as (conceivably) were the secessionists from the Johannine community, attacked by the author of the Johannine epistles, who was himself probably Jewish. Nonetheless, scholars have not infrequently construed Jewish-Christianity in rather monolithic terms, influenced, no doubt, by early heresiologists who demonstrated a remarkable ability to package social groups according to discrete theological categories.[18]

The modern emphasis on theological diversity in the early centuries, however, has brought some sense of reality to the description of Jewish Christianity, forcing scholars to recognize that there were in fact radically different points of view represented by different Jewish Christians, and that various Jewish-Christian groups probably developed their views over time, so that what was believed by the majority of a group's members in the year 180 C.E. may not have been at all what was believed in the year 120 C.E. Nonetheless, there appears to be a tendency even now to think along the lines of several distinct groupings, two or three monoliths instead of one, rather than to recognize that Jewish Christianity probably manifested itself in vastly different ways from one community to the next over time.[19]

My concern here, however, is less with Jewish Christianity as it really was than with Jewish Christianity as it was perceived by the proto-orthodox. For it was their *perception* of their opponents that led scribes to modify their texts of Scripture. Most of our heresiological sources recognize two major groups of Jewish Christians: those who are essentially orthodox, who err only in subscribing to the abiding validity of the Mosaic Law, and those who are patently heretical, particularly in light of their aberrant Christologies.[20] Members of the latter group are frequently labeled "Ebionites" ("those who are poor") by their opponents.[21]

Unfortunately, not even the patristic testimony to the Ebionites is altogether unified, for reasons I have already intimated. On the one hand, the group itself was not internally coherent: Christians calling themselves Ebionite did not all subscribe to the same theological views (any more than all "Christians" did or do), and some of the Ebionite groups may have undergone significant transformations in the course of their history.[22] Moreover, the patristic testimony tended to be both self-perpetuating and progressively distorted over time—later authors invariably adopted views earlier presented by Ireneaus and his contemporaries, modifying them in more or, usually, less reliable ways.[23] Nonetheless, some ideas and practices appear with some regularity in the patristic accounts, making it possible at least to reconstruct how a typical orthodox Christian might have understood the teachings of a typical Ebionite.

According to orthodox sources, the Ebionites self-consciously traced their lineage back to apostolic times, and like the earliest followers of Jesus worked to preserve their Jewish identity and customs, including the practices of circumcision and kashrut.[24] Although a variety of Christologies are attested for such groups,[25] they are most commonly portrayed as adoptionists who rejected both the notion of Jesus' pre-existence and the doctrine of his virgin birth, maintaining instead that Jesus was a "normal" human being, born of natural generation: "They regard [Christ] as plain and ordinary, a man esteemed as righteous through growth of character and nothing more, the child of a normal union between a man and Mary" (Eusebius, *Hist. Eccl.* III, 27).[26] Jesus was distinct only because of his exemplary righteousness, on account of which God chose him to be his Son at his baptism and gave him his messianic mission. This he fulfilled by dying on the cross, after which God raised him from the dead and exalted him to heaven. From there he was expected to return to Jerusalem, the city of God, which still preserved its sacred status.

The heresiological sources agree that the Ebionites accepted the binding authority of the Old Testament (and therefore the continuing validity of the Law) but rejected the authority of the apostate apostle, Paul. The sources do not agree about the character and contours of the gospel used by the Ebionites.[27] Most of the fathers from the early second century (Papias) to the late fourth (Jerome) claimed that it comprised a truncated form of Matthew (outwardly the most Jewish of the four) written in Hebrew, one that lacked its opening chapters, that is, the narrative of Jesus' miraculous birth. But the only quotations preserved from the so-called *Gospel of the Ebionites* are found in the writings of the fourth-century heresiologist Epiphanius—who also claims a personal acquaintance with an Ebionite group in the Trans-Jordan—and these quotations derive from a harmony of the Synoptics written in Greek.[28] The question concerning the character of the Ebionite Gospel is particularly thorny because two other Jewish Christian gospels are attested in the church fathers, the *Gospel of the Hebrews* and the *Gospel of the Nazarenes,* the latter of which may well have been confused with the *Gospel of the Ebionites* by church fathers who had seen neither one.[29]

Theodotus and His Followers

In external appearance, the Roman adoptionists of the second and early third century do not seem at all like the Ebionites. They claimed no Jewish roots; they did not follow the Torah, nor practice circumcision, nor revere Jerusalem. But in other respects they appear strikingly similar: Theodotus and his followers believed that Jesus was completely and only human, born of the sexual union of his parents,[30] a man who, on account of his superior righteousness, came to be adopted as the Son of God at his baptism. They also maintained that their views were apostolic, advocated by the disciples of Jesus and transmitted through true believers down to their own day.[31]

The patristic sources provide a relatively sparse testimony to the views of Theodotus the Cobbler, which is somewhat surprising given his distinction as the "first" to claim that Christ was a "mere man" (ψιλὸς ἄνθρωπος; Eusebius, *Hist. Eccl.* V, 28). Of his two principal disciples, Theodotus the Banker and Artemon, little more is known than that they perpetuated their leader's heresy with intellectual rigor and, as a result, were evidently separated from the Roman church. As might be expected, later heresiological sources supply additional anecdotal material, resting more on pious imagination than on solid evidence.[32]

The earliest accounts are provided by Hippolytus and the so-called Little Labyrinth—three anonymous fragments preserved by Eusebius that are often ascribed, perhaps wrongly, to Hippolytus.[33] Both sources are contemporaneous with their opponents, and despite their differences, provide a basic sketch that coheres with later portrayals.[34] Theodotus the Cobbler came to Rome from Byzantium in the days of Pope Victor (189–198 C.E.). He claimed that Christ was not himself divine, but was a "mere man."[35] Because Jesus was more pious than all others, at his baptism he became empowered by the Holy Spirit to perform a divine mission. According to the report of Hippolytus, Theodotus denied that this empowerment actually elevated Jesus to the level of divinity, although some of his followers claimed that Jesus did become divine in some sense, either at his baptism or at his resurrection. The Little Labyrinth reports that Theodotus's followers insisted that the view of Jesus as fully human but not divine was the majority opinion in the Roman church until the time of Victor's successor Zephyrinus, who "mutilated the truth." The author of the fragment argues quite to the contrary that the belief in Jesus' full divinity is attested both in Scripture and in a wide range of ancient Christian authors, naming in support Justin, Miltiades, Tatian, Clement, Irenaeus, and Melito. Moreover, the author insists that Victor himself had excommunicated Theodotus for his heretical views, a claim that became standard heresiological fare in later times.

The Little Labyrinth also attacks Theodotus's followers for their adoptionistic views, although, as one might expect, it provides some evidence that their theology developed over time. In particular it denounces these troublemakers for preferring secular learning (syllogisms and geometry) to the rule of faith, and secular scholars (Aristotle, Theophrastus, and Galen) to Christ. Furthermore, as we have seen, it accuses them of corrupting their texts of Scripture in order to make them conform to their own views.[36]

Paul of Samosata

I conclude this overview with the notorious Paul of Samosata, not because he actually was an adoptionist, but because the Council of Antioch in 268 C.E. condemned him on these terms, and consequently removed him from his influential post as bishop. In fact, there are reasons for doubting the charge against him.

The sources for Paul's life and the two or three councils held to consider charges against him are relatively sparse and of varying degrees of historical reliability.[37] Although there are fragmentary records of the conciliar investigation—the so-called *Acta,* preserved in manuscripts of the fifth and sixth centuries—most recent investigators have discounted their authenticity.[38] There is also a letter addressed to Paul by six bishops at the council, the *Epistula,* which is now widely considered authentic but which proves problematic for knowing what Paul himself believed because it expresses only the theological affirmations of his orthodox opponents, not the heretical views it was drafted to oppose.[39] Finally, Eusebius had apparently read accounts of the trial, and preserves the synodal letter that came out of it. This letter is normally taken to be authentic, and gives some clues as to Paul's Christology.

What is striking is that while the synodal letter explicitly states that Paul was deposed for his aberrant christological views, it scarcely deals with such issues per se, but instead focuses on Paul's haughty attitude and ethical improprieties.[40] The bishops object to his strutting through the marketplace with bodyguards and adoring crowds, to his suspicious accumulation of wealth, to his decision to build a throne, tribunal, and *secretum,* to his preference of the title *ducenarius* to bishop, and to his indiscreet consorting with women. The fact that the council deposed him in favor of Domnus, the son of the previous bishop, Demetrian, makes one suspect that the proceedings had as much to do with rivalry and personal loyalty as with Christology (Eusebius, *Hist. Eccl.* VII, 30). Here one cannot fail to observe that Paul's christological error was not at all self-evident. At the first council convened to decide his case, his opponents could find no grounds on which to press charges (*Hist. Eccl.* VII, 28); at the second it was only after the skillful verbal maneuverings of Malchion, a professional rhetorician whose services were acquired just for the occasion, that the opposition was able to expose the error of his opinions. It appears that Paul did not so much advocate a particular heresy as take a position with potentially heretical implications. On such terms, one wonders who would have been safe.

In any event, the christological charge against Paul is clear: the synodal letter likens him to the adoptionist Artemon, his spiritual "father." And so Paul was condemned for professing "low, degraded opinions about Christ," namely that Christ was "just an ordinary man" (κοινὸς ἄνθρωπος, *Hist. Eccl.* VII, 27); for disallowing the singing of hymns to Christ (VII, 30); and, most decisively for the council (but enigmatically for us), for refusing to confess that "the Son of God came down from heaven," insisting instead that Jesus Christ derived "from below" ('Ιησοῦν Χριστὸν κάτωθεν VII, 30). In effect, whatever the real agenda at the Council of Antioch in 268 C.E., Paul was condemned for subscribing to the views of Artemon and his forebears among the Roman adoptionists.

Anti-Adoptionist Polemics and the Orthodox Corruption of Scripture

To sum up, orthodox Christians knew of several prominent individuals and groups who denied that Jesus was himself divine and that he pre-existed. For these "heretics," Jesus Christ was a flesh and blood human being without remainder. Several such persons flatly denied that his birth had been miraculous: he had human parents and his mother was not a virgin. According to their view, Jesus was more righteous than other humans and, on account of his righteousness, had been chosen by God to be his Son, adopted at some critical point of his existence, either at his resurrection, or more commonly, at his baptism.

Against such notions the orthodox insisted on their strongly paradoxical Christology. To be sure, Christ *was* human; but he was also divine, the pre-existent Son of God through whom all things were made. It is no surprise to find that the key points of this controversy affected the texts of Scripture over which it was waged: the scribes who copied these texts were by no means immune from the polemical contexts within which they worked. And so, as we will now see, they altered passages that might suggest that Jesus had a human father, or that he came into existence at his birth, or that he was adopted to be the Son of God at his baptism. They changed other passages to accentuate their own views that Jesus was divine, that he pre-existed, and that his mother was a virgin. In each of these textual corruptions we can detect the anonymous workings of orthodox scribes, who through their transcriptions have left us a record of the far-flung impact of the theological controversies of their day.

Jesus the Unique Son of God: The Orthodox Affirmation of the Virgin Birth

Since the orthodox struggle with adoptionists centered in part on the doctrine of Jesus' virgin birth, we might expect to find a theological battle waged over the first two chapters of Matthew and Luke, the only New Testament passages that affirm the belief.[41] As we have seen, some of the heterodox Christians who denied the doctrine were accused of excising these passages from their canon of Scripture altogether.[42] Others were charged with tampering with the texts so as to remove any notion of a virgin birth from them.[43]

So far as we can tell from the surviving evidence, no scribe chose to pursue the latter course with any rigor or consistency. One might conceivably point to the Syriac manuscript discovered at St. Catherine's Monastery on Mt. Sinai as a possible exception. The fifth-century scribe of this manuscript was either thoughtless in the extreme or somewhat inclined to see Joseph as Jesus' actual father, for he concludes Matthew's genealogy of Jesus with the words "Jacob begot Joseph; Joseph, to whom was betrothed the virgin Mary, begot Jesus, who is called the Christ" (Matt 1:16). Similarly, the following pericope ends not with the statement that Joseph "had no relations with her [Mary] until she bore a son," but with the curious observation that Mary "bore to him [i.e., Joseph] a son" (1:25).[44]

Despite the apparent bias of these corruptions, there are reasons for thinking that they were produced from carelessness rather than intent. If the scribe had wanted to show that Joseph was actually Jesus' father, it seems peculiar that he did nothing in the narrative that follows either to eliminate the word "virgin" (παρθένος, v. 23)[45] or to modify the clear statements that Joseph had no sexual relations with Mary so that her child was from the Holy Spirit (vv. 18, 20).[46] Since there is almost no reason to construe any of the manuscript's variant readings as original in these cases,[47] one can only conclude that the scribe was simply inattentive to the doctrinal ramifications of some of his changes.[48]

In none of our other surviving manuscripts is there any clear evidence to suggest that adoptionistic scribes thoroughly revised their texts so as to eliminate the notion of the virgin birth from the opening chapters of Matthew and Luke. The more sensible choice for them, of course, was to do what the patristic sources claimed they did: delete the passages altogether. But even this more radical step would have had a negligible effect on the manuscripts of Scripture that have survived antiquity. For even if thoroughly adoptionistic texts had been created, they would have had very limited currency, limited, that is, to the adoptionistic circles in which they were produced. Once they ceased to serve their function, that is, once adoptionism no longer presented a live option, such manuscripts would naturally not have been preserved, let alone reproduced, among orthodox Christians who by now were thoroughly conversant with the stories of Jesus' miraculous birth.

What have survived are manuscripts produced by the winners of the conflict, Christians who at times went out of their way to guarantee the "correct" (i.e., their) understanding of Jesus' birth in the face of the claims made by adoptionists such as the Ebionites mentioned by Irenaeus, who maintained that Christ "was begotten by Joseph" (*Adv. Haer.* III, 21, 1).[49] Not surprisingly, in virtually every case of possible ambiguity in the passages in question—whenever, for instance, Joseph is called Jesus' "father" or when he and Mary are designated as Jesus' "parents"—one or another scribe has remedied the potential problem by replacing the word in question with an appropriate (i.e., more patently orthodox) substitution. Examining several such passages will provide an entrée into our study of the orthodox corruption of Scripture.[50]

Joseph is called Jesus' father twice in Luke's birth narrative (2:33, 48).[51] In both instances scribes have modified the text to eliminate what must have appeared incongruous with the firmly entrenched notion that although Joseph was Mary's betrothed, he was not the father of Jesus. Thus, Luke 2:33 states that Jesus' "father and mother began to marvel" (ἦν ὁ πατὴρ αὐτοῦ καὶ ἡ μήτηρ θαυμάζοντες) at the things being said about him. The majority of Greek manuscripts, however, along with a number of Old Latin, Syriac, and Coptic witnesses, have changed the text to read "Joseph and his mother ('Ιωσὴφ καὶ ἡ μήτηρ αὐτοῦ) began to marvel."[52] The change makes perfect sense, given the orthodox view that Joseph was in fact not Jesus' father. There can be little doubt that in this case the majority text represents a corruption rather than the original reading: a wide range of early and superior manuscripts consistently give the reading that is also more difficult.[53] The wide attestation of the variant reading and the confluence of ancient versions in its support, however, do show that the text had been changed relatively early in the history of its transmission, at least in the third century and more likely in the second—precisely during the time of the adoptionist controversies.

This widespread evidence of corruption contrasts with the other instance in which Joseph is called Jesus' father in Luke's birth narrative. In 2:48 Jesus' mother finds him in the Temple and upbraids him by saying, "Look, your father and I (ἰδοὺ ὁ πατήρ σου κἀγώ) have been grieved, searching for you." Once again the text has been changed, but this time in no consistent pattern of variation. One important but fragmentary Greek witness of the fifth century and two Old Latin manuscripts read "Your relatives and I (οἱ συγγενεῖς σου κἀγώ) have been grieved . . ." (C[vid] β e); while a number of ancient versional witnesses read simply "*We* have been grieved . . ." (a b ff[2] g[1] l r[1], syr[c]).[54] Here again the character of the attestation—the combination of an Alexandrian witness with Old Latin and Syriac texts—shows that the reading had already suffered corruption during the period of our concern; yet interestingly the change was not adopted by the majority of manuscripts that evidence corruption in verse 33.

Two general observations concerning these units of variation suggest what we will find throughout the course of this study. The changes appear to be made at an early date for theological reasons,[55] yet they occur randomly in various textual witnesses, not at all with the kind of consistency one might expect. Similar results obtain when we cast our nets a little further to consider two kinds of closely related passages: those that speak of Jesus' "parents" (γονεῖς) in the birth narratives, and those that name Joseph as Jesus' father in other contexts.

In each of the three instances that Luke refers to Jesus' "parents," various scribes have effected changes that circumvent a possible misconstrual. The most widely attested instance occurs in Luke 2:43, where "his parents" (γονεῖς αὐτοῦ) is changed to "Joseph and his mother" (Ἰωσὴφ καὶ ἡ μήτηρ αὐτοῦ) in a wide range of Greek and versional witnesses.[56] Virtually the same phrase (οἱ γονεῖς αὐτοῦ) is changed, less frequently, in Luke 2:41, where one late Greek manuscript and a number of Old Latin witnesses read "both Joseph and Mary" (ὅ τε Ἰωσὴφ καὶ ἡ Μαριάμ).[57] The first occurrence of the phrase in 2:27, however, is modified only in several witnesses of the Diatesseron,[58] and is omitted in several Greek minuscules of a later period.[59]

The same kind of sporadic corruption occurs in passages outside the birth narratives. The text of Luke 3:23 would presumably have caused orthodox scribes few problems, since it explicitly states that Joseph was not Jesus' real father, but was only "supposed" to have been. Nonetheless it is striking that in two of our Greek witnesses (W 579) the genealogy of Joseph that follows is deleted altogether.[60] It is difficult to judge what may have led scribes, either those of our manuscripts or those of their exemplars, to omit some fifteen verses from their text; but perhaps they recognized the incongruity of tracing Joseph's ancestry back to Adam in a story about Jesus, when Joseph was in fact not Jesus' father (as the text of v. 23 itself indicates). Some modern scholars have seen in the genealogy an implicit challenge to the notion that Jesus had no earthly father;[61] some such difficulty may have disturbed certain early scribes as well.[62]

The fact that Luke had already indicated in chapter 3 that Jesus was only "supposed" to have been the son of Joseph may explain why scribes were not particularly concerned to change the text of chapter 4, when the townsfolk of Nazareth are amazed at Jesus' rhetorical skill and ask "Is this not the son of Joseph?" (Luke 4:22). Most orthodox Christians would have recognized that the question evidences a simple failure to understand—these unbelievers *thought* they knew who Jesus was, but he was only "supposedly" the son of Joseph—so that in some sense changing the text would have proved self-defeating. All the same, it is worth noting that one important minuscule manuscript that frequently preserves a very ancient form of text (MS 13) omits the question altogether, whereas another later manuscript (MS 1200) modifies the text to read, "Is this not the son of Israel?" The function of both corruptions is clear, even if it is understandable why most scribes simply never deemed similar changes necessary.

Much the same can be said of the comparable rejection scene of John 6:41–51. Here again the Jewish crowds ask, "Is this not Jesus, the son of Joseph, whose father and mother we know?" (6:42), and again the text goes on to indicate that Jesus' real father is in fact not Joseph but God: when Jesus replies to their query in verses 43–44, he refers to "the Father who sent me." Rather than eliminating the unbelievers' misperception that Jesus was the son of Joseph and Mary, several scribes simply modified the text to heighten its irony. The clearest instance occurs in two changes embodied in one of our earliest manuscripts of the Fourth Gospel, $\mathfrak{p}^{66}$ (early third century). Here the crowd's misguided question is changed into a false assertion, "This is Jesus the son of Joseph,"[63] whereas Jesus' reply is changed to strengthen his counterassertion that he comes from heaven. He now refers explicitly to "*my* father ($\pi\alpha\tau\acute{\eta}\rho$ $\mu o\upsilon$) who sent me."[64] A similar effect obtains in a more widely attested corruption of verse 42, where some early Greek, Latin, and Syriac manuscripts omit $\kappa\alpha\grave{\iota}$ $\tau\grave{\eta}\nu$ $\mu\eta\tau\acute{\epsilon}\rho\alpha$, so that the crowd's claim to know Jesus' lineage applies only to his father. The change heightens the irony of the passage: the crowd mistakenly claims to know Jesus' earthly father, but Jesus states that his Father has sent him from above.[65] In both cases the scribal changes function to reinforce the "correct" construal of the passage, so that in fact the orthodox purpose is achieved even more effectively here than in passages in which the reference to Joseph as Jesus' father has simply been deleted.

There is only one other reference to Joseph as Jesus' father in the New Testament (John 1:45), and this one alone appears to be invariant in the tradition.[66] Yet once again, given the clear ironies of the passage ("Can anything good come out of Nazareth?" [1:46]) and the orthodox "knowledge" that Joseph is not really Jesus' father—any more than Jesus really comes from Nazareth—it is not altogether surprising that the passage has been left intact.

We would do well at this point, before going further in the analysis, to reflect on the orthodox tendency to corrupt the text of Scripture, based on this initial sampling. That there was such a tendency should already be clear: in virtually every instance in which Joseph is called Jesus' father or parent, various scribes have changed the text in such a way as to obviate the possibilities of misconstrual. The tendency will become increasingly clear as I begin to survey the surviving data. But this matter of survival itself should give us pause. For scribes do not appear, at least in the materials considered so far, to have been thoroughly consistent or rigorous in their attempts to rid the text of latent ambiguities and so to eliminate the possiblity of interpreting these texts in adoptionistic terms. The reasons for this lack of consistency are not too difficult to find. As I have already argued, the majority of orthodox Christians, and presumably orthodox scribes, could live perfectly well with the text as originally written, interpreting it, that is, according to orthodox criteria and beliefs.[67] Furthermore, the very process of transmitting texts was itself a radically conservative process. These scribes understood that they were conserving rather than creating tradition, however problematic the notion might appear to scholars living in a post-modernist world in which every "conservation" and every "reading" of a text is itself an "interpretation" or "writing" of a text.[68]

I have devoted all my attention so far to textual variants involving Jesus' relationship to Joseph in Luke and John. Joseph is never called Jesus' "father" or "parent" in Matthew's Gospel, but given the circumstance that Matthew also records a birth story, one might expect to find some kinds of orthodox corruption here as well. We have already seen that the scribe of the Sinaitic Syriac manuscript, apparently through carelessness, presents a potentially adoptionistic variation of Jesus' genealogy in Matthew 1:16. It is striking that other witnesses supply different variations of precisely the same verse, and that these variations serve rather well to stress orthodox notions concerning Jesus' birth. The text of most manuscripts reads "Jacob begot Joseph, the husband of Mary, from whom (fem.) was born Jesus, who is called the Christ." But several witnesses of the so-called Caesarean text read "Jacob begot Joseph, to whom being betrothed, a virgin Mary begot Jesus, who is called the Christ" (Θ f[13] OL arm [syr[c]]). The Caesarean changes are patently orthodox: now the text explicitly calls Mary a "virgin" (παρθένος) and it no longer calls Joseph her "husband" (ἀνήρ) but her "betrothed" (ᾧ μνηστευθεῖσα). These changes serve not only to keep the text in line with the rest of the story (esp. vv. 18–25), but also to eliminate the possibility of misconstrual. Mary was not yet living with a man as his wife, she was merely his betrothed; and she was still a virgin, even though pregnant.[69] It should be added that there is little reason to suppose the Caesarean reading to be original. Not only does it lack early and widespread support, it also fails to pass muster on the grounds of transcriptional probabilities. Given the story of verses 18–25, who would have wanted to change the perfectly innocuous Caesarean text of verse 16 into one that could be understood as problematic (by calling Joseph Mary's ἀνήρ and by eliminating the word "virgin")?[70] This Caesarean reading is thus better explained as an early modification of the other, an orthodox corruption that serves to circumvent an adoptionistic construal of the text.[71]

Other textual variants that stress the orthodox doctrine of the virgin birth occur outside the birth narratives of Matthew and Luke. One of the most striking appears in the manuscript tradition of the Fourth Gospel, a Gospel that does not record a birth narrative of its own. Some orthodox Christians of the early church thought that John nonetheless did allude to Jesus' miraculous birth in the opening chapter of his Gospel. The most interesting patristic discussion occurs in Tertullian, who accuses his Valentinian opponents of tampering with the text of John 1:13 (*de carne Christi*, 19). Originally, claimed Tertullian, the text referred to the birth of Jesus: "Who was born, not of blood, nor of the will of the flesh, nor of the will of a human, but of God." The Valentinians, he maintained, sought to replace this reference to Jesus' miraculous birth by making the passage refer to their own. This they did by making the verb plural: "who *were* born, not of blood, nor of the will of flesh, nor of the will of a human, but of God." Tertullian went on to argue that the verse affirms in no uncertain terms both the supernatural character of Jesus' conception (in that it occurred apart from sexual intercourse ["born not from blood . . ."]), and the reality of his birth as a physical event (against the Gnostics).

Is it possible that Tertullian's form of the text, that is, with the singular form of the verb, was generated in an anti-adoptionistic milieu?[72] It is worth observing that in another context Tertullian cites the verse (in the singular) explicitly to counter the teachings of "Ebion" (*de carne Christi*, 24). Somewhat earlier, Irenaeus also quotes the verse in the singular to argue that Jesus was not a mere man, but that he came from God and was born of the virgin (*Adv. Haer.* III, 16, 2; 19, 2). Earlier still, the orthodox forgery, the *Epistula Apostolorum,* uses the verse to sanction belief in the miraculous birth of Jesus, quoting it again in the singular (chap. 3).

Despite the currency of this anti-adoptionistic form of the text in the second century—we can assume from Tertullian's discussion that he, at least, knew of its presence in actual manuscripts of the Fourth Gospel—today the plural is read in every known Greek manuscript and by all the versional evidence, with one solitary exception: the Old Latin manuscript b. This scanty documentary support notwithstanding, the variant reading was championed by a number of textual scholars in the nineteenth century, and perhaps most convincingly by Adolf von Harnack at the beginning of the twentieth.[73] Nonetheless, virtually all recent investigators have been impressed by the overwhelming support of the plural reading in the textual tradition and have recognized the tendentious character of the singular number.[74] Tertullian's protestations notwithstanding, what we have here is not a heretical tampering with the text, but an orthodox one. The corruption serves to locate the orthodox notion of Jesus' birth in a passage that otherwise lacked it.

A comparable textual corruption occurs elsewhere in the Johannine corpus, this time near the end of the first epistle. Establishing a plausible interpretation of 1 John 5:6 has proved more difficult over the years than establishing its text.[75] Nonetheless, the verse's textual problems prove interesting for our investigation, because here the author says something about Jesus' manifestation to the world: "This is the one who came through water and blood, Jesus Christ; not in the water only, but in the water and in the blood." Among the variant readings preserved in the textual tradition, those that affect the introductory clause are particularly germane to the present discussion. For the words "the one who came through water and blood" ($\delta\iota'$ $\mathring{\upsilon}\delta\alpha\tau\circ\varsigma$ $\kappa\alpha\grave{\iota}$ $\alpha\mathring{\iota}\mu\alpha\tau\circ\varsigma$) have been modified in a variety of ways. The following four variants are all attested:[76]

1. "through water and spirit" (MSS 43, 241, 463, 945, 1241, 1831, 1877*, 1891);
2. "through water and spirit and blood" (MSS P 81 88 442 630 915 2492 arm eth);
3. "through water and blood and spirit" (MSS ℵ A 104 424ᶜ 614 1739ᶜ 2412 syrʰ sa bo Or); and
4. "through water and blood and the Holy Spirit" ($\pi\nu\varepsilon\acute{\upsilon}\mu\alpha\tau\circ\varsigma$ $\mathring{\alpha}\gamma\acute{\iota}\upsilon$, MSS 39 61 326 1837).

It might appear at first glance that the first variant is an early assimilation of the text to John 3:5 ("Whoever is not born from water and spirit cannot enter the kingdom of God"), with the others representing different kinds of conflations of this corrupted reading with the one normally understood to be original ("through water and blood").[77] But it should not be overlooked that the *third* variant is in fact the earliest and most widespread of the four, and occurs in witnesses generally acknowledged to be superior to the Byzantine manuscripts attesting the others. With its occurrence in Origen, it can be dated to the early third century, and its variegated attestation shows that it was widely known. It also would have been an easy reading to create out of the original text, since it involves no erasure or substitution, but the simple addition of the two words $\kappa\alpha\grave{\iota}$ $\pi\nu\varepsilon\acute{\upsilon}\mu\alpha\tau\circ\varsigma$ to the end of the clause. Furthermore, the word $\pi\nu\varepsilon\acute{\upsilon}\mu\alpha\tau\circ\varsigma$ would no doubt have been abbreviated as one of the *nomina sacra,* so that the entire corruption could have been made by penning six letters (ΚΑΙΠΝΣ), perhaps above the line. The third variant may therefore represent not a conflation but the earliest form of corruption.

In this case, however, the phrase "water and spirit" is not the earliest modification from which the others derived, so that the parallel to John 3:5 does not explain why the text was changed in the first place. Instead, because the passage refers to "Jesus Christ" and his "coming," one may well suspect that the change was initially made in order to affirm the orthodox doctrine that Jesus did not come into the world through natural means, but through the miraculous working of the Spirit of God (he came "through water and blood and Spirit"). This understanding of the phrase is made yet more explicit in the fourth of the variants, which leaves virtually no room for doubt that the agency of the Holy Spirit is in view (cf. the *locus classicus* of the orthodox doctrine, Luke 1:35). The first two variants, then, simply attest the assimilation of this early and widespread corruption to the familiar words of Jesus to Nicodemus in John, chapter 3.

One other variant reading that may be taken to support the orthodox understanding of Jesus' birth, or at least to circumvent an adoptionistic view, occurs in the unlikely context of Peter's sermon on the day of Pentecost (Acts 2). In speaking of Jesus' resurrection, Peter appeals to a scriptural "proof": David pronounced that God would not allow his holy one to see corruption (Psalm 15). Peter claims that David spoke not of himself but of one to come, for he knew that God would raise up for himself one to sit on David's throne, one who would come "from the fruit of his loins" (ἐκ καρποῦ τῆς ὀσφύος αὐτοῦ, Acts 2:30). An interesting variant is found in codex Bezae, which states instead that David's successor would come "from the fruit of his heart" (ἐκ καρποῦ τῆς καρδίας αὐτοῦ).[78] One might be inclined to see here a simple reference to the well-known saying that David was "a man after God's own heart." In this case the Messiah would be understood to enjoy David's favored status before God. Without denying this possibility, it is worth noting another way the change might function: for now Jesus is no longer said to be a physical descendant of David, but is instead one *like* David.[79] Why would an early scribe want to make such a change?

Some have claimed that the change is accidental, either the mistranslation of an Aramaic source of the speech,[80] or a faulty reversion of the word *praecordis* ("heart" or "belly") by the Greek scribe of codex Bezae from the Latin text on the opposing page (i.e., it[d]).[81] The first possibility depends on the existence of such an Aramaic source for the speeches of Acts, a view everywhere recognized as riddled with problems;[82] the second depends on the influence of Bezae's Latin text on its Greek, an influence that almost certainly occurred in just the reverse direction.[83] It may be more fruitful then to consider the change as deliberate rather than accidental. A plausible explanation is that a scribe who knew that Jesus was born of a virgin recognized that he was not, technically speaking, one of David's line, since he stood in that line only through a legal adoption; so he modified the text to circumvent a misconstrual of Peter's claim. Now Jesus is said to be from David's "heart" rather than his "loins."[84]

More Than Chosen: The Orthodox Opposition to an Adopted Jesus

Representatives of proto-orthodoxy objected to Christian adoptionists not only because they denied that Jesus had been born of a virgin, but also because they claimed that a profound change had occurred in his relationship with God at a critical point of his existence. The righteous man Jesus had been chosen by God, adopted to be his Son. For most adoptionists this had occurred at his baptism. Diametrically opposed to this view was the orthodox notion that Jesus had *always* been the Son of God, prior to his baptism and even to his birth. As the heresiologist Irenaeus states:

That He is Himself . . . God, and Lord, and King Eternal, and the Incarnate Word, proclaimed by all the prophets, the apostles, and by the Spirit Himself, may be seen by all who have attained to even a small portion of the truth. The Scriptures would not have testified these things of Him, if, like others, He had been a mere man." (*Adv. Haer.* III, 19, 2).

One might naturally expect to find that this orthodox view affected the manuscript tradition of the New Testament. And in fact there is evidence precisely where one would anticipate it.

Luke 3:22

A place to begin is with textual corruptions that appear to suppress adoptionistic understandings of Jesus' baptism.[85] One of the most intriguing occurs in early witnesses of Luke's account, in which the voice from heaven is said to proclaim "You are my Son, today I have begotten you" (Luke 3:22). This is the reading of codex Bezae and a number of ecclesiastical writers from the second century onward. I will argue that it is in fact the original text of Luke, and that orthodox scribes who could not abide its adoptionistic overtones "corrected" it into conformity with the parallel in Mark, "You are my beloved Son, in you I am well pleased" (Mark 1:11). Because this particular variant is so central to our discussion, and because most scholars have, in my opinion, wrongly evaluated the competing virtues of the two readings, I will devote a comparatively lengthy discussion to the problem.

External Attestation

The strongest support for the reading of codex Bezae derives from transcriptional and intrinsic probabilities, about which I will be speaking momentarily. But its external attestation should not be discounted, as has frequently happened in earlier treatments.[86] Granting that the reading does not occur extensively after the fifth century, it cannot be overlooked that in witnesses of the second and third centuries, centuries that to be sure have not provided us with any superfluity of Greek manuscripts, it is virtually the only reading that survives. Not only was it the reading of the ancestor of codex Bezae and the Old Latin text of Luke, it appears also to have been the text known to Justin,[87] Clement of Alexandria,[88] and the authors of the *Gospel according to the Hebrews*[89] and the *Didascalia*.[90] It is certainly the text attested by the *Gospel according to the Ebionites,* Origen, and Methodius.[91] Somewhat later it is found in Lactantius, Juvencus, Hilary, Tyconius, Augustine, and several of the later apocryphal Acts.[92] Here I should stress that except for the third-century manuscript 𝔭[4], there is no certain attestation of the other reading, the reading of our later manuscripts, in this early period. The reading of codex Bezae, then, is not an error introduced by an unusually aberrant witness. This manuscript is, in fact, one of the *last* witnesses to preserve it. Nor is it a "Western" variant without adequate attestation. Among sources of the second and third centuries, it is virtually the only reading to be found; down to the sixth century it occurs in witnesses as far-flung as Asia Minor, Palestine, Alexandria, North Africa, Rome, Gaul, and Spain.[93]

How can we account for a textual situation of this sort? The best attested reading of the early period, a reading known throughout the entire Christian world, virtually disappears from sight, displaced by a reading that is, as we shall see, both harmonized to that of another Gospel and less offensive doctrinally. Given what we have seen so far concerning scribal proclivities—and, of course, I have just begun to amass the data—there is every reason to suspect that here we are dealing with an original reading that has been displaced for theological reasons.

Transcriptional Probabilities

This preliminary judgment is rendered more plausible by several pieces of internal evidence. The transcriptional issues are clear and straightforward. One of the two readings harmonizes with the text of Mark and is inoffensive; the other cannot be harmonized with Mark and is doctrinally suspect. Even patristic witnesses that *attest* the reading sometimes reveal their embarassment over it, explaining it away by interpretations that strike modern readers as peculiar in the extreme.[94] If we ask which reading is more likely to have been changed by Christian scribes, how can there be any doubt?

There has been doubt, however, only because *both* readings can be construed as scribal harmonizations: one to Mark's Gospel, the other to the LXX text of Psalm 2:7. This circumstance alone appears to have saved the more widely attested text from the scalpel of commentators and editors. According to the common view, the more difficult reading ("Today I have begotten you") represents a harmonization to the second Psalm.

There are formidable problems with this view, however, as can be seen by probing the transcriptional probabilities through a series of difficult questions: (1) Which is more likely, that a scribe will harmonize a Gospel text to a parallel in another Gospel or to a passage in the Old Testament? Gospel harmonization is virtually ubiquitous in the manuscript tradition of the Synoptics, occurring in nearly every pericope of the double or triple tradition. Furthermore, a scribe who copies Luke will likely have Matthew and Mark on the brain, so to speak, in most cases having recently transcribed them. All things being equal, harmonization to the closest parallel is to be preferred, so that on this score the earliest attested reading appears to be original. (2) Which is more likely—that a scribe will *create* a reading that is doctrinally offensive, or that he will ameliorate a theological problem? To call the words of the Psalm text in Luke 3:22 the more difficult reading is, of course, an accurate kind of shorthand. But we must not lose sight of the compelling logic of the principle, simply because there is a convenient phrase to describe it. The variant reading preserved by the majority of earliest witnesses, the one that has no parallel in the other Gospel accounts, also appears to support a christological view that became anathema in the early Christian centuries. Is it likely that a scribe would have created it? Although this argument might appear circular in the context of the present discussion (which is concerned with *establishing* the presence of theologically oriented corruptions), the same cannot be said of the third question concerning transcriptional probabilities, a question that proves, to my mind at least, to be decisive: If Luke 3:22 was changed by scribes in order to conform its text to the wording of Psalm 2, how is it that the same motivation was never at work in the transmission of the texts of the other Gospels? As common as this explanation of the textual situation might be, no one has ever been able to explain why this particular harmonization occurred in the transcription of Luke, but never in that of Matthew or Mark.

Intrinsic Probabilities

These transcriptional probabilities become particularly compelling when we recognize how well the reading attested in codex Bezae coincides with the theological agenda of Luke himself, even though his agenda may not have been shared by later proto-orthodox scribes. Here there is a powerful confluence of factors, for the reading that proved such an obvious embarassment for orthodox Christians of later times shows remarkable affinities with Luke's own view of Jesus' baptism.

This is not to say that the intrinsic suitability of the reading has been widely recognized. Just to the contrary, in the view of many scholars, it makes little sense for Luke's divine voice to declare that Jesus has *become* the Son of God at his baptism when he had already been *born* the Son of God (from a virgin mother) two chapters earlier. And so, given the angelic pronouncement of Luke's annunciation scene ("the Holy Spirit will come upon you and the power of the Highest will overshadow you, so that the one who is born will be called the Son of God," 1:35) it is virtually inconceivable, in this view, that Jesus would later be told "Today I have begotten you."[95]

Unfortunately, as happens so frequently with arguments of this kind, it is difficult to see which way the knife is more likely to cut. For any perceived discrepancy between Luke chapters 1 and 3 could just as easily have led early scribes to harmonize the text of Luke 3:22 to its parallel in Mark 1:11, thereby circumventing the problem. On this level, it would appear that arguments of intrinsic probabilities (which reading Luke was more likely to have written) and transcriptional probabilities (which reading scribes were more likely to have created) grind to a standstill.

This is not, however, an inevitable outcome of weighing different kinds of probability. It results here only when intrinsic probabilities are evaluated according to the dubious premise that Luke has been (logically) consistent in his use of christological titles and conceptions.[96] The argument assumes, that is, that Luke would not predicate the same christological title to Jesus on the basis of different critical moments, or junctures, of his existence. In fact, the assumption is demonstrably false. When one looks beyond the relationship of Luke 3:22 to 1:32–35 and takes a more panoramic view of this two-volume work, it becomes evident that the words of Psalm 2:7 at Jesus' baptism do not so much create an inadmissable inconsistency as highlight tensions otherwise found—indeed, consistently found—throughout Luke's portrayal of Jesus.

An obvious example comes in Luke's depiction of Jesus as the Messiah. According to Luke's infancy narrative, Jesus was born the Christ (2:11). But in at least one of the speeches of Acts he is understood to have become the Christ at his baptism (10:37–38; possibly 4:27); whereas in another Luke explicitly states that he became the Christ at his resurrection (2:38). It may be that in yet another speech (3:20) Jesus is thought to be the Christ only in his parousia.[97] Similarly "inconsistent" are Luke's predications of the titles Lord and Savior to Jesus. Thus, Jesus is born the Lord in Luke 2:11, and in Luke 10:1 he is designated Lord while living; but in Acts 2:38 he is said to have been *become* Lord at his resurrection. So too, in Luke 2:11 he is born Savior, and in Acts 13:23–24 he is designated Savior while living; but according to Acts 5:31 he is said to have been *made* Savior at the resurrection. Nor does the title Son of God, the title that is directly germane to our present deliberation, escape this seemingly erratic kind of treatment: Jesus is born the Son of God in Luke 1:32–35, descended Son of God according to the genealogy of 3:23–38, and declared to be Son of God while living (e.g., Luke 8:28; 9:35); but Acts 13:33 states that he *became* the Son of God at his resurrection. This kind of titular ambiguity does not inspire confidence in claims that certain readings cannot be Lukan because they stand in tension with Luke's use of christological titles elsewhere.

This does not mean that the broad scope of Luke's narrative is irrelevant to the textual problem of 3:22. It *is* relevant, but not through an appeal to a consistent use of christological notions. More fruitful is an assessment of the other references to Jesus' baptism throughout Luke's work, "backward glances," as it were, that provide clues concerning what happened at that point of the narrative. What is striking is that these other references to Jesus' baptism do not appear to presuppose a simple "identification formula" by which Jesus is acknowledged to be the Son of God ("You are my beloved Son"). They instead assume that God actually *did* something at that moment, that he actually conferred a special status upon Jesus ("Today I have begotten you").

A reasonable place to begin is with the second occurrence of a voice from heaven, that on the Mount of Transfiguration. It is commonly known that for Luke's source, the Gospel of Mark, the heavenly voice at the transfiguration echoes the heavenly voice at the baptism. But whereas the first makes its pronouncement in the second person, apparently addressing only Jesus ("You are my beloved Son," Mark 1:11), the latter occurs in the third person, confirming this disclosure to the disciples ("This is my beloved Son," Mark 9:7). Luke of course used Mark's account in creating his own, and no attempt to reconstruct the heavenly words of Luke's baptism scene can afford to overlook the voice at the transfiguration.[98] Here the textual situation is much clearer. Luke has changed Mark's heavenly voice in the second instance, so that now rather than confirming to the disciples that Jesus is the "beloved" Son, it confirms that Jesus is the "elect" Son: "This is my Son, my chosen one" (ὁ υἱός μου ὁ ἐκλελεγμένος; Luke 9:35).[99] If the voice in Luke's transfiguration scene refers back to the scene of Jesus' baptism and confirms to the disciples what was there revealed to Jesus, that he "has been chosen" (perfect tense), one is hardpressed to see how the more commonly attested text of Luke 3:22 could be original. For this reading ("You are my beloved Son, in whom I am well pleased") constitutes a mere identification formula in which Jesus is recognized as the Son of God. It is only in the variant reading, the one that is attested in virtually all the earliest witnesses, that God is actually said to confer a new status upon Jesus ("Today I have begotten you"). Only in the theologically difficult reading is God said to "elect" Jesus in a manner presupposed in 9:35, that is, through a quotation of the royal adoption formula drawn from the second Psalm.[100]

In further support of this view is Luke's only other reference to Jesus as God's elect. Although Luke never again applies the verbal form ἐκλελεγμένος to Jesus, he does use the synonymous adjective ἐκλεκτός. In the crucifixion scene, in a verse unique to the third Gospel, the crucified Jesus is mocked by the rulers of Israel: "He saved others; let him save himself, if he is the Christ of God, his Chosen One!" (ὁ χριστὸς τοῦ θεοῦ, ὁ ἐκλεκτός, 23:35). Here, interestingly, the title ἐκλεκτός is placed in apposition to χριστός; it is as God's "Christ" that Jesus is his "chosen" one. To this extent, Luke's use of ἐκλέγομαι / ἐκλεκτός corresponds rather closely to the common application of these words to the king of Israel as God's "chosen," his "anointed" throughout the Old Testament.[101] It would not be at all surprising then, to find the clearest expression of an Old Testament "election formula for kings"— namely, Psalm 2:7[102]—applied to Jesus at the point at which he becomes God's elect.

Is this point his baptism? The other Lukan references looking back to the event suggest that it is. One of Luke's striking changes of Mark's narrative sequence occurs in his transferrence of the sermon and rejection at Nazareth to the very outset of Jesus' ministry (Mark 6:1–6; Luke 4:16–30). As is well known, Luke not only changed the narrative context for the account, but he also made a considerable number of internal changes in order to present the scene as a kind of paradigmatic foreshadowing of what was to happen to Jesus in the Gospel and to his followers in Acts. In the preceding context, the Spirit of God comes upon Jesus at his baptism (3:22), then leads him in the wilderness for forty days (4:1). When Jesus returns into Galilee, "in the power of the Spirit" (4:14), he preaches his first sermon. This sermon begins with Jesus' self-declaration in the words of Isaiah 61:1: "The Spirit of the Lord is upon me, because he anointed (ἔχρισεν) me . . . .". Granting that these words are quoted from the Scriptures, one is still left to ask what could be the significance of this aorist tense (ἔχρισεν) for Luke. That is to say, just *when* (prior to Luke 4) did God "anoint" Jesus? The reading that proved more difficult for later scribes provides a clear answer: it was in the preceding chapter when God declared, "Today I have begotten you."[103]

Luke's two other uses of the verb χρίω confirm the point. In Acts 4, Peter refers to Jesus as the one whom God had "anointed" (4:27; ἔχρισας, again aorist tense), after explicitly quoting Psalm 2 with reference to Jesus, the "χριστός" against whom the rulers of the earth were gathered together (Ps 2:1–2). Then in Acts 10 Peter states that God anointed Jesus with the Holy Spirit and power, and this time clearly links the event with "the baptism of John" (10:38).

Together, these texts presuppose that at the baptism God actually *did* something to Jesus. This something is sometimes described as an act of anointing, sometimes as an election. In either case, the action of God is taken to signify his "making" Jesus the Christ. These texts, therefore, show that Luke did not conceive of the baptism as the point at which Jesus was simply "declared" or "identified" or "affirmed" to be the Son of God. The baptism was the point at which Jesus was anointed as the Christ, chosen to be the Son of God.

This understanding of the significance of Jesus' baptism cannot, of course, be unrelated to the words pronounced by the voice in Luke's account. The more commonly attested reading, which happens to be harmonized with Mark's account, involves a declaration or recognition of Jesus' sonship ("You are my Son"). This hardly squares with the significance that Luke attaches to Jesus' baptism elsewhere. The other reading, however, consists of an election formula, in which a king is actually chosen by God upon his anointing ("Today I have begotten you"). Given Luke's indication elsewhere (Acts 4:25–26) that the text of Psalm 2 particularly applies to Jesus' anointing, it should now be clear that the voice in his account actually quoted these words as a proclamation of the momentous election of Jesus as the begotten Son of God at this, the beginning of his ministry.[104]

Orthodox Christians such as Justin recognized the use to which such a view could be made by later adoptionists who denied (now in opposition to Luke) that Jesus had been born of a virgin and claimed that he had been a "mere man." The options open to such orthodox believers were to argue for a nonadoptionistic interpretation of Luke 3:22 or to modify it into conformity with its Synoptic parallel.[105] The latter option seems to have been widely exercised by the anonymous scribes whose handiwork has survived down to the present day.

Other Examples

Having dealt at some length with a passage that proved to be particularly difficult for orthodox scribes, we are now in a position to evaluate several other passages in less detail. One that relates closely to the heavenly voice of Luke 3:22 is the passage already mentioned, the account of the voice at Jesus' transfiguration in Luke 9:35. Here the textual situation is less problematic, because early and superior witnesses (including p⁴⁵ ⁷⁵ ℵ B L Ξ 892 1241) attest the reading that again could have proved susceptible to an adoptionistic construal. In these manuscripts the voice calls Jesus "my Son, the one who has been chosen" (ὁ υἱός μου ὁ ἐκλελεγμένος). One can scarcely account for this text if it is not original. The word ἐκλελεγμένος is not used in this way elsewhere in the New Testament, yet, as has been seen, it portrays a

distinctively Lukan conceptualization of Jesus. And of all the available readings, it alone is not harmonized to one Synoptic parallel or another: the widely
attested ὁ υἱός μου ὁ ἀγαπητός is harmonized to Mark 9:7 (MSS A C* R W
33 565 f¹³ Byz OL syr), the less popular ὁ υἱός μου ὁ ἀγαπητός ἐν ᾧ εὐδόκησα
to Matthew 17:5 (C³ D Ψ d cop^bo[ms] Lect.s), and the Caesarean ἐκλεκτός to
Luke 23:35 (Θ f¹ MS 1365). The vast majority of textual scholars therefore
accept the earliest attested reading as original.

Why, then, was it changed? Not simply to make the Gospel texts har-
monious. If this were the case, one would expect the alternative process to
have happened as well—that is, harmonizations of Mark and Matthew to the
text of Luke. The magnitude of the textual changes in Luke, coupled with
the virtual absence of such changes in Matthew or Mark,[106] suggests that the
change was made for doctrinal reasons pure and simple—to eliminate the
potentially adoptionistic overtones of the text.[107]

One might expect the third related Lukan text to have been similarly
affected by scribes. But given the earlier discussions of passages relating to
the virgin birth, one can posit reasons for scribes not taking particular umbrage at the crowd's mockery of Jesus in Luke 23:35: "Let him save himself
if he is the Christ of God, his elect" (εἰ οὗτός ἐστιν ὁ χριστὸς τοῦ θεοῦ, ὁ
ἐκλεκτός). Although the text suffered various kinds of corruption at different
points of the tradition,[108] the final two words are omitted only sporadically
(e 047). An interesting pattern seems to be emerging here. We have seen that
anti-adoptionistic changes occur rather frequently when Luke's narrator calls
Joseph Jesus' father, but not when unbelievers do. So, too, in references to
Jesus as God's "elect." When the voice from heaven addresses Jesus in these
terms, the text is widely changed; when unbelievers do, it escapes virtually
unscathed. It is difficult to know what to make of these data, except to say
that orthodox scribes appear to have been somewhat sensitive to context and
to have allowed their own interpretive principles to guide their decisions concerning which passages to modify.

One other passage from the Lukan corpus has suffered a similar sort of
early corruption, although in this case the change is considerably more subtle
than those considered to this point. The Apostle Peter begins his speech to
Cornelius's household in Acts 10 by reminding them of what had happened
with respect to "Jesus of Nazareth" after the preaching of baptism by John,
"how God anointed him with the Holy Spirit and power" (ὡς ἔχρισεν αὐτὸν
ὁ θεὸς πνεύματι ἁγίῳ καὶ δυνάμει) before he went about performing his
ministry of doing good and healing those who were oppressed by the devil
(10:38). There is little doubt concerning the text at this point, since it is
supported by virtually the entire Greek tradition, even though it strikes the
reader as grammatically awkward: the ὡς clause ("how God anointed him")
appears to function as a syntactical parallel to the following relative clause
("who went about doing good . . ."). This in itself may explain the change
preserved in codex Bezae and representatives of the Old Latin, Syriac, and
Middle Egyptian traditions, a change from ὡς ἔχρισεν αὐτόν ("how God
anointed him") to ὃν ἔχρισεν ("whom God anointed"). But the change ful-

fills another function as well, for as the original text stands, part of the Gospel message concerns how God anointed Jesus with the Spirit, empowering him for his ministry of doing good and healing. All of this, according to Luke, took place on the heels of John's baptismal activities. As has been seen, such a view was advocated by adoptionists like the second-century Theodotus, who supported his view of Jesus' election by observing that he did no miracles prior to becoming God's anointed Son at the baptism.[109] By transforming the adverbial clause into a relative one, the so-called Western text in effect removes the story of God's anointing of Jesus from the "matter that transpired" in the days of John. Now the text simply identifies Jesus as the one God anointed to do good, without stating, however, that the action of Jesus becoming God's anointed formed part of the Gospel message they had heard.[110]

This interpretation of the change of Acts 10:38 is lent some cogency by a comparable modification of the preceding verse in codex Vaticanus. In this early witness there is no mention of John's baptism at all: "after the baptism that John preached" is changed to "after the preaching of John" ($\mu\epsilon\tau\grave{\alpha}$ $\tau\grave{o}$ $\kappa\acute{\eta}\rho\upsilon\gamma\mu\alpha$ $\grave{o}$ $\grave{\epsilon}\kappa\acute{\eta}\rho\upsilon\xi\epsilon\nu$ $\mathrm{'I}\omega\acute{\alpha}\nu\nu\eta\varsigma$). The change is subtle, but again seems to minimize the connection between the Baptist's activities and Jesus' anointing, making the passage less susceptible to an adoptionistic use. For the orthodox it was less objectionable to concede in a general way that Christ was endowed with God's spirit and power than to associate that endowment with a specific event that transpired at his baptism.

That the issues we have been examining are not restricted to Luke and Acts can be seen by considering one of the intriguing textual variants of the Fourth Gospel. In the majority of textual witnesses, the testimony of John the Baptist to Jesus reads: "And I have seen and borne witness that this is the Son of God" ($o\grave{v}\tau\acute{o}\varsigma$ $\grave{\epsilon}\sigma\tau\iota\nu$ $\grave{o}$ $\upsilon\grave{i}\grave{o}\varsigma$ $\tauo\hat{v}$ $\theta\epsilon o\hat{v}$; 1:34). But there are solid reasons for thinking that the reading preserved in a range of early and significant manuscripts is to be preferred: ". . . that this is the Elect ($\grave{o}$ $\grave{\epsilon}\kappa\lambda\epsilon\kappa\tau\acute{o}\varsigma$) of God" ($\mathfrak{p}^{5\mathrm{vid}}$ ℵ* 77 218 b e ff²* syr$^{s\ c}$).[111]

In terms of textual alignments, codex Sinaiticus belongs to the so-called Western text in this portion of John.[112] This means that even though the reading is not widely attested later in the tradition, it is found in the earliest and best representatives of the "Western" tradition,[113] as well as in one of the early Alexandrian papyri. Furthermore, the reading can boast a fairly widespread attestation, being found in witnesses of Egypt, Syria, and the Latin-speaking West.[114]

Yet more importantly, it is virtually impossible to explain the existence of this early reading if the more commonly attested "Son of God" were original. The term "elect of God" does not occur elsewhere in John's Gospel, making it difficult to see what would have motivated a scribe to use it here—especially since none of the occurrences of "Son" in John's text, and they are legion, were changed similarly.[115] One can readily see, on the other hand, why a scribe might want to change an unusual term to one that is both more familiar and typical in the Gospel. This is particularly so given the scribal proclivities we have already detected, namely to modify texts that could be construed adoptionistically. It should be observed that here again the idea of Jesus' election is associated with his baptism, an association that the orthodox took some pains to eschew. It is striking that this association occurs in both Luke and John. Other similarities between these two Gospels (i.e., in passages that are not textually disputed) have led a number of scholars to posit some kind of common oral tradition behind their accounts.[116] In short, John (as well as Luke) appears to have understood Jesus to be "the elect of God."[117] Scribes who found this description potentially offensive modified it into conformity with standard Johannine usage elsewhere.[118]

The textual corruption of another Johannine passage is somewhat more involved. The text of 1 John 5:18 has traditionally proved to be as difficult to interpret as to establish: "We know that everyone who is born from God (πᾶς ὁ γεγεννημένος ἐκ τοῦ θεοῦ) does not sin, but the one who has been born from God keeps him" (ὁ γεννηθεὶς ἐκ τοῦ θεοῦ τηρεῖ αὐτόν). The issue of interpretation has centered on the object of τηρεῖ, that is, whether it was originally a personal pronoun (αὐτόν) or a reflexive (αὑτόν). This decision depends in part on whether the preceding participial clause "the one who has been born from God" (ὁ γεννηθεὶς ἐκ τοῦ θεοῦ) refers to Christ or the believer. The exegetical choice is of some significance: the verse either means that Christ as the one begotten of God protects the Christian from sin or that a person is enabled to abstain from sin by virtue of a spiritual birth.[119] The choice is complicated by the textual issue. For among a range of Old Latin, Coptic, and later Greek manuscripts, the final clause "the one who has been born of God keeps him" has been changed to read "the birth from God (ὁ γέννησις τοῦ θεοῦ) keeps him."[120] With this wording of the text, spiritual rebirth itself preserves the believer from sin. Why might scribes have sought to make the change?

It must first be said that there is almost nothing to commend the reading ὁ γέννησις as original.[121] The entire Greek manuscript tradition before the Middle Ages, and virtually all the patristic and versional evidence, stands against it, as do intrinsic probabilities: the better attested reading preserves a contrasting parallelism of two participial clauses, ὁ γεγεννημένος ἐκ τοῦ θεοῦ ("the one who *is* born of God," i.e., the believer) and ὁ γεννηθεὶς ἐκ τοῦ θεοῦ ("the one who *has been* born of God," i.e., probably Christ, as I will argue momentarily). The original reading then was ὁ γεννηθείς. Orthodox scribes may well have found the text awkward, for one could readily ask, *"When* was Christ 'born of God'?" The adoptionists, of course, had an answer ready to hand: it was when God chose him and anointed him with his spirit (normally, at the baptism). Transcriptional probabilities, then, also speak in favor of the participial construction.

Orthodox scribes could change the text in two different ways in order to circumvent an adoptionistic reading. The less frequently chosen path involved changing the expression "the one born from God" to "the birth from God." Although, as has been seen, the reading cannot be taken as original, it is nonetheless ancient (Old Latin, Syriac, Coptic). The other possibility was simpler and involved the interchange of the personal pronoun (αὐτόν) with the reflexive (ἑαυτόν) following the main verb. In this case one is more or less forced to understand by ὁ γεννηθείς not Christ but the believer (i.e., as the one who "keeps himself"). In contrast to the other corruption, this one proved popular in the manuscripts of the Greek tradition (ℵ A^c P Ψ 33 81 1739 Byz Lect Or et al.).

Despite its prominence, the reflexive (used here with the aorist participle) can scarcely be original. To be sure, in 1 John γεννάω frequently designates believers, nine times in all; but in each instance the verb is given in the perfect passive, never the aorist.[122] Furthermore, if the aorist were taken to refer to the believer, the point of the verse would be considerably muddled: no longer would it present a clear contrast between the believer who is liable to sin and Christ who keeps from sin. Now it contrasts the believer who *is* born of God and yet liable to sin and, presumably, the same believer who *was* born of God and who protects himself from sin.

Thus, on the basis of Johannine style and the immediate context, one can conclude that the personal pronoun, as attested in manuscripts A* B and a range of other Greek and versional witnesses, must be original. As a result, the change of both the participial clause and the object of τηρεῖ can be seen as secondary corruptions that serve to frustrate a possible adoptionistic reading of the text. With these changes, Christ is no longer the one "who has been born of God."[123]

Several of the orthodox changes that I have considered are directed against adoptionistic views of Jesus' baptism. That this should be the focal point of concern is no surprise: all the known adoptionists of the second and third centuries claimed that it was at his baptism that God adopted Jesus to be his Son. Nonetheless, some of the earliest traditions put the christological moment par excellence at the resurrection. For these traditions, God appointed Jesus to be his Son when he vindicated him and exalted him to heaven. That this was not a live christological option after the first century in part explains why texts such as Acts 13:33, texts that might otherwise appear so problematic, survived the pens of the orthodox scribes virtually unscathed.[124]

In at least one instance, however, such a text *has* been slightly altered, presumably to mitigate its potentially adoptionistic overtones. As we have seen, in the opening of the book of Romans Paul quotes an early christological creed: "[Jesus Christ], who came from the seed of David according to the flesh, who was appointed Son of God in power (τοῦ ὁρισθέντος υἱοῦ θεοῦ ἐν δυνάμει) at the resurrection of the dead" (Rom 1:3–4). One is naturally taken aback to see Paul referring to Jesus' "appointment" as Son of God at the resurrection, but he clearly had reasons for quoting the creed.[125] Moreover, as I have noted, he was himself probably responsible for changing the wording of the creed by interpolating the phrase ἐν δυνάμει. Now Christ does not become the Son of God, but the "Son-of-God-in-power" at the resurrection, an idea compatible with other Pauline (and pre-Pauline) texts (cf., e.g., Phil 2:6–11).

Apparently, however, not even the Pauline modification satisfied Latin scribes of the early centuries. This, at least, seems to be the implication of the standard Latin rendering of the verse, which presupposes the word προορισθέντος, rather than the simple ὁρισθέντος, for the description of God's election of Jesus ("praedestinatus" rather than "destinatus"). That the compounded form of the participle is not original to the text is clear: it has no Greek or other versional support, and in fact makes the thought rather convoluted.[126] The notion seems to be that God "predestined" Jesus to attain his status as Son of God at the resurrection. This would mean, of course, that Jesus already enjoyed a special status before God prior to the event itself (as the one "predestined") so that the resurrection was but the realization of a status proleptically conferred upon him.[127] In short, the variant, which cannot be traced beyond the confines of the Latin West, serves to undermine any assumption that Jesus' resurrection effected an entirely new standing before God.

Jesus, Son of God before His Baptism

Given the adoptionists' view that Jesus' sonship dates from the time of his baptism, it is not surprising to find textual corruptions that speak of him as God's Son even before this revelatory event. Of the various texts to be considered here, the one that has generated by far the most scholarly interest is the opening verse of the Gospel according to Mark.[128]

Mark 1:1

The vast majority of manuscripts introduce the Gospel of Mark with the words: "The beginning of the Gospel of Jesus Christ, the Son of God." But the final phrase, "the Son of God," is lacking in several important witnesses, including manuscripts ℵ Θ 28ᶜ 1555, syrᵖ arm geo, and Origen. In terms of numbers, the support for this shorter text is slight. But in terms of antiquity and character, this is not a confluence of witnesses to be trifled with. It frequently *has* been trifled with, however, and here is where one finds no little confusion in earlier discussions of the problem. Thus, one scholar discounts the evidence as deriving entirely from Caesarea, and as therefore representing a local corruption—even though supporting witnesses include the early Alexandrian codex Sinaiticus and the part of Origen's John Commentary that was written in Alexandria.[129] Another scholar maintains that because Sinaiticus has some affinities with the so-called Western textual tradition (he must have in mind the opening chapters of John, which have no relevance to the issue here), it is to be grouped with the Western text, so that now there is only secondary Western and Caesarean support for the reading.[130] Still other scholars argue that because Origen and Sinaiticus are otherwise so similar, their support must be counted as one witness instead of two, a solitary Alexandrian witness not to be given much weight.[131]

In point of fact, two of the three best Alexandrian witnesses of Mark support this text. Moreover, Origen quotes it in this form not only in Alexandria, but also in the *Contra Celsum,* which he wrote in Caesarea.[132] He may, of course, simply have remembered or used his Alexandrian manuscripts after his move, but it is to be noted that the reading also occurs in other so-called Caesarean texts, including its best representative, codex Koridethi, and the Palestinian, Armenian, and Georgian versions. Furthermore, the reading is found in a later witness that otherwise attests an essentially Western text (MS 1555).[133] This slate of witnesses is diverse both in terms of textual consanguinity and geography. It is this diversity that poses the greatest difficulty for the normal explanation of the problem. Most commonly it is explained that the shorter reading was created by accident: because the words Χριστοῦ and θεοῦ happen to terminate in the same letters (-ου), a scribe's eye inadvertently skipped from one to the other, causing him to leave out the intervening phrase.[134] But since the change occurs in such a wide spread of the tradition, it cannot very easily be explained as an accident. For then the omission would have had to have been made independently by several scribes, in precisely the same way. The explanation is rendered yet more difficult by the circumstance that the same error, so far as our evidence suggests, was not made by later scribes of the Byzantine tradition, many of whom are not known for their overly scrupulous habits of transcription.[135] The upshot is that the change of the text of Mark 1:1, whichever reading should be accepted as original, was probably not created by oversight.

In further support of this view is a practical consideration that until quite recently has been entirely overlooked.[136] It should strike us as somewhat odd that the kind of careless mistake alleged to have occurred here, the omission of two rather important words, should have happened precisely where it does—within the first six words of the beginning of a book. It is certainly not too difficult to see how such carelessness might otherwise occur; indeed, its occurrence is virtually ubiquitous throughout the tradition. Copying texts was a long and arduous process, and fatigue could lead to carelessness and as a result to a host of readings that prove to be utterly nonsensical. But here is a reading that makes perfectly good sense, that occurs at the outset of a text, independently attested in a number of witnesses. This raises an interesting question: *Is* it less likely that a scribe—or rather, that a number of scribes—would make this kind of careless error at the beginning of a book rather than later, say, in the middle? It is a difficult question to answer, because so little is known about the modus operandi of scribes, especially in the early centuries.[137] But it seems at least antecedently probable that a scribe would begin his work on Mark's Gospel only after having made a clean break, say, with Matthew, and that he would plunge into his work with renewed strength and vigor. So that this does not appear simply to be the romantic notion of a twentieth-century critic, I should note that recent manuscript analyses have indeed demonstrated that scribes were more conscientious transcribers at the beginning of a document.[138] Furthermore, and perhaps more significantly, it is worth observing that the scribes who actually produced the two earliest manuscripts that attest the omission, codices Sinaiticus and Koridethi, went to some lengths to decorate the end of their previous work on Matthew and to indicate afresh the beginning of the new work at hand.

For all these reasons, it appears that the textual problem of Mark 1:1 was not created by accident: whether the phrase "Son of God" was added to a text that originally lacked it or deleted from a text that originally had it, the change was made deliberately.

This in itself makes it more likely that the earliest form of Mark's Gospel lacked the phrase. For one can understand why a scribe who did not find the phrase in the book's opening verse might want to add it. Indeed, as we shall see, there may have been more than one reason to do so. But it is very difficult to see why scribes who read the phrase might deliberately seek to eliminate it.

A number of scholars have insisted, nonetheless, that the longer text (i.e., including the phrase "Son of God") must have been original, because it coincides so well with Mark's christology otherwise. This is an interesting claim, because it assumes that if a scribe *were* to change the text of Mark, he would do so in a way that stands at odds with the rest of Mark's account. Needless to say, this assumption is not at all necessary: the way scribes understood Mark's Gospel in antiquity naturally coincides at a number of points with the way it is commonly construed today. Thus, even if the variant reading does evince Mark's understanding of Jesus, it still may not be original—especially if the other reading can make good sense in the context of the Gospel as well.

Other scholars have claimed that because Mark ends his story of Jesus, for all practical purposes, with the centurion's proclamation that Jesus is the Son of God (15:39), he likely would have begun the Gospel on the same note in 1:1. This also is not persuasive, because the opening bracket for which 15:39 provides the closing is not 1:1 but 1:11,[139] where, as in 15:38–39, there is a "ripping" (σχίζομαι, only in these two passages in Mark: of the heavens and of the temple veil), a "voice" (from heaven, from the centurion), and an affirmation of Jesus' divine sonship (by God, by a Gentile).[140]

Thus, although most interpreters agree on the importance of the phrase "Son of God" to Mark's narrative otherwise, this in itself provides no evidence for the text of 1:1. To the contrary, the centrality of the phrase actually highlights the hermeneutical problem confronted by early interpreters of the narrative. For Mark does not state explicitly what he means by calling Jesus the "Son of God," nor does he indicate when this status was conferred upon him. This makes the interpretation of his Christology a somewhat precarious matter, as even the most recent investigations provide ample witness.[141] In the early church, this Gospel could be read by adoptionists who believed that it was at his baptism that Jesus became the Son of God, as well as by the orthodox, who believed that Jesus had always been the Son.

As the textual situation of Mark 1:1 appears not to have been created by sheer accident, and because the shorter text appears in relatively early, unrelated, and widespread witnesses, I can now draw a conclusion concerning the history of its transmission. Scribes would have had little reason to delete the phrase "the Son of God" from Mark 1:1, but they would have had reasons to add it. Just as was the case in the other variant readings previously considered, it may have been the orthodox construal of Mark's Gospel that led to the corruption of the text. Mark entitled his book "The Beginning of the Gospel of Jesus Christ," and proceeded to narrate that first significant event of Jesus' life, his baptism and the accompanying revelatory experience. In order to circumvent an adoptionistic reading of this inaugurating event, early orthodox Christian scribes made a slight modification of Mark's opening words, so that now they affirm Jesus' status as the Son of God prior to his baptism, even prior to the mention of John the Baptist, his forerunner. Now even before he comes forward to be baptized, Jesus is understood by the reader to be the Christ, the Son of God.

Other Examples

The manuscript tradition preserves other instances of exalted views of Jesus in passages that relate his activities prior to baptism. Since the New Testament is scarcely stocked with a large quantity of such passages in the first place, one should not expect to find a high incidence of such variants. And in fact, they occur only sporadically in the tradition. As two examples I can cite the Palestinian Syriac text of Luke 2:43, where the twelve-year-old Jesus ('Ιησοῦς ὁ παῖς) is already identified as "the Lord" (ὁ παῖς ὁ κύριος 'Ιησοῦς) and the reading of Luke 3:21 in the uncial manuscript 0124, where it is "the Lord" who comes to John in order to be baptized. Other variants go a step further and stress that Jesus enjoyed an exalted standing before God not only prior to his baptism, but even before his appearance on earth. Naturally, a number of data could be included under this rubric. Many of the texts to be considered later, for example, affirm that Jesus himself was God. Here I simply examine several corruptions that stress that Jesus' appearance in this world was not his coming into existence.

An interesting instance occurs in Matthew 1:18, a verse whose other textual variants will be discussed in a later context.[142] At this point we can consider a reading that is frequently dismissed as having resulted from the accidental substitution of words. Whereas the earliest and best manuscripts agree in introducing the passage with the words: "The beginning (γένεσις) of Jesus Christ happened in this way,"[143] a large number of witnesses read instead, "The *birth* (γέννησις) of Jesus Christ happened in this way."[144] The orthographic and phonetic similarity between the two words in question could certainly have led to some confusion. It seems unlikely, however, that a simple slipup would have occurred, one way or the other; both variants appear in wide stretches of the textual tradition, a fact difficult to explain as simple coincidence.

The first question to be asked, then, is which of the readings is more likely the original. In addition to claiming the earliest and best manuscript support, the reading γένεσις ("beginning") seems to cohere better with the preceding context. Matthew began his Gospel by detailing the "book of the γένεσις" of Jesus Christ (i.e., his genealogical lineage; 1:1), making it some-what more likely that he would here (v. 18) continue with a description of the γένεσις itself. And so the majority of textual scholars agree that γέννησις represents a textual corruption, created perhaps out of deference to the fol-lowing account of Jesus' birth.[145]

At the same time, something more profound may be occurring here. Both γένεσις and γέννησις can mean "birth," so that either one could be appro-priate in the context. But unlike the corrupted reading, γένεσις can also mean "creation," "beginning," and "origination." When one now asks why scribes might take umbrage at Matthew's description of the "genesis" of Je-sus Christ, the answer immediately suggests itself: the original text could well be taken to imply that this is the moment in which Jesus Christ comes into being. In point of fact, there is nothing in Matthew's narrative, either here or elsewhere throughout the Gospel, to suggest that he knew or subscribed to the notion that Christ had existed prior to his birth. Orthodox scribes found Matthew's account useful nonetheless, particularly in conjunction with state-ments of the Fourth Gospel supporting the notion of Jesus' existence with the Father prior to his appearance in the flesh. The orthodox doctrine, of course, represented a conflation of these early christological views, so that Jesus was confessed to have become "incarnate [Gospel of John] through the virgin Mary [Gospels of Matthew and Luke]." Anyone subscribing to this doctrine might well look askance at the implication that Matthew was here describing Jesus' origination, and might understandably have sought to clar-ify the text by substituting a word that "meant" the same thing, but that was less likely to be misconstrued. And so the term γέννησις in Matthew 1:18 would represent an orthodox corruption.[146]

One other text, this one outside of the Gospels, can be mentioned briefly in this connection. For most interpreters, the corruption of Ephesians 4:9 represents less a shift in meaning or nuance than a heightening of the empha-sis already found in the passage, an emphasis that in fact proved particularly suitable to the orthodox claim of Jesus' pre-existence. In his explanation of Psalm 68:19, "Ascending to the heights, he made captivity captive," the au-thor of Ephesians suggests that only one who had descended into the "lower parts of the earth" could ascend above (4:8–9), that is, that an ascent from earth to heaven presupposes a previous descent in the other direction.[147] This interpretation would support the orthodox claim that Jesus was the pre-existent Son of God who descended for the task of salvation, prior to returning to his heavenly home.

It is interesting to note, however, that some modern commentators have understood the passage not as referring to a descent *prior* to an ascent, but just the opposite, to an ascent that precipitates a descent.[148] According to this interpretation, the passage refers to Christ's exaltation in anticipation of his return. Such an interpretation, however, could well be taken to undermine the notion that the pre-existent Christ came to earth prior to returning to heaven. Whether or not this is the better exegesis of the passage is not a question to be decided here. What is of some significance, however, is the textual situation. A number of witnesses have modified the text in a way that precludes this kind of understanding, emphasizing that Christ's "descent" *was* both prior to and requisite for his "ascent." This they have done simply by adding the adverb πρῶτον to the verse (ℵ² B C³ Ψ Byz OL syr sa al). That this is to be seen as an "improvement" of the text is shown by two of our earliest manuscripts (ℵ C), which attest it only in scribal correction. With the addition there is no ambiguity; even the adoptionists acknowledge that Christ ascended into heaven, and now the conclusion appears unavoidable: to do so he must first have descended thence.[149] This stress on the descent motif, therefore, may well have derived from an orthodox desire to stress the incarnation of the Son of God in his appearance in the world.[150]

Jesus the Divine: The Orthodox Opposition to a Low Christology

Of all the anti-adoptionistic corruptions of Scripture, by far the most common involve the orthodox denial that Jesus was a "mere man" (ψιλὸς ἄνθρωπος). This kind of corruption is not unrelated, of course, to those that have already been considered, namely, variants that oppose adoptionistic views of Jesus' birth, baptism, or election. But the textual variations I will now discuss are, generally speaking, opposed to the basic conception of the adoptionists rather than to their specific doctrines. In these variant readings one finds the stark expression of the orthodox belief that Jesus is far more than a man, that he is in fact divine. In the orthodox tradition, especially as it developed toward the formulations of Nicea and Chalcedon, this divinity was not something that had been bestowed upon Jesus at some point of his earthly existence; it was a divinity that he had shared with God the Father from eternity past. Thus, two kinds of variation can now come under scrutiny: those that heighten Jesus' divine character (he is "God") and those that minimize his human limitations (he is not a "mere man").

Christ, Designated as God: 1 Timothy 3:16

We begin with a particularly intriguing textual problem from the Pastoral Epistles. The author of 1 Timothy is almost certainly quoting an earlier creed when he explicates "the mystery of our religion" (τὸ τῆς εὐσεβείας μυστήριον, 3:16): "Who (ὅς) was manifest in flesh, justified in spirit; seen by angels, proclaimed among nations; believed in the world, taken up in glory." Certain stylistic features make this one of the finest specimens of a preliterary creed in all of the New Testament: its lapidary character (no superfluous words, only verbs, nouns, and the preposition ἐν), the striking syntactical parallelism of its six clauses (each formed with an aorist passive verb followed by a nominal construction in the dative), and the dependence of each clause on the introductory relative pronoun.[151] Precisely here, however, is the textual problem; for the relative has been subjected to alteration in the course of the text's transmission.

In several witnesses the relative has been retained, but changed to the neuter (ὅ, D* 061 d g vg, several church fathers). The change is understandable: the antecedent is μυστήριον, itself neuter. This variant, then, reflects a greater concern for the grammar of the passage than for its contents, since the creed clearly refers to Christ.[152]

The same cannot be said of the other variant, found in a range of witnesses, in which the relative "who" (ὅς) appears as the nominative singular "God" (θεός).[153] The change, of course, may have been created accidentally. As one of the *nomina sacra*, θεός would normally be abbreviated as ΘΣ, making a confusion with the orthographically similar ΟΣ more than intelligible. But there are reasons for suspecting that the change was not an accident.

It should first be observed that four of the uncial witnesses that attest θεός do so only in corrections (ℵ A C D). This shows not only that θεός was the preferred reading of later scribes but also that it did not creep into the tradition unawares.[154] Second, we cannot overlook what the reading θεός provides for the orthodox scribe—a clear affirmation of the doctrine that God became incarnate in the person of Jesus Christ. This certainly is the orthodox "mystery": it was "God" who was "manifest in flesh, justified in spirit," etc.

That the reading θεός cannot be original is shown both by the character of the manuscript attestation—the earliest and superior manuscripts all support the relative—and by the fact that ancient creedal fragments typically begin precisely in this way, that is, with a relative pronoun.[155] The change must have been made fairly early, at least during the third century, given its widespread attestation from the fourth century on.[156] It can therefore best be explained as an anti-adoptionistic corruption that stresses the deity of Christ.

Christ, Designated as God: John 1:18

A comparable corruption appears in the prologue of the Fourth Gospel, although here the issues are far more complicated and have generated substantially more debate and indecision. I will not give an exhaustive study of all the issues surrounding the text of John 1:18; these are competently handled in the commentaries and in several recent studies.[157] I will instead develop my reasons for thinking that the majority of manuscripts are right in ending the prologue with the words: "No one has seen God at any time, but the unique Son (ὁ μονογενὴς υἱός) who is in the bosom of the Father, that one has made him known." The variant reading of the Alexandrian tradition, which substitutes "God" for "Son," represents an orthodox corruption of the text in which the complete deity of Christ is affirmed: "the unique God [(ὁ) μονογενὴς θεός] who is in the bosom of the Father, that one has made him known."[158]

External Evidence

It must be acknowledged at the outset that the Alexandrian reading is more commonly preferred by textual critics, in no small measure because of its external support. Not only is it the reading of the great Alexandrian uncials (א B C), it is also attested by the earliest available witnesses, the Bodmer papyri 𝔭[66] and 𝔭[75], discovered in the middle of the present century. It would be a mistake, however, to consider this external evidence compelling in itself. For in actual fact, contrary to widely held opinion,[159] the discovery of the early papyri has done very little (in this instance) to change the character of the documentary alignments. This is due to the peculiar character of the verse's attestation: even *before* the discovery of the papyri, scholars realized that the bulk of the Alexandrian tradition attested the reading, including witnesses that date back to the beginning of the third century.[160] This means that we already *knew* that it must have been preserved in early Greek manuscripts of Alexandria—even before we had access to any of them. The chance discovery of two such witnesses has consequently done nothing to change the picture, but has simply demonstrated that our theories about transmission are essentially correct.[161]

Here it must be emphasized that outside of the Alexandrian tradition, the reading μονογενὴς θεός has not fared well at all. Virtually every other representative of every other textual grouping—Western, Caesarean, Byzantine—attests ὁ μονογενὴς υἱός. And the reading even occurs in several of the secondary Alexandrian witnesses (e.g., C³ Ψ 892 1241 Ath Alex). This is not simply a case of one reading supported by the earliest and best manuscripts and another supported by late and inferior ones, but of one reading found almost exclusively in the Alexandrian tradition and another found sporadically there and virtually everywhere else. And although the witnesses supporting ὁ μονογενὴς υἱός cannot individually match the antiquity of the Alexandrian papyri, there can be little doubt that this reading must also be dated at least to the time of their production. There is virtually no other way to explain its predominance in the Greek, Latin, and Syriac traditions, not to mention its occurrence in fathers such as Irenaeus, Clement, and Tertullian, who were writing before our earliest surviving manuscripts were produced.[162] Thus, both readings are ancient; one is fairly localized, the other is almost ubiquitous. This in itself does not demonstrate that ὁ μονογενὴς υἱός is original, but it does show the error of automatically accepting the external attestation of the Alexandrian reading as superior.

Intrinsic Probabilities

It is on internal grounds that the real superiority of ὁ μονογενὴς υἱός shines forth. Not only does it conform with established Johannine usage, a point its opponents readily concede, but the Alexandrian variant, although perfectly amenable to scribes for theological reasons, is virtually impossible to understand within a Johannine context. As we shall see, these points are best treated in conjunction with one another rather than independently, for here again arguments of transcriptional and intrinsic probabilities make a rather formidable coalition.

I begin with the question of intrinsic plausibility. One of the insurmountable difficulties of accepting the Alexandrian reading as original involves ascertaining what it might *mean* for a first-century document to say that Jesus is "the unique God" ([ὁ] μονογενὴς θεός). The problem exists whether or not one chooses to read the definite article—although if external support is considered decisive, the article is probably to be preferred.[163] If so, then the problem of translation is simply made more acute, not created, since in some sense the meaning of μονογενής itself embodies the notion of exclusivity conveyed by the use of the article. By definition there can be only *one* μονογενής: the word means "unique," "one of a kind."[164] The problem, of course, is that Jesus can be the *unique* God only if there is no other God; but for the Fourth Gospel, the Father is God as well. Indeed, even in this passage the μονογενής is said to reside in the bosom of the Father. How can the μονογενὴς θεός, the unique God, stand in such a relationship to (another) God?[165]

The problem is avoided, of course, with the reading that is more widely attested. Not only does this reading avoid the contradiction implied by the other, however, it also coincides perfectly well with the way μονογενής is used throughout the Johannine literature. In three other Johannine passages μονογενής serves as a modifier, and on each occasion it is used with υἱός (John 3:16, 18; 1 John 4:9). Proponents of the Alexandrian reading, of course, have often turned this argument on its head by claiming that scribes already conversant with Johannine usage disposed of the more difficult phrase ὁ μονογενὴς θεός by conforming it to the standard expression. This is certainly a possibility; but in fact, the phrase that proves difficult for John was *not* a problem for Christians in the second century and beyond, who, with their increasingly paradoxical understandings of Christology, *could* conceive of ways for Christ to be the unique God himself.[166] It would be a mistake, however, to read these sophisticated forms of Christology back into the pages of the Fourth Gospel, where Jesus is on a par with God (see 10:30, 33), and so can be addressed as God (20:28, perhaps 1:1), but is never identified as "the one and only God" himself.[167] One is left, then, with the problem of how to understand [ὁ] μονογενὴς θεός in the *Johannine* world if it were accepted as original.

Scholars who prefer the reading generally escape the difficulty by proposing alternative ways of construing its meaning or syntax. One common expedient involves claiming that μονογενής itself connotes the idea of "sonship," so that the word υἱός is to be understood even when it is not expressed.[168] In this case, the conflate reading found elsewhere in the tradition (ὁ μονογενὴς υἱός, θεός), although corrupt in wording, is correct in meaning: the Alexandrian text (ὁ μονογενὴς θεός) should then be understood to mean "the unique Son who is God."

The difficulty with this view is that there is nothing about the word μονογενής itself that suggests it. Outside of the New Testament the term simply means "one of a kind" or "unique," and does so with reference to any range of animate or inanimate objects.[169] Therefore, recourse must be made to its usage within the New Testament. Here proponents of the view argue that *in situ* the word implies "sonship," for it always occurs (in the New Testament) either in explicit conjunction with υἱός or in a context where a υἱός is named and then described as μονογενής (Luke 9:38, John 1:14, Heb 11:17). Nonetheless, as suggestive as the argument may appear, it contains the seeds of its own refutation: if the word μονογενής is understood to mean "a unique son," one wonders why it is typically put in attribution to υἱός, an attribution that then creates an unusual kind of redundancy ("the unique-son son"). Given the fact that neither the etymology of the word nor its general usage suggests any such meaning, this solution seems to involve a case of special pleading.

The more common expedient for those who opt for [ὁ] μονογενὴς θεός, but who recognize that its rendering as "the unique God" is virtually impossible in a Johannine context, is to understand the adjective substantivally, and to construe the entire second half of John 1:18 as a series of appositions, so that rather than reading "the unique God who is in the bosom of the Father," the text should be rendered "the unique one, who is also God, who is in the bosom of the Father."[170] There is something attractive about the proposal. It explains what the text might have meant to a Johannine reader and thereby allows for the text of the generally superior textual witnesses. Nonetheless, the solution is entirely implausible.

For one thing, it posits that the "natural" meaning of the Johannine text was not understood by a number of scribes who found it so peculiar that they sought to modify it to established Johannine usage. How is it that modern critics in the German- and English-speaking worlds can make ready sense of a passage that seems to have struck Greek-speaking scribes as so perplexing? Moreover, a moment's reflection shows that the proposed construal is not at all the most natural. It is true that μονογενής can elsewhere be used as a substantive (= the unique one, as in v. 14); all adjectives can. But the proponents of this view have failed to consider that it is never used in this way when it is immediately followed by a noun that agrees with it in gender, number, and case. Indeed one must here press the syntactical point: when is an adjective *ever* used substantivally when it immediately precedes a noun of the same inflection? No Greek reader would construe such a construction as a string of substantives, and no Greek writer would create such an inconcinnity. To the best of my knowledge, no one has cited anything analogous outside of this passage.

The result is that taking the term μονογενὴς θεός as two substantives standing in apposition makes for a nearly impossible syntax, whereas construing their relationship as adjective-noun creates an impossible sense. Given the fact that the established usage of the Johannine literature is known beyond a shadow of a doubt, there seems little reason any longer to dispute the reading found in virtually every witness outside the Alexandrian tradition.[171] The prologue ends with the statement that "the unique Son who is in the bosom of the Father, that one has made him known."

Transcriptional Probabilities

Why then was the text changed? It is striking that Christ as the Logos is called "God" in verse 1 of the prologue and that the burden of the passage is that this pre-existent divine being has become flesh. The word θεός itself occurs some seven times in the passage, the word υἱός never. It may be that the context has decided the issue for some scribes, who conformed the passage to the terminology *ad loc.* But one must still ask what would have motivated them to do so. Here the character of our witnesses cannot be overlooked. In the early period, when the reading was beginning to establish itself in the Alexandrian tradition, it is found not only in Greek manuscripts, but also among a variety of Alexandrian writers, both orthodox and Gnostic. The presence of the reading in authors of a wide range of theological persuasions has actually served to throw investigators off the scent of its genesis; for it has been assumed that if both orthodox and Gnostic writers attest the text, it must not have been generated out of theological concerns. But the key point to register is that all those who support the text attest a "high" Christology: Alexandrians from Clement and Origen to Ptolemy and Heracleon could all affirm that the μονογενής was God. The solution to the problem of the origin of the variant lies not in the orthodox-Gnostic controversy, but in that of both the orthodox and Gnostic Christians against the adoptionists.[172] The variant was created to support a high Christology in the face of widespread claims, found among adoptionists recognized and opposed in Alexandria,[173] that Christ was not God but merely a man, adopted by God. For the scribe who created this variant, Christ is not merely portrayed as the "unique Son." He himself is God, the "unique God," who is to be differentiated from God the Father, in whose bosom he resides, but who nonetheless is his co-equal.[174] This Alexandrian reading derives from an anti-adoptionistic context, and therefore represents an orthodox corruption.[175]

Other Examples

Having dealt with the previous two variants at some length, we will now consider somewhat less extensively other instances of textual corruption that function similarly in designating Christ as "God." A number of such variations occur throughout the textual traditions of the Gospels.

All four Evangelists begin their accounts of Jesus' ministry with the preaching of John the Baptist, the forerunner of the Lord who fulfills the prophecy of Second Isaiah ("A voice crying in the wilderness . . ." Mark 1:3 par.). What is interesting for our purposes is that in each instance one or another manuscript has changed the Gospel text so as to make it clear that the Lord (Jesus) whom John precedes is none other than God himself.[176]

When Mark put the words of Isaiah 40:3 on the lips of the Baptist, he,

or his source, modified the LXX text with an interesting christological result.[177] Whereas the LXX had said "Prepare the way of the Lord, make straight
the paths of our God," Mark's modification allows for a distinctively Christian understanding of the passage: "Prepare the way of the Lord, make straight
his [i.e., Jesus'] paths" (1:3). John is portrayed here as the forerunner of
Jesus, who is presented in this Gospel as the κύριος (2:28; 11:3; cf. 12:36;
13:35).[178] But Mark, standing in good company with most of the other New
Testament authors, does not call Jesus God, either here or elsewhere in his
narrative. Later scribes, however, saw both the opportunity and the importance of reading Jesus' divinity into this text. The opportunity was provided
by the LXX, the importance by the controversy over Jesus' divine status. And
so the change represented by codex Bezae and the early Latin witnesses is not
merely a thoughtless reversion to the LXX.[179] Now, even prior to his baptism, Jesus can rightly be called divine: "Prepare the way of the Lord [i.e.,
Jesus], make straight the paths of our God."

This change might be expected, especially in the manuscript tradition of
Mark, a Gospel particularly susceptible to an adoptionistic construal, in that
it lacks any reference to Jesus' pre-existence with his Father (as in John) or
to his miraculous birth (as in Matthew and Luke). And, indeed, the most
widely attested corruptions of the Isaian text occur here. But each of the
other Gospels has been similarly modified throughout the tradition. Precisely
the same variation occurs at Matthew 3:3 in b syr[c] and Irenaeus, and at Luke
3:5 in r[1], and in Syriac and Diatesseronic witnesses. Even John, which lacks
the relevant portion of Isaiah 40:3, has this lack supplied by Old Latin manuscript e, not surprisingly in the Septuagintal rather than the Marcan form:
"rectas facite semitas dei nostra" (1:23).

It is interesting to note that variant readings that specifically call Jesus
God appear somewhat regularly throughout the manuscript traditions of the
Johannine literature, where the Christology is already relatively exalted. So
far we have considered one significant, if controversial, example in the final
verse of John's prologue. Other examples from the Johannine corpus include
the curious instance of John 19:40, where Joseph of Arimathea and Nicodemus prepare the body of Jesus for burial: "They took the body of Jesus (τὸ
σῶμα τοῦ Ἰησοῦ) and bound it in linen." The scribe of codex Alexandrinus,
perhaps in an inadvertent slip, but one that is nonetheless telling, substitutes
θεοῦ for Ἰησοῦ (as *nomina sacra*, ΘΥ for ΙΥ), with the result that they "took
the body of God and bound it." Whether deliberate or not,[180] this kind of
change could function in a number of ways for orthodox Christians: it could
counter a docetic notion (because Jesus as God really has a body) or even a
separationist view such as that embraced by some groups of Gnostics (because Jesus' "divinity" has not left him, even upon death).[181] But perhaps
above all, the change, whether an accidental slip or a calculated alteration,
functions to express the orthodox notion that Jesus himself is God in the
flesh.

A somewhat different kind of corruption occurs in the manuscript tradition of 1 John 3:23. The immediate context states that believers can have

confidence before God and will receive what they ask of him, if they keep his commandments (3:21–22). The author then explicates the commandment of God: "That we believe in the name of his Son Jesus Christ (ἵνα πιστεύσωμεν τῷ ὀνόματι τοῦ υἱοῦ αὐτοῦ Ἰησοῦ Χριστοῦ) and love one another." Several witnesses, however, including again codex Alexandrinus, lack the words τοῦ υἱοῦ (A 1846 vg^mss). Now the text reads: "That we believe in his name, Jesus Christ, and love one another." Although it is certainly possible that the two words dropped out of the passage by accident, there seems to be no particular reason (e.g., homoeoteleuton) for them to have done so.[182] It is plausible, then, that the scribes of these manuscripts simply took the opportunity to express their orthodox conviction: "Jesus Christ" *is* the name of God.

This doctrine of the deity of Christ—which, to be sure, coincides to some degree with Johannine Christology itself—is emphasized throughout the manuscript tradition of the Fourth Gospel.[183] An example occurs in John 10:33, where Jesus' antagonists, "the Jews," explain why they have been attempting to stone him: "because you, being a man, make yourself a god" (ποιεῖς σεαυτὸν θεόν). This appears to be a correct perception on their part, given Jesus' pronouncement three verses earlier, that "I and the Father are one." But the force of this pronouncement and the clarity of the Jews' understanding of it are enhanced by the addition of the article to θεόν, an addition attested only in our third-century manuscript p^66. Now Jesus is said not merely to proclaim himself "a god," a proclamation that could itself be construed as a blasphemy, but actually to make himself "God."[184] The change is characteristic of the movement in early Christology away from seeing Jesus as one who is in some sense *equal* with God, to seeing him actually *as* God, a movement that culminates in the claim made by such second-century heretics as Noetus and Praxeas that Jesus is to be identified with God the Father himself.[185]

A comparable change occurs in the manuscript tradition of John 12:41, which explains that the famous words of Isaiah 6:10 ("He blinded their eyes and hardened their heart, lest they should see with their eyes, and understand with their heart, and turn, that I might heal them") were spoken because the ancient prophet had seen Jesus' glory and spoken concerning him (ὅτι εἶδεν τὴν δόξαν αὐτοῦ καὶ ἐλάλησεν περὶ αὐτοῦ). A range of early witnesses modify the text to speak no longer of "his glory" but of the "glory of God" (τὴν δόξαν τοῦ θεοῦ, Θ f^13 1 syr^h cop), or of the "glory of his [Isaiah's] God" (τὴν δόξαν τοῦ θεοῦ αὐτοῦ, D). There is no ambiguity in the context concerning John's use of Isaiah's prophecy: it refers to Jesus and his marvelous signs (v. 37). It appears, then, that for the scribes who altered the text, when the prophet Isaiah looked ahead to see Jesus, what he saw was "the glory of God" and he therefore spoke concerning "him" (i.e., the God Jesus).[186]

Similar changes occur throughout the manuscript traditions of the Synoptic Gospels as well, particularly in the birth narratives of Luke 1–2. We have already observed that certain passages of these chapters have been modified so as to protect the orthodox notion of Jesus' miraculous birth. Other verses were occasionally changed to emphasize the orthodox view that this one born of a virgin was in fact God. This is perhaps the best explanation for the interchange of *nomina sacra* in manuscripts of Luke 1:15, where the angel Gabriel assures Zechariah that his son John will be "great before the Lord" (ἐνώπιον τοῦ κυρίου).[187] The context indicates that "the Lord" here is Jesus, before whom (ἐνώπιον αὐτοῦ, v. 17) John will go in the spirit and power of Elijah. This makes the change of verse 15 from κυρίου to θεοῦ (ΚΥ to ΘΥ) appear to be more than accidental.[188] As was the case in the modification of the Baptist's proclamation of the coming of the Lord, so too here: John anticipates not the Lord Jesus, but the God Jesus. The text of Luke 1:17 has also been changed in some manuscripts, so that rather than preceding "him" (αὐτοῦ), John is predicted to precede "the Lord" (Δ Didymus) or, more significantly for our purposes, "God" (Persian Diatesseron and Georgian MSS). So too in Zachariah's song of praise, the Benedictus, where it is again foretold that John will go "before the Lord" (1:76), one manuscript of the Palestinian Syriac reads "before your God." And finally, when Luke 2:26 indicates that the Holy Spirit had revealed to Simeon that he would not die before seeing the the Lord's Christ (τὸν χριστὸν κυρίου), the Old Latin manuscript ff[2] has made the change that we might now anticipate, namely that Simeon is told that he will see "Christ, namely God."

Comparable changes can be found outside the Lukan birth narrative. Rather than providing an exhaustive list, I will simply cite representative examples. When Peter makes his famous confession of Luke 9:20, rather than acknowledging Jesus as "the Christ of God" (τὸν χριστὸν τοῦ θεοῦ), in some Coptic manuscripts he professes him to be "Christ, God" (= τὸν χριστὸν τὸν θεόν). In Mark 3:11, where the demoniac proclaims Jesus' identity, "You are the Son of God," one important minuscule manuscript reads "You are God, the Son of God" (σὺ εἶ ὁ θεός, ὁ υἱὸς τοῦ θεοῦ, MS 69).[189] The statement of Luke 7:9, "when Jesus heard this," has been changed in one minuscule (124) to read "when God heard this." Similarly, manuscript 2766 changes the words of the demoniac in Luke 8:28 from "Jesus Son of the Highest God" to "Jesus, the Highest God" (omit υἱέ). In Luke 8:40, where the crowds welcome Jesus after having awaited him, the first hand of codex Sinaiticus says they welcome him because they have all been awaiting "God" (τὸν θεόν for αὐτόν). Finally, in the quotation from Psalm 110 in Luke 20:42, the text of the Persian Diatesseron has been changed so as not to read "the Lord said to my lord," (i.e., for Luke, God spoke to David's Lord) but instead "God said to my God," (i.e., God the Father spoke to God the Son).[190]

Outside the Gospels one can find instances of this kind of variation occasionally attested in one of our earliest witnesses to the text of the Catholic epistles, 𝔭[72] (third century). A striking example occurs in the salutation of 2 Peter 1:2: "May grace and peace be multiplied to you in the knowledge of God and of our Lord Jesus." 𝔭[72] omits the conjunction "and" (καί), leading to the identification of Jesus as God: "in the knowledge of God, our Lord Jesus." That this omission was not an accident is confirmed by similar modifications in the same manuscript. Thus, in Jude 5, where manuscripts vary over whether it was "the Lord" (most manuscripts), or "Jesus" (A B 33 81

1241 1739 1881), or "God" (C² 623 vg^ms) who saved the people from Egypt (variations that are all explicable from the Old Testament narratives themselves and from early Christian understandings of them, at least as intimated in 1 Corinthians 10), $\mathfrak{p}^{72}$ stands alone in saying that the Savior of the people from Egypt was "the God Christ" (θεὸς Χριστός).[191]

Within the Pauline corpus we find a particularly interesting variation of this kind, one that merits a more prolonged discussion. In Galations 2:20 Paul makes his famous claim: "I live by faith in the Son of God who loved me and gave himself up for me." In a number of early and significant textual witnesses, however, the phrasing is changed from "in the Son of God" (τῇ τοῦ υἱοῦ τοῦ θεοῦ) to "in God (and/even) Christ" (τῇ τοῦ Θεοῦ καὶ Χριστοῦ; MSS $\mathfrak{p}^{46}$ B D F G). I will argue that this, and related corruptions of the text, can best be understood as having arisen from orthodox interests. But first it is important to consider how the text came to be changed in the first place.

Some critics have thought that the corrupted text was created in two stages. The minuscule manuscript 330 attests the corrupted text, but omits the phrase καὶ Χριστοῦ (reading, therefore, ἐν πίστει ζῶ τῇ τοῦ θεοῦ, "I live in the faith of God, who . . ."). This makes for an interesting reading indeed, for now God is said to have loved Paul and given himself up (= died) for him. Here is a clear orthodox statement that Jesus is divine. Metzger has suggested that some such error occurred early in the tradition, when a scribe inadvertently omitted the two words τοῦ υἱοῦ.[192] A later scribe, realizing the error of his exemplar's ways, sought to correct the problem by emending the text. Reasoning that the passage must have originally said something about "Christ," the scribe appended the words "and Christ" to the end, thereby creating a corruption of a corruption, namely, the reading "faith in God (and/even) Christ who loved me. . . ." Furthermore, another scribe corrected the text differently, by adding precisely the words that had earlier been omitted, τοῦ υἱοῦ, but in the wrong place, making the text now read "faith in God the Son (τοῦ θεοῦ τοῦ υἱοῦ, MS 1985) who loved me . . . ."

Metzger is surely right that the original text must have read "faith in the Son of God who loved me." Not only does this reading explain all the others, but it also is the only one that coincides with Paul's theology. Nowhere does Paul speak of God as the object of Christian faith, and neither of the other expressions ("God even Christ," "God the Son") occurs in this way in Paul. Interestingly, for our purposes, even if these various corruptions were generated accidentally, all of them can be construed as orthodox. As we have seen, even accidental changes can function in important ways, and one must always ask what kind of scribe might have created such readings, and how he might have understood them once he did.

Of course the singular readings have no claim to authenticity, and these appear to be the most clearly orthodox of all: the one speaks of "God" and the other of "God the Son" "who . . . gave himself up for me." The more commonly attested variant, however, is also easy to construe as orthodox: here an anarthrous Χριστός is made to follow ὁ θεός. Since "Christ" lacks the article, the erring scribe appears to be equating the two names, using them to refer to the same person, not to two separate individuals.[193] The phrase is probably best translated, then, "faith in God, even Christ, who loved me and gave himself for me." As a result, even if these changes were generated accidentally, they end up conveying a notion that the Christ who effects salvation is none other than God. It is noteworthy that the corruption can be dated firmly to the third century, and that it occurs in early witnesses of both the Alexandrian and "Western" texts (p^{46} B D* F G [b]).[194]

Comparable changes also occur sporadically throughout the manuscript tradition of the Pastoral Epistles. Thus, in the proem of 1 Timothy, several Greek and versional witnesses change the "command of God our savior and Christ Jesus our hope" (1:1) to the "command of God our savior, (i.e.) Jesus Christ our hope";[195] in 2 Timothy 1:10 the reference to salvation that has now become manifest through the "epiphany of our Savior Christ Jesus" has been changed to speak of the salvation now made known through "the epiphany of our Savior, God" (MS I); and in Titus 3:6 a number of lectionaries change the reference to "Jesus Christ our Savior" to read "Jesus Christ our God." In the Old Latin tradition of Hebrews 13:20, "our Lord Jesus" has been changed to "our God Jesus" (MS d). This last example is another instance that can be explained as having occurred by accident (confusion of "deum" for "dominum"), but again one must ask what kind of scribe might have made such a slip and what he might have meant by it once it was made.

Christ as Divine: The Exchange of Predicates

One of the ways that proto-orthodox Christians of the second and third centuries expressed their understanding of Christ involved an "exchange of predicates," in which the attributes and activities of God were predicated of Christ, or, conversely, the characteristics and actions of Christ were predicated of God. Interchanges of this sort occur commonly in such writers as Ignatius, Melito, and Tertullian who speak of the "blood of God" or the "passion of God," or even of God being "crucified" or "murdered."[196]

As might be expected, this is one area where orthodox believers felt compelled to walk a fine line: as these Christians combatted adoptionists on one front, they found themselves besieged by Patripassianists on another.[197] And so, while not at all averse to exchanging predicates between Christ and God, by the end of the second century, proto-orthodox Christians were cautious not to *identify* Christ and God in such a way as to eliminate any distinctions between them. Christ was divine, and as such his activities could be attributed to God; but he was not himself God the Father.[198] The fine line can be detected in a careful thinker like Tertullian, who in one context refers to God as crucified (*de carne Christi* 5) but in another ridicules Praxeas for crucifying the Father (*Adv. Prax.* 1).[199]

The balancing act that ensued is evident in some of the textual changes of the New Testament manuscripts.[200] Perhaps the most striking example occurs in the manuscript tradition of Acts 20:28, where a variety of corruptions appear to circumvent different misconstruals. There is little doubt concerning the original form of the passage: Paul speaks to the Ephesian elders about "the church of God (τὴν ἐκκλησίαν τοῦ θεοῦ) which he obtained through the blood of his own (Son)" (τοῦ αἵματος τοῦ ἰδίου).[201] Of the textual variants germane to our discussion here,[202] the first concerns the genitive "of God," which in a number of witnesses has been changed to read "of the Lord."[203] This latter phrase ("church of the Lord") is almost certainly a corruption. It never occurs elsewhere in the New Testament, although the more commonly attested "church of God" does, some eleven times in the Pauline corpus. Moreover, this more common phrase is supported by Alexandrian witnesses generally regarded as superior in Acts (ℵ B et al.). It is also much to be preferred on transcriptional grounds: the reading τοῦ κυρίου could refer to Christ as well as to God, making it somewhat more acceptable in the minds of certain Christians who were uncomfortable with the potentially Patripassianist implications of the following phrase, τοῦ αἵματος τοῦ ἰδίου, which may naturally be rendered "his own blood." That is to say, orthodox scribes uneasy with the possible interpretation that God the Father shed "his own blood" appear to have changed the text to make it refer instead to Christ, "the Lord," who shed his blood.[204] Scribes working still later were confronted with both readings, and created the conflation attested by the majority of late manuscripts, "the church of the Lord and God."

Given the initial textual problem, the change of τοῦ αἵματος τοῦ ἰδίου at the end of the verse takes on additional significance, showing how orthodox Christologies could effect seemingly contradictory corruptions of a text. For this final phrase has been changed in a number of witnesses precisely along the lines of the "exchange of predicates" mentioned earlier, making the text appear not to *discourage* a Patripassianist misconstrual so much as to *encourage* an orthodox interpretation that Christ, as God, obtained the church by shedding his blood. Thus, in the majority of Greek witnesses, the "blood of his own (Son)" (τοῦ αἵματος τοῦ ἰδίου), has been changed to read "his own blood" (τοῦ ἰδίου αἵματος).[205] Most witnesses to this reading support the earlier conflation "church of the Lord and of God," making "his own" in this case refer back to "God." Now the text states that God has obtained the church through the shedding "of his own blood." The text is nonetheless secondary: it survives in none of the early witnesses to the text and serves a clear theological function.

Another instance of an exchange of predicates occurs in 𝔭⁷², a witness whose anti-adoptionistic tendencies we already have observed.[206] In 1 Peter 5:1, almost the entire textual tradition is unified in speaking of Peter as a witness to "the sufferings of Christ" (τῶν τοῦ Χριστοῦ παθημάτων). This third-century papyrus, however, changes the text by substituting θεός for Χριστός, with the striking result that now Peter is witness to the "sufferings of God" (τῶν τοῦ θεοῦ παθημάτων). The change relates closely to references to "God's sufferings" (or "passion") in proto-orthodox authors of the second and third centuries.[207] Such statements serve two distinct orthodox functions: they affirm that the one who suffered was God (against adoptionists) and they stress that this God, Christ, really did suffer (against, e.g., various groups of Gnostics).[208]

Exchanges of predicates can occur in the opposite direction as well; that is, rather than attributing Christ's activities to God, they can attribute God's activities to Christ. In corruptions of the New Testament manuscripts, this other kind of interchange occurs most frequently in contexts that speak of God's judgment of his people, a judgment that orthodox Christians frequently portrayed as the judgment of Christ. This appears to be the best explanation for several interesting changes within the Pauline corpus.

In 1 Corinthians 10 Paul provides a Christian interpretation of the Pentateuchal account of Israel in the wilderness, claiming that the rock that Moses struck to provide life-giving water was none other than Christ, God's provision of life to the world. Furthermore, in line with a rabbinic midrash, Paul reasons that because Moses struck the rock on more than one occasion, it must have followed the Israelites around during their journeys (1 Cor 10:5).[209] He goes on to note that despite God's provision for the Israelites, most of them were not pleasing to him, leading to their destruction in the wilderness: "But God (ὁ θεός) was not pleased with most of them, for they were laid low (κατεστρώθησαν) in the wilderness." Curiously enough, and significant for the present investigation, the words ὁ θεός are omitted in several witnesses (MS 81 *Clem Iren*[pt]). In these witnesses, the subject of the verb must be taken as ὁ Χριστός, drawn from the end of verse 4. Now it is "Christ" who was displeased with the Israelites, who entered into judgment with them.

On one level this is an extension of the christological focus already present in the passage; but on another level it is somewhat different. For it is one thing to ascribe to Christ the life-giving presence of the "rock," and quite another to attribute to him the execution of divine wrath. The change signifies the orthodox understanding that the God who is involved with his people in salvation as well as in judgment is none other than the divine Christ.

This understanding of scribal tendencies may help resolve the more difficult problem of verse 9 of the same chapter.[210] In this case the vast majority of witnesses attest a change that for a variety of reasons proved far more successful in the tradition than did that of verse 5. Paul exhorts his readers not to tempt the Lord (μηδὲ ἐκπειράζωμεν τὸν κύριον), as the Israelites did, who as a result were destroyed by serpents. A variety of witnesses, however, have changed the word "Lord" to make its referent unambiguous, some opting for "God" (θεός), but the vast majority choosing "Christ" (Χριστός). The latter reading appealed not only to ancient scribes, but also to recent critics: it is the reading, for example, of the UBSGNT[3] (= NA[26]). The argument for its originality is certainly attractive. Although it is not found extensively among Alexandrian witnesses, it is attested by their earliest representative, 𝔓[46], as well as by the majority of Western and Byzantine manuscripts.[211] Moreover, scribes who may have been confused about Christ bringing judgment against the Israelites in the Old Testament may simply have changed the text either to allow for a different understanding (changing "Christ" to "Lord") or to require this understanding (to "God").[212]

These arguments, however, are not persuasive. In fact, we know that most Christians had no difficulty at all in understanding how Christ could have been active in the affairs of the ancient Israelites. Most of them believed he *was* actively involved and read his involvement into Old Testament narratives on every possible occasion.[213] One need simply peruse the commentaries and homilies of the church fathers from the third century onward to see such christological interpretations on virtually every page. It is precisely this proclivity to Christianize the Old Testament, a Christianization that indeed had its roots in the earliest stages of the religion but that intensified with the passing of time, that makes the more commonly attested reading of 1 Corinthians 10:9 so suspect.

It is worth noting, in this connection, that precisely this (modified) form of 1 Corinthians 10:9 ("neither let us put *Christ* to the test, as did some of them . . .") was used to counter adoptionistic Christologies during the period of the text's corruption. Two of our ancient sources cite the text against Paul of Samosata to show that Christ was not a mere man, but that he was alive and active already in Old Testament times.[214] According to the fourth-century scholion found in the margin of manuscript 1739, the opponents of Paul were able to appeal to the interpretation of the text in Origen's lost *Stromateis* to show that Christ appeared in the Old Testament,[215] just as the *Epistle of Hymenaeus,* addressed directly to Paul himself, argues that "Christ is named 'Christ' in the divine Scriptures before his incarnation," quoting 1 Corinthians 10:9 (using Χριστός) as proof.

Is the reading Χριστός, then, a corruption made expressly in order to counteract adoptionistic Christologies?[216] Here we must take serious account of intrinsic probabilities, specifically with regard to the broader literary context. In his study of the problem, Carroll Osburn provides an extensive argument for the superiority of Χριστός on just such contextual grounds. His entire position, however, boils down to a simple contention: because Paul calls Christ the rock in verse 4, he probably has "Christ" in mind still in verse 9.[217] This overlooks a consideration that appears more decisive to me. Even though Paul understands Christ to be the life-giving presence that sustained the Israelites in the wilderness, for him it is explicitly *God* who brought judgment against them when they failed to please him. The subject of verse 5 is unambiguous: "God" laid them low in the wilderness. There is no reason to think that Paul has shifted conceptualities in midstream here. And so, the Israelites were destroyed after putting *God,* not "Christ," to the test in 1 Corinthians 10:9. This means that the reading that is preserved widely among the Alexandrian witnesses otherwise understood to be superior (e.g., ℵ B C 33) is, in fact, original. The text was changed by proto-orthodox scribes who saw "Christ" as the one who exercised divine prerogatives even during the days of the Exodus.[218]

A comparable change occurs in the textual tradition of Romans 14:10, in which Paul states that all Christians will appear before the judgment seat of God (τῷ βήματι τοῦ θεοῦ). A number of witnesses, however, have changed the text to read "the judgment seat of Christ" (ℵ^c C^2 Ψ 048 0209 Byz r syr al). That the change is not a sheer accident is evident from its occurrence in several scribal corrections. The reading may, of course, simply represent a harmonization to 2 Corinthians 5:10, which also speaks of the judgment seat of Christ. But what gives the change an added significance is its context, for the next verse provides a scriptural warrant for this notion of judgment through an appeal to Isaiah 49:18: "As I live, says the Lord, to me every knee shall bow and every tongue shall confess to God." The two clauses of the verse stand in parallel relationship, so that the bowing knees correspond to the confessing tongues, and in both cases the object of worship is the same ("to me" / "to God"). In fact, the confession that is made is precisely a confession that this one before whom we appear for judgment *is* God. By changing verse 9 to "the judgment seat of Christ," scribes have done far more than effect a harmonization to another Pauline epistle, although the availability of the parallel may have suggested the change in the first place. For now the text speaks of Christ to whom every knee will bow in worship, whose deity every tongue will confess. In making this change, scribes have actually gone one step further than Paul's preliterary source of Philippians 2:9–10, which also attributes Isaiah 49:18 to the exalted Christ. Now there is little ambiguity: Christ himself is God.[219]

Christ: No Ordinary Human

Many of the textual corruptions considered to this point have emphasized the orthodox notion that Christ was divine. Other changes of the text effect a comparable result, but do so by modifying passages that could be used to argue that he was merely human. Rather than providing proof texts for the orthodox, this kind of corruption eliminates proof texts of the adoptionists; or, to use imagery suitable to polemical confrontation, these corruptions are not so much weapons that orthodox Christians used to arm themselves as munitions stolen from the arsenals of their opponents.

One of the clearest examples of an orthodox change effected to prevent its heretical "misuse" occurs in the statement of Jesus in Matthew 24:36: "Concerning that day and hour no one knows, neither the angels of heaven nor the Son (οὐδὲ ὁ υἱός), but the Father alone." Although the phrase "nor the Son" is found in the earliest and best representatives of the Alexandrian, Caesarean, and Western traditions,[220] it is lacking in the great bulk of manuscripts, including most of the Byzantine. The omission must have been made quite early, as it is attested in Origen and a number of versional witnesses (most of the Syriac and Coptic, along with the Latin Vulgate). Some critics have argued that this shorter text is original to Matthew, because the disputed phrase οὐδὲ ὁ υἱός occurs in the Markan parallel (Mark 13:32), where its attestation is secure. According to this view, the fact that scribes by and large left the phrase intact in Mark shows they were not troubled by its potentially adoptionistic overtones (viz., that Jesus, as a mere man, did not know when the end would come); they therefore must have modified the Matthean form into conformity with its Marcan parallel.

As plausible as this argument may appear, most textual critics have not found it convincing. For one thing, it is not entirely true to say that scribes did not take offense at the phrase in Mark: it is sometimes omitted there as well (X pc). Furthermore, it is understandably lacking more frequently in manuscripts of Matthew than in those of Mark, because Matthew was copied far more often. The popularity of Matthew, in fact, makes scribal harmonizations towards Mark, the least copied of the Gospels, a relatively rare phenomenon. If there were a harmonization in this case, one would expect it to have worked the other direction; that is, if Matthew originally lacked the phrase and Mark had it, one would expect scribes to omit it in Mark.[221] Moreover, not only is the phrase οὐδὲ ὁ υἱός found in our earliest and best manuscripts of Matthew, it is also necessary on internal grounds. As Metzger notes, the phrase forms the second half of a parenthetical οὐδέ . . . οὐδέ clause, so that without it the phrase οὐδὲ ἄγγελοι τῶν οὐρανῶν stands oddly alone in the sentence. This may explain why Luke attests the material in the surrounding verses (of both Mark and Matthew), but omits this verse altogether. If he found the phrase οὐδὲ ὁ υἱός difficult, he could by no means simply omit it without creating a grammatical inconcinnity.

That the phrase in Matthew was seen as problematic by Christian scribes is demonstrated with particular clarity by the history of codex Sinaiticus. The original hand of the manuscript included the phrase, a corrector erased it, and a second corrector restored it. The reason scribes in general found the phrase problematic should be self-evident: it suggests that the Son of God is not all-knowing and could be used therefore by adoptionists to argue that Jesus was not himself divine. It should be stressed that although the phrase would have continued to be problematic in later times, for example, during the Arian controversy, it was omitted much earlier, before the christological debates of the fourth century: it is lacking in the Diatesseron and Origen, and in a range of versional witnesses whose convergence is inexplicable apart from the existence of their common text at least as early as the late second century. The change that was initially made during the adoptionistic controversies then became the standard text of the Middle Ages.

A textual variant that evidences a similar tendency occurs in the second chapter of Luke, a chapter that has been shown repeatedly to have been problematic for anti-adoptionist scribes. In this instance, however, scholars have widely regarded the original reading to be secondary, largely because it is not attested by Alexandrian witnesses normally judged to be superior. The scholarly consensus notwithstanding, there are sound reasons for thinking that Luke 2:40 did not simply say that the child Jesus "increased and grew," but that he "increased and grew in spirit," [222] and that subsequent scribes changed the text because they recognized its adoptionistic potential (Jesus underwent spiritual development).

The external support for the shorter text is to be sure quite strong. It is found not only in Alexandria but also in important Western witnesses.[223] At the same time, it must be noted that the longer text is attested within these traditions as well: nearly all the secondary Alexandrians (Ψ 33 892 1241) and several Western witnesses (aur f q syr[p.h]) join the entire Caesarean and Byzantine traditions in its support. This widespread attestation may not in itself require the adoption of the reading, but it should at least alert us to the presence of a complicated textual problem.

The complication is heightened when one turns to internal considerations and asks which text Luke was more likely to have written. In the parallel account of Chapter 1, the same words are used of John the Baptist, who "increased and grew in spirit" (1:80). Given general critical principles that urge the shorter and less harmonized text as more likely original, particularly when supported by early and superior witnesses, it is little wonder that critics have generally discounted πνεύματι in 2:40 as a secondary addition created as a harmonization. Despite its clear strength, this argument overlooks several important considerations. First, it is obvious that Luke himself has created the parallel between John and Jesus.[224] Both the shorter and the longer text of 2:40 coincide with 1:80—the words "he grew and increased" (ηὔξα-νεν καὶ ἐκραταιοῦτο) are identical.[225] But the *shorter* text does not coincide conceptually, for now John is said to increase in spirit while Jesus is said to grow physically. Why would Luke go to such lengths to indicate a parallel relationship that is not really parallel? Furthermore, why would scribes have wanted to heighten the parallel in a way that might work against their own interests? With πνεύματι in 2:40, one could say that Jesus and John were not essentially different from one another, and that Jesus, far from being divine, was simply a human who, like all other humans, developed spiritually. It is difficult to believe that scribes would create such problems for themselves, especially on such a wide scale as is attested in our manuscripts (the vast majority supporting the longer reading). But it is not at all difficult to see why scribes might want to eliminate the problem simply by deleting the problematic word. Now John and Jesus are not really alike, and Jesus is not said to grow spiritually.

But there are other reasons for thinking that Luke wrote the longer text found in the bulk of our manuscripts. Little is more distinctive of Luke's portrayal of Jesus in the early chapters of his Gospel than his emphasis on the role of the Spirit. In statements unique to the third Gospel, Jesus is conceived by the Spirit (1:35); his identity is revealed by the Spirit (2:25–35); the Spirit comes upon him in bodily form (3:22); he is said to baptize with the Spirit (3:16); he makes his public appearance full of the Spirit (4:1); he is led around in the wilderness by the Spirit (4:1); he begins his public ministry filled with the Spirit (4:14); he preaches his gospel empowered by the Spirit (4:18). In this context, it makes good sense that even as a young child Jesus grew in relationship to the Spirit, that is, between his entry into the world through the Spirit and the beginning of his ministry in the power of the Spirit.[226]

When the cumulative force of the evidence is taken into consideration, the longer text of Luke 2:40 is almost certainly to be preferred. This text coincides with the emphasis on Jesus' relationship to the Spirit throughout the context, it makes better sense of the clear parallel to John the Baptist in 1:80, and it better explains the textual data, namely, the dominance of the more difficult reading in the manuscript tradition. Why, then, was the text changed in several earlier witnesses? As was the case with Matthew 24:36, orthodox scribes appear to have taken umbrage at the notion that Jesus was not all-knowing or spiritually perfect. The longer, more difficult reading of Luke 2:40, then, was altered to eliminate the possibility of its heretical use.[227]

The orthodox refusal to understand Jesus as "merely" human probably accounts for other textual variants in which references to Jesus as a man are simply deleted. It is not that the orthodox disavowed Jesus' full humanity. Quite to the contrary, one of their fiercest battles was in favor of his "human nature" against various docetic and separationist Christologies that in one way or another denied it. But for orthodox Christians, even though Jesus was a real flesh and blood human being, he was much more than that. As a result, the orthodox defended themselves on two fronts, against those who denied that Jesus was a man and against those who claimed that he nothing more. Orthodox polemics against the latter group may well account for several modifications of texts in which Jesus was originally designated as a "human" ($\check{\alpha}\nu\theta\rho\omega\pi\sigma\varsigma$).

One of the most intriguing examples occurs in John 19:5, the famous passage in which Pilate, after having Jesus beaten, robed in purple, and crowned with thorns, presents him to the Jewish crowds, saying "Behold the man" ($\kappa\alpha\grave{\iota}\ \lambda\acute{\epsilon}\gamma\epsilon\iota\ \alpha\grave{\nu}\tauo\hat{\iota}\varsigma\cdot\ \grave{\iota}\deltao\grave{\nu}\ \grave{o}\ \check{\alpha}\nu\theta\rho\omega\pi\sigma\varsigma$). If this sentence were lacking from just one witness, it could perhaps be explained as an accidental omission. But the fact that it is absent from one of our earliest witnesses, $\mathfrak{p}^{66}$ (third century) and from several otherwise unrelated witnesses (OL ac^2) should alert us to the possibility of a deliberate modification of the text. There is nothing here, such as homoeoteleuton or homoeoarcton, that might account for an accidental agreement in error. If the omission were not made by accident, why would it have been made deliberately?

To answer the question, we do well to observe that a different textual variant is attested in a solitary witness that is rather closely related to $\mathfrak{p}^{66\cdot}$ In codex Vaticanus the definite article has dropped out, so that Pilate is now recorded as saying, "Behold, a man" ($\grave{\iota}\deltao\grave{\nu}\ \check{\alpha}\nu\theta\rho\omega\pi\sigma\varsigma$). While there is nothing to commend this singular reading as original, it does make for an interesting shift in meaning. Now, rather than pointing to Jesus as "the man" that the Jewish leaders want to have destroyed, Pilate indicates that the mocked and beaten Jesus is only a man ("See, he is mortal").[228] If the reading now preserved in codex Vaticanus once had a wider currency, then the deletion of the entire sentence makes considerable sense. Scribes found its implication troubling; for them, even though Jesus had been bloodied and reviled, he was not a mere mortal. Pilate's statement to the contrary could best be dismissed by being excised.

A similar motivation may have led to the series of corruptions in 1 Corinthians 15:47, in which Paul elucidates his famous notion of Christ as a second Adam: "The first man was from the earth, of soil, the second man is from heaven" ($\grave{o}\ \delta\epsilon\acute{\nu}\tau\epsilon\rho\sigma\varsigma\ \check{\alpha}\nu\theta\rho\omega\pi\sigma\varsigma\ \grave{\epsilon}\xi\ o\grave{\nu}\phi\alpha\nuo\hat{\nu}$). Strikingly, the reference to Christ as the "second man" has been variously changed in the tradition:

(1) "the second man, the Lord" (ὁ δεύτερος ἄνθρωπος ὁ κύριος, ℵ 075 Byz syr); (2) "the second, the Lord" (ὁ δεύτερος ὁ κύριος, 630 Marcion); (3) "the second man [is] spiritual" (ὁ δεύτερος ἄνθρωπος πνευματικός, 𝔭[46]); (4) "the second, heavenly man" (ὁ δεύτερος ἄνθρωπος . . . ὁ οὐράνιος, F G OL). Each of these changes functions similarly by emphasizing the difference between Adam and Christ: Christ is not just another man, a second creation of God that surpasses the first. He is the "Lord-man," the "spiritual-man," the "heavenly-man." Again, it is difficult to account for these changes apart from assuming an orthodox tendency to portray Jesus as far more than human.

The same tendency may have effected the more subtle change two verses earlier, in which the "first man Adam" is contrasted with the "last Adam." Several witnesses have omitted the explicit reference to the first Adam as a "man" (ἄνθρωπος, lacking in B K 326 365 Iren[lat] al), perhaps because the contrast with the anti-type Christ might then suggest that he too was a (created) ἄνθρωπος. In both instances, it should once again be stressed that although the corrupted text may have served a useful function in later contexts, such as the Arian controversy, the textual data demonstrate that it was actually generated much earlier, at least by the beginning of the third century.

One final kind of textual variant that can be attributed to anti-adoptionistic concerns involves passages that might suggest that Jesus had the capacity to sin. As Christians became increasingly convinced of Jesus' full deity, they became correspondingly certain not only that he did not sin but that he, as God, was absolutely removed from the realm of sin. In the words of Tertullian:

> Some people are very bad, and some very good; but yet the souls of all form but one genus: even in the worst there is something good, and in the best there is something bad. For God alone is without sin; and the only person without sin is Christ, since Christ is also God (*Treatise on the Soul* 41).

This orthodox conviction made some impact on the text of the New Testament, as scribes modified certain passages that might carry with them the implication that Jesus as a full flesh and blood human being was liable to sin.

Several such modifications appear in manuscripts of the Epistle to the Hebrews. There is little doubt concerning the original text of Hebrews 2:18: "Because [Jesus] himself suffered, having been tempted, he is able to help those who are tempted." In the preceding verse Jesus is described as being like his human kindred in all things, so that he might be merciful to them and become a faithful high priest before God on their behalf, to offer expiation for their sins. In such a context, in which Jesus is said to be like other humans, the statement that he suffered after being "tempted" (πειρασθείς) could understandably cause some confusion.[229] Indeed, one natural way to read verse 18 ("he suffered, having been tempted") is that Jesus' difficulty in withstanding temptation is what led to his suffering. It comes then as no surprise to find the original hand of codex Sinaiticus circumventing the problem simply by deleting the participle πειρασθείς. The omission could have been simply accidental; it was corrected by a later hand. But it is nonetheless intriguing: without it the text does not say that Jesus was tempted, only that he suffered.[230]

Other changes in the text of Hebrews point in the same general direction, serving to eliminate any notion of imperfection in Jesus. This seems to be the best explanation of the omission found in an Alexandrian manuscript of Hebrews 10:29. The original text speaks of the one who "spurns the Son of God and disregards the blood of the covenant by which he was sanctified" (ἐν ᾧ ἡγιάσθη). In codex Alexandrinus, however, the final clause ("by which he was sanctified") is omitted.[231] Once again one might consider the possibility of a simple scribal error; but there is nothing in particular that might have caused such a slip, and the shorter text makes perfectly good sense in the context. Indeed, the omission can be construed as a clarification, for the subject of the verb sanctified (ἡγιάσθη) in the original text may be seen as ambiguous. Who is sanctified, the one who spurns Christ or Christ himself? The closest antecedent is "the Son of God," and it may be that the orthodox scribe of codex Alexandrinus, recognizing that the Son of God was not sanctified by the blood of the covenant, simply eliminated the possibility of interpreting the text in this way by deleting the words in question.

A similar situation occurs in the opening verses of the book, where the Son of God is said to have made "a cleansing for sins" (1:3).[232] The majority of manuscripts in the Byzantine tradition have added a possessive pronoun for clarification, so that now the text states that Christ made a cleansing for "our" sins. The modification serves to differentiate Christ from the Levitical priests who make cleansing for their *own* sins before offering a sacrifice of atonement for the people (7:27).

Outside of the Epistle to the Hebrews a similar kind of change is preserved in several manuscripts of Colossians 1:22. The text appears originally to have read, "But now he has made a reconciliation (ἀποκατήλλαξεν) in the body of his flesh (τῆς σαρκὸς αὐτοῦ) through death." In several witnesses the main verb (ἀποκατήλλαξεν, third person singular) is changed to an aorist passive participle in the plural (ἀποκαταλλαγέντες, D* F G b), shifting the focus away from Christ, who brought about the reconciliation, onto believers who have been reconciled. What is striking is that some of these witnesses also omit the pronoun αὐτοῦ, so that the verse now reads "but now having been reconciled in the body of the flesh" (F G). In these manuscripts, the text speaks no longer of Christ's body of flesh, but instead of the believers' fleshly bodies. But why make such a change? It appears to have been made deliberately, and perhaps the best explanation is that it prevents the text from referring to Christ's "body of flesh." Given the negative connotations of "flesh," especially in the Pauline corpus, one could well understand why orthodox scribes who believed that Christ was in fact human, but not susceptible to sin and the lusts of the flesh, might have wanted to make the change, circumventing thereby any possible interpretation that might see Christ as human and nothing more.[233]

Summary and Conclusions

I bring this discussion of the anti-adoptionistic corruptions of Scripture to a close by summarizing its principal concerns and restating its salient conclusions. My overarching thesis is that christological controversies in the second and third centuries affected the transmission of the New Testament, as Christian scribes modified their texts of Scripture so as to make them more serviceable for the theological conflicts of their day. One of the "heretical" views evidenced throughout the period understood Jesus to be the Son of God only by adoption. Advocates of this position included certain Jewish Christians (Ebionites) and the Roman followers of Theodotus the Cobbler. Paul of Samosata was deposed from his Antiochan bishopric for espousing some such view, whether or not he actually did; other Christians may have done so, even though our ancient sources pass over them in silence.

For adoptionists, Jesus was a flesh and blood human being, born of the natural union of Joseph and Mary. An extraordinary man, without peer in righteousness or wisdom, Jesus was chosen to be the unique Son of God, the savior of the world. Some of the early adoptionists situated Jesus' election at his resurrection; by the second century most believed it had occurred at his baptism. Advocates of both positions agreed that Jesus was not himself divine, but was, as their opponents put it, a "mere man."

In opposition to this kind of low Christology, proto-orthodox Christians insisted that Christ was far more than a man, that he was himself divine. Much of the controversy centered on the nature of Christ's uniqueness, as the proto-orthodox claimed that he had pre-existed, that he had been virginally conceived, that he was God on earth. A variety of passages from the emerging New Testament could be used by both sides of this debate; and, significantly for this investigation, the wording of these passages was by no means etched in stone. To the contrary, scribes who transmitted the texts occasionally changed them to make them "say" what they were already known to "mean."

Because it was the victorious party of later centuries that by and large produced the manuscripts that have survived antiquity, we should not expect to find in them a large number of textual modifications that support an adoptionistic Christology. Indeed, such corruptions occur in only rare instances, and even these are not above question (e.g., Matt 1:16 in syr[s]). The *opposition* to adoptionism, on the other hand, did make a significant impact on the textual tradition. In several passages (e.g., Mark 1:1 and Luke 3:22) such corruptions virtually displaced the original text.

Our investigation of these changes has followed the rubrics provided by the proto-orthodox polemicists themselves. Some scribal changes emphasized that Jesus was born of a virgin; others circumvented the adoptionist claim that he was not. One regular target for such changes were passages that originally spoke of Joseph as Jesus' father or parent (e.g., Luke 2:33, 43, 48). Other changes served to emphasize Mary's virginity (e.g., Matt 1:16). In several instances, the idea of Jesus' miraculous birth was imported into passages that originally said nothing about it (John 1:13; 1 John 5:16).

Orthodox scribes not infrequently altered texts that might be taken to suggest that Jesus became the Son of God only at his baptism (Luke 3:22; Acts 10:37, 38; John 1:34), or at his resurrection (Rom 1:4), or at some unspecified moment (e.g., Luke 9:35; 1 John 5:18). Correspondingly, they changed other passages so as to highlight their view that Jesus was already the Son of God before his baptism (Mark 1:1) or even before his coming into the world (Matt 1:18).

By far the most common anti-adoptionistic corruptions simply designate Christ as "God." Sometimes these variants are widely attested (1 Tim 3:16; John 1:18); more frequently they occur in a restricted portion of the tradition (e.g., Mark 1:3; 1 John 3:23; John 10:33; 19:40), or exclusively among the early versions (e.g., Luke 1:17, 76; 2:26). On occasion, such changes occur in manuscripts that can actually be dated to the period of concern (e.g., 2 Pet 1:2; Jude 5). Even when the supporting witnesses are uniformly late, however, they appear to represent vestiges of an earlier age (e.g., Mark 3:11; Luke 7:9; 8:28).[234] Moreover, Christ's divinity is sometimes affirmed through an exchange of predicates, in which his characteristics and activities are attributed to God (e.g., references to God's blood or passion, cf. Acts 20:28; 1 Pet 5:1), or conversely, God's are attributed to him (e.g., Christ as "judge of the earth," cf. 1 Cor 10:5, 9).

Finally, the orthodox emphasis on Jesus' divinity occasionally led to a de-emphasis on his humanity. So far as we can judge, scribes never *eliminated* the notion that Jesus was fully human. This would have embroiled them in a different set of problems, for then the text could be taken to support the docetic Christologies that the proto-orthodox opposed on another front.[235] But scribes did modify texts that could implicate Christ in human weaknesses and frailties that were not appropriate to one understood to be divine, occasionally changing passages that suggest that Christ was not all-knowing (Matt 24:36) or spiritually perfect (Luke 2:40), and passages that suggest that he was purely mortal (John 19:5) or susceptible to human temptations and sin (Heb 2:18; 10:29).

I have observed that the anti-adoptionist changes of the text occur sporadically throughout the tradition, not at all with the kind of consistency for which one might have hoped. Given the character of our evidence, however, this uneven distribution and irregular attestation are not surprising. The scribes of our surviving manuscripts more commonly *preserved* theological variations than created them, and none of these scribes appears to have made a concerted effort to adopt such readings with rigorous consistency. Almost certainly there was no attempt to create an anti-adoptionistic recension of the New Testament. Indeed, the Christians of the proto-orthodox camp did not, on one level, *need* to change their texts; they believed that the texts, in whatever form they came, already attested their christological views. Most of the debates over Christology, then, centered on the correct *interpretation* of the texts rather than on their wording. But to some degree the debates did impact the physical dimensions of the manuscripts, as scribes periodically—if not rigorously—modified the words of the New Testament to make them more serviceable for the orthodox cause, effecting thereby the orthodox corruption of Scripture.

Notes

1. E.g., Marcion and many Gnostics on the one hand, and Irenaeus, Hippolytus, and Tertullian on the other. As we have already seen, proto-orthodox Christians emphasized quite early that Christ was somehow both divine and human. See, for example, the third-century author of the so-called Little Labyrinth cited in Eusebius, *Hist. Eccl.* V, 28, who insists that Christ's dual nature was affirmed by such authors as Justin, Miltiades, Tatian, Clement, Irenaeus, and Melito.

2. Although the second question is couched in distinctively Irenaean terms, its notion that salvation required Jesus to be divine was widely shared.

3. By implication, of course, the author's own interpretations are supported by the *unadulterated* text of Scripture.

4. See, for example, the discussion of Matthew 1:16, pp. 54–55.

5. This is patently true of the Roman adoptionists, according to Eusebius, *Hist. Eccl.* V, 28, and presumably also of the Ebionites, who traced their lineage back to the Jerusalem apostles of Jesus.

6. Significant full-length treatments include Vernon Neufeld, *The Earliest Christian Confessions;* Reinhard Deichgräber, *Gotteshymnus und Christushymnus in der frühen Christenheit;* Jack Sanders, *The New Testament Christological Hymns;* and Klaus Wengst *Christologische Formeln und Lieder des Urchristentums.* See also the works cited in notes 7 and 12.

7. The creedal character of the passage was recognized earlier in this century by Johannes Weiss, *Das Urchristentum,* 86. Among the best discussions are Eduard Schweizer, "Röm. 1:3f und der Gegensatz von Fleisch und Geist vor und bei Paulus"; E. Linnemann, "Tradition und Interpretation in Röm 1:3f"; H. Schlier, "Zu Röm 1,3f"; James D. G. Dunn, "Jesus—Flesh and Spirit"; and Wengst, *Christologische Formeln,* 112–17. The following commentaries also have useful discussions and bibliographies: Ernst Käsemann, *Commentary on Romans,* 10–13; Walter Schmithals *Der Römerbrief: Ein Kommentar,* 48–51; and especially Ulrich Wilckens, *Der Brief an der Römer,* 57–61.

8. Each of the other nine occurrences of σπέρμα in Paul refers to Christ or Israel as the seed of Abraham (but cf. 2 Tim 2:8). It should also be noted that the contrast κατὰ σάρκα / κατὰ πνεῦμα in this passage is not Pauline, for in none of its other occurrences does the term "spirit" receive a modifier and in no other instance does the contrast refer to the person of Christ, rather than to human existence.

9. See, for example, the lapidary constructions of 1 Corinthians 15:3–5 and 1 Timothy 3:16, both of which also represent preliterary creedal materials incorporated into Pauline texts. See the works cited in notes 6 and 7.

10. The phrase occurs two other times in Romans, an additional five times elsewhere in Paul. On its insertion here by Paul, see especially Schlier, "Zu Röm 1,3f," 209–11, and Werner Kramer, *Christ, Lord, Son of God,* 108–10, *contra* Schmithals, *Der Römerbrief,* 50–51. The addition of the phrase serves to make the creed Pauline because now it states that Jesus became "Son of God *in power*" at the

resurrection (cf. Phil 2:8f) rather than "Son of God." That it is intrusive in the creed itself is shown by the fact that there is nothing in the first clause with which it is parallel, unlike every other component of the second clause. Schmithals observes that even if the phrase is original, it can still be read adoptionistically (*Der Römerbrief*, 51).

11. See further the discussion of the textual variant on ὁρισθέντος, pp. 71–72.

12. See the terse discussion of James D. G. Dunn, *Christology in the Making*, 35–36, and the literature he cites there. The judgment concerning earlier materials in the speeches of Acts holds true even though the speeches themselves are by and large Luke's own compositions. The classical study is Martin Dibelius, "The Speeches of Acts and Ancient Historiography"; of the burgeoning literature since then, I mention only two of the more insightful studies: Eduard Schweizer "Concerning the Speeches in Acts," and Ulrich Wilckens, *Die Missionsrede der Apostelgeschichte*. For a more recent, brief discussion, see Marinus de Jonge, *Christology in Context*, 108–11.

13. See Dunn, *Christology in the Making*, 35–36.

14. See the discussion of the text of Luke 3:22, pp. 62–67.

15. Here it should be stressed that an adoptionist could well affirm that Jesus is the "Son of God" without at all considering him to be "God," just as Solomon was known to be the son of God (2 Sam 7:14). On Mark's Christology generally, see the works cited in note 141.

16. For a brief overview of the movement of early Christology away from the earliest conception that God adopted Jesus to be his Son at the resurrection or at the baptism, on to the higher christology of John, see Raymond E. Brown, *The Birth of the Messiah*, 29–32.

17. For up-to-date discussions and bibliographies, see Burton L. Visotzky, "Prolegomenon to the Study of Jewish Christianities in Rabbinic Literature," and Joan E. Taylor, "The Phenomenon of Early Jewish-Christianity."

18. See the discussion of Chapter 1. Even those who recognize the diversity sometimes provide deceptively unified portrayals: for example, Richard N. Longenecker, *The Christology of Early Jewish Christianity*, and, above all, Jean Danielou, *The Theology of Jewish Christianity*. Danielou's book has been particularly influential. See the critical review by Robert A. Kraft, "In Search of 'Jewish Christianity' and Its 'Theology': Problems of Definition and Methodology."

19. This is one problem with the otherwise interesting study of Ray A. Pritz, *Nazarene Jewish Christianity*.

20. Thus, for example, Justin, *Trypho* 46–47; Origen, *Contra Celsum* 61; Eusebius, *Hist. Eccl.* III, 27. See the discussion of Pritz (*Nazarene Jewish Christianity*) for this differentiation. All the patristic texts are collected and critically assessed in A. F. J. Klijn and G. J. Reinink, *Patristic Evidence for Jewish-Christian Sects*.

21. See the patristic discussions of the name given in Klijn and Reinink, *Patristic Evidence*, 19–43.

22. See Klijn and Reinink, *Patristic Evidence*, 42–43, for the effects of these changes on the external perceptions of the group.

23. Clearly shown in Klijn and Reinink, *Patristic Evidence*, 19–43, 67–73; and the discussion in Taylor, "Phenomenon of Early Jewish Christianity," 321.

24. Taylor, in particular ("Phenomenon of Early Jewish-Christianity"), makes a convincing case that "Jewish-Christianity" comprises those groups of Christians (ethnically Jewish or not) who adhere to Jewish norms of praxis in the face of widespread

opposition by the rest of the Christian movement. And so, at least according to Iren-aeus, the Ebionites practice circumcision, pay special reverence to Jerusalem, and commemorate Jesus' first coming with a Eucharistic meal of bread and water (cf. Irenaeus, *Adv. Haer.* I, 26, 2; V, 1, 3); the latter practice perhaps derived from their view that Christ had abolished all sacrifice. See Hans Joiachim Schoeps, *Theologie und Geschichte des Judenchristentums.*

25. See Klijn and Reinink, *Patristic Evidence* 42–43, 67–73. For an attempt to coordinate these various Christologies by tracing a chronological development of the-ology within Ebionite circles, see Hans Joiachim Schoeps, *Jewish Christianity: Fac-tional Disputes in the early Church*, especially Chapters 4–6.

26. Compare Irenaeus: "The Ebionites . . . assert that [Christ] was begotten by Joseph; thus destroying, as far as in them lies, such a marvellous dispensation of God, and setting aside the testimony of the prophets which proceeded from God" (*Adv. Haer.* III, 21, 1). Other patristic texts, including the one from Eusebius, acknowledge the existence of other Ebionites ("who go under the same name") who admit that "the Lord was born of a virgin and the Holy Spirit," while denying "His pre-existence as God" (III, 27; cf. also, e.g., Origen *Contra Celsum* V, 61). This latter group of Ebionites, then, was not adoptionistic, and thus is not a part of my present concern.

27. See the recent discussions of George Howard, "The Gospel of the Ebionites"; and P. Vielhauer and Georg Strecker, "Judenchristliche Evangelien," in Hennecke-Schneemelcher, *Neutestamentliche Apokryphen* I. 114–28, 138–42.

28. That the gospel was written in Greek is demonstrated by the description of the Baptist's diet: the canonical account that he ate locusts (ἀγκρίδες) is brought into conformity with the Ebionites' vegetarian ways by changing one letter in the (Greek) description of Matthew 3:4 par. Now John is said to eat honey-cakes (ἐγκρίδες). For the gospel's harmonizing tendencies, see the discussion of Luke 3:22 in note 91.

29. See A. F. J. Klijn, "Das Hebraer- und Nazoraerevangelium."

30. See note 35 below.

31. Eusebius, *Hist. Eccl.* V, 28.

32. Thus Epiphanius's story that Theodotus apostacized in the face of torture and afterwards devised a theological rationale for his cowardice, claiming that he had denied only a man (Christ), not God. According to Ephiphanius, this then led him to develop a full theology of Christ as a "mere man" (ψιλὸς ἄνθρωπος; *Pan.* 54, 1, 3–8).

33. See especially R. H. Connolly, "Eusebius *Hist. eccl.* V. 28," where the Hip-polytan authorship championed by Lightfoot and Harnack is accepted. What the ear-lier investigations have failed to consider adequately, however, is precisely the chris-tological views of the fragments in relationship to Hippolytus's own claims. The fragments attack a purely adoptionistic Christology (Christ is a "mere man"), whereas Hippolytus claims that Theodotus espoused a separationist view comparable to the Gnostics and Cerinthians. Hippolytus appears to have gotten the facts of the case wrong in this instance—as often happens when he combines disparate views in order to demonstrate a common source of deviation (he claims, e.g., that the Ebionites also share this separationist view). But quite apart from the accuracy of his description of the Theodotians, it appears that his view is *not* what is envisaged by Eusebius's anon-ymous source. For a *"Tendenz-kritik"* of Hippolytus's *Refutation,* see especially Kos-chorke, *Hippolyt's Ketzerbekampfung.*

34. Hippolytus, *Ref.* 7, 35f, 10, 23f; Eusebius, *Hist. Eccl.* V, 28; compare Ps.Tertullian, *Adv. Haer.* 8 (in dependence on Hippolytus?) and Epiphanius, *Pan.* 54.

35. Hippolytus's report is not only tendentious (see note 33), it is also somewhat

confused. Thus, he claims that Theodotus taught that Jesus was born of a virgin, yet that he was like all other humans (*Ref.* 7, 35). Nothing in the fragments cited by Eusebius suggests that Theodotus subscribed to the doctrine of the virgin birth. On the general unreliability of Hippolytus in such details, see Koschorke, *Hippolyt's Ketz-erbekampfung.*

36. See further my article, "The Theodotians as Corruptors of Scripture."

37. For older works see Gustav Bardy, *Paul de Samosate;* Adolf von Harnack, "Die Reden Pauls von Samosata an Sabinus (Zenobia?) und seine Christologie" and especially Fridriech Loofs, *Paulus von Samosata* and Henri de Riedmatten, *Les Actes du procès de Paul de Samosate.* On the deliberations of the Council of Antioch, see, more recently, Frederick W. Norris, "Paul of Samosata"; and Robert L. Sample, "The Christology of the Council of Antioch (268 C.E.) Reconsidered."

38. See especially Sample ("Council of Antioch," 17–21), who argues for the growing consensus that the *Acta* represent Apollinarian forgeries designed to condemn Nestorian views in the person of Paul, and Norris ("Paul of Samosata," 52), who summarizes the debate and draws a similarly negative conclusion.

39. Sample argues strongly for authenticity. For problems in using the *Epistula* to reconstruct Paul's views, see Norris, "Paul of Samosata," 56–57.

40. See especially Norris, "Paul of Samosata."

41. For a discussion of the development of the orthodox view, see especially Hans von Campenhausen, *The Virgin Birth in the Theology of the Ancient Church.*

42. Thus, the adoptionistic Ebionites were commonly accused of using a trun-cated form of the first Gospel. Moreover, the docetist Marcion, who denied the virgin birth for entirely different reasons, used a version of Luke that was similarly abbre-viated (because Christ could not have been a part of the material world, he could not have been born; he therefore descended fully grown from heaven in the fifteenth year of the reign of Tiberius Caesar). See the discussion in Adolph von Harnack, *Marcion: The Gospel of the Alien God,* 25–51.

43. For other textual changes of the birth narratives, effected in the face of Gnostic "separationist" christologies, see the discussion on pp. 137–40 in Chapter 3.

44. Similarly in verse 21, the Sinaitic Syriac joins with the Curetonian Syriac in giving as the angelic pronouncement to Joseph that "[Mary] will bear to you a son."

45. See the discussions cited in note 46 below (Metzger, Brown, Globe). On the meaning of παρθένος for early Christians, see note 69.

46. See the discussions of Bruce M. Metzger, "The Text of Matthew 1:16"; *id., A Textual Commentary on the Greek New Testament,* 2–7; Brown, *The Birth of the Messiah,* 61–64; and Alexander Globe, "Some Doctrinal Variants in Matthew 1 and Luke 2, and the Authority of the Neutral Text," 63–66.

47. It is to be recalled that I am using the term "original" to refer to the readings of the autographs. In a different sense, of course, these variant readings may be "orig-inal" *to this manuscript* (or scribe).

48. The easiest explanation of verse 16 is that the scribe simply wanted to retain the format of the rest of the genealogy at its very end, so that the formula "X begot Y" was mechanically applied to Joseph and Jesus (See Metzger, *Textual Commentary,* 7). Given the scribe's failure to corrupt verses 18–25 similarly, he appears to have understood his own formulation—if he understood it at all—in the sense that Joseph became Jesus' father (through adoption?), although he was not his actual father.

49. Irenaeus opposes this view by referring to the prophecy of Daniel that the advent of Christ would be like a stone cut without hands (Dan 2:34), which he takes

to be a reference to the birth of Christ in which Joseph (the stonecutter) took no part (*Adv. Haer.* III, 21, 7).

50. The fullest treatment of the textual problems in the birth narratives is Globe, "Some Doctrinal Variants in Matthew 1 and Luke 2." For fuller citation of evidence than I provide here, see his apparatus (pp. 68–72). See also the balanced discussions of Brown, *The Birth of the Messiah.*

51. Some commentators have argued that the incongruity of these verses with Luke's infancy narrative otherwise can be explained by their compositional history, that is, that Luke used different sources for parts of his account. If these views are right, then the proto-orthodox scribes' decision to change the texts could be said to be due to a correct insight into their "original" intent. See, for example, Joseph A. Fitzmyer, *The Gospel According to Luke,* 305–13.

52. Including manuscripts A E Θ Π Ψ 33 565 579 892 f¹³ Byz. The omission of the pronoun αὐτοῦ after μήτηρ in some witnesses makes sense only if the reading ὁ πατὴρ αὐτοῦ is original.

53. See Metzger, *Textual Commentary,* 134.

54. All except syrᶜ simply omit the entire phrase beginning with ἰδού, while the latter attests the opening words ἰδοὺ ἡμεῖς.

55. How do I *know* that the changes were made for "theological reasons"? It is important to recall the comments found in Chapter 1. Of course it is no more possible (in any actual sense) to know "why" a scribe changed a text than to know "why" anyone does anything. By saying that there were theological "reasons" I am simply using a kind of shorthand, which is to be understood as meaning that the changes can *function* in theological ways, in this case, in ways particularly amenable to the proto-orthodox cause. See pp. 28–31. Moreover, if we *were* to speculate on personal motivations for variations of this kind, we should probably ask why *else* a scribe would choose to change the text so that it no longer calls Joseph Jesus' father.

56. Including manuscripts A C E Π Ψ 0130 565 f¹³ Byz and various Latin, Syriac, and Coptic witnesses.

57. Manuscripts 1012 a b g¹ l r¹ (along with some Diatesseronic witnesses). The Old Latin manuscripts c and ff² append "his mother" to the corrupted text. In addition, the Syriac tradition changes the text to read "his kinsfolk" (syrˢ ᵖ; also the Arabic harmony of the Diatesseron).

58. Middle English, Tuscan, Liège harmonies: "Joseph and Mary"; Venetian harmony: "They."

59. NA²⁶ cites only manuscript 245; the International Greek New Testament Project volume on Luke cites manuscripts 1347, 1510, and 2643. Neither apparatus, of course, is exhaustive. It should be noted that precisely the opposite pattern of corruption occurs in the text of Luke 2:42, where codex Bezae and several Old Latin manuscripts change the text from "they went up to the feast" to read "his parents went up to the feast, taking him with them." In this case the change was apparently not made for theological but for literary reasons, simply to clarify what is assumed in the rest of the pericope, that Jesus accompanied his parents on the occasion. Because the scribe of codex Bezae reads γονεῖς in verse 41, there can be no question of his importing an adoptionistic tone to the account. The same conclusion must also be drawn for the addition of οἱ γονεῖς to the text of Luke 2:22 in several late witnesses (MSS X Θᵐᵍ 4 50 64 273).

60. The old uncial W omits the genealogy of verses 23b–38; manuscript 579 deletes verse 23a as well.

61. See Marshall D. Johnson, *The Purpose of the Biblical Genealogies,* 230–31.

62. An alternative explanation is suggested by Irenaeus's comment that Jesus could *not* have been literally Joseph's son if he was the Messiah, because among Joseph's ancestors in Matthew's genealogy is found Jechoniah, son of Joachim, king of Judah, of whom it was prophesied in Jeremiah 22:28 that none of his descendents would sit on the throne (*Adv. Haer.* III, 21, 9). The problem would be avoided by simply omitting the genealogy from Matthew's Gospel.

63. Effected by replacing the negative οὐχ with ὅτι to indicate direct address, a change also made in one manuscript of the Sahidic. That this is not an *adoptionistic* corruption is shown by the corresponding modification made in Jesus' response.

64. The propensity of the scribe of 𝔭⁶⁶ to omit short words rather than add them increases the likelihood that this particular change was made deliberately. See E. C. Colwell, "Method in Evaluating Scribal Habits: A Study of P⁴⁵, P⁶⁶, P⁷⁵."

65. ℵ* W b syrˢ· ᶜ. The heightening of the irony by the omission renders the other possible explanation less likely, namely, that it occurred by parablepsis occasioned by homoeoteleuton (i.e., that the scribe's eye inadvertently skipped from the end of πα-τέρα to the end of μητέρα, thereby leaving out the intervening words).

66. Insofar as the present evidence indicates. Several witnesses (A L [Wˢ] Θ Ψ f¹· ¹³ Byz Or) do supply the article before υἱόν, but this change does not affect the issue.

67. It should also be observed that, at least on the basis of the limited inquiry to this point, texts that appear in the most problematic contexts seem most likely to be changed. Thus, when Joseph is called Jesus' father by the narrator of Luke's birth narrative, it is more frequently changed than when he is "erroneously" called his father by unbelievers who simply do not know any better.

68. Whether or not there were orthodox scribes who altered the text with more rigor is something we will probably never be able to determine. If there were, the distinctive character of their texts would have tended to become leveled out as they were recopied by subsequent scribes who also referred to less radically modified exemplars. Similar conclusions concerning the consistency of theological modifications of the text have been cogently argued by Epp, *Theological Tendency of Codex Bezae.*

69. The term παρθένος, of course, could simply mean "young woman" or "maiden." But in the writings of the early church, especially when the term came to be applied to Jesus' mother, it took on the modern connotations of the word "virgin," designating, that is, a woman who had never engaged in sexual intercourse. See *LPGL* 1037–38.

70. In addition to the works cited in note 46 above (i.e., Metzger, Brown, and Globe), see the penetrating discussion of Theodor Zahn, *Das Evangelium des Matthäus,* 66–67, n. 34.

71. Other variants that function to protect the notion of the virgin birth in Matthew 1 modify passages that speak of Mary as Joseph's wife ("wife" is changed to "betrothed" or "companion" in Syriac, Ethiopic, and Diatesseronic witnesses of Matt 1:20; it is changed to "Mary" or "her" in Syriac, Coptic, and Latin witnesses of Matt 1:24); so too descriptions of Joseph as Mary's husband are modified in the Syriac traditions of Matthew 1:19. On these, compare Globe, "Some Doctrinal Variants." Globe sees similar forces at work behind the changes of Matthew 1:18 (omit "before they came together") and 1:25 (change "he did not know her until . . ."), only here, it is the orthodox desire to preserve the notion of Mary's perpetual virginity that is at work. The confluence of versional support (e.g., Syriac and Latin as independent traditions) demonstrates an early date for such modifications. A similar motivation may

lay behind the omission of τὸν πρωτότοκον from Luke 2:7 in manuscript W. Now Jesus is not called Mary's *first*born son.

72. As I have noted, Tertullian accused the Valentinians of the corruption. This might suggest that the variant would be better treated later in my discussion of "anti-separationist" or "anti-docetic" corruptions. And, in fact, there is nothing implausible about the singular reading being generated simply to show that Jesus really was born. But there is also nothing in Tertullian's discussion to indicate that he really *knew* whence the variant derived, and as I have argued that it is in fact the original text, there is no reason to think that either reading originated in the Valentinian controversy. All that Tertullian knew was that the Valentinians were using the verse to their own end; he addressed the problem by claiming that they themselves had created their own authoritative text. Since the singular number functions to stress that Jesus' birth was unusual (not of blood . . .), rather than that it was a real birth, it probably makes better sense to understand the variant reading as originating in an attempt to demonstrate that Jesus came into the world in a miraculous way.

73. "Zur Textkritik und Christologie der Schriften Johannes." For the older literature, see Josef Schmid, "Joh 1,13." Among modern translations, the Jerusalem Bible renders the verb in the singular.

74. See, for example, Metzger, *Textual Commentary*, 196–97.

75. See, for example, the discussion of p. 132.

76. See Metzger, *Textual Commentary*, 714–15.

77. See Brown, *The Epistles of John*, 573.

78. Other Western witnesses presuppose κοιλίας, borrowed from the LXX of Psalm 15 (MSS gig p r syr[p] and *Iren.*[lat]).

79. Even though, in codex Bezae, he is called "the Christ according to the flesh." Of course, even the proto-orthodox who confessed Jesus' virgin birth—and therefore who acknowledged that he did not *literally* descend from David (at least through an earthly father)—nonetheless acknowledged his real bodily existence.

80. C. C. Torrey, *Documents of the Primitive Church*, 145.

81. E.g., Ernst Haenchen, *The Acts of the Apostles*, 182, n. 5.

82. See, for example, Haenchen, *The Acts of the Apostles*, 73–75.

83. So Bonifatius Fischer: "Today it is nearly universally recognized that the (Latin) text [of MS d] is almost completely dependent on its parallel Greek text, whether it be described as a Latin version so thoroughly corrected to the Greek text that its character as a Latin witness is valid only when supported by other Latin witnesses, or as itself a slavish translation of the parallel Greek text or its ancestor in a diglot manuscript" ("Die Neue Testament in lateinischer Sprache," 42; quoted in Aland and Aland, *Text of the New Testament*, 189).

84. The plausibility is heightened by the uneasiness already evidenced by some proto-orthodox Christians in the mid-second century over their paradoxical claims concerning Jesus' descendency, that is, that he was from the line of David even though born of a virgin. Thus, for example, Justin Martyr's opponent in the *Dialogue with Trypho* objects that Jesus must have been born of natural generation (from "human seed") because "the Word says to David that out of his loins God shall take to Himself a Son, and shall establish His kingdom" (*Dial.* 68). Justin replies that some prophecies are "written obscurely, or parabolically, or mysteriously," and interprets the idea of the Messiah's descent from David in light of what he sees to be a clear prophecy of his virgin birth in Isaiah 7:14.

85. I will discuss other textual variants relating to Jesus' baptism in Chapter 3,

because Gnostics who subscribed to a kind of separationist Christology agreed with the adoptionists in pointing to the baptism as the christological moment par excellence. For them, however, the baptism was not the moment of Jesus' adoption or election, but the point of his infusion with the heavenly Christ, who remained with him until his passion. The parallels between the two views are striking and naturally led to some mutual interaction. It comes as no surprise to see that the patristic sources sometimes describe adoptionists such as the Ebionites in separationist terms. What this means for the present investigation is that some of the materials dealt with in this chapter could have easily been treated in Chapter 3, and vice versa.

86. There are, of course, exceptions. Among earlier discussions, Theodor Zahn, a scholar intimately familiar with complexities of the textual tradition, provides a brilliant discussion, arguing for the originality of the Western reading over the more frequently attested variant (*Das Evangelium des Lucas,* 199–202). See also B. F. Streeter (*The Four Gospels*). Among more recent advocates of the Western reading, the following provide insightful comments: Walter Grundmann, *Das Evangelium nach Lukas,* and Augustin George, "Jesus Fils de Dieu dans l'Évangile selon saint Luc," reprinted in *Études sur l'oeuvre de Luc.* For dissenting opinions, in addition to the scholars cited in I. Howard Marshall, *Commentary on Luke,* 154–56, and Fitzmyer, *The Gospel According to Luke,* 485–86, see John S. Kloppenberg, *The Formation of Q,* 84–85; George E. Rice, "Lk. 3:22–38 in codex Bezae"; A. Feullet, "Le baptême de Jésus"; and Joseph Ernst, *Das Evangelium nach Lukas,* 151–52.

87. *Dial.* 88 (cf. 103). There seems to be little doubt that Justin refers here to the text of Luke. He states that after the Holy Spirit alighted on Jesus in the "form" (εἴδει) of a dove (a phrase unique to Luke) a voice came from heaven, using the very words uttered by David when he was impersonating Christ: "You are my Son, today I have begotten you." What is particularly significant is that Justin appears to feel a need to explain away the text of Psalm 2 by saying that this "generation of Christ" is not his "becoming" Christ, it is the "generation" of people who come to know him. It is easiest to assume that he felt compelled to explain away the text, that is, to show that it was not really meant adoptionistically, because in a sense he *had* to: his explanation makes sense only if he knew that the voice at Jesus' baptism quoted the second Psalm.

88. *Paed.* I, 25, 2. Clement indicates that at Christ's baptism a voice from heaven came forth as a witness to the Beloved, saying "You are my beloved Son, today I have begotten you." The quotation represents a slight conflation, but the second half clearly derives from the Lukan account.

89. Quoted in Jerome, *Comm in Isa.* 11, 12: "Later on in the Gospel (*According to the Hebrews*), of which we made previous mention, this writing occurs 'And it came to pass when the Lord ascended from the water, the entire font of the Holy Spirit descended, and rested upon him, and said to him: You are my Son; in all the prophets I was expecting you, that you might come and I might rest in you. Indeed, you are my rest, you are my first-born Son, who will reign forever.'" The reference is allusive, but given the statement that Jesus is the "first-born Son" it seems to refer to the words of Psalm 2: *tu es filius meus primogenitus.* In any case, the voice does not say "beloved Son," making it less likely to be a reference to the other reading of the Synoptic tradition.

90. "The Lord in baptism, by the laying on of the bishop's hand, bore witness to each one of you and caused his holy voice to be heard that said 'You are my Son. This day I have begotten you' " (93:26)

91. The *Gospel of the Ebionites:* Epiphanius, *Pan.* 30. 13, 7–8. The gospel provides a clear conflation of the three Synoptic accounts of the voice from heaven. When Jesus comes out of the water he hears the voice of God (quoting Mark), "You are my beloved Son . . . ." The voice then adds (καὶ πάλιν), "today I have begotten you." This text must derive from Luke, for the text subsequently states that John the Baptist saw the brilliant light and asked, "Who are you?" In reply the voice from heaven iterates the words of Matthew, "This is my beloved Son . . . ." Origen, *Jn.Com.* I, 29, and *Contra Celsum* I, 41; Methodius, *Symposium* 9.

92. Lactantius, *Div. Inst.* IV, 15; Juvencus, *Evangeliorum Libri Quattuor* I, 360–64; Hilary, *de trinitate* VIII, 25; Tyconius, *Reg* 1. Apocryphal Acts: compare *The Martyrdom of Peter and Paul,* par. 1; *The Acts of Peter and Paul,* par. 29. With respect to Augustine, the evidence is a bit more difficult to evaluate. When he wants to harmonize the Gospels he doubts that the voice quoted Psalm 2 but allows for the possibility (*de consensu evv.* II, 14), suggesting that the voice may have said more than one thing (cf. the *Gospel of the Ebionites!*). When he is not concerned with Gospel harmonization, Augustine seems to support the Psalm 2 form of the text. In *Enchiridion* 49 he gives it as "This day have I begotten you," and then explains that Jesus did not really become God's Son on that "day"; the "today" is an eternal today! This shows that Augustine, like Justin, felt some embarrassment over the reading. Finally, in the *Adv. Faust.* there is little doubt that Faustus attests this text, for he is quoted as saying, "(Matthew) tells us that the person of whom he spoke at the outset as the son of David was baptized by John and became the Son of God on this particular occasion. He was about thirty years old at that time, according to Luke, when also the voice was heard to say to Him, "You are my Son; today I have begotten you" (Chap. 23).

93. See further note 110.

94. See, for example, the comments of Justin and Augustine in notes 87 and 92.

95. Thus, for example, Walter Schmithals, *Das Evangelium nach Lukas,* 55.

96. Logical, that is, in a twentieth-century modernist sense. Luke certainly has a logic of his own, whether or not it is one that most moderns would subscribe to.

97. See John A. T. Robinson, "The Earliest Christology of All?"

98. On the parallels between Luke's baptism and transfiguration scenes, see Allison A. Trites, "The Transfiguration in the Theology of Luke: Some Redactional Links."

99. For the textual problem here, see pp. 67–68.

100. See the study of Evald Lövestam, *Son and Savior.*

101. See G. Schrenk on "ἐκλέγομαι."

102. Hans-Joachim Kraus, *Psalms 1–59: A Commentary.*

103. This construal of the significance of the baptism scene is perhaps even more plausible if scholars such as Fitzmyer (*Gospel According to Luke,* 309–11) and Brown (*Birth of the Messiah,* 242–43) are correct in seeing the infancy narrative of Chapters 1–2 as a secondary addition to the Gospel. If there was an earlier edition of Luke in which the opening scenes were the appearance of John the Baptist and the baptism of Jesus (in which the words of the Psalm were quoted by the heavenly voice), then the christological similarity to Mark's Gospel would be quite remarkable: the first mention of Jesus' sonship comes at his baptism.

104. The possible objection that Luke would not apply the words of Psalm 2 to the account of Jesus' baptism when he planned to apply them to his resurrection in Acts (13:33) is no more valid than the claim that he must have applied the christolog-

ical titles consistently. Luke was simply not interested in strict consistency—or at least in what modern scholars would construe as strict consistency—when it came to matters of Christology.

105. See note 94. The reason for conforming the text to Mark rather than Matthew is self-evident: in both Mark and Luke the heavenly voice addresses Jesus in the second person; in Matthew it uses the third person. It was therefore easiest simply to keep the second person pronoun and harmonize the words to the familiar form of the second Gospel.

106. One possible exception might be the ninth-century manuscript 0131 in Mark 9:7, which reads ὁ ἀγαπητὸς ὃν ἐξελεξάμην. At the same time, although this does seem to harmonize Mark's account to the basic notion of Luke's, it does not at all conform to Luke's wording, which is the real matter of concern here.

107. The Caesarean text (ἐκλεκτός), on the other hand, does appear to be a pure harmonization, because it does not serve to eliminate the doctrinal problem.

108. In almost every instance the change has involved the addition of the phrase "Son of God" to the designations of Jesus. Thus $\mathfrak{p}^{75}$ B D f[13] et al., in different locations within the verse.

109. See the discussion above, pp. 51–52.

110. It will be remembered that codex Bezae also attests the words of Psalm 2 at Jesus' baptism. This may appear to stand at odds with the corruption of the present text to achieve an anti-adoptionistic rendering in a such a highly subtle manner. But here it must be recalled, yet again, that of all witnesses to the original text of Luke 3:22, codex Bezae is virtually the *last*. Far from creating the variant, the scribe of Bezae simply reproduced it. The change he has made in Acts 10:38 indicates that in doing so he interpreted the baptismal voice in a perfectly orthodox way: that is, he did not construe the text as signifying the moment at which God made Jesus his Son.

111. One of the best discussions remains von Harnack, "Zur Textkritik und Christologie," I. 127–32. For a concise statement, and a list of older scholars who support the more difficult reading, see Rudolph Schnackenburg, *The Gospel According to St. John*, 305–06.

112. See Gordon D. Fee, "Codex Sinaiticus in the Gospel of John."

113. Codex Bezae is not extant in this portion of John.

114. A conflated text occurs in the OL witnesses a ff[2c], the Sahidic, and manuscripts of the Palestinian Syriac: "This is the chosen Son of God."

115. Along the lines of intrinsic probabilities, Ernst Haenchen notes, but dismisses, the interesting circumstance that if the text is taken to read "the Elect of God," then seven titles of Jesus are mentioned in the chapter: Lamb of God, Rabbi, Messiah, Son of God, King of Israel, Son of Man, Elect of God. *Das Johannesevangelium*, 169.

116. See, for example, the clearheaded discussion by Robert Maddox, *The Purpose of Luke-Acts*, 158–79.

117. Francis Watson ("Is John's Christology Adoptionistic?") argues that John's Christology *is* in fact adoptionistic (i.e., that the offending scribes understood the text correctly), but curiously does not accept ἐκλεκτός as original.

118. Jeremias (*TWNT*, art. παῖς; V. 687) proposed that the change was made by fourth-century scribes in order to combat adoptionistic Christologies. His recognition of the problem was on target, but his dating of the corruption was not: by the fourth century the adoptionist controversy was virtually a thing of the past. Moreover, subsequent discoveries have shown that the variant occurred already in the third,

or more likely the second, century ($\mathfrak{p}^{66,\ 75}$ both attest it), that is, during the period of the adoptionist debates themselves.

119. For a fuller discussion of the possible interpretations, along with comments on the textual problems, see Brown, *The Epistles of John*, 620–22.

120. Manuscripts 1505 1852 2138 2495; Latin vulgate, sy[h], cop[bo], Chromatius of Aquilea.

121. For an argument to the contrary, see Harnack, "Zur Textkritik und Christologie," I. 105–52.

122. 2:29; 3:9 *(bis)*; 4:7; 5:1 *(tris)*, 4, 18.

123. Another text of the Johannine literature apparently proved far less difficult for orthodox scribes. When Jesus speaks of the one whom "God sanctified and sent into the world" (ὃν ὁ πατὴρ ἡγίασεν καὶ ἀπέστειλεν εἰς τὸν κόσμον, 10:36) he could easily be understood as referring to God's action in eternity past in which He set apart his Son for the redemption of the world. If the word about God's "sanctifying" Jesus had been spoken in a baptismal context, it may well have proved more unsettling. For some scribes, however, it appears to have been unsettling enough; for in some late Greek manuscripts (U 47) the verb is changed from "sanctified" (ἡγίασεν) to "loved" (ἠγάπησεν). The change is probably not to be understood merely as an accidental confusion of orthographically similar words, for the original term could well have proved discomfiting for those who could not conceive of a time when Christ was *not* sanctified. All the same, it is nearly impossible to decide *when* the change was introduced into the tradition, given the limitations of our evidence.

124. Here as well one needs to recognize that some texts were more readily corrupted than others. Acts 13:33, for example, would require fairly heavy editing to alter its message. At the same time, because it is already embedded in a document that could hardly be construed as acceptable to adoptionists (e.g., the birth narratives), and because its particular *form* of adoptionism was no longer in vogue, orthodox scribes apparently saw no need to modify its claims radically. For the slight alterations of the verse, see p. 156.

125. See the commentaries and the works cited in note 7.

126. Even with the change, the text still says that it was at the resurrection that God "predestined" or "pre-appointed" Jesus.

127. See, for example, Schmithals, *Der Römerbrief*, 52. This understanding of the change is given added cogency by recognizing the possible adoptionistic message of the creed taken in isolation: "Unlike Paul himself the formula does not presuppose the preexistence and divine sonship of the earthly Jesus" (Käsemann, *Commentary*, 12).

128. Much of the following discussion can also be found in my contribution to the Symposium on the History of Biblical Exegesis ("Viva Vox Scripturae") held at Princeton Theological Seminary in 1990, and published as "The Text of Mark in the Hands of the Orthodox." See further, note 136. Here I will not be considering the minor variants, such as the use of the article in some manuscripts that attest υἱοῦ θεοῦ. These have no direct bearing on the particular issue of anti-adoptionist corruptions.

129. Jan Slomp, "Are the Words 'Son of God' in Mark 1.1 Original?". Slomp nonetheless adopts the shorter text.

130. Alexander Globe, "The Caesarean Omission of the Phrase 'Son of God' in Mark 1:1."

131. Thus C. H. Turner, "A Textual Commentary on Mark 1," 150; followed,

for example, by William Lane, *The Gospel According to Mark,* and Wolfgang Fene-berg, *Der Markusprolog,* 151–52.

132. *Comm. on John* 1.13 and 6.24; *Contra Celsum* 2.4.

133. Thus Globe, "The Caesarean Omission," 216.

134. That is, that it was an error of parablepsis (an "eye-skip") occasioned by homoeoteleuton (words "ending in the same way"). It is sometimes argued that this kind of mistake is particularly likely here, because the words Ἰησοῦ Χριστοῦ υἱοῦ θεοῦ would have been abbreviated as *nomina sacra,* making the accidental skip of the eye from the word Χριστοῦ to the following καθώς more than understandable. Thus, for example, Feneberg, *Der Markusprolog*; Turner, "A Textual Commentary"; Joachim Gnilka, *Das Evangelium nach Markus;* Carl Kazmierski, *Jesus the Son of God;* and Vincent Taylor, *The Gospel According to St. Mark.* See, however, note 135.

135. Yet more curiously, the words Ἰησοῦ Χριστοῦ, which have the same po-tential for omission as *nomina sacra* ending in omicron-upsilon, are not omitted in the tradition, either individually or as a phrase, except in the first hand of 28, which has been corrected.

136. To my knowledge, no one brought forth this argument until Peter M. Head and I, simultaneously and independently of one another, published articles on the problem. See my "Text of Mark in the Hands of the Orthodox," and Peter M. Head, "A Text-Critical Study of Mark 1.1."

137. On this issue, see E. C. Colwell, "Method in Evaluating Scribal Habits," in *Studies in Methodology,* and James A. Royse, "Scribal Habits in the Transmission of New Testament Texts."

138. Paul McReynolds, "Establishing Text Families," based on his collations of manuscripts of Luke for the International Greek New Testament Project.

139. See, most recently, David Ulansey, "The Heavenly Veil Torn," and the lit-erature he cites on p. 123 n. 1. See further, note 140.

140. It could be pointed out in reply that 1:1 and 15:39 are the only instances of an anarthrous υἱὸς θεοῦ in Mark. Although this is true, it scarcely counts as evi-dence for the longer reading in 1:1. On the one hand, it is difficult to conceive of an author indicating an *inclusio* simply by omitting an article at two points of his nar-rative, as opposed, say, to structuring two entire scenes around parallel motifs (such as in 1:9–11 and 15:38–39). Moreover, there may have been other reasons for the phrase to be left anarthrous in both places. With respect to 1:1, if the phrase "Son of God" was not original, a scribe who wanted to add it would no doubt have sought to make the insertion as unobtrusive as possible, and could have accomplished his goal simply by adding the four letters ΥΥΘΥ. (It is to be observed that the name Ἰησοῦ Χριστοῦ, which immediately precedes, is anarthrous as well.) As to 15:39, it may be of some significance that this is the only time in the Gospel that a pagan calls Jesus "Son of God," and it may well be that the author left the phrase anarthrous to effect a nice ambiguity: it is not altogether clear whether the centurion is proclaiming Jesus to be "The Son of the only true God" (as it is normally taken), or to be a "divine man," that is, one of the sons of the gods. Moreover, it should be observed that if an *inclusio* were formed by 1:1 and 15:39 it would be somewhat out of joint, since it would begin at the very beginning of the story but conclude before its very end— before this Son of God had been raised! If, on the other hand, the *inclusio* were formed by 1:11 and 15:39, it would bracket Jesus' public life with proclamations of his divine sonship, first by God at his baptism, after the ripping of the heavens, then by the Gospel's first real convert, the Gentile centurion, at Jesus' execution, after the ripping of the Temple veil.

141. For recent work on the thorny issue of Mark's Messianic Secret, see James L. Blevins, *The Messianic Secret in Markan Research,* and the essays collected in C. Tuckett, ed., *The Messianic Secret.* For challenges to the notion of a "corrective" Christology in Mark, that is, a conscientious attempt to rectify a flawed understanding of Jesus found otherwise in the Markan community, and probably represented in Mark's own Gospel sources (a view popularized by Theodore Weeden, *Mark: Traditions in Conflict*), see the balanced statement of Jack Kingsbury, *The Christology of Mark's Gospel.* For a more general account, see Frank J. Matera, *What Are They Saying About Mark?*

142. See pp. 137–39.

143. p¹ ℵ B C W Δ Θ f¹ syr^(h. pal) cop^(bo) arm geo.

144. K L Π f¹³ 892 Byz OL syr^(s. c. p) cop^(sa).

145. See, for example, Metzger, *Textual Commentary,* 8.

146. Similar changes occur in other texts—most significantly Romans 1:3 and Galatians 4:4—but I will argue in those instances that the corruption is not directed against adoptionistic Christologies but against docetic. For discussion, see pp. 238–39. A comparable change of γένεσις to γέννησις occurs with reference to John the Baptist in Luke 1:14 in a number of later witnesses (Γ Ψ f¹³ 28 33 700 1241 1424). There the issues are altogether different, however, with the change best accounted for on the ground that later scribes simply accommodated the noun of verse 14 to the verb γεννάω used in reference to John's birth in the preceding verse.

147. For arguments against the view that the text refers to the "descent into hell," see Markus Barth, *Ephesians* II. 434–35.

148. Barth, *Ephesians* II. 443 refers to Hermann von Soden, *Der Brief an die Kolosser, Epheser, Philemon.* See also G. B. Caird, "The Descent of the Messiah in Ephesians 4:7–11."

149. I should point out that the reference to Christ's "descent" here, irrespective of its meaning in the book of Ephesians itself (on which see note 147), was often taken in patristic circles to mean his three-day sojourn in Hades, where he preached to the "spirits in prison" (1 Pet 3:19). See Irenaeus, *Adv. Haer.* IV, 22, 1; V, 31, 1. Nonetheless, the corruption does not seem to move in this direction, for if the scribes who made it understood the text in this way, they scarcely would have needed to emphasize that Christ descended to Hades prior to his ascension, because *this* sequence was agreed to by all hands.

150. So too Barth, *Ephesians* II. 433, n. 43.

151. See Sanders, *Christological Hymns,* 15-17; Wengst, *Christologische Formeln,* 156-60; and Wolfgang Metzger, *Der Christushymnus,* 12-16.

152. The inconcinnity created by the use of the masculine is itself evidence that an earlier creedal fragment has been incorporated. See Wengst, *Christologische Formeln,* 157; and W. Metzger, *Der Christushymnus,* 13.

153. Manuscripts ℵᶜ A² C² Dᶜ K L P Ψ 81 [88] 330 614 1739 Byz Lect, fathers from the fourth century onwards.

154. The change was almost certainly no accident for the later scribe of manuscript 88, who gives as his text ὁ θεός, leaving no ambiguity concerning his understanding of the passage.

155. Compare Phillippians 2:6; Colossians 1:15. See the works cited in note 151.

156. Of all the witnesses attesting either variant, only Origen antedates the fourth century; and his witness is found only in the fourth-century translation of his works.

157. See especially Paul R. McReynolds, "John 1:18 in Textual Variation and

Translation." McReynolds gives an exhaustive listing of the textual sources, a full review of external and internal arguments, and a citation of the various renderings of the verse in modern English translations. For another recent discussion with useful bibliographical notes, see D. A. Fennema, "John 1:18." Of the older discussions, still valuable is the analysis of F. J. A. Hort, *Two Dissertations*, 1–72.

158. For fuller apparatus, see UBSGNT[3] and McReynolds, "John 1:18." In short, the textual options in the passage are as follows:

(1) ὁ μονογενὴς θεός, 𝔭[75] ℵ[c] 33 cop[bo] Or[pt]

(2) μονογενὴς θεός, 𝔭[66] ℵ[*] B C[*] L syr[p. h(mg)] and a range of fathers, including most of the Alexandrians

(3) ὁ μονογενής, vg[ms] Diatesseron and other fathers

(4) ὁ μονογενὴς υἱός, A C[3] K X Δ Θ Π Ψ f[1. 13] 565 700 892 1241 Byz Lect OL syr[c. h. pal] arm eth[pp] geo and most fathers

(5) μονογενὴς υἱὸς θεοῦ, Iren[pt] and Or[pt]

(6) μονογενὴς υἱὸς θεός, cop[sa]

Clearly the third, fifth, and sixth variants can make no claim to being original on documentary grounds, and can each be explained rather easily as corruptions of another reading attested more fully in the tradition. We are left with two considerations, whether the original text spoke of "the unique Son who is in the bosom of the Father" or of "the unique God who is in the bosom of the Father," and if the latter, whether the phrase originally had the definite article.

159. For example, Fennema, "John 1:18," 128.

160. Origen is cited in support of three of the five variants listed in the apparatus of UBSGNT[3,] but not for the one variant that he actually attests. A thorough assessment of the evidence shows that he supports ὁ μονογενὴς θεός. See Bart D. Ehrman, et al., *The Text of the Fourth Gospel in the Writings of Origen*, 60.

161. See my comments on the external evidence for the so-called Western non-interpolations in the excursus, pp. 223–27.

162. That Ireneaus and Clement attest the other reading as well is readily explained by its theological usefulness. See p. 82.

163. Among all the witnesses, 𝔭[75] is generally understood to be the strongest; 𝔭[66], which supports the shorter text, is notoriously unreliable when it comes to articles and other short words, so that the omission here simply corroborates what one finds elsewhere throughout the manuscript. Thus Colwell, "Method in Evaluating Scribal Habits." See further, pp. 265–66.

164. See Dale Moody, "God's Only Son." Among other things, Moody argues convincingly against the rendering "only-begotten," on the grounds of etymology and usage.

165. This cannot be construed as meaning that the reading is more likely original because it is "difficult." In fact, it was *not* difficult for scribes, who embraced it as a useful statement of Christ's full deity. See notes 172 and 173.

166. See, e.g., T. E. Pollard, *Johannine Christology and the Early Church*.

167. See further, note 171.

168. Thus Fennema, "John 1:18." This also appears to be the expedient of Raymond Brown (*The Gospel According to John*, 1.17), who adopts the translation "God the only Son" without comment. Interestingly, he renders the variant μονογενὴς υἱός quite similarly as "the Son, the only one." This would seem to suggest that the nominal υἱός is in fact otiose to the phrase.

169. LSJ, *in loc.* See also Moody, "God's Only Son."

170. Thus, recently, McReynolds, "John 1:18." For a list of other scholars, see

Fennema, "John 1:18," p. 133, n. 27. That this view is hardening into a kind of orthodoxy is evident in its casual acceptance by recent authors. See, for example, Otfried Hofius, "Der in des Vaters Schoß ist."

171. A final argument has occasionally been adduced in support of μονογενὴς θεός, namely, that the literary structure of the prologue more or less requires the reading, because the three statements of the opening verse are paralleled, in inverse order, by the final verse. Thus "the Word" (v. 1) is echoed by "that one has made him known" (v. 18; both relating to Christ's revelatory function); "was with God" by "in the bosom of the Father" (both explaining his relation to the Father); and "was God" by "the unique God" (both affirming his divine character). This is an interesting argument, but one that fails to persuade me—not because the parallels do not in fact exist, but because of the way they are effected. In *neither* of the first two instances are the statements of verse 1 actually repeated in verse 18. As there is no reason to think that the author has changed his style with regard to the final element, the reader should expect an equivalent term, not a repetition. And that is precisely what one does find in the phrase ὁ μονογενὴς υἱός, a phrase that affirms Christ's unique divine character, without stating that he is the one and only God himself (which not even v. 1 asserts, because θεός lacks the article).

172. McReynolds ("John 1:18," 115) chides M.-É. Boismard (*St. John's Prologue,* 65) for drawing this conclusion, but misses the point when he argues that the Gnostics would have been particularly inclined to the text. Naturally they would have been, but they are not the ones the reading functions to oppose. It is also pointless to argue that the more commonly attested reading does not fit well into an anti-Arian context (cf. Brown, *The Gospel According to John,* 17); clearly both readings were well worn before Arius arrived on the scene.

173. Compare Origen, *Dialogue with Heraclides,* 128, which condemns the "blasphemous doctrine which denies the deity of Christ," as well as *Hom. in Luke,* 17, and *in Epistula ad Titum,* which speaks of the Ebionites who say that Christ was born of a man and woman like everyone else, and was, as a consequence, only human.

174. See note 166.

175. Why was this the only occurrence of ὁ μονογενὴς υἱός to be changed in the textual tradition of the Fourth Gospel? The answer may lie in the central position it occupies within the prologue, setting the stage for the Christology of the rest of the Gospel.

176. See the discussion of Erich Fascher, *Textgeschichte,* 14.

177. My comments on this passage can also be found in "The Text of Mark in the Hands of the Orthodox."

178. The term can also be used of God, of course (e.g., 13:20, 36), especially in quotations of Scripture (e.g., 11:9; 12:11, 29). In other passages the reference is ambiguous (e.g., 5:19).

179. This is especially true of codex Bezae, where the ἡμῶν of the LXX text is (unwittingly?) changed to ὑμῶν.

180. As I have argued, even if the change was unconscious, one would still need to ask what kind of scribe might have been likely to make it, and how, having done so, he might have understood it.

181. See Chapter 3, pp. 122–23.

182. The words τοῦ υἱοῦ αὐτοῦ of course all end in the same letters. But if the mistake were made accidentally by confusing their endings, the *final* word(s) would have been omitted by an eye-skip, not the first.

183. Another example may occur in the textual tradition of John 18:32. Here

the original text states that "the Jews" refused Pilate's request to take Jesus and try him under their own law, so as to fulfill Jesus' statement concerning his own death (i.e., that it would be by crucifixion, the Roman mode of execution). Some elements of the tradition, however, rather than stating that the Jewish opposition fulfilled "the word of Jesus which he spoke" (ὁ λόγος τοῦ Ἰησοῦ πληρωθῇ ὃν εἶπεν), declare that their actions fulfilled "the word of God which he spoke" (ὁ λόγος τοῦ θεοῦ πληρωθῇ ὃν εἶπεν, MSS L Δ pc). Since the verse refers back to Jesus' earlier claims that he would be "lifted up," the conclusion seems most natural that the scribes who made the change did so simply because they understood that when Jesus spoke, God spoke. Other minuscule manuscripts read "the word of the Lord," which could represent either a direct corruption of the original "word of Jesus" or of the later corruption "word of God."

184. The change appears not to have been made by accident, in view of the tendency of the scribe of 𝔭⁶⁶ to omit short words far more readily than to add them. On this see Colwell, "Method in Evaluating Scribal Habits."

185. Such a Patripassianist position does not seem to be fully embraced in this simple change of John 10:33. But it should be observed that a later hand corrected the text of 𝔭⁶⁶ by deleting the article. This may demonstrate the *potentially* Patripassianistic undertones of the earlier change. Thus, a variety of christological positions played their role in the transmission of the New Testament text: orthodox scribes who believed that Jesus was both God (*contra* the adoptionists) and distinct from the Father (*contra* the Patripassianists), sporadically modified texts that could be used by heretical opponents of either persuasion. See further the discussion of Acts 20:28, pp. 87–88.

186. The orthodox claim that Jesus was both human and divine may also be evidenced in an interesting combination of changes in John 9:33 and 35. In verse 33, the crowd claims that "if this one were not from God, he would be able to do nothing." The text, however, is changed in some witnesses to read "if this man (ὁ ἄνθρωπος) were not from God" (𝔭⁶⁶ Θ N 1241 pc). Some of these same witnesses (e.g., Θ N) also attest the change found in verse 35, in which Jesus' question is sometimes modified from "Do you believe in the son of Man?" to "Do you believe in the Son of God?" In both cases Jesus proceeds to identify himself as the proper object of belief. What this means, however, is that manuscripts Θ and N have incorporated a purely orthodox Christology into the text by their *sequence* of corruptions. Now, in close proximity to one another, the text affirms that Jesus is rightly understood to be both human (ἄνθρωπος, v. 33) and divine (υἱὸς τοῦ θεοῦ, v. 35).

187. Reading the article before κυρίου, with B D K L W 565 892 al.

188. So Θ Ψ f¹³ 700 1424, the Persian Diatessaron, and Old Slavonic^mss.

189. A comparable change occurs in Mark 5. After Jesus heals the demoniac, he instructs him to return home and tell what the Lord (ὁ κύριος) has done for him (5:19); in some witnesses, however, the man is to tell what "God" (ὁ θεός) has done for him (D [1241]). As for the possibility that this particular variant is a simple harmonization to Luke 8:39, one should question why such a harmonization has been made in this case, especially in light of the orthodox tendency to emphasize that the one who does these things is God himself. Moreover, even in Luke 8:39 a change has been made that encourages the reader to identify Jesus as God. Here, after the demoniac receives his instruction to proclaim what God has done for him (i.e., for Luke, through Jesus), he goes about preaching what "Jesus had done to him" (ὅσα ἐποίησεν αὐτῷ ὁ Ἰησοῦς). For Luke the tradition does not suggest that Jesus, as God, had healed the man. Jesus is not identified as God in this Gospel, although he is under-

stood to be the one through whom God works. Later scribes, however, understood the implications of the text somewhat differently; the passage is slightly modified in a number of Greek and Coptic witnesses to state that the man went about preaching what "God" (i.e., Jesus) had done for him.

190. That this change is not accidental is borne out by a corruption pointing in the same orthodox direction in the Persian Diatesseron's account of the Baptist's preaching in Luke 3:4, where the text of Isaiah 40 is modified to highlight the divinity of the one to come: "Prepare the way of the Lord *God*" (= κυρίου θεοῦ).

191. For another instance of the tendency of 𝔭⁷² to stress an exalted Christology, see the discussion of 1 Peter 5:1 below.

192. Via parablepsis occasioned by homoeoteleuton. Metzger, *Textual Commentary, 593*.

193. See BAGD, art. ὁ II 10 b; art. καί I 1 a; less firmly, Nigel Turner, *Grammar of New Testament Greek*, vol. III, 181-82.

194. Another subtle but intriguing variant occurs in Paul's Second letter to the Corinthians. In the opening chapter, Paul speaks of having within himself the "judgment of death" that compels him not to have confidence in himself but "in the God who raises the dead" (ἐπὶ τῷ θεῷ τῷ ἐγείροντι τοὺς νεκρούς, 1:9). Our earliest manuscript, however, in company with a handful of later witnesses, gives the participle in the orthographically and phonetically similar aorist form, ἐγείραντι (𝔭⁴⁶ 326 365 614 1881 2495 boᵐˢ vgᵐˢ). The subject of the participle is θεός and the object is in the plural. What could it mean to speak of "the God who raised (past tense) those who were dead?" In the biblical record God himself raises only Jesus, unless one thinks of the Matthean account of the aftereffects of Jesus' crucifixion (27:52). All other accounts of the dead being raised occur through human agency. But of course, Jesus raises the dead in several of the Gospel traditions (e.g., Mark 5, Luke 7, John 11). Given the orthodox proclivity to see Jesus as divine and the widespread knowledge that he had raised the dead, could the corruption be explained in part as a reference to Jesus as the God in whom Paul places his confidence?

195. ἐπιταγὴν θεοῦ σωτῆρος ἡμῶν, Ἰησοῦ Χριστοῦ τῆς ἐλπίδος ἡμῶν (MSS 42 51 104 234 327 463 fu ethʳᵒ).

196. Blood of God (αἷμα τοῦ θεοῦ, Ign. *Eph.* 1:1; *sanguine dei*, Tertullian, *ad uxor* II. 3); the suffering of God *(passiones dei)* and God crucified (Tertullian, *de carne Christi* 5); "God is murdered" (ὁ θεὸς πεφόνευται; Melito, *Paschal Homily*). For other references, see Adolf von Harnack, *History of Dogma*, I. 187.

197. See the discussion of Chapter 5.

198. Compare, for example, Origen, *Dial. with Heraclides*, 118–24.

199. This is not to impute an inconsistency to Tertullian, as in both treatises he is cautious to speak of Christ as both divine and human. See the discussion in Chapter 5.

200. The change of Galatians 2:20, already discussed, can be considered to be one such change, in that "God" is now described as "the one who loved me and gave himself up for me." See pp. 86–87.

201. On the translation, see Metzger, *Textual Commentary*, 480–81, and the literature cited there.

202. For another reading *in loc.*, see p. 264.

203. Manuscripts 𝔭⁷⁴ A C* D E Ψ 33 1739 cop al.

204. See the discussion of pp. 264–66. This is where the textual problem differs from that of John 1:18 discussed previously. Although the orthodox were perfectly willing to talk about Christ as the μονογενὴς θεός, since he was, after all, the true

God, they were extremely reluctant to talk about him as God the Father, especially when it came to the shedding of blood. The controversy with Patripassianists revolved around precisely this issue of whether it was the Father who suffered.

205. The reading occurs in the fourth-century Alexandrians Athanasius and Didymus, and throughout the Byzantine textual tradition.

206. See pp. 85–86.

207. For example, 1 *Clem.* 2:10 (τὰ παθήματα αὐτοῦ, antecedent: θεός); Ign. *Rom.* 6:3 (τοῦ πάθους τοῦ θεοῦ μου); Tertullian, *ad uxor* II, 3 *(passiones dei)*.

208. See Chapters 3 and 4 for further instances of textual changes that emphasize Christ's real suffering.

209. See the discussion and references in Gordon D. Fee, *The First Epistle to the Corinthians,* 448.

210. For a complete apparatus, see Osburn, "The Text of 1 Corinthians 10:9."

211. On the other hand, the best witnesses of the Alexandrian tradition attest κύριος (א B C 33). Osburn's decision ("The Text of 1 Corinthians 10:9," 201–02) to list upwards of 450 witnesses in support of the Byzantine text gives a somewhat skewed view of the textual situation, as it lends itself too readily to the impression that the reading is more likely original because it is so widely attested. (To be sure, this is not the conclusion Osburn draws in his analysis; but why else list all the manuscripts?). In fact, the vast majority of these witnesses are close relatives of one another, making their independent evidential value nil.

212. So, Metzger, *Textual Commentary,* 560, and more recently, Fee, *The First Epistle to the Corinthians,* 457.

213. See the polemic directed against Paul of Samosata, discussed on p. 90. In addition, to cite but one other example, compare the use of 1 Corinthians 10 by Eusebius of Caesarea in his confrontation with Marcellus of Ancyra (*De Ecclesiastic Theologia* 1, 20; cited by Maurice Wiles, "Person or Personification?", 287). See also the discussion of J. E. L. van der Geest, *Le Christ et l'ancien testament chez Tertullian,* especially Chapter 5, "Le Christ préexistant dans l'ancien testament," in which he shows a number of other polemical grounds for the proto-orthodox insistence that Christ appeared already in the Old Testament.

214. See Osburn, "The Text of 1 Corinthians 10:9," 209–11, and the literature he cites there.

215. For the text, see Eduard von der Goltz, *Eine textkritische Arbeit des zehnten bezw. Sechsten Jahrhunderts,* 66.

216. It would be a mistake to think that the text had been modified simply to subvert the teachings of the third-century Paul. The change is attested already in the time of our earlier adoptionistic controversies (e.g., in Clement of Alexandria and the anonymous presbyter quoted by Irenaeus [*Adv. Haer.* IV, 27, 3]).

217. "The Text of 1 Corinthians 10:9," 208.

218. Osburn ("The Text of 1 Corinthians 10:9," 203–05) has effectively discounted Epiphanius's claim that the text was corrupted by Marcion (i.e., from κύριος to χριστός). But Osburn's own view, that Antiochan opponents of Alexandrian exegesis, or more likely adoptionists, modified the text to keep Christ *out* of the Old Testament does not accord well with the textual alignments. The reading is best attested among the *opponents* of adoptionism (e.g., Epiphanius) and precisely in Alexandria (MSS א B C 33), *not* predominantly in the Byzantine (i.e., Antiochan) tradition!

219. It is possible that the corruptions of 2 Corinthians 5:6 and 8 in several witnesses derive from the same motivation, although here there can be less ground for certainty. The passage states that being present in the body is to be absent from "the

Lord," (v. 6), whereas being absent from the body is to be present with "the Lord" (v. 8). In both instances "the Lord" has been changed to "God" (τοῦ κυρίου / τοῦ θεοῦ, v. 6; τὸν κύριον / τὸν θεόν, v. 8). At first the change appears innocuous enough, and scarcely christological. But the passage goes on to identify who it is before whom people are present when "absent" from the body: they appear before the "judgment seat of Christ." By changing "the Lord" to "God" in verses 6 and 8, while retaining the notion of "the judgment seat of Christ" in verse 11, scribes have shown that being absent from the body means being present before the God Christ.

220. Manuscripts ℵ*· ᵇ B D Θ f¹³ 28 OL syrᵖᵃˡ arm geo¹· ᴮ eth al.

221. Furthermore—to put a twist on the argument—if it is true that Matthew originally did lack the phrase, that is, that he deleted it when he took over the logion from Mark, one would then have grounds for arguing that from the earliest of times it *was* seen as problematic, precisely the point that supporters of the Byzantine text of Matthew need to avoid!

222. ηὔξανεν καὶ ἐκραταιοῦτο πνεύματι, with manuscripts A Δ Θ Ψ 053 33 565 892 1241 f¹· ¹³ Byz aur f q syrᵖ· ʰ boᵐˢ· Both variant readings complete the verse by indicating that Jesus was "full of wisdom." See note 225.

223. Leading witnesses: the so-called great uncials (ℵ B D, along with L N W) and most of the Latin and Coptic manuscripts.

224. Or Luke's source did. The point is not affected either way.

225. The emphasis on 2:40 is on Jesus becoming "full of wisdom," perhaps in contrast to the Baptist, about whom the same is not said. The subsequent narrative— Jesus as a twelve-year-old in the temple—serves to demonstrate the point. Because *this* is the shift of emphasis, the *rest* of the phrase ("increased and grew in spirit") probably conformed with 1:80.

226. Given the widespread occurrence of πνεῦμα in the context, always meaning "the Spirit of God," it is best to understand it here as referring not simply to Jesus' own personal growth ("in spirit") but to his growth in relationship to the Spirit, that is, his development in relationship to God.

227. A similar motivation may have led later scribes to omit the phrase πληρού μενον σοφίᾳ in Luke 2:40 (MSS 472 903 983 1009 Theodoret). Now Jesus is not said to become filled with wisdom, a difficult statement to understand if, as God, Jesus is already "all wise."

228. This interpretation is even preferred by some commentators who read the article in 19:5. See Charles Panackel, ΙΔΟΥ Ο ΑΝΘΡΩΠΟΣ, 336–37.

229. The word πειράζω, of course, could also be rendered "put to the test." But this does not appear to be the way scribes who modified the text took it.

230. It should be pointed out that precisely this problem of misconstrual is obviated in the parallel passage of Hebrews 4:15. For there, unlike here, it is made crystal clear that the one who was tempted was without sin. A scribe uncomfortable with the possible implications of 2:18 may well have modified the earlier passage in the same direction.

231. Compare the text of John 10:36, discussed earlier in another context. See note 123.

232. For another orthodox corruption of this verse, see pp. 150–51.

233. Interestingly, when Tertullian was intent on demonstrating to Marcion that Jesus *did* have a real, fleshly body, he turned to precisely this verse as proof (i.e., in its original formulation; *Adv. Marc.* V, 19).

234. As I have argued, even when a solitary later witness preserves an orthodox modification of this kind, it is either reproducing an earlier corruption or is reflecting

the successful resolution of the conflict. That is to say, even if a medieval scribe did introduce such a corruption on his own, by doing so he simply demonstrates the strength of the orthodox victory over the adoptionistic Christologies of a bygone era: the conquest was so complete that "orthodoxy" had become second nature in an age when the controversy itself was little more than a faded memory.

235. See the comments in Chapter 6 concerning the seemingly contradictory impulses evidenced in the manuscripts and their relationship to the paradoxical affirmations of the proto-orthodox Christology.

3

Anti-Separationist Corruptions of Scripture

Introduction: Separationist Christologies in Early Christianity

The transition from the adoptionistic Christologies embraced by such groups as the Jewish-Christian Ebionites to the separationist views advanced by Gnostic Christians is not so abrupt as one might expect. To be sure, the early adoptionists have struck modern investigators as somewhat primitive, unsullied by the fantastic mythological speculations underlying the Gnostic systems.[1] To the orthodox church fathers, however, these kinds of Christology appeared closely related.[2] This can be seen with particular clarity in the patristic accounts of the archheretic, Cerinthus.

Cerinthus is a shadowy figure of the early second century, around whom there accumulated several interesting, if apocryphal, tales.[3] It was precisely the proximity of his views to those of the adoptionists that led later heresiologists such as Pseudo-Tertullian (*Adv. Omn. Haer.,* 3) and Epiphanius (*Pan.* 28) to consider him the progenitor of the Ebionites. But recent scholarship inclines more toward our older sources, which depict him as an early Gnostic.[4] Like the adoptionists, Cerinthus believed that Jesus was a full flesh and blood son of Joseph and Mary, a man distinguished by neither a divine nature nor a miraculous birth, remarkable only for his exemplary righteousness and wisdom. Also like them, Cerinthus maintained that Jesus' baptism marked a turning point; he did not, however, regard it as the time of Jesus' adoption to sonship. Instead, at his baptism, Jesus received into himself a portion of the Godhead, the divine Christ who came upon him in the form of a dove. This indwelling Christ empowered Jesus for ministry and remained in him until the very end; then, when Jesus was about to suffer, the Christ withdrew to return to heaven, leaving Jesus to endure his passion alone.

This understanding of the relationship between Jesus and the Christ represents, *in nuce,* the views developed with considerable complexity by other Gnostic Christians of the period. For orthodox Christians bent on unity, such views impugned the very essence of Christian truth. For them, God was one, the church was one, and Jesus Christ was one. As a result, Gnostics who, in

119

their opinion, dissected the divine realm, severed the material world from the true God, and created schisms within the church, came under persistent attack for advancing divisive doctrines, including those that differentiated Jesus from the Christ.[5] According to the constant refrain of the orthodox opposition, Jesus Christ is "one and the same."[6] In this chapter I will show how this orthodox response came to affect the transmission of Scripture, as scribes modified their sacred texts in light of the controversy. As a preliminary step, we do well to learn something more about the terms of the debate.

The Orthodox Perception of Christian Gnosticism

To understand why gnostic Christologies aroused such passionate opposition, we must first explore the ideological foundations upon which they were constructed. This will involve a thumbnail sketch of the notoriously complex world of Christian Gnosticism. Given the central focus of our investigation— the activities of orthodox Christian scribes—we have little reason to examine non-Christian forms of Gnosticism, and can also leave aside the thorny question of gnostic origins (i.e., whether Gnosticism developed before, after, or simultaneously with Christianity).[7] Moreover, as was the case with adoptionism, it is far less important for us to see Christian Gnosticism "as it really was" than to recognize how it was "perceived."[8] For it was their *perception* of Gnostic Christologies that led proto-orthodox scribes to corrupt their sacred texts.

Even restricting ourselves to what the orthodox heresiologists have to say about the Gnostics does not leave us a simple task. While the church fathers of the second and third centuries saw Gnosticism as the greatest threat to the internal well-being of the Christian church,[9] they did not look upon the movement as at all monolithic; even from their stereotyping perspective, representatives of the view appeared wildly divergent at every turn. As Irenaeus pronounces in his famous lament over the Valentinians: "Since they differ so widely among themselves both as respects doctrine and tradition, and since those of them who are recognised as being most modern make it their effort daily to invent some new opinion, and to bring out what no one ever before thought of, it is a difficult matter to describe all their opinions" (*Adv. Haer.* I, 21, 5).

It is hard to engage an opponent who cannot be grasped. Faced with a cacophony of disparate myths, beliefs, and practices, the heresiologists undertook to restore a semblance of coherence to the disparate groups of Gnostics by tracing (or better, creating) their various genealogical relationships. These genealogies explained why Gnostics appeared so similar in outline yet so increasingly complex and discrepant in detail.[10] Most of the heresiological accounts draw the Gnostic line back to Simon Magus, the contemporary of the apostles who has already been discussed.[11] Simon's willful disposition and passion for magic led to a remarkably self-serving form of heresy, in which he claimed to be God himself, come to bring salvation to the world.[12] Simon's successors did not share their master's exalted image of himself, and his own divine status faded quickly into oblivion. But they retained the basic components of his soteriological system, modifying and expanding them with fantastic cosmological and cosmogonical details. The pedigree of such systems forms the backbone of much of the orthodox slander: Ptolemaeus and Marcus, the chief culprits of Irenaeus's five-volume attack, stand condemned both for their tarnished ancestry and for their own godless innovations.[13]

For our purposes, the discrepant mythologies of these various Gnostic groups are less important than what lies behind them, namely, the Gnostic understanding of the world and of human existence within it (at least as these were perceived by the orthodox polemicists).[14] Gnostics were regularly attacked for taking a radically anti-cosmic stand that struck at the heart of the orthodox belief that the God who created the world and reigns as its Lord is also the God who has redeemed it. For the Gnostics, the true God did not create this world at all. The world emerged from a cosmic disaster in which a lower deity or a group of angels, either out of malice or ignorance, created the material universe and entrapped elements of the divine within it. The mythologies that these Gnostics espoused served to explain how these lower deities came into being (often as emanations from the true God) and how conflicts among their ranks led both to the catastrophic concoction of matter and to its aftermath, the imprisonment of divine sparks. While these cosmogonies struck the fathers as puzzling in their complexity and bizarre in their detail, they proved particularly disturbing in their guiding premise, that the Creator and Ruler of this world is not the true God but a lower deity whose creation comprises the realm of evil and ignorance.

The material world is prison to the sparks of the divine, and the goal of the Gnostic systems is to liberate them. It is, in fact, within human bodies that the sparks have become imprisoned and from which they must be released. This release can only come when the divine sparks are awakened, brought back to life by acquiring the true knowledge (Greek: *gnosis*) of their origin and destiny. The Gnostic religion, therefore, entails the revelation of salvific knowledge, "knowledge of who we were and what we have become, of where we were and where we have been made to fall, of whither we are hastening and whence we are being redeemed, of what birth is and what rebirth."[15] When persons within whom the divine sparks reside learn the mysteries of their own existence, of their fall into matter and the secret way of escape, then they have become "Gnostics," that is, "Knowers," those who have been set free from the ignorance and evil of the material world and enabled to return to their home.

Because this salvific knowledge provides a way to escape this world, it cannot be attained through normal "worldly" means. The God of this world has certainly not provided it, as he is either evil and thus intent on keeping the divine sparks perpetually entrapped, or ignorant of any realm superior to his own. One can only acquire the knowledge necessary for salvation through a revelation of the true God himself. This salvific knowledge, then, is revealed by an emissary from the divine realm to a select group of followers, who in turn convey it to those deemed able to receive it.

It is within this context of Gnostic revelation that we can situate the development of Gnostic Christologies. The emissary who provides the knowledge requisite for salvation must come from the divine realm, else he would have no access to the true *gnosis*. Moreover, he cannot actually participate in the material world, else he would himself be entrapped within it. Given the logic of this system, at least as it was perceived by the church fathers, Gnostic Christians had two basic christological options: they could claim either that Christ was a divine being who came into this world in the semblance, but not the reality, of human flesh,[16] that is, that he was a phantom who only appeared to be human, or that he descended from the fullness of the divine realm, the Pleroma, to indwell a human being temporarily, in order to communicate his message of salvation before returning to his heavenly home.[17] I will explore the former option, the one more appropriately labeled "docetic," in the chapter that follows, and devote the present discussion to the second view, the "separationist" Christology that was embraced by the majority of Gnostic Christians.[18]

According to separationist Christologies, Christ was one of the divine aeons of the Pleroma, who entered into the man Jesus at his baptism, through whom he conveyed salvific *gnosis* to the disciples during his public ministry, and from whom he departed at some time prior to the crucifixion. The view is found in relatively pure form in Irenaeus's description of an unnamed group of heretics near the end of Book 1 of his *Adversus Haereses:*

> Jesus, by being begotten of a virgin through the agency of god, was wiser, purer, and more righteous than all other human beings. The anointed (Christ) in combination with wisdom (Sophia) descended into him, and thus was made Jesus Christ. Accordingly many of his disciples—they say—did not recognize that the anointed (Christ) had descended into him; but when the anointed (Christ) did descend into Jesus, he began to perform miracles, heal, proclaim the unrecognizable parent, and openly confess himself to be the child of the first human being. . . . And while he was being led away (to death)—they say—the anointed (Christ) himself, along with the wisdom (Sophia), departed for the incorruptible realm, but Jesus was crucified (*Adv. Haer.* I. 30, 12–13).[19]

This was not the end of the story, however, for these Gnostics maintained that Christ raised the man Jesus from the dead, and over an extended period of time revealed through him the *gnosis* necessary for salvation.

> The anointed (Christ) was not unmindful of its own, but sent down into him a certain power, which raised him up in a (kind of) body that they call animate and spiritual, for he let the worldly parts return to the world. . . . Now after his resurrection he remained (on earth) for eighteen months. And because perception had descended into him (from above), he taught the plain truth. He taught these things to a small number of his disciples, who, he knew, were able to receive such great mysteries (*Adv. Haer.* I. 30, 13–14).

Thus, according to opponents of the view, Jesus' teachings were said to be preserved only among the elect, only, that is, among those who had the divine spark within them and so were able to receive the *gnosis* requisite for salvation. In the typical Gnostic anthropology, such persons were called "pneumatics" ("spiritual"). All others were understood to be either "psychic" ("animal") or "hylic" ("material"). The latter were creations of the world's "Demiurge" pure and simple, and had no possibility for existence beyond this world. Upon death, they simply ceased to exist. The psychics, however, could hope for a limited kind of salvation, though not one so glorious as that reserved for the pneumatics. Included among the psychics were members of the Christian church at large, who accepted the literal teachings of Christ, but who erred in understanding their surface meaning alone, not their deeper ("real") significance. Such persons would be saved by faith and good works. Only the pneumatics, the Gnostics themselves, could truly understand the revelation from God; on the basis of that revelatory knowledge, they were destined to escape this material world.

In part, then, *gnosis* involved understanding the true but hidden teachings of Scripture.[20] Given the rest of their system, it is not surprising that Gnostics typically understood the Old Testament to be the book of the Demiurge, the God of the Jews who created the world and received the worship of most Christians, ignorant believers who mistook him for the true God. But even within the Demiurge's book had been secreted important revelations that could be discerned when one moved beyond the literal meaning to the allegorical. The opening chapters of Genesis were particularly to be cherished, for here the mysterious beginnings of the universe lay hidden in allegorical form. Even more significantly, the writings of Jesus' own apostles conveyed secret revelations not accessible to the literal-minded psychics of the church. Only true Knowers could unravel the meanings embedded in seemingly unrelated details of the text, meanings that comprised the secret teachings of the Gnostic system.[21]

This refusal to subscribe to a literal understanding of the text was a source of perennial frustration for the proto-orthodox church fathers.[22] The frustration strikes a cord of sympathy with most moderns: if a "common-sensical" or "straightforward" reading of a text (i.e., a literal interpretation) has no bearing on what the text actually means, then the text can scarcely be used to arbitrate disputes. Since the Gnostics already knew what the text meant (Christ had told them!) they were no longer constrained by what the text "said" (or at least by what the orthodox said it said).

As should be clear from this description, the Gnostics who were attacked by such heresiologists as Irenaeus, Hippolytus, and Tertullian did not consider themselves to be a religion distinct from Christianity. They instead claimed to possess the correct interpretation of Christianity itself, an interpretation allegedly transmitted secretly from Jesus to his disciples. It is for this reason that their opponents found such persons so difficult to track down and up-root.[23] Gnostics could remain within their Christian communities and confess everything that any orthodox Christian confessed. But the Gnostics understood even these standard confessions allegorically, professing the orthodox faith with their lips, but redefining the terms in their hearts: "Such persons are to outward appearance sheep; for they appear to be like us, by what they say in public, repeating the same words as we do; but inwardly they are wolves" (Irenaeus, *Adv. Haer.* III, 16, 8; see also IV, 33, 3). Thus, as a solitary example, Valentinians could confess the "resurrection of the flesh," even though they believed that the flesh was evil and bound for destruction. For them, the confession "meant" that people who are in the flesh (entrapped sparks) can ascend to the Pleroma through *gnosis.*

Anti-Gnostic Polemics and the Orthodox Corruption of Scripture

Rather than discuss the entire compass of the orthodox opposition to Gnosticism, I will focus on the christological controversy per se.[24] In response to the Gnostic separationist Christologies, orthodox writers evoked numerous texts of Scripture to demonstrate that Jesus Christ was "one and the same," that there was no division between Jesus and the Christ, and that there was no time in which Jesus was not the Christ. Thus, in a trenchant discussion in Book III of his *Adversus Haereses,* Irenaeus attacks those "blasphemous systems which divide the Lord, as far as lies in their power, saying that he was formed of two different substances" (III, 16, 5). Both the Gospels and Paul, claims Irenaeus, contravene the Gnostic notion that the heavenly Christ entered into Jesus only at his baptism and left him before his passion. To the contrary, Scripture affirms that Jesus was actually *born* the Christ (III, 16, 2), that he was *recognized* as the Christ while yet an infant (III, 16, 4), that he *suffered* as the Christ (III, 16, 5), and that he *died* as the Christ (III, 16, 5). In contrast to the variegated separationist views, "the Gospel knew no other son of man but Him who was of Mary, who also suffered; and no Christ who flew away from Jesus before the Passion; but Him who was born it knew as Jesus Christ the Son of God, and that this same one suffered and rose again" (III, 16, 5).

If orthodox scribes were disposed to modify their biblical texts in light of the Gnostic controversies, their corruptions might be expected to emphasize precisely these points, that Jesus Christ is one being not two, that the Christ did not enter into Jesus at his baptism or leave him before his crucifixion, that Jesus was born the Christ and crucified as the Christ. At the same time, one might not anticipate a superfluity of such corruptions; the Gnostics, after all, were widely thought to disdain the literal wording of the text.[25] Why modify a text if its wording has little bearing on the debate? In point of fact, however, scribes did have their reasons, as I will show in the conclusion to this chapter. For now, it is enough to observe that such corruptions do indeed occur, and precisely in texts that appear critical to the debate.

Jesus Christ: One and the Same

I begin by considering one of the thorniest textual problems of the Johannine literature. Because the resolution of this problem can illuminate so well the orthodox opposition to separationist Christologies, I have chosen to devote some sustained effort to unpacking the various complexities of the text of 1 John 4:3.[26]

1 John 4:3

In the majority of manuscripts, 1 John 4:3a reads "every spirit that does not confess Jesus (πᾶν πνεῦμα ὃ μὴ ὁμολογεῖ τὸν Ἰησοῦν) is not from God." Other witnesses, however, as early as the second century, read "every spirit that looses (or "separates") Jesus (πᾶν πνεῦμα ὃ λύει τὸν Ἰησοῦν) is not from God." This reading does not, to be sure, figure prominently among the surviving New Testament manuscripts.[27] Quite to the contrary, the more familiar text is found in every Greek uncial and minuscule manuscript of 1 John,[28] every Greek lectionary with the passage, every manuscript of the Syriac, Coptic, and Armenian versions, the oldest Latin manuscript of 1 John, and virtually all the Greek and many of the Latin fathers who cite the passage.[29] The tantalizing *varia lectio* has nonetheless enjoyed a favored status among modern critics and commentators, having been championed by such eminent scholars as Theodor Zahn and Adolf von Harnack earlier in this century, and by the influential commentaries of Rudolf Bultmann, Rudolf Schnackenburg, and Raymond Brown more recently.[30] The attractiveness of the reading is not hard to explain. On the one hand, it is extremely difficult to understand and therefore likely to be changed by scribes. Moreover, at least in the view of its modern supporters, it is also pregnant with meaning, unlike the seemingly flaccid reading attested by the Greek witnesses, a reading that indeed could be taken to represent a scribal harmonization of 4:3 to its immediate context (4:2 ὁμολογεῖ; 4:3a μὴ ὁμολογεῖ).

Despite the widespread endorsement of this less attested reading, there are compelling reasons to reject it as a corruption of the text, made in direct opposition to Gnostic Christologies that "separated" (or "loosed") Jesus from the Christ.

Documentary Considerations

In weighing the competing merits of the two readings, the first and most obvious observation to make is that one of them absolutely dominates the textual tradition. It is difficult to explain a dominance this complete on any terms, apart, that is, from supposing the reading to be original; that this particular reading should so dominate the tradition is especially impressive, given its extraordinary grammatical construction. It is one of the curiosities of scholarship that commentators have blithely labeled the *other* reading—"every spirit that looses Jesus" (λύει τὸν Ἰησοῦν)—more difficult, and therefore likely original, immediately after observing that the use of μή with the indicative ὁμολογεῖ is grammatically bizarre and therefore textually suspect![31] But precisely here is the critical point: the puzzling phrase λύει τὸν Ἰησοῦν is not the only difficult reading in 1 John 4:3. The use of μή with the indicative makes μὴ ὁμολογεῖ τὸν Ἰησοῦν difficult as well, although for a different reason.[32]

The grammatical peculiarity of the reading should at least raise an initial suspicion that this is not a simple scribal assimilation of 4:3a to the phrasing of 4:2.[33] A scribe who wanted to ease a difficult reading would scarcely have created such a grammatical enigma, but would simply have inserted an antonym[34] or negated the preceding verb with the common οὐχ. The real question to be addressed, then, is why one of the two difficult readings has come to dominate the Greek manuscript tradition of 1 John so thoroughly as virtually to exclude the other reading altogether.[35]

There are only three possibilities. Either μὴ ὁμολογεῖ τὸν Ἰησοῦν represents a corruption created independently by a number of different scribes in an effort to ameliorate the difficulties of λύει τὸν Ἰησοῦν by harmonizing the verse (in an unusual way) to its immediate context; or this same corruption was made for the same reason in only one manuscript, which happens to be the archetype of the entire Greek (and Syriac, Coptic, and Armenian) tradition; or the reading is, in fact, original. This is the point at which the grammatically incongruous character of ὃ μὴ ὁμολογεῖ τὸν Ἰησοῦν becomes decisive. The idea that the reading represents an "accidental agreement in error," that is, that different scribes independently and repeatedly corrupted the text to read μὴ ὁμολογεῖ τὸν Ἰησοῦν, is altogether implausible. This would mean that the exemplars used by each of these scribes—exemplars that all read λύει τὸν Ἰησοῦν—were never copied correctly, at least in any copies that have survived. Even more incredibly, it would mean that scribes, independently of one another, chose to conform 4:3a to 4:2 by using a grammatical construction so peculiar as to send New Testament scholars scurrying to their Greek grammars to decide if the construction is even possible.[36] While, as I have already suggested, it is unlikely that any scribe would have made such a change, it is absolutely incredible that a number of scribes would have hit upon it coincidentally.

This means that the reading μὴ ὁμολογεῖ τὸν Ἰησοῦν must have derived from a solitary manuscript, either the autograph or a corrupted copy of it. This determination is significant for its historical implications, implications too often overlooked by scholars who fail to consider manuscript alignments as *historical* phenomena.[37] For this solitary manuscript was the archetype of every extant Greek manuscript at 1 John 4:3, whatever its textual character otherwise. Indeed, since none of our Greek manuscripts of 1 John, manuscripts known to be wildly divergent in other respects,[38] attests any other reading, the reading μὴ ὁμολογεῖ τὸν Ἰησοῦν must have been introduced at the very earliest stages of the transmission of 1 John. If it is not the original reading, it must have been a corruption of one of the first copies of the original.

Once the matter is put in these terms, the case for λύει τὸν Ἰησοῦν as the original text is irreparably damaged. Advocates of the reading commonly argue that it was changed by later scribes who could no longer understand what the text might have meant and so harmonized it to the context, creating the more familiar reading preserved in the majority of manuscripts, μὴ ὁμολογεῖ τὸν Ἰησοῦν. This argument overlooks the enigma created by the unusual grammar of the resultant text and the circumstance that, as we shall see, church fathers evidence no difficulty at all with the meaning of λύει τὸν Ἰησοῦν. Even worse, it flies in the face of the historical realities posed by the data: for, in fact, even if μὴ ὁμολογεῖ τὸν Ἰησοῦν *were* a corruption of the text, it could *not* have been made by "later" scribes but, necessarily, in the earliest stages of the transmission of 1 John, probably within the Johannine community itself. There is no other way, historically, to account for its total domination of the Greek textual tradition, both early and late. The meaning of λύει τὸν Ἰησοῦν, however, would presumably not have been lost at the very inception of the tradition, within the community that actually produced the document. This leaves little historical ground, then, for understanding how the reading "every spirit that looses Jesus" (λύει τὸν Ἰησοῦν) could be original if it was virtually lost to the tradition.[39] As a consequence, the documentary support for the other reading (μὴ ὁμολογεῖ τὸν Ἰησοῦν) is even stronger than its complete dominance of the textual tradition might otherwise indicate. This dominance can scarcely be explained apart from the supposition that the reading is original.

Linguistic Considerations

We can now turn to an evaluation of several linguistic features of the variant reading ("Every spirit that looses Jesus is not from God") that confirm its secondary character and suggest something about its provenance. What was stated earlier with regard to the more commonly attested reading applies to the variant as well: it either derives from an accidental agreement in error by various scribes, or from a solitary archetype—either the autograph or a corrupted copy of it. Since it too is such a puzzling reading, difficult to understand in all respects, one can be reasonably certain that the individual witnesses who attest it did not hit upon it by chance. This means that it must have ultimately derived from a solitary source, which, since it could scarcely have been the autograph, must have been subsequent to it. The linguistic considerations that support this assessment and that presage my conclusion that the reading was in fact generated by proto-orthodox scribes in the context of christological polemics can be simply stated: the early witnesses who attest the reading "Every spirit that looses Jesus is not from God" take it to mean exactly what its modern champions agree it could *not* have meant in a Johannine context, whereas these same scholars ascribe meanings to it that it cannot bear linguistically. What the reading must have meant makes sense only in a later historical setting.

I begin, then, with a brief assessment of the attestation of the variant. It is worth noting that for the first two hundred years of its existence, the reading is found exclusively in the context of christological polemics. The Greek attestation of the variant, as previously indicated, is practically nonexistent. Some scholars have made a great deal of its presence in a marginal note of an important tenth-century manuscript, 1739.[40] But in point of fact, this scholion simply informs us that λύει τὸν Ἰησοῦν was the text known to Irenaeus, Origen, and Clement. In other words, despite its great value in other respects,[41] manuscript 1739 provides no independent support for this reading and reveals little that was not already known simply from the writings of the fathers it mentions.

Among the Greek fathers, the clearest supporter of the variant is the fifth-century church historian Socrates, who cites it in an anti-Nestorian polemic. Socrates informs his reader that Nestorius errs in spurning the title *Theotokos* ("Bearer of God") for the Virgin Mary because in doing so he unwittingly divides Jesus' humanity from his deity. He does this, asserts Socrates, not knowing that "in the ancient copies" (ἐν ταῖς παλαίας ἀντιγραφαῖς) of 1 John it is written that every spirit that "looses" Jesus (i.e., for Socrates, divides his humanity from his deity) is not from God.[42] Thus, Socrates shows that in the fifth century the reading could be found in earlier sources but that, nonetheless, it was a reading not generally known. Moreover, Socrates takes the phrase λύει τὸν Ἰησοῦν to mean "loosing" Jesus by positing a distinction between Christ's natures.

Interestingly enough, the reading was taken in a similar way from the very beginning. Thus, Irenaeus, our earliest Greek source for the reading, whose citation of it has unfortunately come down to us only in Latin translation, quotes it against Valentinian Gnostics who "divide" Jesus Christ into multiple substances (*substantiae*) by claiming that the Christ descended from the Pleroma into the man Jesus, and then left him prior to his crucifixion.[43] So too Origen, who knows both readings, cites the verse to claim that he himself is not violating its teaching by "dividing up" Jesus, despite his unusual views on the relationship between Jesus' human and divine substances.[44]

This is the extent of the evidence of the reading in Greek.[45] Although the evidence is sparse, it is enough to show that (a) the reading was known by the end the second century, (b) it was cited in the context of christological polemics, and (c) it was taken to confute any separation of Christ's "substances."

On the Latin side of the evidence much the same can be said. The reading *solvit Iesum*, the most common Latin translation of λύει τὸν Ἰησοῦν, appears not to have been the earliest reading of the tradition.[46] When it *is* quoted by the fathers, it is always in a highly charged polemical context and is understood in its literal sense of "loosing" or "separating" Jesus. Thus, Tertullian, who knows both readings and attests the variant *solvit Iesum* only in a conflated form, directs it against Marcion, whose Christology denies that Jesus Christ came "in the flesh" and therefore, in Tertullian's view, "looses" or "separates" Jesus from the Creator God.[47] A century and a half later, the modalist Priscillian (c. 370), who more frequently attests the other reading ("does not confess Jesus"), cites the variant as a Scriptural warrant for spurning a Christology that "separates" Jesus from the divine realm.[48] Most of the later Latin witnesses, many of whom know both forms of the text, regularly cite the variant (*solvit Iesum*) when opposing aberrant Christologies. For them, the reading provides a standard refutation of anyone who appears to deny the deity of Christ.[49]

How do these witnesses confirm the secondary character of the variant? Two critical points need to be made. The first is so obvious that it seems to have escaped general notice. From the late second century on, church fathers evidence no embarrassment at all over this reading. They quote it at will, whenever they find it appropriate. This puts the lie to the universal notion that πᾶν πνεῦμα ὃ λύει τὸν Ἰησοῦν is the *lectio difficilior* in this passage. It may be the more difficult reading to modern scholars who cannot understand what it originally could have meant, but it was not difficult at all, so far as the evidence suggests, to the early witnesses. They knew exactly what it "meant," and had no difficulty in applying its meaning to the various christological controversies they faced. "To loose Jesus" meant, for them, to effect any kind of separation within Jesus Christ. True believers (i.e., the "orthodox") confessed that Jesus Christ came in the flesh (1 John 4:2). Whoever maintained a christological view that "loosed" or "separated" Jesus—either from the heavenly Christ (Valentinians), or from the Creator God (Marcion), or from true Deity (Arians)—denied that confession. It is no accident that in the Latin tradition *solvit Iesum* alternates with *dividere Iesum* in the citation of this reading.[50] It was the notion of "dividing" or "separating" Jesus that the reading was widely taken to condemn.

But this "metaphysical" interpretation of λύει τὸν Ἰησοῦν is precisely the problem for modern interpreters who opt for the reading, because they generally concede that it is anachronistic to posit such a meaning for the Johannine community at the end of the first century or the beginning of the second.[51] This is a striking irony of modern-day discussions of the problem: critics who accept the early witnesses' attestation of the reading refuse to accept their interpretation of it. How then do modern scholars construe its meaning? While there have been several unusual proposals, none of which has received any kind of following,[52] most scholars have understood the phrase to mean "to destroy, annihilate, or annul" Jesus. Since no one thinks that the secessionists literally "destroyed" or "annihilated" Jesus, even those who subscribe to this particular nuance of the term understand it figuratively. The Johannine opponents, then, "destroy" Jesus by denying his, the man Jesus', value or worth—or in the expression of Raymond Brown, they "negate the importance of [the man] Jesus."[53]

This way of construing the term certainly makes better sense in a Johannine context than the patristic interpretation of "divide" or "separate." But the supporters of this rendering appear not to have asked the obvious question of whether the phrase λύει τὸν Ἰησοῦν can *mean* to "nullify" or "negate the importance of" Jesus.[54] It is striking that none of the early witnesses that attest the reading, including the earliest Greek-speaking witnesses, attributes any such meaning to it. But now the question is purely linguistic: what does it mean in Greek to "loose" (λύειν) a person?

I do not need to belabor the point here. As anyone can see by surveying the literature—whether the Johannine writings, the rest of the New Testament, the early patristic literature, the LXX, or contemporary Hellenistic writings—"to loose" a person never means to nullify or negate his or her importance. The frequently cited parallel in 1 John 3:8 is not analogous, for there it is the "works" of the devil that are destroyed, not the devil himself. In fact, wherever λύειν is used with a personal object in the New Testament, it always denotes a releasing, or a setting free (i.e., "separating"), of a person from some sort of bondage, whether physical (e.g., fetters),[55] social (e.g., a marriage contract),[56] or spiritual (e.g., sins).[57] This is also the meaning of the term in the writings of the early church fathers,[58] of the LXX,[59] and of the Hellenistic world at large.[60] So far as I know, there is no parallel to the understanding of λύει τὸν Ἰησοῦν as "nullifying," or "negating the importance of" Jesus.

Thus, if we were to accept this reading as original—which we can scarcely do, given the manuscript alignments—we must take it to mean what the earliest sources claim it means: λύει τὸν Ἰησοῦν means to release or separate Jesus, perhaps from the Christ (so, the Gnostics Valentinus and Cerinthus), perhaps from the Creator God (Marcion), or perhaps from his divine nature (Nestorius, according to Socrates). But, as is commonly acknowledged even by the proponents of this reading, one can scarcely speak of such concerns over Jesus' "unity" in the early Johannine community, where the controversies raged on an entirely different front. On the one hand, this confirms the judgment that the reading λύει τὸν Ἰησοῦν is not original. On the other, it urges us to consider more closely how the theological climate of the Johannine writings differs from that presupposed by the variant reading. As this matter will prove significant for other aspects of our study,[61] it is not out of place to delve into the issue at some length.

Theological Considerations

Here again my basic thesis can be stated plainly: although the less frequently attested reading, "every spirit that looses Jesus is not from God," makes sense in later controversies over Christologies that separated Jesus (e.g., from the Christ), it does not make equal sense in the context of the Johannine community near the end of the first century. Here we are thrown into the wider debate concerning the history of the Johannine community, specifically concerning the theological controversies that created a rift in the church, causing one group of Christians to secede sometime prior to the writing of 1 John.[62] The relevance of the secession to the present discussion is limited to the christological views that were involved. Unfortunately, as is well known, the investigation is somewhat hampered by our restricted access to the competing views. While the Christology of the author of 1 John (and presumably of the group he represents) is reasonably clear, that of his opponents can only be deduced from the polemical arguments he levels against them. He calls his opponents "antichrists" because they refuse to confess that Jesus is the Christ, the Son (of God) (2:22–23).[63] The charge has led some interpreters to assume that the opponents were non-Christian Jews who failed to acknowledge the messiahship of Jesus. But because these opponents formerly belonged to the Johannine community (2:19), it seems more likely that they were in fact Christians who had developed their christological views to an extreme that for the author amounted to a denial of the community's basic confession that the Christ, or the Son of God, is actually the man Jesus (cf. John 20:30–31). Most commentators, therefore, speak of the secessionists in terms of a "high" Christology that minimizes or eliminates the community's belief that the man Jesus was himself the Christ.[64]

In what sense did the secessionists deny this communal belief? Some important clues are provided by the author's other ostensibly polemical comments. In one other place he calls his opponents "antichrists." In 4:1–3 he sets the "spirit" of the "false prophets," the antichrists gone out into the world, against those who have the spirit of God. Only the latter confess that Jesus Christ has come "in flesh." Whichever reading is adopted for 4:3, the antichrists' denial that the Christ is the man Jesus appears to derive from their denial of his fleshly manifestation. This, no doubt, is why the author begins his epistle as he does, with a prologue (reminiscent of the more eloquent prologue of the Fourth Gospel) that emphasizes that the "Word of Life" that was revealed could be perceived by the senses: he was seen and heard and touched (1:1–3), that is, he was a real person of real flesh.

Elsewhere too the author emphasizes the "fleshly" character of Jesus Christ, particularly with respect to his real death. Thus, in his final explicit polemic against the secessionists, the author informs his readers that Jesus Christ did not "come in water only," but "in water and in blood." Whatever the precise meaning of the formula "Jesus Christ came in water"—and the matter is widely debated and far from certain[65]—it seems clear that its modification by the author of 1 John ("in water and in blood") involves the confession that Jesus Christ experienced a real death in which he shed real blood. Apparently, then, the secessionists' refusal to acknowledge that Jesus Christ had suffered real death by shedding blood was connected with their denials that the Christ was the man Jesus and that Jesus Christ had come in the flesh. This point of contention also explains, then, the importance attached by the author to the "blood of Jesus" and to his work of "expiation" (cf. 1:7, 2:2, 4:10).

The polemical statements of 1 John have led some commentators to postulate connections between the secessionists and other known groups opposed by the precursors of orthodoxy. It is understandable, if unfortunate, that most previous investigators have seen in the secessionists' position an adumbration of a Cerinthian Christology, the separationist view described at the beginning of the present chapter.[66] Specific support for this view is thought to derive from 1 John 5:6, where the secessionists are said to confess that Jesus Christ came in water but not in blood. This, it is claimed, relates to the Cerinthian notion that the Christ was manifested to Jesus at his baptism (water), but left him prior to the crucifixion (blood). In a creative defense of this understanding, Klaus Wengst has argued that the secessionists could have located this very notion within the community's common traditions, as preserved in the Fourth Gospel. At the outset of that narrative the Spirit descends and remains on Jesus at his baptism (1:32) and departs from him immediately prior to his death (19:30).[67]

Despite its popularity, this identification of the secessionists' views with those of Cerinthus or other Gnostic separationists founders on a number of points. On the one hand, as Schnackenburg has pointed out, the polemics of 1 John provide no intimation of the metaphysical speculation upon which such Christologies are constructed.[68] Furthermore, the linchpin of the argument, 1 John 5:6, actually works against the interpretation. Martinus de Boer has recently shown that the verse can only be understood as citing the *secessionist* position, "Jesus Christ came in water," in order to correct it: "not in water only, but in water and in blood."[69] Thus, the secessionists believed that "Jesus Christ" was manifested "in water." But that is not at all the same thing as saying that "the Christ" was manifested to "Jesus" in water (i.e., at his baptism). Whatever the precise meaning of 1 John 5:6, no Cerinthian would say that "Jesus Christ" came in water, for this confession would entail a denial of their standard claim that Jesus and the Christ were distinct entities.

Moreover, Wengst's attempt to see a precursor of the Cerinthian view in the Gospel of John is totally unconvincing. Jesus' baptism is not even narrated in the Gospel. Worse yet, Jesus gives up the spirit in John of his own volition (John 10:17–18; 19:30) and only *after* he has suffered and shed blood! Wengst acknowledges that a Cerinthian exegesis of these texts would need to be forced, because among other things it would involve blatant misconstruals of their grammar.[70] In actuality, if the secessionists appealed to these traditions to support their views, it would be a marvel that they posed any threat to the community at all: this kind of Christology is virtually insupportable from the Johannine traditions as they have come down to us.[71]

Finally, although a Cerinthian separationist Christology may explain the polemical emphasis in 1 John on Christ's expiation and real death, it cannot adequately explain the author's emphasis on the real fleshly existence of Jesus Christ (4:2). The prologue, which emphasizes the tangible, fleshly character of the Word of Life made manifest, must certainly be regarded as a critical component in the overall polemic of the letter. But the Cerinthians did not deny that Jesus could be heard, seen, and felt, which makes this polemical introduction virtually inexplicable if in fact the secessionists embraced the kind of Christology that "separated" Jesus from the Christ.

In point of fact, as can be inferred from the preceding remarks, these secessionists must have developed views that corresponded to the other "christological option" taken by Gnostics in the second century: the docetic Christology that claimed that Jesus was not a real flesh and blood human being, but only appeared to be so. As I will point out again in the next chapter, a heterodox group with precisely such views was attacked several years later by Ignatius.[72] So far as I can see, a Christology of this kind explains all the polemic of 1 John and is itself a plausible development of the kind of high Christology evidenced already in the Fourth Gospel. The author of 1 John calls the secessionists false prophets who refuse to acknowledge that "Jesus Christ has come in the flesh" (ἐν σαρκί 4:2). Ignatius's opponents in Smyrna and Tralles also rejected the notion that Jesus Christ truly (ἀληθῶς) came "in the flesh" and was killed and raised "in flesh" (ἐν σαρκί). Instead, they taught that he only "seemed" (δοκεῖν) to be what he was and to do what he did (see especially Ign. *Smyrn.* 1:1–2; 3:1; 4:2, Ign. *Trall.* 9:1–2). For them, Jesus was a spirit without a real fleshly body, who only assumed a human form for a time (cf. Ign. *Smyrn.* 3:2; 4:1).[73] Significantly, in his rebuttal of these docetists, Ignatius emphasizes that Jesus' real body could be perceived and handled (ψηλαφάω Ign. *Smyrn.* 3:2), much as the prologue of 1 John stresses that the Word of Life could be heard and handled (ψηλα-φάω). A particularly striking parallel comes in Ignatius's condemnation of his opponents for "not confessing that he bore flesh" (Ign. *Smyrn.* 5:2 μὴ ὁμο-λογῶν αὐτὸν σαρκοφόρον; cf. 1 John 4:2 "every spirit that confesses Jesus Christ having come in the flesh . . . ," πᾶν πνεῦμα ὃ ὁμολογεῖ Ἰησοῦν Χριστὸν ἐν σαρκὶ ἐληλυθότα).

Moreover, just as in 1 John, Ignatius emphasizes the reality and importance of Jesus' real death by shedding real blood. The opponents in Smyrna and Tralles are explicitly said to believe that Christ, who was not of real flesh, only "appeared to suffer" (λέγουσιν τὸ δοκεῖν αὐτὸν πεπονθέναι Ign. *Smyrn.* 2:2; Ign. *Trall.* 10:1), whereas Ignatius emphasizes that Christ truly (ἀληθῶς) suffered, died, and was raised, and that anyone who fails to believe in Jesus' blood is subject to judgment (Ign. *Smyrn.* 6:1), because Christ's real suffering is what effects salvation (Ign. *Smyrn.* 1:1; 2:1; cf. 1 John 1:7; 2:2; 5:6). Interestingly, just as the aberrant Christology of the secessionists allegedly led to a deviant system of ethics, in which love of the brothers and sisters was neglected, so too Ignatius explicitly connects the docetists' heterodoxy with their failure to love (Ign. *Smyrn.* 5:2; 7:1, cf. 1 John 2:9–11; 3:14–18; 4:7–8).

Thus, the polemical emphases of 1 John seem to parallel those found soon thereafter in Ignatius's opposition to the docetic Christians of Smyrna and Tralles. It would be foolish, of course, to insist that the Johannine secessionists should be *identified* with these later groups; there is simply no evidence. But at least they are moving along a heterodox trajectory that eventuates in a full-blown expression of docetism. What, then, would the author of 1 John have meant when he accused the secessionists of refusing to make the community's confessions that the Son of God/the Christ is Jesus? He must have meant, as intimated earlier, that the secessionists could not truly make these confessions because they devalued the fleshly existence of Jesus, that is, they denied that he was a real human being of flesh and blood. The emphasis of the Johannine homology, then, falls either on the predicate noun, that the "Son of God is *Jesus*" (the man), or perhaps on the verb itself, that the "Son of God *is* Jesus" (since in the secessionists' view the Son of God only appears to be the man Jesus).[74]

To sum up: the epistle of 1 John counters a docetic Christology that is comparable to the one later espoused by the opponents of Ignatius. In this view Jesus only appeared to be human and to suffer and die, for he was not really made of flesh. This differs significantly from the Cerinthian separationist Christology, which does not seem to be attacked by the author of 1 John, a Christology that divides Jesus and the Christ into distinct entities, so that the Christ came into Jesus at his baptism and separated from him prior to his death.

The difference between these christological views is crucial for the textual problem in 1 John 4:3. The reading I have preferred on other grounds, "every spirit that does not confess Jesus [having come in the flesh] is not from God" (πᾶν πνεῦμα ὃ μὴ ὁμολογεῖ τὸν Ἰησοῦν [ἐν σαρκὶ ἐληλυθότα] ἐκ τοῦ θεοῦ οὐκ ἔστιν),[75] presupposes the same kind of docetic tendency evidenced elsewhere throughout the letter, whereas the variant reading, "every spirit that looses Jesus is not from God" (πᾶν πνεῦμα ὃ λύει τὸν Ἰησοῦν ἐκ τοῦ θεοῦ οὐκ ἔστιν) presupposes precisely the *other* christological tendency, a tendency that does not appear to lie within the author's purview. My conclusion now appears unavoidable: the variant reading, a reading found in none of the surviving Greek manuscripts, cannot have been the original reading of 1 John 4:3.

Conclusion

How then can we account for the origin and propogation of this variant reading, which, although no longer found in the Greek manuscript tradition 1 John, does survive in some of the Latin evidence? Many of the fathers who cited the text attested it in both forms, quoting one form or the other for contextual reasons, or, on occasion, conflating them. This suggests that these fathers found the *varia lectio* to be a particularly appropriate weapon against certain heretical Christologies, namely, those that involved some kind of metaphysical separation, either of the earthly Jesus from the heavenly Christ (Cerinthus, Valentinus), or of Christ from the Creator God (Marcion), or of Christ's humanity from his deity (Nestorius, according to Socrates). Whence, then, did the reading come?

In all likelihood it did not originate as a simple scribal error. In fact, it may well have not originated as a textual variant at all, but as a recapitulation of the text's "meaning" in the context of proto-orthodox christological polemics, that is, as an interpretive paraphrase that was later incorporated as an orthodox corruption. "Not to confess Jesus" during the Gnostic controversies meant (for the proto-orthodox) to adopt a Gnostic Christology, a Christology that separated Jesus from the Christ. Anyone who accepted such a view was "not from God." The earliest datable occurrence of this paraphrase was in Irenaeus's opposition to Valentinian Gnosticism. This may have been its originating context. Subsequently, wherever Gnosticism proved to be a problem, the paraphrase (insofar as it was known) proved useful, even prior to its incorporation in any manuscript of the New Testament. Thus, it is no surprise to find the reading attested in Alexandria, for example, in the writings of Origen and perhaps also in those of his predecessor, Clement.[76] Other fathers found the interpretation useful for combatting other christological heresies that, like Valentinian Gnosticism, involved some kind of "separation" in Christ, as opposed to the orthodox insistence on "unity."

At some point prior to the fourth century the interpretive paraphrase was placed in the margin of a manuscript—much as it was later placed in the scholion of the tenth-century manuscript 1739. The marginal note was evidently transferred into the text at some stage, in a manuscript that was itself copied on occasion. By the early fifth century the reading could be found in a few Greek manuscripts known to Socrates. How the reading came to be incorporated into the Latin Vulgate is only one of the many mysteries surrounding that most influential of all versions. The unknown translator of the Catholic epistles probably found it either in a Latin manuscript that he otherwise regarded as reliable, or in a Greek manuscript that he used to correct his Latin tradition. In any case, once the reading became part of the Vulgate, its position in the Latin tradition was secure, making it all the more noteworthy that later Latin writers still cite the passage in its original form, except when using it against certain christological heresies. Thus, the polemical context that created the corruption proved also to be the matrix within which it was perpetuated throughout the course of its existence, until it captured the attention and imagination of modern scholars.

Other Examples

Having now considered at some length an orthodox corruption that proves significant far beyond its modest appearance—it does after all concern the single word λύειν—we are in a position to examine with greater brevity other variant readings that function similarly. The vast majority of textual corruptions that serve to counter Gnostic tendencies apply to particular points of the controversy, such as the meaning of Christ's birth, baptism, and death. By comparison, those that condemn the Gnostics' separationist tendencies per se are relatively sparse. One textual change attested in the Synoptic tradition, however, does relate to this aspect of our study. In the familiar logion of Matthew 12:30 and Luke 11:23, Jesus declares, "The one who is not with me is against me, and the one who does not gather with me scatters."[77] Commentators have generally overlooked a change of the saying that is attested in significant witnesses of the Alexandrian text. In both Gospel accounts codex Sinaiticus joins other manuscripts in appending the personal pronoun με to the final clause, making it read, "The one who does not gather with me scatters me."[78]

There is little reason to consider the variant original. The bulk of the Alexandrian tradition reads against it, the support of codex Sinaiticus notwithstanding, as does virtually every other witness of every other textual group. Nor are there convincing arguments for its authenticity on internal grounds. To the contrary, there are solid reasons for considering it a second-century corruption effected for theological reasons. Not that the Gnostic controversies have typically been invoked to explain its genesis. The few commentators who deal with the matter generally concur with Bruce Metzger: the reading represents an attempt to balance the logion by providing its fourth verb with a personal object corresponding to those of the previous three.[79]

While this explanation has a kind of immediate appeal, a closer examination of the matter reveals its problems. Each of the preceding verbs is followed by a *prepositional phrase* (μετ' ἐμου / κατ' ἐμου / μετ' ἐμου). A scribe wanting to balance the sentence would simply have iterated the words κατ' ἐμου. It can scarcely be objected that the addition of the parallel phrase κατ' ἐμου would make little sense in the context, because the addition of με itself is labeled "disasterous" and "meaningless."[80] Nor should it be explained that the final verb is transitive and so requires a direct object; the preceding verb (συνάγει) is transitive as well, yet lacks an object. Even with the scribal addition, then, one is left with a "balanced" clause that is in fact asymetrical.

It is true that for Jesus to have said "the one who does not gather with me scatters me" would have made little sense in the context of the canonical Gospels. The solution to the problem emerges only when it is recognized that in a *different* context, outside the concerns of Matthew, Luke, and their common source, the saying can in fact be readily construed. I have already shown that proto-orthodox Christians of the second century were concerned with Gnostic Christologies that separated or divided Jesus Christ into multiple entities.[81] For these representatives of orthodoxy, Gnostics who differentiated between Jesus and the Christ, who split him into distinct beings, were Jesus' real enemies. Far from being those who "gathered with" him, that is, who joined with him in mission and fellowship, those who divided or scattered Jesus were "against him" (κατ' ἐμου). The corruption of Matthew 12:30/ Luke 11:23 embodies the orthodox rejection of anyone who denies the unity of Jesus Christ.[82]

As a final variant reading of this kind, we may consider the corruption attested in several witnesses of 2 Corinthians 11:4. Here again there is little doubt concerning the original text: "If one comes who preaches a different Jesus (ἄλλον Ἰησοῦν) from the one we preached . . . you bear it well." In a reading preserved in both Greek and Latin manuscripts, however, the text has been changed to speak not of a different "Jesus" but of a different "Christ" (MSS F G 4 Vg arm Ambrst al). An exchange of names is easy to understand under any circumstances, and such variants occur throughout the tradition.[83] In this case, however, we are not dealing with a scribal harmonization, either to another passage or to a more familiar mode of expression: the phrase "another Christ" occurs nowhere else in the New Testament. Furthermore, we should not overlook what this particular change provides for the proto-orthodox scribe. The problem raised by the Gnostic controversies was not over a multiplicity of "Jesuses," but over a multiplicity of Christs. Some Gnostics Christians advocated not simply a different Christ from the one espoused by the orthodox (i.e., Jesus Christ as unitary person) but several Christs who differed even one from another. The Valentinians, as we have seen, claimed that there were three.[84] Given the nature of this controversy, it does not seem at all implausible that the change effected in the text of 2 Corinthians 11 was far from accidental. It functions to counteract precisely the separationist idea that proto-orthodox Christians found so distressing,[85] namely, that in addition to Jesus, there was "another" Christ (or even "other Christs").

Jesus, Born the Christ

The textual modifications considered to this point reflect a direct challenge to those who contended that Jesus and the Christ represented distinct entities. As I have observed, these are by no means the most frequent kind of anti-Gnostic corruptions. More commonly, scribes altered their texts so as to undermine specific aspects of the separationist Christologies.

We have seen that proto-orthodox Christians had to defend their understanding of Jesus' birth not only against adoptionists, who spurned the miraculous character of the event, but also against Gnostics, who denied that Jesus was himself the Christ from his mother's womb. Irenaeus explicitly attacks this view by citing passages of the New Testament to show "that the Son of God was born of a virgin, and that He Himself was Christ the Savior whom the prophets had foretold; not, as these persons assert, that Jesus was He who was born of Mary, but that Christ was He who descended from above" (*Adv. Haer.* III, 16, 2). Does this orthodox position come to be reflected in the transcriptions of the relevant passages? To be sure, not many passages *are* relevant; two of the Gospels do not contain birth narratives.[86] As a consequence, texts that might prove vulnerable to this kind of scribal activity appear primarily in the opening chapters of Matthew and Luke, where one does find evidence of orthodox tampering.[87]

I have already discussed the anti-adoptionist corruptions of Matthew 1:16.[88] The verse also proved susceptible to the kind of modification envisaged here, although in this case the resulting corruption has generated little interest among the commentators. The vast majority of manuscripts speak of Mary giving birth to "Jesus, the one who is called Christ" ('Ιησοῦς ὁ λεγόμενος Χριστός). Several witnesses, however, lack the participle (and its article), making the text now refer to the birth of "Jesus Christ" (64 [d] k syr^c Dial Tim and Aqu^3). The variation appears also to be attested by Tertullian, who, in his only citation of the verse, uses it against Valentinian Gnostics and their Christology. In arguing that, because of his real birth from Mary, Christ had real flesh, Tertullian notes that "Matthew also, when tracing down the Lord's descent from Abraham to Mary, says 'Jacob begat Joseph the husband of Mary, of whom was born the Christ' " (*de carne Christi* 20).[89]

A motivation for the omission of the participle readily suggests itself from the context of Tertullian's own polemic, that is, in the confrontation with heretics who maintained that Jesus and the Christ were distinct entities. Even these heretics acknowledged, of course, that Jesus was "called" Christ, but for them, Jesus himself was *not* the Christ.[90] It makes sense, then, that one or more orthodox scribe "improved" the text by deleting the ambiguous participle, thereby strengthening the orthodox character of the verse as a whole. For them, Matthew speaks of the birth of the unified Jesus Christ himself, not simply of Jesus "who was called" Christ.[91]

It proves more difficult to establish the text of Matthew 1:18, another verse whose problematic character has already been discussed.[92] For the present concern I should note a variation in Matthew's declaration that "the birth of Jesus Christ happened in this way." As shall be seen at greater length near the end of this chapter, in the New Testament manuscripts the names and titles of Jesus Christ fluctuate extensively for reasons that appear closely related to the theological proclivities of orthodox scribes. With respect to the text at hand, the surviving manuscripts present several variations: "the birth of Jesus" (W 4 74 270 pc), "the birth of Christ Jesus" (B), the "birth of Christ" (OL, Vg, syrˢˑ ᶜ Theoph Iren Aug pc) and "the birth of Jesus Christ" (most witnesses).

The first two readings can make little claim to authenticity: they lack adequate documentary support and are readily explained as alterations of the more commonly attested forms of the text.[93] This leaves the reading found in parts of the so-called Western tradition ("the birth of Christ," OL, Vg, syr) and the one found virtually everywhere else ("the birth of Jesus Christ"). Scholars have vacillated on the intrinsic suitability of these two readings. Some have argued that Ἰησοῦ Χριστοῦ is original because it recalls the opening verse of the book: "The book of the genealogy of Jesus Christ" (βίβλος γενέσεως Ἰησοῦ Χριστοῦ, v. 1; τοῦ δὲ Ἰησοῦ Χριστοῦ ἡ γένεσις, v. 18). In this case, the text would have been corrupted into conformity with the name as it appears in the preceding verse (v. 17, "until the Christ," ἕως τοῦ Χριστοῦ).[94] Other scholars, as one might anticipate, argue just the reverse, that the usage of verse 17 demonstrates that the text of verse 18 originally read Χριστοῦ and was corrupted to conform with the opening statement of the book (Ἰησοῦ Χριστοῦ).[95] Clearly such arguments lead to a standoff.[96]

The surest basis for resolving a textual dispute of this kind is to consider the external support. The phrase Ἰησοῦ Χριστοῦ is not only attested by the earliest Greek witness (𝔭[1]), it is preserved in every Greek manuscript of every textual group and subgroup from every region of early Christendom. In contrast, there is not a solitary Greek manuscript—uncial, minuscule, or lectionary—that attests the shorter reading. Given the ambiguities of the internal evidence, this kind of manuscript alignment must be seen as decisive for the original text, especially when one can posit a viable explanation for the variant that survives in only a fraction of the tradition.

We know that this verse was important for orthodox heresiologists: they quote it explicitly to confute Gnostic Christologies that separate Jesus from the Christ. Irenaeus in particular accrues some significant mileage from the Western reading: "The birth of Christ occurred in this way." Irenaeus argues that because the text speaks specifically of the birth "of Christ," it directly confutes those who "assert that Jesus was he who was born of Mary but that Christ was he who descended from above" (*Adv. Haer.* III, 16, 2). Thus, the shorter text proved particularly amenable for the proto-orthodox in their struggles against Gnostic Christologies: Mary's infant was the Christ.

At the same time, one might wonder why the longer text, which speaks after all of the birth of "Jesus Christ," might not have proved equally accommodating. The explanation may be found in the circumstance that Christians, from at least the time of the Apostle Paul, widely construed "Jesus Christ" as a proper name. This was demonstrably the case for various groups of

Gnostics.[97] For Irenaeus, however, the designation Χριστός is to be read as a title. It is not, that is, simply one of Jesus' names; it actually identifies Jesus as the Christ of God. Because the corruption enjoyed a wide distribution among patristic and versional sources, we can assume that Irenaeus was not its creator, but had already found it in the manuscript tradition of the Gospel. If my theory of its provenance is correct, the change was made some time earlier in the second century by an orthodox scribe who shared Irenaeus's concern to emphasize against the separationists that it was precisely the Christ who was born of Mary.[98]

A different aspect of the Gnostic understanding of Jesus' birth appears to be under attack in an orthodox corruption of the opening chapter of Luke. In the familiar verse of the Annunciation, the angel Gabriel informs Mary that because of her miraculous conception, "the child that will be born will be called holy, the Son of God" (τὸ γεννώμενον ἅγιον κληθήσεται υἱὸς θεοῦ, 1:35). A number of witnesses emend this declaration to include a significant prepositional phrase: "the child that will be born *from you* (ἐκ σου) will be called holy . . ." (C* Θ f¹ 33 a c e g¹ gat syrᵖ Iren Tert Ad Epiph al). Scholars are virtually unanimous in considering this longer text secondary.[99] Despite its support in Western, Caesarean, and secondary Alexandrian witnesses, it is not found in the earliest and best manuscripts, which demonstrate an even more remarkable range in terms of both geography and textual consanguinity. Moreover, if the variant were original, it would be difficult to explain its omission throughout so much of the tradition. It certainly presents nothing that could be construed as objectionable to the prevailing tastes of early scribes. The shorter text is therefore more likely original.

Why was the text changed? Some have argued that a scribe or scribes felt the literary imbalance of the angelic pronouncement: in the two preceding clauses the angel spoke of God's action specifically upon Mary ("will come *upon you*" / "will overshadow *you*") making it understandable that the third and final clause should be provided with a corresponding personal pronoun of its own ("the child that will be born *from you*").[100] Others have thought that the parallel in Matthew 1:20 ("for that which is conceived *in her*") proved influential.[101] While these factors are not to be overlooked, we would be remiss to neglect what otherwise has passed by the boards unnoticed—the theological possibilities of the longer text.

In point of fact, the longer text could prove to be significant for opponents of certain kinds of separationist Christology. Both Irenaeus and Tertullian took offense at the Valentinian claim that Christ (i.e., Jesus, the so-called "dispensational" Christ of the Demiurge, upon whom the Christ from the Pleroma descended at baptism), did not come *from* Mary, but came *through* her "like water through a pipe" (Iren., *Adv. Haer.* I, 7, 2; Tert., dependent on Irenaeus, *Adv. Val.* 27). In this view, the "dispensational" Christ used Mary as a simple conduit into the world, receiving nothing from her, least of all a physical human nature. In contrast to this, the heresiologists urged that Christ came *from* Mary, because otherwise he neither experienced a real human birth nor received a full human nature, without which he would be unable to bring salvation to those who *are* fully human (*Adv. Haer.* III, 22, 1–2). And so, in an explicit attack on the Valentinians, Irenaeus urges that

> It is the same thing to say that he [Christ] appeared merely to outward seem-
> ing and to affirm that he received nothing from Mary. For he would not
> have been one truly possessing flesh and blood by which he redeemed us,
> unless he summed up in himself the ancient formulation of Adam. Vain
> therefore are the disciples of Valentinus who put forth their opinions, in
> order that they may exclude the flesh from salvation, and cast aside what
> God has fashioned (*Adv. Haer.* V, 1, 2).

The importance of the *varia lectio* of Luke 1:35 (ἐκ σου) in such controversies, then, is that it supports the orthodox notion that Christ actually came
from Mary. Tertullian appears to preserve an allusion to this very text. With
characteristic verve he castigates Valentinians who deny that Christ assumed
real flesh:

> But to what shifts you resort, in your attempt to rob the syllable "of" [Latin
> *ex*, Greek ἐκ] of its proper force as a preposition, and to substitute another
> for it in a sense not found throughout the Holy Scriptures! You say that he
> was born *through* [Latin *per*] a virgin, not *of* [Latin *ex*] a virgin, and *in* a
> womb, not *of* a womb (*de carne Christi* 20).[102]

And so the corruption of Luke 1:35 appears to reflect controversies over the
Valentinian Christology, which both asserted a distinction between Jesus and
the Christ and posited a Jesus who, as a direct creation of the Demiurge, did
not assume complete humanity.[103] An anonymous orthodox scribe of the second century inserted the phrase ἐκ σου, a phrase whose theological significance is cloaked by its innocent literary virtue: it provides a symmetrical
balance for the angelic pronouncement to Mary while confuting the Christology of Valentinian Gnostics.[104]

Jesus, the Christ at His Baptism

As we have seen, the baptism of Jesus figures prominently in separationist
Christologies as the christological moment par excellence.[105] It was then that
the Christ entered into Jesus, empowering him to perform his earthly ministry. From the perspective of the history of religions, this idea is of interest for
its conspicuous affinities with the adoptionist views shared by such groups as
the Ebionites and the Roman Theodotians. Proto-orthodox Christians opposed the view in all its manifestations, arguing against the Gnostics that it
contradicted the "self-evident" teachings of Scripture. In the words of Irenaeus, "It certainly was in the power of the apostles to declare that Christ
descended upon Jesus. . . . but they neither knew nor said anything of the
kind: for, had they known it, they would have also certainly stated it. But
what really was the case, that did they record, namely, that the Spirit of God
as a dove descended upon him" (*Adv. Haer.* III, 17, 1).

How did this debate affect the scribes who reproduced the biblical accounts? Here again one should not anticipate an abundance of corruptions: only three brief passages of the New Testament actually record the event.[106] It is all the more striking to find that each of the passages has been modified in ways that appear amenable to the orthodox cause.

Mark's account is the earliest, and because of its particular mode of expression, it proved to be the most susceptible to corruption. When Jesus comes up from the waters, the Spirit descends to him as a dove, and a voice from heaven proclaims, "You are my beloved Son; in you I am well pleased" (Mark 1:11). Mark's narrative as a whole does little to discourage the Gnostic understanding of the event, that the dove represents the divine Christ who descended from the heavenly realm and entered into Jesus, empowering him for his ministry.[107] As I have repeatedly observed, Jesus is not said to have experienced a miraculous birth in this Gospel, nor to have done anything extraordinary before receiving the Spirit at his baptism. In fact, the Gospel says nothing at all about his life prior to the appearance of the Baptist in the wilderness. It is only after he is baptized and receives the Spirit that Jesus begins to perform miracles and to convey his teachings. It comes then as no surprise that, as Irenaeus informs us, heretics "who separate Jesus from the Christ" used Mark's Gospel to the exclusion of all the others (*Adv. Haer.* III, 11, 7).

This circumstance makes the textual problem of Mark 1:11 all the more interesting.[108] There is virtual unanimity among textual scholars that Mark originally spoke of "the Spirit as a dove descending unto him" (τὸ πνεῦμα ὡς περιστερὰν καταβαῖνον εἰς αὐτόν).[109] This is the text found in the earliest and best representatives of the Alexandrian and Western traditions, and it is nearly impossible to explain its provenance if the variant tradition found in the bulk of Byzantine manuscripts is original.[110] In these latter witnesses, the spirit is said to descend as a dove "upon" (ἐπί) Jesus rather than "unto" (εἰς) him. The difficulty of this reading is fairly obvious. The preposition εἰς commonly means "into," so that the text as Mark originally wrote it is especially vulnerable to the Gnostic claim that at Jesus' baptism a divine being entered into him. Whether Mark himself understood the event in this way is not the question I am concerned to address here. It *is* worth noting, however, that both Matthew and Luke changed the preposition to ἐπί ("upon").[111] The existence of this variant expression within the Synoptic tradition provided scribes of the second century with just the opportunity they needed to circumvent a possible "misuse" of the account in Mark.[112] It would thus be a mistake to see the change reflected in the Byzantine tradition as a simple harmonization; as in all such cases, one must ask *why* scribes would have wanted to modify a reading peculiar to one of the Gospels. In this instance the reason is not at all difficult to locate. The text as originally written could be used by Gnostic Christians who, as Irenaeus informs us, appealed to this Gospel in particular to support their separationist Christologies.[113]

Nor was Mark's the only account susceptible to such changes. Not even the preposition ἐπί could escape a Gnostic construal, because the Spirit "coming upon" Jesus could well be taken to mean that it "empowered" him. And so it is not surprising to find that a number of the early witnesses change the preposition in Matthew 3:16 to the still less ambiguous πρός. Now the Spirit simply comes "to" Jesus.[114]

One other change that Matthew made when redacting his Marcan source concerns the intriguing comparative particle ὡς (the Spirit descended "like" a dove), which he modified to ὡσεί. Although the terms appear to have been interchangeable throughout the manuscript tradition of the New Testament,[115] it is difficult to maintain that there is absolutely no difference in nuance. Outside the writings of the New Testament, at least, ὡσεί is generally to be construed as the less definite and more hypothetical of the two,[116] and if the New Testament authors themselves saw the words as identical, it is somewhat difficult to explain why Matthew made the change in the first place. By using ὡσεί, Matthew may be distancing himself from the possible understanding that the Spirit actually assumed the form of a dove when he descended upon Jesus. Now the Spirit descends "as if" it were a dove. This understanding of the change leads to an important question for the textual tradition: When later scribes changed the ὡς of Mark 1:11 and Luke 3:22 to make it conform with Matthew's ὡσεί, were they motivated in part by a comparable interest, especially in light of the Gnostic construal of the event?

There is some evidence to suggest that the actual manifestation of the Spirit "as a dove" proved amenable to certain groups of Gnostics, who used the text to authorize their separationist construal of the event. We are best informed of the Marcosians, a group of Valentinian Gnostics attuned to the numerological significance of the divinely inspired words of the biblical text. In a passage filled with invective and wit, Irenaeus details the Marcosian exegesis of the descent of the dove.[117] When the letters in the Greek word for dove (π-ε-ρ-ι-σ-τ-ε-ρ-α) are given their numerical equivalences, they add up to 801.[118] This, remarkably, is also the number of deity, which comprises the Alpha and the Omega (α and ω, representing the Greek numerals one and eight hundred). Therefore, in the Marcosians' view, the descent of the dove shows that Jesus received into himself the fullness of deity at his baptism.[119]

We have no way of knowing how many other Christians of the second and third centuries subscribed to this construal of the event.[120] What is clear is that both Mark and Luke are susceptible to it. And so the change of the phrase ὡς περιστεράν to ὡσει περιστεράν, in numerous witnesses of both Gospels, may reflect something more than the linguistic predilection or harmonistic tendencies of scribes.[121] It may reflect the strategy detected throughout the manuscript tradition of the Gospels of distancing the text from possible Gnostic construals by means of slight literary modifications. Now rather than descending "as a dove" the Spirit descends "as if it were a dove."

In this connection, finally, we do well to observe that Luke's account of the baptism is the least ambiguous concerning the physical nature of the "Holy Spirit" (τὸ πνεῦμα τὸ ἅγιον). For here the Spirit is said to descend upon Jesus "in bodily form, as a dove" (3:22, σωματικῷ εἴδει ὡς περιστεράν). The changes in this description that are scattered throughout the textual tradition may have been accidental, but when they appear to serve theological ends as well, one is surely justified in harboring some doubt. Particularly striking is the complete inversion of the sense by the earliest manuscript, $\mathfrak{p}^4$, where the Spirit is said to descend upon Jesus in "spiritual" ($\pi\nu\varepsilon\acute{\upsilon}\mu\alpha\tau\iota\ \varepsilon\ddot{\iota}\delta\varepsilon\iota$) rather than "bodily" form. This early Alexandrian witness thus undercuts a potentially Gnostic construal of the text because there is now no "real" or "bodily" descent of a divine being upon Jesus. A similar result obtains in the later Alexandrian witness, manuscript 579. Here the phrase $\tau\grave{o}\ \pi\nu\varepsilon\hat{\upsilon}\mu\alpha\ \tau\grave{o}\ \ddot{\alpha}\gamma\iota\upsilon$ $\sigma\omega\mu\alpha\tau\iota\kappa\hat{\omega}\ \varepsilon\ddot{\iota}\delta\varepsilon\iota$ is omitted altogether, making the text say that "something like a dove descended" upon Jesus. There is no mention of God's Spirit at all, obviating the interpretation that this Spirit was in fact the divine Christ who entered into Jesus.

Jesus, Crucified as the Christ

To this point of the discussion I have examined orthodox modifications that serve to undercut the Gnostic notion that Jesus came to be indwelt by the Christ at his baptism. For proto-orthodox Christians, Jesus was born the Christ, and his baptism did not change his essential relationship with God. The other significant christological moment for most Gnostic Christians came at the end of Jesus' ministry, when the Christ departed from him to return to the Pleroma, leaving Jesus alone to suffer and die. Irenaeus summarizes the view as follows:

> They understand that Christ was one and Jesus another; and they teach that there was not one Christ but many. And if they speak of them as united, they do again separate them: for they show that one did indeed undergo sufferings, but that the other remained impassible; that the one truly did ascend to the Pleroma, but the other remained in the intermediate place (*Adv. Haer.* III, 17, 4).

In general, orthodox Christians countered this view by stressing the unity of Jesus Christ and enumerating passages of the New Testament that speak of "Christ" or "Jesus Christ" shedding his blood and dying. As Irenaeus reiterates throughout his refutation, neither Jesus himself, nor Paul, nor any of the other apostles "knew anything of that Christ who flew away from Jesus, nor of the Savior above, whom they hold to be impassible," for "the same being who was laid hold of and underwent suffering and shed his blood for us was both Christ and the Son of God" (*Adv. Haer.* III, 16, 9).

Mark 15:34

It will be significant for our deliberations to recognize the role played by the Gospel accounts, especially Mark's, in this debate between the proto-orthodox and the Gnostics. As is well known, Jesus' last words in Mark are his "cry of dereliction": $\varepsilon\lambda\omega\iota\ \varepsilon\lambda\omega\iota\ \lambda\varepsilon\mu\alpha\ \sigma\alpha\beta\alpha\chi\theta\alpha\nu\iota$, an Aramaic quotation of Psalm 22:2, for which the author supplies the LXX translation, "My God, my God, why have you forsaken me?" (ὁ θεός μου ὁ θεός μου, εἰς τί ἐγκατέλιπές με; Mark 15:34). At stake in the Gnostic controversy was the meaning of the word ἐγκατέλιπες. The proto-orthodox took it to mean "forsake," and argued that because Christ had taken the sins of the world upon himself, he felt forsaken by God; the Gnostics, on the other hand, understood the word in its more literal sense of "leave behind," so that for them, Jesus was lamenting the departure of the divine Christ: "My God, my God, why have you left me behind?"[122]

This is clearly the interpretation given by the Gnostic *Gospel of Philip*, one version of which was familiar to orthodox heresiologists.[123] The anonymous author quotes the verse before proffering his explanation: "'My God, my God, why O Lord have you forsaken me?' It was on the cross that he said these words, for it was there that he was divided."[124] The words are similarly construed in their reformulation in the *Gospel of Peter*, where on the cross Jesus cries out, "My power, O power, you have left me."[125] It is to be recalled that this book played a role in the struggles for orthodoxy: upon reading it, the bishop Serapion condemned its heretical Christology and banned its use in his congregations.[126] The significance of Mark 15:34 for Gnostic Christologies is also attested by Irenaeus, who in his refutation of the separationist view observes that Valentinians used the text to show that Jesus' fate on the cross mirrored the tragic events of the divine realm, when the last of the aeons, Sophia, became separated from the Pleroma (*Adv. Haer.* I, 8, 2).

Previous investigators have failed to recognize how this controversy over the meaning of Jesus' last words in Mark relates to the famous textual problem of the verse. For here, in a reading that has intrigued scholars since Adolf von Harnack championed it as original earlier in the century, occurs one of the truly striking modifications of the Gospel.[127] In significant elements of the Western text, rather than crying out "My God, my God, why have you forsaken me?" the dying Jesus cries "My God, my God, why have you reviled me?" (ὁ θεός μου ὁ θεός μου, εἰς τί ὠνείδισάς με; D c i k syr[h]; Porph).[128]

Von Harnack's arguments for the authenticity of the reading are worth recounting. Given the agreement of codex Bezae and the Old Latin manuscripts, along with the apparent attestation of the verse by Porphyry, the reading appears to have had a wide circulation already in the second century. Moreover, it is difficult to explain the creation of the reading if it is not original. It appears unlikely, according to von Harnack, that a scribe took offense at ἐγκατέλιπες in Mark 15:34, and so changed it to ὠνείδισας; the parallel text in Matthew 27:46 is invariant, and if scribes took offense at the word in Mark they surely would have been offended by its occurrence in Matthew as well. Furthermore, scribes typically harmonized Mark to the more frequently read (and copied) Matthew. Such a harmonization, according to von Harnack, appears therefore to have happened here fairly early in the tradition. Mark derived his text of Psalm 22 from the LXX, but modified its rendition of the Hebrew, so that rather than "forsaking" Jesus, God is said to "revile" or "mock" him. This is appropriate, claims von Harnack, because in the Marcan passion narrative everyone *else* mocks Jesus as well, including the two criminals crucified with him (v. 32, ὠνείδιζον αὐτόν; cf. 14:65; 15:16–20, 29–31). Matthew then, who used Mark as his source, retranslated the Psalm reference according to its LXX rendering. Later scribes followed suit by harmonizing Mark's text to Matthew.

The ingenuity of von Harnack's argument has done little to create for it a following. On the one hand, Matthew had as much reason as Mark to stress the mockery of Jesus in his passion; he reproduces, for example, Mark's reference to the robbers and others "reviling him" (27:44, ὠνείδιζον αὐτόν; cf. also 26:67–68; 27:27–31, 39–43). Why would he not also, then, retain the words of Jesus as Mark records them? Moreover, in both Synoptic accounts the phrase ἐγκατέλιπές με (or ὠνείδισάς με) is presented as a *translation* of the Scripture text given in Aramaic (Hebrew, in Matthew). Presumably Mark (or his source) knew as well as Matthew that σαβαχθανι does not mean "revile me" but "forsake me." [129] Why, then, does Mark even preserve the Aramaic form of the cry? If he wanted to highlight God's mockery of Jesus, a mistranslation of the Psalm would scarcely have been necessary: Jesus' final cry could simply have been given in Greek.

The argument for ἐγκατέλιπες is cinched by its overwhelmingly superior external attestation. The reading is found in every Greek manuscript of every textual group and subgroup, with the solitary exception of codex Bezae. Moreover, the patristic sources attest this reading virtually without dissent, as do all of the versions, apart from four of Bezae's Western allies. For most critics, this confluence of internal and external arguments makes the case against the variant reading virtually airtight: Mark did not quote the Psalm and then mistranslate it.

If the Western reading of Mark 15:34 is secondary, why was the change made? Von Harnack is right to see that the theology of the verse caused scribes problems, although not the problems he thinks;[130] and the theme of mockery does explain the change, but not the change he assumes. In fact, the problem with the cry of dereliction was that Gnostics had used it to support their separationist Christology. For them, Jesus' despair at being "left behind" by God demonstrated that the Christ had separated from him and returned into the Pleroma, leaving him to die alone. Not only do we know that this was the Gnostic understanding of the verse, we also know that the orthodox found this exegesis both unsound and offensive. The change of ἐγκατέλιπες to ὠνείδισας, then, was made to circumvent the "misuse" of the text, and naturally suggested itself from the context. Just as Jesus was reviled by his opponents, those for whom he died, so too he bore the reproach of God himself, for whose sake he went to the cross in the first place. As to why the same change was not made in Matthew as well, I can simply observe again both the sporadic nature of such corruptions and the fact that proto-orthodox Christians recognized that the Gospel of Mark proved singularly useful for those who espoused a separationist Christology.[131]

Hebrews 2:9

A comparable motivation for changing a text may lie behind one of the most famous and intriguing corruptions of the Epistle to the Hebrews. In this case, however, the corruption carried with it so much the sense of an obvious improvement that it had already overwhelmed the manuscript tradition of the epistle prior to the penning of the earliest surviving witnesses. In most of my earlier discussions of textual variants I have shown the importance of both external and internal evidence, especially when they work together in tandem. In the case of Hebrews 2:9 there is a direct clash between these two kinds of evidence. Although the surviving documents are virtually uniform in stating that Jesus died for all people "by the grace of God" (χάριτι θεοῦ), the force of internal evidence compels us to accept as original the poorly attested variant reading, which states that Jesus died "apart from God" (χωρὶς θεοῦ).

Despite the general paucity of the reading's documentary support, there are several points of interest to be noted. Among Greek manuscripts, the reading occurs only in two documents of the tenth century (0121b 1739).[132] But the latter is a curiosity among medieval manuscripts, in that its scribe reproduces a prescript to the Pauline epistles found in his exemplar, which states that the text had been copied from a "very ancient exemplar" that contained an Origenian text. The manuscript also reproduces its exemplar's marginal notes. These record the exegetical and textual comments of several church fathers, none of whom lived beyond the fourth century. The conclusion is close to hand that manuscript 1739 is the conscientious transcription of a fourth-century exemplar, whose text derives from a manuscript at least as ancient as our earliest papyri.[133] It comes as no surprise to find that its reading of Hebrews 2:9 (Jesus died "apart from God"), although virtually excluded from other surviving witnesses, was acknowledged by Origen himself as the reading of the majority of manuscripts of his own day, manuscripts that consequently must have been produced no later than the end of the second century or the very beginning of the third.[134] Other evidence also suggests its early popularity: it was found in manuscripts known to Ambrose and Jerome in the Latin West, and is quoted by a range of ecclesiastical writers down to the eleventh century.[135] Among the versions it is represented in both Latin (Vg MS G) and Syriac (Peshitta). The results of this quick survey should give us pause. The surviving manuscripts have virtually eliminated the reading χωρὶς θεοῦ, even though it was at one time widely attested, particularly in Origen's Alexandria and Caesarea, where it appears to have comprised the majority text.

When one turns from external to internal evidence, there can be no doubt concerning the superiority of this poorly attested variant. To start with the obvious, the reading provides a textbook case of the *lectio difficilior*. Christians in the early centuries commonly regarded Jesus' death as the supreme manifestation of God's grace. But to say that Jesus died "apart from God" could be taken to mean any number of things, most of them unpalatable.

Since scribes must have created one of these readings out of the other, there is little question concerning which of the two is more likely the corruption.

But was the corruption deliberate? Advocates of the more common text (χάριτι θεοῦ) have naturally had to claim that it was not (otherwise their favored text would almost certainly be secondary). By virtue of necessity, then, they have devised alternative, if unlikely, scenarios to explain the origin of the more difficult reading. Most commonly it is simply supposed that because the words in question are so similar orthographically (XΩPIΣ / XAP-ITI), a scribe inadvertently mistook the word "grace" for the preposition "apart from." This is a possibility, although, as I will emphasize momentarily, a change of this kind would more likely have occurred in the reverse direction. Before pressing the point, however, I should state my general reservations: it strains credulity to think that the modification—whichever way it occurred—represents a simple scribal blunder. For now the meaning of the text, at least on the surface (which is where accidents of this sort invariably occur), is not even proximately the same as the original. Even if we grant that scribes were sometimes (many times?) inattentive to their work, and so produced nonsensical readings, in this instance neither reading is nonsensical. Both readings make perfectly good sense, but the sense they make is not at all equivalent. The corruption, therefore, was more likely made "intentionally." [136]

If we were to grant, for the sake of argument, that the textual problem resulted from some kind of confusion or haphazard, where would that leave us? Because both readings make "sense," the most we could say is that an "accidental" change would have been made by a scribe who was only partially (not absolutely) inattentive to his work. This now raises some interesting questions of its own. Is a negligent or absentminded scribe likely to have changed his text by writing a word used *less* frequently in the New Testament (χωρίς) or one used *more* frequently (χάριτι, four times as common)? Is he likely to have created a phrase that never occurs elsewhere in the New Testament (χωρὶς θεοῦ) or one that occurs over twenty times (χάριτι θεοῦ)? Is he likely to produce a statement that is bizarre and troubling or one that is familiar and easy? Surely it is the latter: readers typically confuse unusual words for common ones and make simple what is complex, especially when their minds have partially strayed. Thus, even a theory of carelessness supports the less attested reading.

How else then might χωρὶς θεοῦ be explained, if it was not original (granting the premise) and was not created by simple oversight? The most popular theory argues that the reading was created as a marginal note: a scribe who read in Hebrews 2:8 that "all things" are to be subjected to the lordship of Christ recalled from 1 Corinthians 15:27 that "the one who subjects all things" was not himself to be included among the "all things"—that is, that at the end, God the Father is to remain ultimately sovereign. To protect the text from misconstrual, the scribe then inserted an explanatory note in the margin of Hebrews 2:8, pointing out that nothing is left unsubjected to Christ, "except for God" (χωρὶς θεοῦ). [137] This note was subsequently transferred into the text of a manuscript, leading to its attestation at random points of the tradition.

Despite the popularity of the solution, it is altogether too clever, and requires too many dubious steps to work. There is no manuscript that attests *both* readings in the text (i.e., the correction in the margin or text of v. 8, where it "belongs," *and* the original text of verse 9). Why would a scribe have *replaced* the text of verse 9 with the marginal note? Did he think it was a marginal *correction*? If so, why was it in the margin next to verse 8 rather than verse 9? Moreover, if the scribe who created the note had done so in reference to 1 Corinthians, would he not have written ἐκτὸς θεοῦ?

In sum, it is extremely difficult to account for χωρὶς θεοῦ if χάριτι θεοῦ was the original reading of Hebrews 2:9; on the other hand, as shall be seen momentarily, there is every good reason to think that scribes would have substituted the more familiar and comforting phrase for the notion that Christ died "apart from God," a view they found confusing and potentially offensive.

Before moving to other transcriptional issues, however, we do well to confirm our preliminary conclusions by considering the intrinsic probabilities of both readings. For here is another instance in which the *confluence* of arguments itself proves convincing: although a *scribe* could scarcely be expected to have said that Christ died "apart from God," there is every reason to think that this is precisely what the author of Hebrews said. I begin by considering word frequencies. χωρίς is used more often in Hebrews than in any other book of the New Testament, and occurs far more frequently here than χάρις (thirteen occurrences to seven), even though, as I have observed, their relative frequencies are significantly reversed in the New Testament as a whole. Statistical probabilities, of course, mean little apart from considerations of style. But these too favor the minority reading. As J. K. Elliott has observed, χωρίς is always followed by an anarthrous noun in Hebrews (as it is here: θεοῦ); on the other hand, the only real parallel to the reading χάριτι θεοῦ occurs in Hebrews 12:15, where both nouns have the article (τῆς χάριτος τοῦ θεοῦ).[138] The result: the reading that was more common in Origen's day conforms closely with the vocabulary and linguistic usage of Hebrews; the reading attested more commonly in manuscripts produced since then does not.

The less attested reading is also more consistent with the theology of Hebrews. Never in this entire epistle does the word χάρις refer to Jesus' death or to the salvific benefits that accrue as a result of it.[139] Instead, it is consistently connected with the gift of salvation that is yet to be bestowed upon the believer by the goodness of God. The key text is Hebrews 4:16: "Let us draw near to the throne of grace, that we may receive mercy and find grace to help in the time of need" (see also 10:29; 12:15; 13:25). To be sure, Christians historically have been more influenced by other New Testament authors, notably Paul, who saw Jesus' sacrifice on the cross as the supreme manifestation of the χάρις θεοῦ. But Hebrews does not use the term in this way, even though scribes who identified this author as Paul may not have realized it.

On the other hand, the statement that Jesus died "apart from God"—enigmatic when made in isolation—makes compelling sense in its broader literary context. Indeed, it is not at all difficult to see what the author of Hebrews might have meant by the phrase, so long as one leaves aside the Pauline understanding of Jesus' death. Whereas this author never refers to Jesus' death as a manifestation of divine "grace," he repeatedly emphasizes that Jesus died a fully human, shameful death, totally removed from the realm whence he came, the realm of God. His sacrifice, as a result, was accepted as the perfect expiation for sin. Moreover, God did not intervene in his passion and did nothing to minimize his pain. Jesus died "apart from God."

The references are scattered throughout the epistle. Hebrews 5:7 speaks of Jesus, in the face of death, beseeching God with loud cries and tears.[140] In 12:2 he is said to endure the "shame" of his death, not because God sustained him, but because he hoped for vindication.[141] Jesus had to suffer and die to become the perfect sacrifice and to learn obedience to the will of God while experiencing real human suffering (5:7–8). He thereby became the equal of suffering humans whom he could then sanctify (2:11), delivering them from the death in which he equally participated (2:14) and setting an example for them in their own sufferings (12:3). Throughout this epistle, Jesus is said to experience human pain and death, like other humans "in every respect." His was not an agony attenuated by special dispensation.

Yet more significantly, this is a major theme of the immediate context of Hebrews 2:9. The passage focuses on Christ's condescension prior to his exaltation.[142] He was made lower than the angels (v. 9), he became the equal of human beings (v. 11) and shared with them in blood and flesh (v. 14), he experienced human sufferings (v. 10), and he died a human death (v. 15). His condescension allows him now to call humans his "brothers" (v. 12), and it is his human sufferings that have made him "perfect" (v. 10). To be sure, his death is known to have salvific effects: it was a sacrifice for sins (v. 17) that destroyed the devil who had the power over death (v. 14) and delivered those in bondage to their fear of death (v. 15). But the passage says not a word about *God's grace* as manifest in Christ's work of atonement. It focuses instead on Christology, on *Christ's condescension* into the transitory realm of suffering and death. It is as a full human that Jesus experienced his passion, apart from any succor that might have been his as an exalted being. The work he began at his condescension he completes in his death, a death that had to be "apart from God."[143]

How is it that the reading χωρὶς θεοῦ, which can scarcely be explained as a scribal corruption, conforms to the linguistic preferences, style, and theology of the Epistle to the Hebrews, whereas the alternative reading χάριτι θεοῦ, which would have caused scribes no difficulties at all, stands at odds both with what Hebrews says about the death of Christ and with the ways it says it? The external evidence notwithstanding, Hebrews 2:9 must have originally said that Jesus died "apart from God."

How now do I account for the variant reading attested in the bulk of the manuscripts? Scribes were not simply puzzled by the statement that Jesus died apart from God. The real situation was far more troubling than that.

We know that the text must have been changed already in the second century: our earliest manuscript, 𝔓⁴⁶, attests the corruption. It was in this period that proto-orthodox and Gnostic Christians engaged in debates over the significance of Jesus' death, Gnostics claiming that prior to the crucifixion the Christ had left the man Jesus, and the proto-orthodox insisting that Jesus and the Christ were one and the same, in life and in death. Given this context and the effect it had on other passages of the New Testament (e.g., Mark 15:34), the motivation for the change of the text of Hebrews 2:9 becomes all too clear. Whereas the Epistle to the Hebrews stressed that Jesus had been made lower than the angels for a brief time and suffered as a partaker of humanity in its totality, the Gnostics could readily take the original text to mean that the divine element within Jesus had already left him prior to his death, so that he died "apart" from God, that is, abandoned by that divine being who had sustained him during his ministry. It appears that scribes of the second century who recognized the heretical potential of the phrase χωρὶς θεοῦ changed it by making the simple substitution of the orthographically similar and altogether acceptable, if contextually less appropriate, χάριτι θεοῦ, thereby effecting an orthodox corruption that came to dominate the textual tradition of the New Testament.

Other Examples

Less dominant in the tradition is a corruption that occurs in the preceding chapter of the Epistle to the Hebrews, which, to his credit, Günther Zuntz recognized as evidencing a similar orthodox *Tendenz*.[144] The hymnic fragment cited in 1:3 refers to the Son of God, who "bearing all things by the word of [his] power (τῆς δυνάμεως [αὐτοῦ]), through himself having made a cleansing of sins (δι' ἑαυτοῦ καθαρισμὸν τῶν ἁμαρτιῶν ποιησάμενος), sat down at the right hand of majesty on high."[145] The passage contains several interesting textual variants,[146] of which the prepositional phrase "through himself" (δι' ἑαυτοῦ) is of particular relevance to the present discussion. The phrase is wanting in a number of important manuscripts of predominantly Alexandrian cast (ℵ B Ψ 33 81), but is present in the earliest form of that tradition (𝔓⁴⁶ 1739 Ath) as well as in the leading representatives of other text types (D 0121b Byz a b syr cop). Witnesses that lack the phrase have in its stead the personal pronoun αὐτοῦ, which is to be understood as going with the preceding clause ("*his* power"); codex Bezae and nearly the entire Byzantine tradition conflate the two readings.

The antiquity and diversity of the witnesses that support the prepositional phrase ("through himself") speak in its favor, and here it should be observed that the two manuscripts that appear to have stood against the rest of the Greek tradition in 2:9 (0121b 1739) stand together here as well, both of them including the phrase to the exclusion of the pronoun, this time in the company of our earliest manuscript, 𝔓⁴⁶.[147] One can readily understand how the prepositional phrase, coming at the beginning of the clause, could cause some confusion for scribes unaccustomed to the classical style. This may have led to its modification into the possessive attached to the preceding clause ("his power"); the change is easier to explain as having occurred in this direction, with the omission of the preposition, than in the other, with its addition. But as Zuntz notes, the resulting construction destroys the hendiadys of the original (τὸ ῥῆμα τῆς δυνάμεως, "the powerful word") and shifts the focus away from its subject, the Son of God. In fact, precisely this shift suggests that scribes found more than the grammatical style of the original problematic; indeed, in view of the comparable pattern of attestation in 2:9 (0121b 1739), one has grounds for suspecting a theological motivation for the corruption. The phrase δι' ἑαυτοῦ would normally be taken to mean "by his own effort, with no assistance from outside."[148] In other words, Jesus is said to have taken on himself the task of procuring a cleansing for sins without any (divine) assistance. After accomplishing his work, he was exalted to God's right hand. This understanding of the ancient hymn makes good sense in Hebrews, but given its serviceabilty in the hands of Gnostics, one can understand the natural inclination of scribes to effect a modification. For if Jesus' work was accomplished δι' ἑαυτοῦ, one might infer that the divine element had left him prior to its consummation. To avoid such a construal, orthodox scribes simply dropped the preposition and changed the reflexive to a personal pronoun. By omitting two or three letters[149] they obviated a potential problem, much as they eliminated the problem of 2:9 by making a comparably unobtrusive change. It comes as no surprise to find the corruption attested predominantly in manuscripts of Alexandria, where Gnostics made such significant inroads during the second century, when the change must have been effected.

Other textual modifications that work to circumvent the Gnostic idea that the Christ departed from Jesus prior to his death occur in a series of changes in a solitary verse of Paul's letter to the Romans, changes that at first glance appear insignificant but at closer quarters reveal their true colors. In Romans 8:34 Paul states that "Christ Jesus is the one who died, but rather is the one who has been raised, who sits at the right hand of God." Due to some considerable variation among the manuscripts, the text is difficult to establish at several points. First to be noted is the name "Christ Jesus," which is shortened to "Christ" in codices Vaticanus and Bezae and a number of later manuscripts, most of them Byzantine. The attestation of the longer text is equally impressive, however, finding support in the majority of the earliest Greek and Latin witnesses. This configuration of external support and the ambiguity of internal evidence has led the UBSGNT[3] editors to enclose the word in brackets.

An argument that has not been given its due can prove decisive for the shorter text ("*Christ* is the one who died"), particularly in light of two other changes, yet to be considered, that appeared during the course of the verse's transmission. We do well to remember that Gnostic Christians expressed a particular fondness for Paul's letters and interpreted them in support of their own theological views.[150] It is not difficult to see how the shorter text of the present verse might be construed by interpreters who wished to see in it a confirmation of their notion that the Christ was exalted (i.e., raised back into the Pleroma; see, for example, Irenaeus, *Adv. Haer.* III, 17, 4) without dying. The first clause can indeed be understood as a question that is confuted by the statement of the second: "Is Christ the one who died? No, rather he is the one who was exalted [i.e., to heaven to dwell with God]." In this construal of the words, Christ is *not* the one who died; Jesus is. Christ on the other hand is the one who is exalted, who ascends into the Pleroma. One of the ways that orthodox scribes could disallow this construal of the verse was simply to add the name Ἰησοῦς to the text, so that now it speaks of the unified Christ Jesus who both died and was raised, rather than of the Christ in implicit contradistinction to Jesus.[151] That this was in fact the orthodox understanding of the verse is known from Irenaeus, who explicitly quotes it in order to show that "the same Being who was laid hold of, and underwent suffering, and shed his blood for us, was both Christ and the Son of God, who did also rise again and was taken up into heaven" (*Adv. Haer.* III, 16, 9).

Two other changes of the verse work along a similar vein and serve to support the theory that the text was modified to circumvent a Gnostic construal. Part of the ambiguity of the original text lies in the uncertain relationship between the notions of Christ "being raised" and his being exalted to "the right hand." Do these statements refer to the same event (the Gnostic understanding, since for them, Christ was raised/exalted without dying) or are they sequential (the orthodox view: he died, then he was raised)? To eliminate the confusion was actually a simple matter: a number of manuscripts of largely Alexandrian provenance add the phrase ἐκ νεκρῶν, so that now it is clear that the resurrection *from the dead* is understood, making it certain that Christ himself died and went to the place of the dead.[152] The same motivation can be detected in the simple addition of the conjunction καί to the phrase μᾶλλον δέ. As has been seen, the original text can be read as adversative, with the second participle ("having been raised") being construed as a correction of the first ("having died"), so that Gnostic Christians could take the verse to mean that "rather than" dying, Christ was raised. The addition of the conjunction precludes this construal, for now the text affirms that Christ did die, "and yes also" was raised. It appears, then, that all three modifications work toward the same end of frustrating the possible misinterpretation of Romans 8:34 by those who were all too ready to affirm Christ's exaltation without acknowledging his death.

The variant readings considered to this stage work to counter separationist views of Jesus' death by arguing the unity of Jesus Christ, even in his passion. Another way the orthodox polemicists repelled Gnostic Christologies was to quote New Testament passages that speak specifically of "Christ" suffering, shedding blood, and dying. Irenaeus provides a particularly clear example of the strategem in the third book of his *Adversus Haereses*, where he strings together a large number of the sayings of Jesus (e.g., "thus it was fitting for Christ to suffer," Luke 24:46) and the teachings of Paul (e.g., "for in due time, Christ died for the ungodly," Rom 5:6) with the express purpose of showing that "when referring to the passion of our Lord . . . and his subjection to death, [they] employ the name of Christ" (*Adv. Haer.* III, 18, 3). For Irenaeus, the conclusion is clear: "the impassible Christ did not descend upon Jesus, but he himself, because he was Jesus Christ, suffered for us."

The heresiologists were not alone in emphasizing the New Testament usage of the name "Christ" in statements related to the passion. Their scribal counterparts attest this form of polemic as well, so that among the more common anti-Gnostic corruptions can be numbered interpolations of the name "Christ" into passages that originally referred to the suffering and death of Jesus.[153] Because very few of these corruptions bear the marks of authenticity, I will simply note some prominent examples to establish the dominant pattern. As one might expect, the vast majority of instances occur in the Gospels and in Paul. One that is no less expected occurs in the well-known statement of 1 John 1:7: "And the blood of Jesus his Son cleanses us from all sin." There is little doubt that this is the original wording of the text: it is attested in the earliest and best Greek manuscripts (e.g., ‬א B C II 1241 1739) and is preserved as well in Latin, Coptic, and Syriac documents. Some of the versional evidence, however, and the entire Byzantine tradition, supplies Χριστός, so that now it is not just Jesus' blood, but the blood of Jesus *Christ* (one and the same) that brings cleansing for sin.[154] The dominance of the reading in late manuscripts and its presence in some of the early versions suggests its ancient provenance, but scarcely its originality.[155] A comparable variation occurs in another Johannine text, the famous pronouncement of the Baptizer in John 1:36: "Behold the Lamb of God." In two uncial and several minuscule manuscripts, as well as in Armenian manuscripts and the Curetonian Syriac, the verse is modified to read "Behold the Christ, the Lamb of God."[156] Given the commonly understood sacrificial connotation of the title, the reason for the change appears plain. One need only ask, what kind of Christian might want to emphasize that it was specifically "Christ" who was the sacrificial lamb?

In the Gospels, changes of this kind affect both the predictions of Jesus' passion that are found on his own lips and the descriptions of the event itself. An example of the former occurs in Matthew 16:21, "From that time Jesus (ὁ Ἰησοῦς) began to reveal to his disciples that he must go to Jerusalem to suffer many things . . . and be killed." In the early Alexandrian tradition the text is changed to read, "From that time Jesus Christ (Ἰησοῦς Χριστός) began to reveal . . ." (‬א B cop^sa mss bo). The reading is attractive in view of its support by such high-quality manuscripts. The external evidence is not at all unambiguous, however, given the attestation of the shorter reading in every Greek manuscript except the two Alexandrians. And since the double name occurs nowhere else in Matthew outside of the birth narrative, it appears anomalous here. It was not at all anomalous to orthodox scribes, however, who saw in the text the prediction that it was the one man Jesus Christ who was to travel to Jerusalem to his death.[157]

Within the passion narrative, one naturally finds that a considerable degree of harmonization has occurred among the New Testament manuscripts. Nonetheless, the changes in the descriptions of Jesus' suffering may reflect more than simple harmonistic tendencies. In the Gospel of Mark, Jesus is condemned for blasphemy by the Sanhedrin, and then spat upon, beaten, and mockingly told to "Prophesy" (14:65). This final terse expression is expanded by Luke: "Prophesy, who is it that struck you?" (22:64) and differently by Matthew: "Prophesy to us, Christ, who is it that struck you?" (26:68). When scribes follow Matthew in adding the title Χριστέ to their texts of Luke and Mark, the addition serves not only to fill out the phrase but also to emphasize that it was the Christ who experienced these sufferings.[158]

Paul's letters provided ample opportunity to stress the orthodox doctrine that "Christ" himself suffered and died, as the doctrine can be found even in the unadulterated text of his letters. Subsequent corruptions simply drive the point home.[159] When Paul speaks of "carrying about in the body the death of Jesus" in 2 Corinthians 4:10, scribes were not at all indisposed to modify the text to speak of ". . . the death of Christ," a modification still reflected in the famous bilingual uncials of the Western tradition (D F G);[160] when in the next chapter Paul says that "he died for all" (5:15) two of the same uncials are joined with a number of other witnesses in specifying instead that "Christ died for all" (F G 51 93 234 1911 dem arm al); so too in the earlier correspondence with the Corinthians, when Paul refers to the bread and cup of the Christian eucharist in terms of "the body and blood of the Lord" (1 Cor 11:27), some witnesses modify the text to read "the body and blood of Christ" (A 33 eth^ro);[161] when he speaks to the Galatians of "the scandal of the cross" (5:11), several of our witnesses dutifully make yet more plain the real scandal, that it is "the scandal of the cross of Christ" (MSS A C 76 102 218 326 cop eth^utr). As suggested, these corruptions appear to coincide rather closely with the rest of Paul's teachings; at the same time, as I have had occasion to observe, Paul was claimed by the Gnostic Christians as much as by the orthodox. Scribes of the latter persuasion, therefore, may well have wanted to heighten what they saw as the Pauline emphasis that Jesus and the Christ were not distinct entities, and that when Paul said Jesus died he meant that Christ died.[162]

One other textual phenomenon that is somewhat more difficult to assess is the occasional substitution of ἀποθνῄσκω for πάσχω in passages that refer to Christ's salvific work; in the modified texts Christ is said not merely to have "suffered" but actually to have "died." Of course, the two words may simply have been confused because of their lexical similarity (cf. αποθανειν / παθειν). But it is peculiar that when 1 Peter uses πάσχω to refer to Christ's suffering, three out of four texts were changed (2:21, 3:18, 4:1; the exception is 2:23), whereas when it uses the same word to describe the suffering of Christians—eight occurrences in all—it is *never* changed (2:19, 20; 3:14, 17; 4:1b [?], 15, 19; 5:10). This appears to be more than an accident. Moreover, the changes can be traced back to the period of concern—directly in 3:18, with the attestation of 𝔭^72 and a wide range of early Greek and versional evidence; indirectly in 2:21 with codex Sinaiticus, the Palestinian Syriac, and a smattering of Greek, Latin, and Armenian witnesses.[163] The same change, it should also be noted, occurs in Hebrews 9:26 in Sahidic and several medieval Greek manuscripts.

If the tendency to make this change can be traced back to the late second or third century and is not accidental but intentional, how can it be explained? Certainly the notion that Christ "suffered" ($\pi\alpha\theta\epsilon\hat{\iota}\nu$) is orthodox. But one wonders if it is not also susceptible to a peculiarly Gnostic construal as well, since the time of his indwelling of Jesus is for the Christ a time of suffering.[164] To say that Christ actually "died," however, is a clearly orthodox notion, even though, to be sure, it too could be reinterpreted by Gnostic Christians in any way they might choose. The point, of course, is not that the orthodox emphasis may or may not have proved rhetorically effective. The point is that we know what the orthodox emphasis was. The changes in 1 Peter and Hebrews, then, may well be attributed to the orthodox emphasis on the "death" of Christ.

Jesus, the Christ Raised from the Dead

We have seen that orthodox Christians of the second and third centuries opposed separationist Christologies by emphasizing that Christ himself suffered and died. They also emphasized that the one raised from the dead was Christ, a doctrine that seemed to them the natural corollary. The point was not to be taken for granted, however, given the Gnostic claim that the Christ had departed from Jesus before his passion, so that it was only Jesus who died and was raised from the dead. A concise statement of the separationist view is found in Irenaeus's summary at the end of Book I of his *Adversus Haereses* in which an unnamed group of Gnostics claimed that the divine Christ "departed from him [Jesus] into the state of an incorruptible Aeon, while Jesus was crucified. Christ however, was not forgetful of his Jesus, but sent down a certain energy into him from above, which raised him up again in the body" (*Adv. Haer.* I, 30, 13). For Irenaeus and his orthodox associates, however, it was the unified Jesus Christ who died on the cross, and the unified Jesus Christ who rose from the dead: "Do not err. Jesus Christ, the Son of God, is one and the same, who did by suffering reconcile us to God, and rose from the dead" (*Adv. Haer.* III, 16, 9).[165]

Given the orthodox view of Christ's resurrection, one can fairly well anticipate the ways orthodox scribes might change their texts of the New Testament.[166] Likely candidates for such changes would be passages that could be taken to say that it was only the man Jesus, not the one Jesus Christ, who was raised from the dead. Moreover, since even the Gnostics could claim that "Christ was raised" (meaning that he was exalted to heaven before the death of Jesus, not that he was raised "from the dead"),[167] we might expect alterations of passages whose ambiguity could be taken to support such a view—passages that indicate that "Christ" was raised without stating that he was raised "from the dead." Obviously, changes of this kind will be slight—the addition of a word or phrase here or there—and there is little reason to expect them to occur with any greater consistency or rigor than any of the other orthodox corruptions considered so far. Rather than citing every instance of the phenomenon, I will again be selective and simply establish the dominant pattern. The changes typically appear exactly where one might expect them, in the Gospels, Paul, and the speeches of Acts that mention Jesus' resurrection from the dead.

We begin with the speeches of Acts. An example occurs already in chapter 3, where Peter alludes to Isaiah 52:13 to show that after the crucifixion God "glorified his servant Jesus" ($\dot{\epsilon}\delta\delta\xi\alpha\sigma\epsilon\nu$ $\tau\delta\nu$ $\pi\alpha\hat{\iota}\delta\alpha$ $\alpha\upsilon\tau\upsilon\hat{\upsilon}$ $'I\eta\sigma\upsilon\hat{\upsilon}\nu$) by raising him from the dead (Acts 3:13). The statement would not be objectionable, of course, to Gnostics who affirmed just this point, that it was precisely the man Jesus who was raised from the dead (not the Christ, who never died). Small wonder, then, that orthodox scribes might adjust the text slightly to preclude such a construal,[168] as appears to have happened in codex Bezae and some elements of the Ethiopic tradition. These witnesses insert the title $X\rho\iota\sigma\tau\delta\varsigma$ into the text, so that now it speaks of "Jesus Christ" as the one whom God glorified.

Better attested is the change made in the idyllic assessment of the early Christian community found in the following chapter. Here we are told that the apostles were "delivering with great power the witness of the resurrection of the Lord Jesus" ($\tau\hat{\eta}\varsigma$ $\dot{\alpha}\nu\alpha\sigma\tau\dot{\alpha}\sigma\epsilon\omega\varsigma$ $\tau\upsilon\hat{\upsilon}$ $\kappa\upsilon\rho\dot{\iota}\upsilon\upsilon$ $'I\eta\sigma\upsilon\hat{\upsilon}$, v. 33). This at least is the text of the earliest manuscripts ($\mathfrak{p}^8$ B),[169] along with a number of other important witnesses and the entire Byzantine tradition.[170] But a group of other manuscripts, including codices Sinaiticus and Bezae, along with a wide range of versional witnesses, again insert the title $X\rho\iota\sigma\tau\upsilon\hat{\upsilon}$ ("the resurrection of Jesus Christ"). The change, however, is made differently throughout the tradition; some seven forms of the text diverge from one another, primarily in the matter of word order and the inclusion/exclusion of $\dot{\eta}\mu\hat{\omega}\nu$ with "Lord." While the double name "Jesus Christ," therefore, has early and widespread support, its variable attestation and its absence in both the earliest manuscripts and the broadest stream of late manuscripts combine to suggest its secondary character.[171]

A comparable change occurs in the speech of Paul in the synagogue of Pisidian Antioch. Here Paul declares that the resurrection of Jesus has fulfilled the promises that God made to the Jewish ancestors: "We proclaim the good news to you, that the promise given to the fathers, God has fulfilled to us their children, by raising Jesus, as it is written in the second Psalm, 'You are my son, today I have begotten you'" (Acts 13:32–33). The addition of $X\rho\iota\sigma\tau\delta\varsigma$ to the name Jesus (D 614 sy^h) appears to resolve two potential christological problems simultaneously: it makes it clear that Christ was the one who was raised, against the early form of adoptionism that maintained that Jesus became the Christ only *at* the resurrection, and, more germane to my purpose here, it demonstrates the unity of Jesus Christ in his resurrection against those who claimed that the Christ returned to the Pleroma before Jesus' death.[172]

In Paul's own letters we find comparable changes where they might be expected. In his famous claim to apostolic authority based on his vision of the resurrected Jesus, Paul asks (rhetorically), "Am I not an apostle? Have I not seen our Lord Jesus?" (1 Cor 9:1). A number of manuscripts, for reasons that by now are becoming clearer, have specified that it was the unified "Jesus Christ" (D E K L P syr^p cop arm geo al) or "Christ Jesus" (F G demid pc) that Paul saw. A somewhat different situation confronted scribes in Romans 8:10–11, where Paul speaks both of the "Christ who is in you" and of "Jesus" who was "raised from the dead." One can well imagine the Gnostic inclination to see in this text a differentiation between the Christ and Jesus. It would appear, however, that when Paul goes on to name "Christ" as the one who was raised (v. 11b), the (orthodox) identification of Jesus as the Christ would be assured.[173] Nonetheless, it is to be noted with respect to the latter verse that along with a large number of other witnesses, the Valentinians did not read the name with the article (Χριστός rather than ὁ Χριστός).[174] It may be, then, that they understood (or rather, that they were thought to understand) Χριστός as a personal name that was interchangeable with Jesus instead of a titular designation of "the Christ" (who, for them, was *not* "raised from the dead").[175] This in itself may have led to the widespread insertion of the article by orthodox scribes seeking to obviate any ambiguities. Yet more significant is the addition of Ἰησοῦν in a large number of witnesses in a wide variety of ways (five forms of the text of v. 11b attested among such manuscripts as ℵ* A C D syr^pal 103 d e dem x ar). Now the unity of "Jesus Christ [or Christ Jesus] who was raised from the dead" is stated unequivocally, giving the change all the appearance of an orthodox corruption.[176]

The widespread alteration of 1 Corinthians 15:15 does not fit the precise pattern we have observed so far, although it does achieve a similar end. In this passage Paul attacks those who do not subscribe to the future resurrection but maintain that believers already enjoy the full benefits of salvation here and now. Paul's response to these "enthusiasts" takes as its starting point the confession they share in common, that Christ "was raised on the third day according to the Scriptures." In verse 15 he argues that if there is in fact no resurrection of the dead, then contrary to their common confession, Christ himself has not been raised: "And also we have been found to be false witnesses of God, because we have testified of God that he raised Christ whom he did not raise, if indeed the dead are not raised." The last clause (εἴπερ ἄρα νεκροὶ οὐκ ἐγείρονται) appears otiose in the context, because its entire premise is none other than that of the entire argument. This makes it interesting that in one stream of tradition the clause is omitted (D a b r Vg^mss al).

Most critics have assumed that a scribe of the Western tradition deleted the clause because it did appear so extraneous.[177] But this explanation is not altogether satisfying. Indeed, the clause *appears* unnecessary to the argument precisely because it *is* unnecessary. Here it may be important to observe a stylistic peculiarity: nowhere else in his writings does Paul use the phrase εἴπερ ἄρα, or even its counterpart, εἴ ἄρα. The style appears, then, to be non-Pauline, and the clause appears otiose. If we *were* to take it as a scribal addition to the passage, the question becomes, what might have generated the change? It is not at all difficult to understand why the shorter text is the *lectio ardua:* apart from the dictates of its literary context, verse 15 states that God did not raise Christ from the dead, a view perhaps amenable to the Gnostics (who accepted Paul as their apostolic authority), but not at all the view of their orthodox opponents. In light of the solid entrenchment of the shorter text in the Western tradition, the stylistic peculiarity of the clause in question, and the peculiar circumstance that while it appears superfluous in the context, the clause nevertheless guarantees that its context not be over-looked in making sense of it, it is perhaps best to understand the longer text as a corruption effected by a scribe seeking to prevent the possibility of mis-interpreting the verse as a denial of Christ's resurrection.

As might be imagined, changes that stress the orthodox doctrine of the resurrection are not altogether lacking from the resurrection narratives of the Gospels. Even though the longer ending of Mark is itself secondary, its word-ing was no more immune to corruption than any other portion of the New Testament text (as scribes would normally not know they were corrupting a corruption). And so when the text mentions the resurrected "Lord Jesus" prior to his ascension into heaven (16:19), a large number of witnesses sim-ply omit the name "Jesus," obviating thereby the problem of talking about Jesus but not Christ (A D[3] C[3] X Θ Π[supp] Ψ f[13] 28 565 700 892 1241 Byz cop[bo] eth al); several others attest the change one has more customarily come to expect, the creation of the double name "Jesus Christ" as a designation of the one who ascends to heaven (W o bo[mss]).[178] Somewhat earlier in Mark's narrative, in the original ending of the Gospel, the women at the tomb are told that Jesus is no longer there but has been raised. They are to tell Jesus' disciples and Peter "that he will go before you into Galilee" (Mark 16:7). Here several witnesses amend the text to make it perfectly clear that this one who precedes them into Galilee "has been raised from the dead" (f[1] pc). This emphasis may have been deemed particularly appropriate since Mark other-wise never speaks of Jesus' resurrection "from the dead."

A comparable change occurs in the final chapter of the Gospel according to Matthew. When the women arrive at the tomb, they are told by the angelic witness that Jesus "has been raised from the dead" (Matt 28:4). Interestingly, the prepositional phrase ("from the dead") is lacking from both the Western tradition (D OL syr[s]) and Origen, one of our earliest and best witnesses to the Alexandrian text. Even though the shorter text is sparsely attested, it is difficult to explain as a corruption. The simple fact that the same phrase is not found with ἠγέρθη in verse 6 would hardly account for its deletion here.[179] On the other hand, it is relatively easy to see why scribes might have wanted to *insert* the phrase, as it now makes clear that Jesus has not simply been exalted but actually raised "from the dead."

A different kind of change occurs somewhat later in Matthew's account. When Jesus appears to his eleven remaining disciples on the Mount of Olives, the original text of Matthew 28:17 states that they responded to his presence by "worshipping" (καὶ ἰδόντες αὐτὸν προσεκύνησαν). But it is left ambig-

uous as to whether they bow down before *him,* bestowing on him the ado-
ration otherwise reserved for God, or if upon seeing him they bless the God
who raised him from the dead. The ambiguity is resolved in a change preserved in the vast majority of manuscripts, a change difficult to construe apart
from an orthodox milieu in which the Jesus who was raised is himself the
divine Christ worthy of worship. In these manuscripts the third person pronoun is provided as an object for the verb, so that now the disciples are said
unequivocally to worship "him," the resurrected Jesus himself. That the pronoun is not original is evident both in the impressive concatenation of Alexandrian and Western witnesses arrayed against it [180] and in the fact that those
manuscripts that attest it, some as early the second century, differ among
themselves with respect to its case (i.e., whether it should be genitive, dative,
or accusative). It appears that scribes agreed on the necessity of the change,
but not on how it should be made. Here again, then, we must entertain the
possiblity of an early orthodox corruption of Scripture, "designed" to counter
those who distinguish between the man Jesus and the divine Christ. [181]

Jesus Christ, Son of God

As we have seen, representatives of orthodoxy did not latch onto the doctrine
of the unity of Jesus Christ by mere happenstance. They found the doctrine
appealing precisely because it was challenged in some quarters, specifically
by groups of Gnostic Christians who distinguished between Jesus and the
Christ. Nor did the propensity to use the dual name "Jesus Christ" derive
simply from usage established early on in some circles, such as that surrounding the Apostle Paul. This established usage provided orthodox Christians
with ammunition they needed to combat the claims of their Gnostic opponents. But they stockpiled this ammunition as much because of its utility in
these debates as because of the precedent of earlier authorities.

And so the orthodox penchant for identifying Jesus as the Christ in the
accounts of his birth, baptism, death, and resurrection derives from a polemical context. [182] Outside these particular narratives, one can posit a comparable motivation for a slew of corruptions that appear to function similarly.
The identification of Jesus as the Christ is made explicit, for example, in
numerous texts that refer to Jesus' ministry, particularly those in which others acknowledge his identity. Thus, when Jesus confronts demons who "know
him" in Mark 1:34, orthodox scribes interpolated the affirmation essential to
their own Christology, so that now the demons are said to know "him [i.e.,
Jesus] to be the Christ." [183] The same kind of corruption, interestingly enough,
is evidenced in Old Latin manuscripts of Mark 3:11, where Jesus commands
the demons to be silent concerning him, because, according to the altered
reading, "they knew that he was the Christ himself" (b g[1. 2] q). This emphasis
coincides in turn with the change made in the previous verse by an entirely
different set of witnesses, which by interpolating the words ὁ Χριστός have
recorded the demons' initial acclamation in the words of the orthodox formula "You [Jesus] are the Christ, the Son of God" (C M P syr[p] c pc). Nor

is this acknowledgment restricted to demons. Upon Peter's confession in the Gospel of Matthew, Jesus commands his disciples that they should tell no one that he is the Christ (ὅτι αὐτός ἐστιν ὁ Χριστός). Apparently not content to leave it at that, a number of scribes have underscored the point by augmenting the text with the name Jesus, so that now the disciples are specifically told not to divulge the truth that "he himself is Jesus the Christ."[184]

Such examples from the Synoptic Gospels could be multiplied at will. They occur elsewhere in the New Testament as well, for instance, in the famous interpolation in the story of Philip and the Ethiopian eunuch in Acts 8. Upon hearing that the Old Testament scriptures were fulfilled by Jesus, the eunuch asks Philip what there is to prevent him from undergoing baptism (8:36). In the original text, there is apparently no obstacle at all, for he immediately descends to the water. But in the addition attested by a wide range of Greek and versional witnesses, Philip tells the eunuch that he first must profess (the orthodox) faith: "And Philip said, 'If you believe from your whole heart, it is possible [to be baptized].' And he answered, 'I believe Jesus Christ to be the Son of God.' "[185] Now the text embraces yet more clearly the confession insisted on by the orthodox, that Jesus Christ is the Son of God (one and the same), a confession essential for those who wish to join the people of God. It is no surprise to find that Irenaeus quotes the interpolated text against his Gnostic opponents (*Adv. Haer.* III, 12, 8).

Changes in the Johannine literature appear to function similarly. Thus, when the author of 1 John claims that God abides in the one who "confesses that Jesus is the Son of God" (4:15), codex Vaticanus specifies that it is "Jesus Christ" who is the Son of God. So too, in 5:5, where conquering the world involves confessing that Jesus is the Son of God, some manuscripts have rephrased the confession to coincide with the orthodox unitary doctrine that "Jesus Christ is the Son of God" (33 378 arm). Furthermore, several changes in our earliest manuscripts of the Fourth Gospel serve to emphasize that Jesus himself *is* the Christ, the Son of God. This appears the best way to explain the addition of ἀληθῶς to 1:49 in p⁶⁶* 1241 (reading "You really *are* the Son of God!")[186] and of the definite article to 10:36 in p⁴⁵ (reading "because I said 'I am *the* Son of God' "). One can simply wonder how many other instances occurred in other third-century manuscripts that have *not* managed to survive the ravages of time.[187]

Similar trends are in evidence throughout the Pauline corpus. In one of those rare passages in which Paul mentions the life of Christ without reference to his death and resurrection, he notes that he came as a minister to the circumcision (Rom 15:8, λέγω γὰρ Χριστὸν διάκονον γεγενῆσθαι περιτομῆς). Gnostics who understood this to mean that the Christ came to Jesus for the sake of the elect would have no difficulty with such a passage, although their unease might increase when the text is changed to speak of the unified "Jesus Christ" (D E F G OL pc) or "Christ Jesus" (L P vg go al) coming for this purpose. With respect to a different passage, we have already seen what scribes did with Paul's reference to carrying about in the body the "death of Jesus" (2 Cor 4:10).[188] Some scribes similarly saw fit to modify his words concerning the "life of Jesus" in the same passage, by changing it to coincide with the orthodox unitary stress on "Jesus Christ."[189] So too, when Hebrews names "Jesus" as the "apostle and high priest of our confession" (3:1), we find a plethora of manuscripts changing the text to indicate that it is "Christ Jesus" (Byz) or "Jesus Christ" (MSS C^c D^c E K L arm al) who is so called.

The Unity of the Name: Our Lord Jesus Christ

The preceding discussion encourages a brief reflection on a phenomenon that has been occasionally observed, although not convincingly explained, in earlier investigations of the theological proclivities of Christian scribes. As we have already seen, early scribes were far from averse to extending the names and/or titles of Jesus in the texts of Scripture. This applies not only to the terms "Christ" and "Son of God," but also and in particular to the title "Lord." Not infrequently, two or more of these titles will find their way into texts in combination, so that the resulting "Jesus Christ our Lord" ('Ιησοῦς Χριστὸς τοῦ κυρίου ἡμῶν) is regularly attested as a corruption among the New Testament manuscripts. How is this phenomenon to be explained?

Most critics have simply assumed that scribes preferred to provide for Jesus his full name and title. There is clearly something to this assumption, since, after all, the variants do not seem particular with respect to when and where they occur. It nonetheless fails to explain *why* scribes preferred to preserve the name and title in its fullness. Moreover, the idea that later scribes were moved to do so by the force of tradition raises its own query concerning the inception of that tradition.

The most persuasive discussion to date is that of Eldon Epp, who in his much cited treatment of the theological tendency of codex Bezae argues that the full name of "our Lord Jesus Christ" reflects the bias of the Western text against the Jews, because the emphasis on who Jesus is—as provided in the full name—shows how insidious the Jews are in rejecting him.[190] It is an intriguing theory, but not altogether satisfying. For one thing, by restricting himself to the occurrences of the phrase in the so-called Western tradition, Epp overlooks the circumstance that it occurs everywhere else as well.[191] Furthermore, one wonders what kind of *Sitz im Leben* might be in view for the generation and perpetuation of this kind of corruption. Was the scribal predecessor of the text of codex Bezae, for instance, actively engaged in polemics against his counterparts in the synagogue? If not, did he simply dislike Jews in general and decide to exercise his antipathy whenever possible? Regrettably, Epp is reluctant to say anything about the social context within which such an anti-Judaic bias might have functioned, a reluctance that leads one not so much to suspect the evidence as to question, in this case, its interpretation.[192]

As might be expected, an alternative explanation for the phenomenon suggests itself within the context of the present study, an explanation that is firmly rooted in a historical milieu about which we have some considerable knowledge and that accounts for the presence of the full name and title of

Jesus *throughout* the textual tradition. According to Irenaeus, whose views were widely shared and often simply replicated, Gnostic Christians confessed with their mouths the unity of Jesus Christ but did not really believe it: "Although they certainly do with their tongue confess one Jesus Christ, [they] make fools of themselves, thinking one thing and saying another. . . . They thus wander from the truth, because their doctrine departs from Him who is truly God, being ignorant that his only-begotten Word . . . is Himself Jesus Christ our Lord" (*Adv. Haer.* III, 16, 6). Throughout his polemic Irenaeus insists that the various epithets applied to Jesus in the New Testament do not refer to different components of the Divine Pleroma, different aeons that each had a different name and function (e.g., Logos, Only-Begotten, Truth, Life, Christ). Instead, they apply equally to the One who became man, Jesus Christ (e.g., I, 9, 2–3). It is of particular interest to our present discussion that Irenaeus explicitly states that although the Valentinian Gnostics call Jesus the "Savior," they refuse to call him "Lord" (κύριος; *Adv. Haer.* I, 1, 3). Whether or not Irenaeus is right is of little consequence for my purposes here. For if orthodox heresiologists *believed* that their Gnostic opponents did not use this title for Jesus, it is understandable why they themselves *would* use it, especially in conjunction with the other names and titles that came to accumulate around Jesus. The upshot is that the well-documented predilection for the title "Lord" among the proto-orthodox scribes, and the combination of this title with the unitary name "Jesus Christ," may well have arisen within the context of anti-Gnostic polemics.

Given the plethora of examples, I will here simply indicate the detectable trends by citing a few cases chosen more or less at random. One trend is merely to add κύριος, either to the name Jesus (e.g., Luke 5:19 syr^pal),[193] or to another designation of Jesus such as "Son of David" (Matt 9:27)[194] or "Rabbi" (Mark 10:51),[195] or to a text in which Jesus is the subject but is left unnamed (e.g., Matt 4:18).[196] The same effect can be created, conversely, by adding the name Ἰησοῦς to the title κύριος, as happens in several Alexandrian manuscripts of Matthew 20:30.[197]

More frequent still is the tendency to create the full appellation "Jesus Christ the Lord" or "Jesus Christ our Lord" out of any of its components that happen to appear in the original text. In a passage I have previously discussed, Paul speaks of bearing the "stigmata of Jesus" (Gal 6:17).[198] I earlier observed that some scribes changed the text to speak of the "stigmata of Christ," apparently in order to show that it was Christ who suffered death. Others used the text to stress the full unity of the one who suffered by inserting the title κύριος, making it speak of the stigmata of the Lord Jesus (MSS C^c D^c[1739] Byz [syr^p]); yet other scribes went further in speaking of "the stigmata of the Lord Jesus Christ" (ℵ d e); while still others completed the title to make the text read "the stigmata of our Lord Jesus Christ" (D* F G OL [sa^mss]). In Acts 2:38, where Peter speaks of being baptized "in the name of Jesus Christ," a number of scribes have added the title τοῦ κυρίου, so that baptism is now in the name of "the Lord Jesus Christ."[199] When Stephen looks up into heaven in Acts 7:59, he cries out "Lord Jesus, receive my spirit," except in a handful of manuscripts in which he instead addresses the "Lord Jesus Christ."[200] In Romans 6:11 the name Christ Jesus becomes "Christ Jesus our Lord" in some witnesses (ℵ C Byz [syr^p] bo); just as, in others, the statement of Romans 10:9, that one must make confession in the name of "the Lord Jesus," becomes confession in the name of "the Lord Jesus Christ" (p^46 a t). So too the phrase "our Lord Christ" in Romans 16:8 becomes "our Lord Jesus Christ" (in manuscripts L cop arm), whereas the phrase "our Lord Jesus" two verses later becomes "our Lord Jesus Christ" (in A C Ψ Byz OL syr cop). These kinds of changes recur throughout the entire New Testament, up to the final verse of the book of Revelation, where "the grace of the Lord Jesus" is modified to read "the grace of Jesus Christ" in most manuscripts (051^s Byz) but "the grace of our Lord Jesus Christ" in others (2067 OL syr).

As suggested by this smattering of examples, the designation of Jesus as Lord and the concatenation of titles in his honor pervade the manuscript tradition of the New Testament. These changes are not to be regarded as merely incidental to the tradition, nor as deriving from an unreflective desire on the part of Christian scribes to say everything possible about Jesus at every available turn. The scribal tendency to call Jesus κύριος and to apply to him a string of exalted appellations ultimately stems from theological disputes of the second century, in which proto-orthodox Christians emphasized the unity of Jesus Christ in the face of separationist Christologies that claimed that each of Jesus' names and titles referred to distinct divine entities. Such changes in the manuscript tradition of the New Testament represent orthodox corruptions of Scripture.

Summary and Conclusions

In this chapter I have examined the orthodox reaction to separationist Christologies espoused by Gnostic Christians, especially as the controversy came to affect the text of the emerging New Testament. Gnostic Christianity comprised a plethora of divergent groups that manifested a wild array of mythologies, beliefs, and cultic practices. These groups nonetheless appear to have shared some basic notions about the nature of the world and of human existence within it. Intrinsic to all such systems, at least as understood by their orthodox opponents, was a redeemer figure who descended from heaven to bring the divine knowledge *(gnosis)* requisite for salvation to souls imprisoned in the realm of matter. In the Gnostic view, this figure could not belong to this world, as this would involve an entrapment in matter and enslavement to the evil (or ignorant) deities that created it. The redeemer was normally thought, therefore, to have made temporary residence here, entering into the man Jesus at his baptism, empowering him for a ministry of teaching and healing and departing from him prior to his inglorious execution.

In the opinion of the proto-orthodox, this differentiation between the man Jesus and the divine Christ was just one of the divisive doctrines of the Gnostics, who also severed the creator of the world from its redeemer, detached the Old Testament from the New, and created schisms within the Christian community. "Orthodox" Christianity, on the other hand, took pride in its affirmations of the unity of the faith: that there is one God, one canon of Scripture, one church, and one Jesus Christ.

As we have seen, proto-orthodox Christians disputed the scriptural basis for the Gnostics' doctrines and even denied them the right to appeal to Scripture in their support.[201] At the same time, they knew that such "prescriptions" had little real effect—the Gnostics could simply ignore them—and they took quite seriously their opponents' ability to manipulate Scripture to their own ends, not simply by altering its words (a practice with which they were occasionally charged), but also by interpreting them according to their own hermeneutical principles, principles that by and large denied any ultimate authority to the literal words of the text and sought to uncover the "true" meaning embedded allegorically within them.

It is interesting to observe that the heresiologists continued to apply their own historico-grammatical techniques of exegesis to the Scriptures, even though they realized that their opponents denied their validity. This is to say, both sides refused to grant not only the appropriateness of their opponents' exegetical conclusions, but also the validity of their exegetical methods. It may seem odd that the two sides argued past each other in this way; they rarely appear to be fighting on common ground. This is, nonetheless, one of the securely attested features of the controversy. We may be justified in thinking, then, that the scriptural arguments mounted by both sides were intended not so much to convert one's opponents as to edify one's own constituency and thereby to minimize, perhaps, the number of defections.

The same may be true of the scribal alterations of these scriptural texts. Indeed, it seems unlikely that proto-orthodox scribes could be overly sanguine about the effect of such changes on their actual opponents. One can scarcely imagine them expecting to convert Gnostic Christians simply by altering a word here or there in the text of the New Testament. Perhaps it is better, then, not to see these textual corruptions as a polemical strategem *per se,* but instead as a *by-product* of the debates. By changing their texts, scribes were incorporating their own "readings" into them, showing how they *should* be read in the face of other interpreters who read them differently.

We have seen that several such corruptions directly challenge the gnostic claim that Jesus and the Christ were distinct beings, namely, by pronouncing an apostolic or dominical anathema on anyone foolhardy enough to advance such a view (1 John 4:2, Matt 12:30, Luke 11:23, 2 Cor 11:4). More commonly, orthodox scribes modified texts that may have served their opponents well as proof texts. In their altered form, these texts emphasize that Jesus was the Christ from birth, not from the time of his baptism (Matt 1:16, 18; Luke 1:35), that the Christ did not enter into Jesus when the spirit descended upon him as a dove (Mark 1:11; Matt 3:16; Luke 3:22) nor leave him before his passion (e.g., Mark 15:34; Heb 1:3; 2:9; Rom 8:34). Orthodox scribes also affirmed their belief in *Christ's* death and resurrection by inserting the title "Christ" into relevant passages that otherwise lacked it (e.g., 1 John 1:17;

Matt 16:21; 2 Cor 4:10; Acts 3:13; 4:33; 13:33; 1 Cor 9:1). Finally, and perhaps most frequently of all, they stressed the unity of the redeemer by altering his name as it occurred in the biblical text, revealing thereby their predilection for the phrase "our Lord Jesus Christ." This concatenation of titles stated with particular clarity the orthodox belief in the face of Gnostics who were known to disdain the title "Lord" and to deny the unity of Jesus and the Christ. Thus, even changes that might otherwise appear slight or unworthy of notice testify to the wide-ranging influence of the proto-orthodox Christology, a Christology that gained ascendency near the end of our period and that was soon to emerge as victorious during the theological struggles of the fourth century.

Notes

1. I have chosen not to deal here with the complicated question of whether "Gnostic" is an appropriate designation for the various groups to be considered in this chapter, partly because Irenaeus, for example, applies it as a blanket term—rightly or wrongly—for all the groups he attacks (see the title of his work: "The Refutation and Overthrow of Falsely-Named Gnosis"), and partly because my thesis does not depend on what such groups are called. On the controversy over the appropriateness of the term, see M. J. Edwards, "Gnostics and Valentinians in the Church Fathers," in response to the spirited claims of Morton Smith, "The History of the Term Gnostikos."

2. Indeed, they are at times nearly indistinguishable. Thus, Irenaeus presents the Ebionite Christology as separationist (*Adv. Haer.* I, 26), apparently relying upon a source. For the purposes of the present study, however, it will prove heuristically useful to keep distinct the "ideal types" of Christology, recognizing at all times that the permutations and conflations in actual or reputed proponents of the period make the matter far more complicated. On "hybrid" Christologies, see note 17.

3. For analyses of the traditions surrounding Cerinthus, see Gustav Bardy, "Cerinthe," and Raymond Brown, "Cerinthus," in Appendix II, *The Epistles of John,* 760–71.

4. I do not mean to draw an absolute line between Jewish and Gnostic Christians; these categories naturally overlap in significant ways, not least because some of the Gnostics may well have been Jews. With respect specifically to Cerinthus, the earliest reference occurs in the *Epistula Apostolorum,* the orthodox pseudepigraph of the early second century that explicitly directs its polemic against the Gnostic Simon (Magus) and Cerinthus. Moreover, the first extensive discussion, by Irenaeus (*Adv. Haer.* I, 26, 1), describes Cerinthus in patently Gnostic terms. On the Gnostic affinities of the "historical Cerinthus," in addition to the works cited in note 3, see Klaus Wengst, *Häresie und Orthodoxie,* 26.

5. Irenaeus attributes comparable notions, for example, to the Ptolemeans (I, 7, 2), the Marcosians (I, 21, 2), the Carpocratians (I, 25, 1), and (perhaps) the Barbelognostics (I, 30, 12–14), and claims that even the Ebionites have "similar" views (I, 26, 2). His most strident attack on the position is found in III, 16–18. See also, for example, Tertullian, *Adv. Val.* 27, and Hippolytus, *Ref.* 6, 46; 7, 15, 21–24.

6. See especially Irenaeus, *Adv. Haer.* III, 16–18.

7. The literature on these issues is immense. See the studies cited in Chapter 1, note 29.

8. This is a particularly important caveat because, as was seen in an earlier context, our knowledge of Gnosticism "as it really was" has changed dramatically over the past several decades, especially with the discovery of primary Gnostic materials near Nag Hammadi, Egypt. As I have already observed, even before the discovery of the Nag Hammadi library there were reasons for thinking that the heresiological reports were not altogether reliable. Antagonists can rarely be trusted to provide dispassionate information. But the Nag Hammadi materials have shown just how far afield some of the patristic claims were, although scholars continue to debate why this might be—whether, that is, the church fathers were sometimes misinformed or whether the quality of their sources outstripped their capacity to understand them. It may well be, as Frederik Wisse has cogently argued ("Nag Hammadi Library and the Heresiologists"), that heresiologists such as Irenaeus simply misconstrued the nature of the materials available to them; mistaking sublime expressions of Gnostic poetry for attempts at propositional theology, the fathers themselves constructed the Gnostic "systems" that were then readily susceptible to attack as hopelessly complex, inconsistent, and contrary to all "common" sense. Similarly, Koschorke *(Die Polemik)* argues that the orthodox erred in taking the myths as central, rather than as simple expressions of the ultimate concerns of "otherworldliness" shared by various Gnostic groups. See further pp. 15–17.

9. Apart, that is, from the Marcionites, who were normally associated with Gnosticism despite their radically different positions on critical issues of cosmology, anthropology, soteriology, and Scripture. See note 37 in Chapter 4.

10. Scholars have long recognized that the relatively consistent descriptions of the Gnostic systems among the church fathers derives from their literary interdependence (see Wisse, "Nag Hammadi and the Heresiologists"). The fathers themselves occasionally acknowledged their indebtedness to one another; Irenaeus, for example, claims to have used Justin's lost *Syntagma,* whereas both Tertullian and Hippolytus rely almost exclusively on Irenaeus for their descriptions of the Valentinians. Of considerably more interest to scholars, therefore, are instances in which two fathers describe the same Gnostic sect in irreconcilable terms. See further, Chapter 1, note 51. In such instances, it is not necessarily the case that later discussions are less accurate. Some scholars, for example, consider Hippolytus's treatment of Basilides historically superior to Irenaeus's. See Robert M. Grant, "Gnostic Origins and the Basilidians of Irenaeus."

11. See pp. 5–6.

12. According to Irenaeus, Simon claimed that "it was himself who appeared among the Jews as the Son, but descended in Samaria as the Father, while he came to other nations in the character of the Holy Spirit. He represented himself, in a word, as being the loftiest of all powers, that is, the Being who is the Father over all" (*Adv. Haer.* I, 23, 1).

13. Irenaeus finds other Gnostics liable on the same grounds, of course; Tertullian more or less repeats the charge, whereas Hippolytus elevates it to a self-evident truth: in his *Refutation* it is enough simply to show whence a heresy comes (for him, it is always from a Greek philosophy) in order to demonstrate its heinous character. See further Vallée, *A Study in Anti-Gnostic Polemics,* 41–62, and especially Koschorke, *Hippolyt's Ketzerbekämpfung.*

14. As set forth, for example, in Irenaeus, *Adv. Haer.* I, on which subsequent heresiologists themselves depended, sometimes with acknowledgment (cf. Tertullian,

Adv.Val. 5; see note 10). A convenient collection of the patristic texts can be found in Werner Foerster, *Gnosis: A Selection of Gnostic Texts.* For more detailed sketches of the basic Gnostic systems, see Jonas, *The Gnostic Religion,* and, especially, Rudolph, *Gnosis.* For the orthodox perception of such systems and their polemics against them, see the works cited in Chapter 1, notes 50, 52, 53, and 55.

15. Clement of Alexandria, *Exc. Theod.* 78, 2.

16. This, of course, is the docetic Christology allegedly espoused by such Gnostics as Simon Magus and Saturninus, as well as by Marcion, whose Gnostic credentials I will later dispute.

17. As I have indicated, Gnostic Christianity was quite complex, never cut and dried, even when systematized by its orthodox opponents. And so it is no surprise to find that a number of groups, including the Valentinians, about whom we are best informed, espoused a kind of "hybrid" Christology, maintaining the separationist view that the Christ descended upon Jesus at his baptism, while asserting that Jesus himself was not actually a flesh and blood human being, but was "specially made" by the Demiurge (Irenaeus, *Adv. Haer.* I, 6, 1; see also Tertullian, *de carne Christi* 15). According to Hippolytus, there were actually two schools of Valentinian thought: the Italian, represented by Heracleon and Ptolemaeus, which claimed that Jesus' body was made out of "psychic" substance, and the Oriental, headed by Axionicus and Bardesanes, which maintained it was "pneumatic" (*Ref.* 6, 30). In neither system was he a real flesh and blood human, a "mere man." See further the discussion of Luke 1:35, pp. 139–40. For ease of presentation, I will discuss the separationist aspects of such hybrid Christologies in this chapter, reserving unequivocally docetic views for the chapter that follows.

18. That this view, rather than the docetic, more typically characterized the Gnostics was already recognized by von Harnack, who, however, somewhat anachronistically labeled it a "two-nature" Christology (see, e.g., *History of Dogma* II, 286). In fact, if one chooses to speak of it in these later terms, it is more like a "two-person" Christology.

19. I borrow here the translation of Layton, *Gnostic Scriptures,* 180. For a brief discussion of the relation to the group that Irenaeus actually designates as "Gnostics" in *Adv. Haer.* I, 29, see Layton, p. 170.

20. See the discussion of pp. 20–22.

21. See the examples I cite on pp. 21–22.

22. Although, as I have pointed out, the fathers themselves regularly interpreted the text in nonliteral ways as well. See the discussion of pp. 20–22.

23. See especially Koschorke, *Polemik der Gnostiker,* Teil IV, "Zur Struktur der gnostischen Polemik" and Lüdemann, "Zur Geschichte des ältesten Christentums in Rom." It is worth noting that Irenaeus found his own proto-orthodox predecessors particularly inept in exposing Gnostics and removing them from their churches (*Adv. Haer.* IV, 2, Pref.).

24. As a rule, the heresiologists, beginning with Irenaeus, attacked the Gnostic systems as a whole by emphasizing the unity of the orthodox tradition versus the divisive doctrines of the Gnostics. For an accessible overview, see Vallée, *A Study in Anti-Gnostic Polemics,* 1–33.

25. See Pagels, *The Gnostic Paul,* 163, and Wisse, "The Nature and Purpose of Redactional Changes," 47. The frustration is evidenced, for example, by Tertullian, *Prescription,* 38.

26. Much of the following treatment is drawn from my article, "1 John 4.3 and the Orthodox Corruption of Scripture," slightly revised.

27. Only 1739^mg ar c dem div p vg, and the fathers discussed on pp. 128–30.

28. Except for two manuscripts that attempt to ameliorate the obvious difficulties of the grammar: 1898 (ὃ ἂν μὴ ὁμολογεῖ) and 242 (οὐκ ὁμολογεῖ).

29. The manuscripts that support this majority reading themselves diverge on several telling points, particularly with respect to the titles and descriptive phrases attached to the name Ἰησοῦν.

30. For a fuller list of scholars who support the reading, see Brown, *The Epistles of John*, 496.

31. As, for instance, Alfred Rahlfs ("Mitteilungen"), who concurs with von Harnack's vigorous support of λύει τὸν Ἰησοῦν as the more difficult reading ("Zur Textkritik und Christologie," 556–61), but sees confirmation of this view on the grammatical ground that μή is almost never used with the indicative in the New Testament.

32. Although the construction is not at all impossible (John 3:18 [!], 2 Pet 1:9, 1 Tim 6:3, Tit 1:11, and Acts 15:29 in MS D).

33. Contra R. Schnackenburg, *Die Johannesbriefe*, 222.

34. In this case ἀρνέομαι ("deny"), as in 1 John 2:22–23.

35. A word concerning the nature of this tradition would be in order here. It should not be supposed, as it might well be otherwise, that the Greek text of 1 John is some sort of monolith, so that its uniform attestation of a reading simply represents a single textual form to be compared with other textual forms, such as that represented by the Latin. In point of fact, the Greek manuscript tradition of 1 John is extremely complex, evidencing widespread corruption and cross-fertilization of textual groups. The complexity of this tradition has been demonstrated in William Larry Richards' classification of the Greek manuscripts of 1 John on the basis of their textual affinities (*The Classification of the Greek Manuscripts of the Johannine Epistles*). Richards was able to isolate three major groups of related manuscripts of 1 John, groups that divide themselves up into a total of fourteen subgroups, one of which comprises manuscripts of such complex textual relations as to defy classification altogether. What is striking for our purposes is that in the midst of this complicated nexus of widely variant texts and mixed texts, the reading πᾶν πνεῦμα ὃ μὴ ὁμολογεῖ τὸν Ἰησοῦν ἐκ τοῦ θεοῦ οὐκ ἔστιν at 1 John 4:3b is absolutely secure: it is not only the majority reading of all three divergent groups of manuscripts and of all fourteen subgroups, it is attested by every manuscript of every single group and subgroup.

36. Schnackenburg, for example, notes that μή with the indicative is out of the ordinary, but then goes on to say that μὴ ὁμολογεῖ τὸν Ἰησοῦν was mechanically created by scribal changes of the difficult reading (!) and then came to dominate the entire tradition (*Johannesbriefe*, 222). Similarly, see R. Bultmann, *Johannine Epistles*, 62.

37. Scholars cannot be allowed simply to bypass the historical issues raised by an absolute domination of one reading in the manuscript tradition of the New Testament, particularly when the reading is "difficult." Some critics, like von Harnack, seem content to trace readings as far back as possible into the tradition and, having established, say, that two readings both reach back into the second century, assume that the readings are thereby on equal footing in terms of their antiquity. Of course, this is not the case at all. Most variant readings can be traced back into the early centuries—but that does not mean that all readings are equally ancient. The historical question of how one reading dominated the text of the New Testament in later cen-

turies is also, in the present case, the question of how it came to dominate the text of the second century.

38. Richards, *Classification, passim.*

39. Von Harnack provided the most serious, if overly ingenious, solution to the problem of how μὴ ὁμολογεῖ τὸν Ἰησοῦν entered into the tradition if λύει τὸν Ἰησοῦν is original. For the shortcomings of von Harnack's theory, see Ehrman, "1 John 4:3," 226–27.

40. E.g. von Harnack, "Zur Textkritik." See also F. Büchsel, *Die Johannesbriefe,* 63.

41. See especially Zuntz, *The Text of the Epistles,* 68–86.

42. *Hist. Eccl.* VII, 32. Socrates claimed that the Nestorians changed the text of 1 John 4:3 because they "wanted to separate the man [Jesus] from God" (λύειν ἀπὸ τοῦ θεοῦ τὸν ἄνθρωπον θέλοντες).

43. *Adv. Haer.* III, 16, 8; *substantia:* III, 16, 5.

44. *Matt. Com.* 65. He quotes the more commonly attested wording in the *catena* on 1 Corinthians 12:3 and, significantly, seems to presuppose the wording μὴ ὁμολογεῖ in his comments. See C. Jenkins, "Origen on 1 Corinthians," 30. Origen also attests the traditional reading in *Exod. Hom.* 3, 2, where the context indicates that he is quoting 1 John rather than 2 John 7.

45. As previously noted, Origen's mentor, Clement, *may* have had the reading as well. This is evidenced not only in the scholion in manuscript 1739, but also by his discussion of the closely related 2 John 7. See the discussion of note 76.

46. This, at least, is the conclusion drawn by the editors of the *Vetus Latina* after an exhaustive study of all the evidence (W. Thiele, ed., *Vetus Latina* 26, 1, 330–31). In any case, it was not the reading known to Cyprian and is not found in the earliest Old Latin manuscript of 1 John, a manuscript that appears to stand alone among Old Latin manuscripts in withstanding contamination by the Vulgate at this point. Only six Old Latin manuscripts contain the passage: q (6–7th century), ar (9th century), p (9th century), div (13th century), c (12–13th century), and dem (13th century). Two of these simply preserve the Vulgate text of the Catholic epistles (ar div), whereas three preserve the Vulgate text with a greater or lesser smattering of Old Latin readings (p c dem). Only one manuscript—the earliest by two or three centuries—preserves a pre- (or non-) Vulgate text of the Catholic epistles to any great extent: manuscript q, which happens to support the reading μὴ ὁμολογεῖ in 1 John 4:3. See the discussion of these manuscripts in Bruce Metzger, *The Early Versions of the New Testament,* 285–322.

47. *Adv. Marc.* V, 16, 4; compare *Prescription* 23.

48. *Tract.* 1, 31, 3. The other reading is found in *Tract.* 2, 42, 4–5 and 2, 52, 27–29. For the debate over the Priscillian authorship of these tractates and a cogent defense of the traditional view, see Henry Chadwick, *Priscillian of Arila,* 62–69.

49. See the helpful synopsis of references provided *in loc.* by J. Wordsworth and H. J. White, *Novum Testamentum Domini Nostri Iesu Christi.*

50. Thus, the Latin translations of Irenaeus (*Adv. Haer.* III, 16, 1, 5, 8) and Clement of Alexandria (see note 76).

51. From two widely divergent points of view, see Büchsel, *Die Johannesbriefe,* 64, and I. Henry Marshall, *The Epistles of John,* 207–08.

52. For example, that of Otto Piper ("1 John and the Primitive Church"), who understood the phrase, in light of 1 Corinthians 12:3, to mean to "curse" Jesus so as to rob him of his supernatural power.

53. This way of wording the phrase fits into Brown's entire reconstruction of the secessionists' Christology. In his opinion, the secessionists do not deny Jesus' humanity per se, but only the salvific *significance* of that humanity; they therefore "nullify" or "negate" the importance of Jesus. For an evaluation of this view, see note 66. Other scholars who do not share this particular understanding of the secessionists' views, but who nonetheless subscribe to a similar rendering of λύει τὸν Ἰησοῦν as "annul Jesus," "nullify Jesus," or "render Jesus ineffectual," are Bultmann, *Johannine Epistles,* 62; Büchsel, *Die Johannesbriefe,* 64; and Schnackenburg, *Die Johannesbriefe,* 222.

54. I do not mean to retract the opinion I advanced in Chapter 1, that a word can "mean" anything a reader *wants* it to mean. The question I am raising here, however, is the more traditional one posed by exegetes and historical critics: if one speaks of "loosing" Jesus in Greek, how would these words normally be construed?

55. For example, Paul in Acts 20.30. See also John 11:44; Revelation 8:14, 15; 20:3, 7.

56. 1 Corinthians 7:27.

57. For example, Revelation 1:5 and, probably, Luke 13:16.

58. For example, *1 Clem.* 56:9 (quotation of Job 5:20); Ign. *Magn.* 12:1; Ign. *Smyrn.* 6:2. In addition, the term came to mean "releasing" the body from tension, that is, relaxing and "releasing" a person from this life: dying. See the listing in *LPGL* 817.

59. Tobit 3:17; Judith 6:14; Job 5:20; Psalms 101:20; 104:20; 145:7; Isaiah 14:17; Jeremiah 47:4; Daniel 3:25; 3 Maccabees 6:29.

60. I have not checked every solitary occurrence in every Greek author. But in addition to the New Testament, the LXX, and the Apostolic Fathers, I have checked every reference in the standard lexica (*LSJ,* BAGD, *LPGL*) and every occurrence of the term in Epictetus, Josephus, Philo, and the inscriptions currently available through the *Thesaurus Linguae Graecae.*

61. In particular, the discussion of docetic Christologies in Chapter 4.

62. The literature on this subject is extensive and adequate summaries can be found in the commentaries. See especially Brown, *Epistles,* 47–68. Several more recent attempts to understand the theology of the secessionists take different tacks and come to different conclusions. See, for example, Martinus C. de Boer, "Jesus the Baptizer: 1 John 5:5–8 and the Gospel of John," and J. Painter, "The 'Opponents' in 1 John."

63. It is widely recognized that the terms "Christ" and "Son of God" appear to be interchangable for this author (e.g., 3:23; 4:25; 5:1, 13). At the same time, it is *not* frequently enough recognized that in this christological confession it is the *subject,* not the predicate, that takes the article. This is therefore an identification formula that answers the question "*who* is the Christ (or the Son of God)?" On this grammatical point, see de Boer, "Jesus the Baptizer," who in turn depends on the comments of E. V. N. Goetchius, "Review of L. C. McGaughy."

64. Because the epistle's explicit polemics are always directed against this one christological notion, there is little reason to adopt Stephen Smalley's recent resuscitation of the view that the author is actually fighting on two fronts, one against the high Christology of proto-Gnostics and the other against the low Christology of Jewish Christians (*1, 2, and 3 John*). See my review of Smalley's commentary.

65. See below, p. 132.

66. As I earlier noted, Raymond Brown takes a different position, contending that the secessionists do not actually deny Christ's humanity but simply assert that it

has no salvific importance. For my part, I do not see how this position explains all the polemical emphases of the letter. The prologue, in particular, seems designed to show that the "Word that has been manifested" could be sensibly perceived: he could be seen, heard, and handled. What would be the point of this emphasis if it were not to counteract the claim of the secessionists that Jesus Christ was not fully human, a man of flesh? As I read this letter, the author does not emphasize merely that Jesus' death was salvifically important; he stresses *that* he died and in doing so shed real blood.

67. So Wengst, *Häresie und Orthodoxie*.

68. See his other criticisms as well. *Die Johannesbriefe*, 15–23.

69. See note 62. It will be seen that in other respects I do not agree with de Boer's reconstruction of the historical situation.

70. Wengst, *Häresie und Orthodoxie*, 24.

71. Again, given my understanding of how texts and meanings "work," I am not saying that the Fourth Gospel could not be *used* to support such a Christology. As anyone can see by perusing patristic exegesis, nearly any passage can be taken to support nearly any position, so long as a person *wants* it to, regardless of what it might "mean" when considered from the literal (i.e., the historico-grammatical) point of view. My point, however, is that Wengst is wrong to say that the traditions of the Fourth Gospel could naturally lead to the Cerinthian Christology. The Gospel of John is neither more nor less likely to do so than any *other* document that appears unrelated to the Cerinthian view.

72. See pp. 182–83.

73. I am taking these references as sarcastic uses of the opponents' own slogans: δαιμόνιον ἀσώματον (Ign. *Smyrn.* 3:2); ἀνθρωπομόρφων (Ign. *Smyrn.* 4:1).

74. Is it conceivable that the secessionists would have moved so far from the original beliefs of the Johannine community? Given the high Christology embedded in the later traditions of the Gospel of John, it is not difficult to see how further developments toward a non-human Jesus could have occurred very soon within this community. Indeed, the Gospel of John itself is sometimes read as naively docetic in its portrayal of Jesus (see especially Ernst Käsemann, *The Testament of Jesus: A Study of the Gospel of John in the Light of Chapter 17*). If modern scholars with all the critical tools at their disposal can read the Gospel this way, it would be no surprise to find that earlier, less critical readers saw the Jesus of these traditions in a similar light.

75. The ellipsis is to be supplied from verse 2.

76. As I have previously noted, Clement never cited 1 John 4:3 in any of his surviving works. But in fragments preserved in the Latin translation of Commodius, he did cite 2 John 7 *(ut . . . unum credat Iesum Christum venisse in carne)* as the scriptural opposition to false teachers who are said to "divide Jesus Christ" *(dividat Iesum Christum)*. Some have inferred from this that Clement knew of the reading λύει τὸν Ἰησοῦν from his Greek manuscripts of 1 John. But the reference could just as easily suggest that Clement understood that "failing to confess Jesus Christ come in the flesh" involved "dividing" Jesus. Or to put the matter in the proper chronological sequence, when Clement was confronted with "heretics" who posited a "separation" in Christ, he claimed that they had failed to "confess Jesus Christ come in the flesh" and simply quoted the biblical text against them. It is just this kind of simple equation of the text with contemporary christological problems that then led to the incorporation of the variant reading into the margin of a manuscript and from there into the text itself. On this, see below, pp.134–35.

77. ὁ μὴ ὢν μετ᾽ ἐμοῦ κατ᾽ ἐμοῦ ἐστιν, καὶ ὁ μὴ συνάγων μετ᾽ ἐμοῦ σκορπίζει. The text is identical in Matthew and Luke.

78. In Matthew the longer text occurs in ℵ 33 bo syr^(h(mg)) Or Ath; in Luke in ℵ* C' L Θ Ψ 33 892 1071 syr^s bo^mss.

79. Metzger, *Textual Commentary,* 32 (Matthew) and 158 (Luke). So too, for example, Marshall, *Commentary on Luke,* 428.

80. Metzger, *Textual Commentary,* 32, 158.

81. It is to be remembered that, according to Irenaeus, the Valentinians espoused three different Christs: one that helped restore order to the Pleroma after the fall of Sophia, one that represented the combined attributes of all the other aeons, and one that was created by the Demiurge into whom the second entered at his baptism.

82. It comes as no surprise that this *varia lectio* made particular inroads into the copies of the New Testament produced and preserved in Alexandria, one of the bastions of Gnostic Christianity, where orthodox scribes were constantly confronted by the claims of their heretical opponents. Not only several Alexandrian manuscripts, but also Alexandrian fathers of the stature of Origen and Athanasius attest the corruption. Its prevalence in these circles must mean that it crept into the text at a relatively early date, certainly before Origen's literary output at the beginning of the third century, and that it continued to affect the text there long after the Gnostic threat had passed into the annals of orthodox history.

83. The change is facilitated by the use of the *nomina sacra,* so that it involves simply the substitution of IY for XY. On the common exchange of names, see the discussion below, pp. 161–63.

84. See note 81.

85. The evidence itself goes back to the fourth century in the Latin West, and there is every good reason to believe that the variant attested at that time was actually generated earlier, that it had Greek precedents in the East. The historical *Sitz im Leben* that would make sense of this substitution of names, therefore, appears to coincide with its provenance.

86. Although the variant in John 1:13, which I discussed under the rubric of anti-adoptionist corruptions, could also function to counter a Valentinian Christology. As has been seen, the reading is used by Tertullian to argue that Jesus, though himself divine, was actually born with real flesh. See Chapter 2, note 72.

87. See also, however, the corruptions involving γεννάω that are discussed in Chapter 4, pp. 238–39.

88. See above, pp. 58–59.

89. Not only did Tertullian eliminate the participial clause, he removed the name Jesus as well, thereby heightening the usefulness of the text for the orthodox cause. It will be noted that I am suggesting a slightly different motivation for the change than Tertullian's evidence, taken in isolation, might suggest. He used the verse to show that Christ was actually born of Mary and therefore had real flesh; the corruption, though, may have functioned originally to emphasize that the birth of Jesus was itself the birth of Christ. For a corruption that clearly does evidence some of Tertullian's concerns here, see the discussion of Luke 1:35, pp. 139–40.

90. See the discussion on Matthew 1:18, pp. 137–38.

91. That the same phrase was not also changed in 27:17 gives no occasion for surprise: we have already seen the sporadic nature of this kind of variation. Moreover, the latter occurrence appears on the lips of Pilate, who indeed does *not* understand that Jesus really is the Christ, as opposed to the narrator of 1:16, who does. In this sense, the pattern of attestation resembles what we found earlier with respect to affir-

mations of Jesus' miraculous birth: when unbelievers called Joseph Jesus' father the text was almost invariably left intact, when the evangelist did, it was commonly changed. See the discussion on pp. 55–58.

92. On the textual problem of γένεσις / γέννησις see pp. 75–76.

93. It is striking, however, that W and its allies here preserve precisely the text that Irenaeus claims might have been useful to Gnostics had it existed ("the birth of Jesus"). But the reading appears to have come from a shortening of the majority text ("the birth of Jesus Christ"), made in view of verse 17 ("from whom was born Jesus . . .") and 2:1 ("when Jesus was born . . ."). The text of codex Vaticanus not only lacks other documentary support, but appears to be a simple inversion of the majority reading "Jesus Christ" to "Christ Jesus," a sequence common in Paul but found nowhere in the Gospels.

94. A possibility considered by Metzger, *Textual Commentary*, 7.

95. Most cogently by Zahn, *Das Evangelium des Matthäus*, 66–67.

96. The strongest internal argument against the longer text is the observation that Ἰησοῦ Χριστοῦ normally lacks the article in the New Testament. See Brown, *The Birth of the Messiah*, 123; Dale Allison and W. D. Davies, *A Critical and Exegetical Commentary on the Gospel according to Matthew* 1.198, n. 3; and, with reservations, Metzger, *Textual Commentary*, 7. Against this it should be noted that the wording of the entire clause is peculiar. Perhaps the best way to resolve the problems of both sequence and terminology is to observe that the clause provides the transition between the genealogy of verses 2–17 and the birth narrative of verses 18–25. The article, then, serves as a weak relative whose antecedent is the subject of the preceding pericope (Ἰησοῦ Χριστοῦ, v. 1).

97. As is evident in the Gnostic literature itself, for example, the *Gospel of Philip*, 62, and is implicit throughout Irenaeus's own discussion. See, for example, *Adv. Haer.* III, 16, 6.

98. That the name Jesus Christ could perform a similar anti-separationist function is evident in the modifications of Matthew 2:1 attested elsewhere in the tradition. In several late manuscripts the statement that "Jesus was born in Bethlehem" has been changed to "Jesus Christ was born in Bethlehem."

99. It is scarcely mentioned, for example, by Fitzmyer, *Gospel According to Luke*, I. 351, and Marshall, *Commentary on Luke*, 71. See Metzger, *Textual Commentary*, 129–30.

100. So, for example, Westcott and Hort, *The New Testament in the Original Greek*, II. Appendix, 52; Marshall, *Commentary on Luke*, 71; Metzger, *Textual Commentary*, 129–30.

101. Brown, *Birth of the Messiah*, 291.

102. Similarly, Tertullian mocked the Valentinian Christ, "whose position must be decided by prepositions; in other words, [Christ] was produced *by means of* a virgin, rather than *of* a virgin! On the ground that, having descended into the virgin rather in the manner of a passage through her than of a birth by her, he came into existence *through* her, not *of* her—not experiencing a mother in her, but nothing more than a way" (*Adv. Val.* 27).

103. That the corruption may also reflect the orthodox controversy with a docetic Christology may be suggested by the quotation of the longer form of the text by Tertullian in an attempt to demonstrate to Marcion that Christ entered into the world by being born, not as a full-grown adult (*Adv. Marc.* IV, 7).

104. We do well to recall that Gnostics were notorious among the orthodox for overlooking the "straightforward" meaning of the words of the biblical text (straight-

forward, that is, to the orthodox). Among other things, this means that even were a scribe to make such a corruption in light of the heretical position, the Gnostics (at least according to the heresiologists) would have remained undisturbed, because for them the words of the text were ultimately unimportant on the literal level. We should not be taken aback, then, to find that among the witnesses to the longer text of Luke 1:35 is Valentinus himself, if we can trust that Hippolytus faithfully reproduced his source in *Ref* 6:30. Given what we know about the Gnostic appropriation of the New Testament text, we can assume that Valentinus simply used whatever manuscripts were available to him in the churches.

105. See the groups named in note 5.

106. John's Gospel does not describe the scene itself, but simply the Baptist's recollection of what he saw (1:32–34).

107. Here I do not go into the full history of interpretation of the Spirit as a dove at Jesus' baptism. Among the many studies, see especially W. Telfer, "The Form of a Dove," and Leander Keck, "The Spirit and the Dove."

108. For a briefer discussion of this problem, see my article "The Text of Mark in the Hands of the Orthodox."

109. A gauge of this consensus: the variant reading is neither cited in UBSGNT[3] nor discussed in Metzger's *Textual Commentary.*

110. The addition of καὶ μένον in ℵ (W) 33 OL bo^mss al is a clear harmonization to John 1:33, and is of no concern here.

111. That they did so independently of one another has been plausibly argued, for example, by Allison and Davies, *Gospel According to Saint Matthew,* I, 334; but this is an issue relevant more to discussions of Synoptic relationships than to my textual concerns.

112. The reading is readily datable to the second century in view of its diverse and widespread attestation. Not only is it found in the bulk of surviving Greek manuscripts, it is also the reading of the fourth-century codex Sinaiticus, of the early Syriac, and of almost all the Latin evidence.

113. See further the discussion of Bauer, *Das Leben Jesu,* 118–19.

114. Manuscripts C, E, and several others. The change in codex Bezae to εἰς can only be seen as a harmonization to Mark (there is scant trace of any adoptionistic corruptions in Bezae otherwise). Interestingly, Irenaeus uses the Matthean text specifically to show that "Christ did not at that time descend upon Jesus, neither was Christ one and Jesus another" (*Adv. Haer.* III, 9, 3).

115. So BAGD, 905; see also W. D. Davies, *Jewish and Pauline Studies,* p. 378, n. 60.

116. See *LSJ ad loc.*

117. *Adv. Haer.* I, 14, 6. That they understood the Spirit to have actually assumed the form of a dove is suggested in I, 15, 3.

118. Following ancient methods of calculating the numerical significance of words and names, premised on the use of the alphabet for numerals in Greek. Thus in περιστερά, the π is worth eighty, the ε five, and so forth. See Bruce Metzger, *Manuscripts of the Greek Bible: An Introduction to Palaeography,* 7–9.

119. Irenaeus's scorn notwithstanding, we would be ill-advised to see in this kind of exegesis anything but a serious attempt at doing theology. See the similar argument of Ps-Tertullian, *Adv. Omn. Haer.* 5, in reliance upon Irenaeus.

120. Irenaeus does mention other groups that speak explicitly of the dove descending upon Jesus, whereas his position is that it was the Spirit that came to him "as a dove." Contrast *Adv. Haer.* I, 7, 2 with III, 17, 1.

121. Manuscripts M P and a number of Byzantine witnesses in Mark; A Θ Ψ f[1.13] and the entire Byzantine tradition in Luke.

122. For the orthodox, this verse also proved an important weapon in the dispute with Patripassianists, because it appears to differentiate so clearly between the Son and the Father who had forsaken him. So Tertullian, *Adv. Prax.* 25, 27.

123. Epiphanius, *Pan.* 26, 13, 2.

124. *Gospel of Philip* 68. The translation is by Wesley W. Isenberg, in Robinson, *The Nag Hammadi Library in English*, 2nd edition, 141; in the 3rd edition, Isenberg renders the final clause "for he had departed from that place," a change in nuance, but equally applicable to this discussion.

125. Although some scholars have argued that the narration of this Gospel in fact antedates canonical Mark (for example, John Dominic Crossan, *The Cross that Spoke: The Origins of the Passion Narrative*), the balance of evidence suggests a second-century provenance. See especially Raymond Brown, "The *Gospel of Peter* and Canonical Authority." Other recent discussions can be found in Helmut Koester, *Ancient Christian Gospels: Their History and Development*, 216–40, and Christian Maurer and Wilhelm Schneemelcher, in Hennecke-Schneemelcher, *Neutestamentliche Apocryphen* I. 180–88.

126. Eusebius, *Hist. Eccl.* VI, 12. There are other indications of a heretical Christology in the fragments of the *Gospel of Peter* that are extant. It claims, for example, that Jesus was silent on the cross "as if he felt no pain," a statement sometimes understood as docetic. For a discussion of the relevant texts from a different perspective, see Jerry McCant, "The Gospel of Peter: Docetism Reconsidered." McCant's major objective is to show that the *Gospel of Peter* can be understood without assuming a separationist Christology because it mentions neither a distinction between "Jesus" and "Christ" (names that do not even occur in the fragment that survives) nor Jesus' baptism. Regrettably, McCant confuses phantasmal Christologies (which I have argued are properly labeled docetic) with separationist (which he terms "Cerinthian"). A more significant weakness in McCant's position, in my judgment, is evident when he admits that he does not see (given his construal) what Serapion might have found objectionable in the surviving fragment. The puzzle, however, is readily solved when the text is read through the lenses provided by the polemical concerns of Serapion's day, rather than simply in light of the Synoptics and the Old Testament (McCant's own approach to construing the text). We know that Serapion found the document objectionable for its heretical Christology and that Gnostic groups were maligned by orthodox leaders for their separationist views. Yet more significantly, we know that the "cry of dereliction" figured prominently in this controversy. Thus, because the *Gospel of Peter* makes considerable sense when read in light of a Cerinthian Christology, the traditional construal of its text retains its heuristic force.

127. Von Harnack, "Probleme im Texte der Leidengeschichte Jesu."

128. For a briefer discussion of the variant, see my article, "The Text of Mark in the Hands of the Orthodox."

129. A number of scholars have argued that the change in the Western text actually represents a misunderstanding of the Hebrew word σαβαχθανι by a scribe who mistook it as a transliteration of זעפחני, "revile." See M. -J. Lagrange, *Évangile selon Saint Marc*, 9th ed. (Paris: J. Gabalda, 1966) 433 and the literature cited there. Since Mark is the one who actually quotes the Aramaic text, however, it is unlikely that such a misunderstanding can be assigned to him (he knew which word he quoted).

130. Namely, that scribes could not abide the notion of God "mocking" Jesus.

In fact, the notion is not so difficult to construe, given the dominant influence of the Suffering Servant songs of 2 Isaiah on the developing notions of atonement.

131. At least Irenaeus did, the only one who bothered to mention the fact (*Adv. Haer.* III, 11, 7).

132. Along with the corrector of the eleventh-century manuscript 424.

133. See Zuntz, *Text of the Epistles* 69, ". . . 1739 represents a manuscript comparable, in age and quality, to 𝔓⁴⁶." See his discussion on pp. 69–84, 153–56.

134. *Jn. Com.* 1.35; 28.18; 32.28.

135. Including Eusebius, Ambrosiaster, Ambrose, Theodore of Mopsuestia, Theodoret, Vigilius, Fulgentius, Anastasius-Abbot, Ps-Oecumenius, and Theophylact.

136. See the discussion on "intentionality" in Chapter 1, pp. 28–31.

137. See, for example, F. F. Bruce, *The Epistle to the Hebrews*, 32, n. 15 and the literature he cites there.

138. "When Jesus was Apart from God: An Examination of Hebrews 2:9," 339.

139. See especially von Harnack, "Zwei alte dogmatische Korrekturen im Hebräerbrief."

140. Alluding, perhaps, to a tradition not recorded in the canonical Gospel traditions. See the discussion of Harold W. Attridge, *The Epistle to the Hebrews*, 148–52. The text does indicate that he was "heard" because of his piety, but this does not mean that God intervened on his behalf. It means that God, the one "who was able to save him from death," did so by raising him from the dead after he had experienced his human passion. Misconstruing the sense, von Harnack found an incompatibility between Hebrews 2:9 and 5:7, leading to his famous emendation of the latter in which he supplied the negative οὐκ, so that Jesus "was *not* heard. . . ." See von Harnack "Zwei alten dogmatische Korrekturen."

141. According to 13:12, Jesus died "outside the gate," a statement often understood as a historical recollection of the place of Jesus' crucifixion. It is perhaps better, given the other emphases of Hebrews, to interpret it symbolically as referring to Jesus' death in the realm of shame and reproach, beyond the purview of God's special favor, outside the city that stands under God's protection.

142. The passage is based, of course, on a christological interpretation of Psalm 2. For a more detailed exposition, see Attridge, *Epistle to the Hebrews*, 69–102.

143. As Elliott has pointed out, this theology of Christ's passion appears to be rooted in Old Testament notions of death as representing a force that is opposed to God, or an entity removed from God: "In death there is no remembrance of you" (Ps 6:5). It is at least conceivable that the author has Psalm 22 specifically in mind: "My God, my God, why have you forsaken me?" It should not be overlooked that he does cite the Psalm explicitly in the immediate context (v. 12).

144. *Text of the Epistles*, 43–45.

145. On the hymnic character of the passage, see Attridge, *Epistle to the Hebrews*, 41, and the literature he cites there.

146. On another variant, see p. 96.

147. It will be noted that 𝔓⁴⁶, along with codex Bezae and 365, attests the alternative form of the reflexive, δι' αὑτου rather than δι' ἑαυτοῦ, which is thus not to be construed as the personal pronoun (αὑτοῦ). Zuntz, *Text of the Epistles*, 43–45.

148. So Zuntz, *Text of the Epistles*, 44, with reference to Polybius and Epictetus, noting a particularly apt parallel in Polybius's description of Hieron, king of Syracuse (VII. 8. 2): καὶ μὴν οὐκ ἀποκτείνας, οὐ φυγαδεύσας, οὐ λυπήσας οὐδένα τῶν πολιτῶν, δι' αὑτοῦ βασιλεὺς κατέστη τῶν Συρακοσίων.

149. Depending, that is, on which form of the reflexive they read.

150. Indeed, there is some evidence to suggest that prior to Irenaeus it was the Gnostics more than the proto-orthodox who claimed Paul as their own apostle. See especially Pagels, *The Gnostic Paul*, 1–13.

151. As happens in ℵ A C F G L Ψ 33 81 OL cop^bo.

152. Again, I stress that rhetorical effectiveness is not the issue; a Gnostic could well consider this material world the place "of the dead," so that Christ's exaltation could be described as a resurrection from the dead. See further, note 104.

153. This tendency cannot be used to argue for the originality of "Jesus Christ" in Romans 8:34 because of the specific grammar of the verse; if "Christ" were found alone in the text there, it could be taken to mean precisely that he did *not* die (see the discussion on pp. 151–52). Among other things, this simply confirms that the orthodox scribes did not take any kind of rigid or mechanical approach to modifying their texts, so that each instance needs to be decided on the basis of its own merits.

154. Other witnesses read "the blood of his son" (1243 and one Vg manuscript) or "the blood of Jesus Christ" (i.e., omit "his Son"; pc Cass).

155. The reading is not mentioned in UBSGNT[3] or Metzger's *Textual Commentary*.

156. G 039 124 230 262 syr^c al. The Syriac repeats "Behold" before each title.

157. The variant was evidently unknown to Irenaeus, who speaks of the text in reference to Christ, without however citing any expressed subject ("From that time he began . . ."; so too ℵ^c 892 pc). He cites the text, then, precisely in order to show what the variant makes more certain, that "Christ" is the one who suffered (*Adv. Haer.* III, 18, 4).

158. Rarely in Luke, but in both Greek and Latin manuscripts (X 131 g² l); more frequently in Mark (W X Δ Θ f^13 33 565 700 892 cop goth arm eth geo al).

159. Here I might emphasize that by the second century, proto-orthodox Christians could speak of "Christ's" passion almost by theological instinct, so that there is no need to posit any special "intentionality" about these changes. This orthodox reflex in itself, however, should give us pause, as it attests the importance of the proto-orthodox emphasis on Christ's real passion. Certainly those disinclined to stress (or even affirm) this passion would not be expected to create textual modifications of this kind. For this reason, where such changes do occur, as slight and natural as they might appear, they can well be classified as orthodox corruptions.

160. Tertullian, *de resur.* 44, referring to this text, speaks of the "death of Jesus Christ," in order to show that Christ had real flesh like the rest of humanity. The same form of the text occurs in D^c pc. Other modifications speak of the "death of the Lord Jesus Christ."

161. As might be imagined, the Institution narrative proved important to the orthodox opposition to docetists as well. See Tertullian's sardonic treatment in *Adv. Marc.* IV, 40. On a significant corruption of the Lukan account, see the discussion in Chapter 4, pp. 198–209.

162. See note 159. Examples of this kind of corruption could easily be multiplied. One of particular interest is Galatians 6:17, where Paul speaks of bearing the "stigmata of Jesus" in his body. As might be expected, some scribes have modified the text to speak of the "stigmata of Christ" (P Ψ 81 365 1175 2464 pc) or of "the stigmata of our Lord Jesus Christ" (ℵ D* F G it).

163. And perhaps in 4:1 with codex Sinaiticus alone.

164. Compare, for example, the Valentinian notion that Jesus' apparent sufferings on earth were allegorical reflections of the catastrophic passions of Sophia within the Pleroma (Irenaeus, *Adv. Haer.* I, 8, 2).

165. The orthodox emphasis on the resurrection of Jesus, of course, relates to broader soteriological issues in the Gnostic controversies. As we have seen, the Gnostics claimed that deliverance was to come *from* the body, the material part of the human that imprisons the spirit. Naturally they would not stress that Christ's own body was raised immortal. The orthodox urged just to the contrary that salvation was *of* the body, that the God who had created the body would also redeem it. For them, Christ's raised body was the first fruits of the resurrection of all people, a bodily resurrection anticipating the physical redemption of the world. In Irenaeus's words, "The Lord observed the law of the dead, that he might become the first-begotten from the dead, and tarried until the third day 'in the lower parts of the earth'; then afterwards rising in the flesh, so that he even showed the print of the nails to his disciples, he thus ascended to the Father" (V, 31, 2).

166. On the conflict between the orthodox and Gnostic views of the resurrection, see Pagels, "Gnostic and Orthodox Views of Christ's Passion." Compare also the discussion of docetic interpretations of the resurrection in Chapter 4.

167. As has already been seen with respect to Romans 8:34. See pp. 151–52.

168. That the similar expression in Acts 2:32 was not similarly changed in the tradition (so far as we know) may be due to the lack of ambiguity in the context; verse 31 speaks of the "resurrection of Christ" (περὶ τῆς ἀναστάσεως τοῦ Χριστοῦ), which is picked up by the demonstrative of verse 32, "*This* Jesus, God raised" (τοῦτον τὸν Ἰησοῦν ἀνέστησεν ὁ θεός).

169. With an inversion of words in codex Vaticanus that is immaterial for the present consideration: τοῦ κυρίου Ἰησοῦ τῆς ἀναστάσεως.

170. P Ψ 049 956 0142 88 cop^sa syr^h gig Byz al.

171. Surely some of the later scribes added a reference to Χριστός to the text because it seemed natural to do so. As I have argued before, however, the change would have seemed "natural" *only* because by the time these scribes had begun to engage in their labors, to talk of the resurrection of "Jesus Christ" was less exceptional than to speak simply of the resurrection of Jesus. This is one of the legacies the early proto-orthodox Christians bestowed upon their posterity. It was, nonetheless, a legacy acquired through long and hard battles with groups of Gnostic Christians who could admit the exaltation of Christ and the resurrection of Jesus, but scarcely the resurrection of Jesus Christ (at least as understood by the orthodox).

172. Joel Marcus has pointed out to me that the change is provided an additional kind of plausibility by the description in Psalm 2 of the Davidic king as the Lord's "anointed" (χριστός).

173. Or so Irenaeus thought (*Adv. Haer.* III, 16, 9). One can see from the context of his arguments that his opponents did not agree.

174. So UBSGNT[3]. In this the Valentinians agree with ℵ* A B C D 81 1739 al against ℵ^c K P Ψ 33 88 181 2495 Byz al.

175. As was seen, for example, with respect to Matthew 1:18, pp. 137–38. For other aspects of their interpretation of the verse, see Pagels, *The Gnostic Paul*, 34.

176. It is to be noted that Hippolytus used this corrupted form to show that there is a distinction between God the Father and God the Son, because one performed the act of raising upon the other (*Adv. Noet.* 4); Tertullian uses the more common form of the text to the same end (*Adv. Prax.* 28), as well as to show Marcion that Christ, as one who was raised from the dead, had a real body (*Adv. Marc.* V, 14).

177. There is nothing (such as homoeoteleuton) to suggest an accidental omission.

178. Similarly, in the longer ending of Mark, Jesus upbraids his disciples for not believing those who had acknowledged that "he had been raised." A corruption of this secondary ending entered the tradition rather early (as evidenced by its attestation in such witnesses as A C* Δ f[1. 13] 33 565 892 1241). Here Jesus is acknowledged again as having "been raised from the dead."

179. *Contra* Metzger, *Textual Commentary,* 71–72.

180. ℵ B D L 33 a aur b c d e f ff[1. 2] g[1] b l n vg syr[pal ms].

181. Again, the language of "intention" is used advisedly; see especially my comments in note 159 concerning the "natural" tendencies of proto-orthodox scribes to emphasize their Christology in texts that speak of "Christ's" death. *Mutatis mutandi,* the same can be said of corruptions that refer to his resurrection.

182. Orthodox corruptions that emphasize the notion of Christ's parousia will be dealt with in the following chapter, as these appear to emphasize more his real contact with the realm of flesh and blood than his unity within himself.

183. Manuscripts B L W Θ f[1] 33 565 syr[h] cop[bo] arm eth geo al. To be sure, the change reflects a harmonization with the parallel account in Luke. But here, as always, one must ask what drove scribes to create the harmonization. We cannot simply assume that it was a harmonization for harmonization's sake. The widespread attestation of the corruption demonstrates that it originated in the period of our concern. Moreover, we know that proto-orthodox Christians of this period acknowledged Mark as the Gospel of choice among those who differentiated between Jesus and the Christ. Given the serviceability of the harmonized text in attacking separationist Christologies, one must consider it at least plausible that the text was changed in light of this historical context. Of some interest here is the fact that in some of the corrupted witnesses, including the earliest among the Alexandrians (MS C), the change does not bring the text into harmony with its Lukan counterpart but emphasizes yet more strongly the orthodox point, that Jesus "was the Christ himself" (τὸν Χριστὸν αὐτὸν εἶναι). It appears that the change can be attributed to the theological propensities of scribes.

184. αὐτός ἐστιν Ἰησοῦς ὁ Χριστός; ℵ[2] C [D] W Byz OL syr[h] cop[sa ms. bo] al.

185. πιστεύω τὸν υἱὸν τοῦ θεοῦ εἶναι τὸν Ἰησοῦν Χριστόν; attested with numerous variations in 88[c] 630 945 1739 1877 c l (m) r gig syr[h] arm geo and fathers as early as Irenaeus and Tertullian.

186. If the variant were an assimilation to Mark 15:39, one would expect the adverb to be interpolated before the pronoun, rather than after the verb.

187. I should observe that a similar addition of the article occurs in the eighth century Alexandrian manuscript L of John 1:1, so that the text now reads ὁ θεὸς ἦν ὁ λόγος—making it clear that the Word actually was God himself (not simply divine). I am somewhat reluctant to exclude this singular reading from consideration here, but am nonetheless under the distinct impression that it derives from the later Arian controversies. At the same time, it is worth pointing out that Origen already used the *absence* of the article in John 1:1 to demonstrate Christ's subordination to God (*Jn. Com* 2.2.17–18).

188. See p. 154.

189. MSS D F G al, including, interestingly, Irenaeus in a polemical context (*Adv. Haer.* V, 13, 4).

190. *The Theological Tendency of Codex Bezae,* 61–63, in partial reliance on P. H. Menoud, "The Western Text and the Theology of Acts."

191. As can be seen in the examples I cite below.

192. Moreover, even if a social context for this polemic can be located, one must

still wonder whether the title "our Lord Jesus Christ" actually suggests a more strongly anti-Jewish position than any other string of appellations.

193. That is, τοῦ ᾿Ιησοῦ becomes τοῦ κυρίου ᾿Ιησοῦ.

194. υἱὲ Δαυίδ becomes κύριε υἱὲ Δαυίδ in manuscripts N f¹³ 892ᶜ.

195. Where ῥαββουνί becomes κύριε ῥαββουνί, D OL.

196. δέ becomes δὲ ὁ κύριος in syrᶜ.

197. Where κύριε, ἐλέησον ἡμᾶς, υἱὸς Δαυίδ becomes κύριε, ἐλέησον ἡμᾶς, ᾿Ιησοῦ υἱὲ Δαυίδ in L 892 copᵇᵒ ˢᵃ ᵐˢˢ pc.

198. See note 162.

199. D E 614 945 1739 1891 r (p) syr al.

200. C 61 90 181 322 323 326 464 pc.

201. See Chapter 1, pp. 17–22, especially pp. 18–19.

4

Anti-Docetic Corruptions of Scripture

Introduction: Docetic Christologies in Early Christianity

Although adoptionism could rightly claim the oldest pedigree among christological heresies, the representatives of docetism proved far more pestiferous
for the second- and third-century defenders of orthodoxy.[1] As we have seen,
the term docetism derives from the Greek δοκεῖν, meaning "to seem" or "to
appear," and is normally used to designate Christologies that deny the reality
of Christ's fleshly existence. According to these views, Christ only "seemed"
or "appeared" to be human and to experience suffering.[2] In a general way,
of course, the separationist Christologies we have already examined could be
said to fit this description since they claimed that the divine Christ, contrary
to appearances, departed from Jesus prior to his crucifixion. There has consequently been no shortage of scholars who have chosen to label this Gnostic
view docetic.[3] For our purposes, however, it is better to maintain the distinction, sometimes drawn by the orthodox polemicists themselves, between separationist Christologies, which saw Jesus and the Christ as distinct entities,
and docetism, which argued that the one (indivisible) Jesus Christ was completely and absolutely divine, and for that reason not a real flesh and blood
human being.[4] According to this view, Jesus Christ was a phantom, human
in appearance only.

Docetism was not the view of one particular social group, but a christological tendency that characterized several groups, some of them unrelated.[5]
As already seen, the tendency was in evidence among some members of the
Johannine community, the secessionists denounced by the author of 1 John
near the end of the first century.[6] Several decades later, the church of Rome
expelled Marcion of Pontus from their fellowship, in part for advancing a
similar view. There is no trace of a historical connection between Marcion
and the opponents of 1 John. In the intervening years, between the aspersions
of the Johannine secessionists and the castigation of Marcion, stands the sharp
polemic of Ignatius, directed in no small measure against heretics of Asia
Minor who maintained that Christ only "appeared" to be a human and to
suffer. The latter group may well have been connected with certain Gnostics
denounced by Irenaeus some seventy years later, heretics whose Christology
moved along docetic rather than separationist lines.

181

Examining these various expressions of docetism will enable us to uncover their common characteristics, at least as these were perceived by the
orthodox polemicists. As we shall see, the debates that ensued played a significant role in the transcription of Scripture, as scribes altered their sacred
texts in order to highlight the proto-orthodox belief that Jesus Christ was a
flesh and blood human being who shed real blood and experienced real death
for the salvation of the world.

Docetism among the Johannine Secessionists and the Opponents of Ignatius

I have already discussed the Johannine secessionists at some length and do
not need to repeat my analysis here.[7] In seeking to understand the secessionists' Christology, however, it may prove useful to reflect on the sociohistorical factors that influenced its genesis. The matter is complex, and here I can
do no more than sketch the views that have come to constitute a fair consensus among Johannine scholars.[8]

Whether or not the Fourth Gospel is itself "naively docetic"—the controversial claim of Ernst Käsemann—there is no real doubt that it preserves an
understanding of Jesus that is distinctive among the canonical Gospels and
that this understanding elevates his divine character.[9] Furthermore, there are
reasons for thinking that this heightened Christology was linked to particular
historical and social conditions of the Johannine community, that is, that it
was not a purely theological development (if such a thing indeed could be
imagined). More specifically, it appears that the Johannine community originally comprised a group of Jews who worshipped in a local synagogue, even
after having come to believe in Jesus as the Messiah. At some point in its
history, prior to the penning of the Fourth Gospel, the group's new set of
beliefs created friction with nonbelievers among the Jews. The resulting tensions eventuated in a permanent estrangement: those who believed that Jesus
was the Christ were "cast out of the synagogue" (ἀποσυνάγωγος, John 9:22).
More or less in exile, these estranged Christians formed their own insular
community. As a consequence, their theological views developed within a
context of rejection and exclusion. One result was a Christology that accounted for the repudiation of the Christian message by Jews outside the
group. Why had "the Jews" not accepted the message of Jesus? In the thinking of the estranged party, it was because those who were accustomed to
darkness could not see the light; those who belonged to *this* world could not
recognize the one who came from the world above, the world of God. As the
Christology of the community developed, Jesus came to be portrayed not
simply as a Jewish rabbi, or as the Jewish Messiah, or even as the Savior of
the world. To be sure, he was all these things, but he was also much more.
He was the one who came from God, the very Word of God made flesh, who
always existed with God and was equal with him (e.g., 1:1–14; 8:58; 10:30;
20:28), who had come to call his own out of this world by revealing to them
the truth of God that could set them free (e.g., 8:31–32; 14:1–11). At the

same time, the identity of this one sent from God was not public knowledge; only those who had experienced a birth from the world above could recognize him and the truth of his message, and thereby receive the salvation that he had brought (cf. 3:3, 5).

The christological notions embodied in the Gospel of John, then, developed over a period of time and represent reflections inspired by the internal struggles of an ostracized Christian community. Moreover, neither the community's history nor its theological reflections came to a standstill with the completion of the Gospel. To the contrary, as Raymond Brown, in particular, has shown, it was precisely such views as are encapsulated in the Fourth Gospel that led to the secession from the community that we have already discussed.[10] Some members of the group took the community's high Christology to an extreme deemed inappropriate by others. And so, sometime prior to the writing of 1 John, the community again split over christological issues, with the "extremists" (in the view of the author of 1 John) leaving the community to form a group of their own (2:18–19). In the preceding chapter I argued that the Christology of these secessionists was in fact docetic,[11] that they claimed that Jesus, the Savior from above, was so much the equal of God that he could not have been manifest in the flesh in any real sense (he only "appeared" to be fleshly) and that, as a consequence, he did not actually shed blood (he only "appeared" to suffer). Against these secessionist claims, the author of 1 John argued that Christ really did come in the flesh (4:2–3), that he could be sensibly perceived (1:1–4), that he shed blood (5:6), and that it was this shed blood alone that effected a right standing before God (1:7; 2:2; 4:10).

As we have also seen, the position embraced by this author, and presumably by his community as well, finds a close parallel in the writings of Ignatius, particularly in his opposition to the heretics of Smyrna and Tralles.[12] It is difficult to determine the historical relationship of these two groups; there is simply no way to know, for instance, whether the secessionists from the Johannine community (in Antioch? in Ephesus?) either founded or encouraged the heretical movements that Ignatius attacked in Asia Minor on his road to martyrdom. But given the remarkable similarities between the polemics of 1 John and Ignatius, similarities that extend beyond basic conceptualizations to the terminology itself,[13] one can be reasonably certain that if the groups under attack were not linked socially or historically, they at least represented comparable ideological developments and evoked comparable responses from proto-orthodox opponents.[14]

In sum, by the beginning of the second century, proto-orthodox Christians actively engaged in polemics against docetic types of Christology. The orthodox view stressed that Jesus Christ really was a man; that he really was born and really did suffer, shed blood, and die; and that this passion proved salvifically efficacious. This emphasis on the true humanity and suffering of Jesus became the hallmark of the orthodox opposition to docetism throughout the second and third centuries.[15]

Docetism among the Gnostics

Although Ignatius does not call his opponents Gnostic, most scholars have concluded that this is what they were.[16] As I have indicated, docetism was one of two major possibilities for Gnostic Christians who wanted to maintain that Christ brought redemption into the world without himself actually belonging to it. By the latter part of the second century, proto-orthodox polemicists attacked a wide range of Gnostics for espousing such a view, occasionally recognizing it as part of a far more complex christological picture that included separationist elements as well.[17] Chief among the "purely" docetic culprits that the heresiologist Irenaeus names is none other than the father of all heretics, Simon Magus. According to Irenaeus, Simon claimed to be God himself, come down to bring salvation to the world. He had previously appeared as Jesus, even though this was nothing but an "appearance"; as Jesus he had not really been a man, and had appeared to suffer even though he had not really suffered (*Adv. Haer.* I, 23, 3). For Irenaeus this was only the first of several, genealogically related docetic Christologies. Simon's disciple was Menander, whose two most notorious followers, Saturninus and Basilides, were also docetists. According to Saturninus, Jesus came to destroy the God of the Jews and to liberate the sparks of the divine from their bodily prisons. He was not actually born and did not actually have a body, but was only mistakenly supposed to be a material, visible being (*Adv. Haer.* I, 24, 2). The Christology of Basilides appears to have been somewhat more developed. According to Irenaeus,[18] Basilides claimed that one of the divine aeons, Nous (Mind), also called Christ, appeared on earth as a man in order to bring salvation from the powers that created the world. But this appearance was a pure deception, which climaxed at the scene of Jesus' crucifixion. On his path to crucifixion, Christ effected a remarkable and (to Irenaeus's mind) cruel transformation, assuming the appearance of Simon of Cyrene, the bearer of his cross, while transforming Simon into his own likeness. Simon was then mistakenly crucified in Christ's stead, while Christ stood aside, laughing at those he had deceived. As a result, for Basilides, confessing "the crucified man" is an error; those who do so (e.g., the orthodox) worship Simon of Cyrene rather than Christ, and show themselves still to be slaves, under the power of the creator who formed bodies (*Adv. Haer.* I, 24, 3).

Whether or not the historical Basilides actually held to such a remarkable view is less germane to our discussion than the undisputed fact that several of the orthodox church fathers believed he did.[19] It is nonetheless striking that precisely such an idea (a peculiar twist on the concept of vicarious atonement!) has now turned up in some of the literature uncovered at Nag Hammadi. The so-called Second Treatise of the Great Seth also portrays a Jesus who miraculously exchanges places with Simon of Cyrene and mocks his opponents who think they have crucified him.[20] Other Gnostic documents known to the orthodox polemicists advance comparably docetic views.[21]

Marcion of Pontus

Particular infamy surrounds the best-known representative of doceticism, Marcion of Pontus.[22] No other heretic evoked such vitriol, or, interestingly enough, proved so instrumental for counterdevelopments within orthodoxy.[23] It is striking for our deliberations that Marcion's views developed independently of the earliest form of docetism of which we are aware—that of the Johannine community—and almost certainly under a different set of social and ideological precedents.[24] Marcion's relation to the Gnostic docetists is a more disputed matter, to which we will turn in due course.[25]

None of Marcion's own writings has survived, but from the orthodox attacks against him, particularly those of Tertullian and, less reliably, Epiphanius, some biographical details can be reconstructed with varying degrees of certainty.[26] Marcion came from Sinope in Pontus, where his father was allegedly an orthodox bishop of the church. He himself made a living as a commercial shipper, and as a young man amassed a small fortune. At some point in his adulthood he left Sinope; according to the patristic sources, which are difficult to trust on this point, it was under duress: his father excommunicated him from the church for propounding deviant teachings.[27] After spending some time in Asia Minor, Marcion came to Rome, probably around the year 139 C.E. Here he gained admission to the church and donated to its work a substantial sum—some 200,000 sesterces.[28] Little is known of Marcion's activities in Rome, although there is good reason to think that he devoted most of his time to developing his theological system and establishing its basis in two literary projects, the production of his own work, the *Antitheses* (so named because it set the works of the Old Testament God in opposition to the God of Jesus and Paul) and the expurgation of what he considered to be heretical Jewish interpolations in the sacred text of Scripture (comprising, for him, a version of Luke and ten Pauline epistles). Around the year 144 C.E., Marcion chose to make his theological system public, possibly with a view to swaying the church at large. He called a council of Roman presbyters to hear his case, the first such council on record. The outcome of the proceedings, however, was not at all what he had envisaged. The Roman presbyters rejected his views, returned his contribution to their work, (the 200,000 sesterces) and excommunicated him from the church.

From this time on we lose track of Marcion, although there are reasons for thinking that he returned to Asia Minor to begin a series of missionary campaigns. It is known that within a few short years he had acquired a considerable following. By 156 C.E., Justin could say that he had already deceived "many people of every nation" (*Apol.* I, 26). Marcion's missionary success can be gauged by the extent of his opposition; over the course of three centuries his views were attacked throughout the Mediterranean East and West by such notables as Hegessipus, Justin, Theophilus of Antioch, Irenaeus, Clement of Alexandria, Tertullian, Ephraem, Epiphanius, Theodoret, and Eznik de Kolb.[29]

As can be inferred from my brief description of Marcion's literary activities, he is best understood not as a philosopher but as a biblical theologian, specifically as an interpreter of the Apostle Paul. His theological system took its cues from the Pauline epistles, especially Romans and Galatians, in which he found a clear and emphatic contrast between the Gospel of Christ and the Law of the Old Testament, a contrast evident above all in Paul's violent opposition to those who sought to follow the Law after having come to faith in Christ.[30] For Marcion, these basic dichotomies between Law and Gospel, Jewish Christianity and Pauline Christianity, required yet other, more serious, dichotomies. If the Law of the Old Testament is a hindrance to salvation in Christ, then Christ must have no relation to the God who inspired that Law; moreover, because the God who inspired the Law is also the God who made the world, Christ must have no relation to the Creator. In short, there must be two Gods. One is the God of the Jews, who created the world, chose Israel to be his people, and gave them his law. The other is the God of Jesus, previously unknown before his coming into the world. This is also the God whom Paul knew and preached, a God with no relation to the God of the Old Testament, a Stranger both to the world and to its Creator.

Because Christ came from the Stranger-God, he must have had no real ties with the world of the Creator. This means, for Marcion, that Christ was not really a flesh and blood human being, else he would share in the materiality of the Creator's realm. Christ was therefore not born. He descended in the appearance of a full-grown man during the reign of the Emperor Tiberius[31] and ministered among his disciples before being crucified under Pontius Pilate. It is difficult to know what Marcion actually thought about the crucifixion, although the cross remained a central component of his system. It would appear, though, that Christ did not really suffer in the sense that other crucified humans suffered, in that he did not possess a real body of flesh and blood. This at least was the orthodox construal of Marcion's position (the only construal that matters for our purpose), as evidenced in the anti-Marcionite polemic of Tertullian: "For He suffered nothing who did not truly suffer; and a phantom could not truly suffer" (*Adv. Marc.* III, 8).[32]

I have already discussed the implications of Marcion's theology for his canon and text of Scripture.[33] Marcion was evidently the first to insist on a closed canon, a canon that excluded the Old Testament in its entirety and accepted only one Gospel (a form of Luke) and ten letters of Paul.[34] Marcion edited each of these books heavily, not in order to "corrupt" them but in order to "correct" them—to return them to the pristine state they had lost when transcribed by the Christian Judaizers, heretics who inserted passages that affirm the goodness of creation or that quote the Old Testament as a work of the good God or that suggest that Christ came in fulfillment of the predictions of the Hebrew prophets. Marcion deleted such passages as contaminations of the text. Among other things, this means that Marcion's canon contained neither Luke's birth narrative nor Paul's affirmations of the Old Testament, including his reflections on the parallels between Adam and Christ.[35]

As can well be imagined, Marcion's system proved problematic for orthodox Christians on virtually every ground. It divided the creator of this world from its redeemer, it treated Scripture capriciously (in Tertullian's words, Marcion did exegesis with a knife),[36] and it made Jesus a phantom who merely appeared to be human. The christological charges are particularly significant for our purpose. In the eyes of his orthodox opponents, Marcion denied that Christ was really born, that he had real flesh, and that his crucifixion involved real pain and suffering.[37] In no small measure, orthodox scribes who altered their texts of Scripture did so precisely to counter such claims.

Anti-Docetic Polemics and the Orthodox Corruption of Scripture

To sum up: A number of Christian individuals and groups were known to oppose the orthodox notion that Jesus was a real flesh and blood human being. The reasons that various docetists adopted their views are not always easy to discern. In no case can we insist that the matrix was purely ideological or purely sociological, as if these represent discrete categories. What is clear is that all such groups were opposed by proto-orthodox Christians who insisted that even though Christ was divine, he nonetheless had a real human body, a body that was actually born; that became hungry and thirsty and tired; that suffered, shed blood, and died for the sins of the world; that was raised from the dead and ascended into heaven; and that was soon to return from heaven in glory.

As might be expected, orthodox Christians did not restrict their opposition to the polemical treatises they produced. Among the docetists, Marcion, in particular, was known to appeal to Scripture in support of his views and was charged with corrupting its text as a consequence. The charge no doubt could be sustained, even though scant evidence of his transcriptions has survived the copying practices of the proto-orthodox scribes. What have survived are their own productions, manuscripts that attest just the opposite concerns. Indeed, in a number of passages that might have proved critical to the debate—in statements pertaining, for example, to the reality of Jesus' flesh or to his real suffering and death—one can find ample evidence of the orthodox perspective, embodied in the anti-docetic corruptions of Scripture.

The Christ Who Suffered in the Flesh

I begin the investigation with variant readings that go to the heart of the debate over docetic Christologies, namely, those that emphasize that far from being phantasmal, Christ's sufferings were real: he felt pain, shed blood, and died.[38] None of these passages has proved more controversial than the narrative of Jesus' agony in the garden in Luke 22, a complicated text that deserves a relatively prolonged discussion.

Luke 22:43–44

The disputed passage occurs in the context of Jesus' prayer on the Mount of Olives prior to his betrayal and arrest (Luke 22:39–46). After enjoining his disciples to "pray, lest you enter into temptation," Jesus leaves them, bows to his knees, and prays, "Father, if it be your will, remove this cup from me. Except not my will, but yours be done." In a large number of manuscripts the prayer is followed by the account, found nowhere else among our Gospels, of Jesus' heightened agony and so-called "bloody sweat": "and an angel from heaven appeared to him, strengthening him. And being in agony he began to pray yet more fervently, and his sweat became like drops of blood falling to the ground" (vv. 43–44). The scene closes (for all textual witnesses, regardless of their attestation of the disputed verses) with Jesus rising from prayer and returning to his disciples to find them asleep. He then repeats his initial injunction for them to "pray, lest you enter into temptation." Immediately Judas arrives with the crowds, and Jesus is arrested.

Several years ago, Mark A. Plunkett and I subjected the textual problem of 22:43–44 to a full-length analysis and concluded that the verses were secondary to the account, that they had been interpolated by second-century scribes who found their emphatic portrayal of Jesus experiencing real human agony useful for their repudiation of docetic Christologies. Very little has been done to change the status of this debate; here I can simply summarize the evidence that appeared then and still appears now to be compelling.[39]

In this particular instance, the manuscript alignments prove inconclusive for resolving the textual problem. The majority of witnesses, including some of particular textual or historical merit, attest the verses (ℵ*·ᵇ D L Δ* f¹ 565 892*), but they are omitted by the earliest Greek manuscripts and by most of the Alexandrian tradition, beginning with Clement and Origen and including such notable witnesses as p⁶⁶ᵛⁱᵈ·⁷⁵ A B T W 579. Most critics, if compelled to consider this external evidence in isolation, would probably grant the shorter text a slight edge; its supporting documents include the earliest and generally superior manuscripts of the Alexandrian family, along with significant versional and patristic sources. At the same time, other early witnesses attest the longer text, a reading distributed yet more widely throughout the tradition. As a result, arguments over external evidence are unable to decide the issue. The manuscript alignments *do,* however, assist in one respect: they show beyond reasonable doubt when the corruption—whichever reading is the corruption—must have been made. If the verses are secondary, they must have been interpolated into Luke by the middle of the second century, for they are attested by fathers beginning with Justin and Irenaeus and by early Latin and Syriac witnesses. If they are original, they must have been deleted by roughly the same period, since they are absent from Clement at the end of the second century and from other Alexandrian witnesses of the early third, witnesses that represent a stream of tradition that is itself much older.

The ambiguities afforded by the manuscript alignments are only heightened, not resolved, by the style and diction of the longer text. Von Harnack argued for its authenticity on just such grounds, noting that angelic appearances and constructions with $\gamma\acute{\iota}\nu\epsilon\sigma\theta\alpha\iota$ are common in Luke, whereas several other words and phrases occur in Luke and nowhere else: $\mathring{\omega}\phi\theta\eta\ \delta\grave{\epsilon}\ \alpha\mathring{\upsilon}\tau\mathring{\omega}$ $\mathring{\alpha}\gamma\gamma\epsilon\lambda o\varsigma$, $\mathring{\epsilon}\nu\iota\sigma\chi\acute{\upsilon}\epsilon\iota\nu$, and $\mathring{\epsilon}\kappa\tau\epsilon\nu\acute{\epsilon}\sigma\tau\epsilon\rho o\nu\ \pi\rho o\sigma\epsilon\acute{\upsilon}\chi\epsilon\sigma\theta\alpha\iota$.[40] The argument did not prove convincing to Lyder Brun, however, who pointed out that most of these "characteristically Lukan" ideas, constructions, and phrases are either formulated in *uncharacteristically* Lukan ways[41] or are common in Jewish and Christian texts outside of the New Testament.[42] Moreover, as Brun also pointed out, there is an unusually high concentration of hapax legomena in these verses (ἀγωνία, ἱδρώς, and θρόμβος—three of the key words), making their Lukan character actually appear somewhat suspect. At the end of the day, probably the most that can be said is that arguments based on syntax and vocabulary, as with those based on external attestation, ultimately prove inconclusive.[43]

Because the authenticity of the verses cannot be determined on the basis of these traditional kinds of text-critical arguments, we are compelled to turn to other, more decisive, considerations. The fact is that this account of Jesus' heightened agony in the face of his passion—an agony that can be ameliorated only by a ministering angel, that results in his sweating great drops as if of blood—this account is theologically intrusive in Luke's Gospel as a whole and literarily intrusive in its immediate context.[44]

With respect to theology, both within this passage and throughout the Gospel, Luke has gone to considerable lengths to counter precisely the view of Jesus that these verses embrace. Rather than entering his passion with fear and trembling, in anguish over his coming fate, the Jesus of Luke goes to his death calm and in control, confident of his Father's will until the very end. It is a striking fact, of particular relevance to our textual problem, that Luke could produce this image of Jesus only by eliminating traditions offensive to it from his sources (e.g., the Gospel according to Mark). Only the longer text of 22:43–44 stands out as anomalous.

A simple redactional comparison with Mark in the pericope at hand can prove instructive. As is well known, Luke has omitted Mark's statement that Jesus "began to be distressed and agitated" (Mark 14:33), as well as Jesus' own comment to his disciples, "My soul is deeply troubled, even unto death" (Mark 14:34). Rather than falling to the ground in anguish (Mark 14:35), Luke's Jesus bows to his knees (Luke 22:41). In Luke, Jesus does not ask that the hour might pass from him (cf. Mark 14:35); and rather than praying three times for the cup to be removed (Mark 14:36, 39, 41), he asks only once (Luke 22:42), prefacing his prayer, only in Luke, with the important condition, "If it be your will" (εἰ βούλει). And so, although Luke's source, the Gospel of Mark, portrays Jesus in anguish as he prays in the garden, Luke himself does not. Luke has effaced Mark's distinctive features and remodeled the scene to show Jesus at peace in the face of death. The only exception is the account of Jesus' "bloody sweat," an account absent from our earliest and best witnesses. Why would Luke have gone to such lengths to eliminate Mark's portrayal of an anguished Jesus if in fact Jesus' anguish were the point of his story?

Luke in fact does *not* share Mark's understanding that Jesus was in anguish, bordering on despair. Nowhere can this be seen more clearly than in their subsequent accounts of Jesus' crucifixion. Mark portrays Jesus as silent on his path to Golgotha. His disciples have all fled; even the faithful women look on only "from a distance." All those present deride him—passersby, Jewish leaders, and both robbers. Here is a man who has been beaten, mocked, deserted, and forsaken, not just by his followers but finally by God himself. His only words in the entire proceding come at the very end, when he cries aloud, "Eloi, Eloi, lema sabachthani ('My God, my God, why have *you* forsaken me?')." He then utters a loud cry and dies.

Of course Mark has his reasons for narrating the event the way he does. His portrayal of Jesus in agony and doubt, rejected at the end by his people, his followers, and even his God, sets the stage for the salvific events that transpire immediately upon his death: the tearing of the temple's curtain and the centurion's recognition that he was the Son of God.[45] As we will see in a later context, Luke modifies *both* of these subsequent events in ways amenable to his own purposes. What is more important for our study here, however, is the way he has modified the portrayal of Jesus' last hours itself, for his changes reflect an altogether different understanding of Jesus' demeanor in the face of death.

In Luke's account, Jesus is far from silent. Indeed, the sayings ascribed to him throughout these procedings show that he is still in control, trustful of God his Father, confident of his fate, concerned for the fate of others. Seeing a group of women bewailing his misfortune, Jesus tells them not to weep for him, but for themselves and their children, because of the disaster that is soon to befall them (23:27–31). While being nailed to the cross, he prays to God his "Father" to "forgive them, for they do not know what they are doing" (23:34).[46] While on the cross, in the throes of his passion, Jesus engages in an intelligent conversation with one of those crucified beside him, assuring him that they will be together that day in paradise.[47] Most telling of all, rather than uttering his pathetic cry of dereliction at the end, Luke's Jesus, in full confidence of his standing before God ("today you will be with me in paradise"!), commends his soul to his loving Father: "Father, into your hands I commend my spirit" (24:46).

It would be difficult to overestimate the significance of these changes for the textual problem at hand. At no point in Luke's passion narrative does Jesus lose control; never is he in deep and debilitating anguish over his fate. He is in charge of his own destiny; he knows what he must do and what will happen to him once he does it. This is a man who is at peace with himself and tranquil in the face of death.

What, then, shall we say about our disputed verses? These are the only verses in the entire Gospel that undermine this clear portrayal.[48] Only here does Jesus agonize over his coming fate; only here does he appear out of control, unable to bear the burden of his destiny. Why would Luke have totally eliminated all remnants of Jesus' agony elsewhere if he meant to emphasize it here in yet stronger terms? Why remove compatible material from his source, both before and after the verses in question? Either this author has arbitrarily redacted his materials with inexplicable disregard for his own purposes, or the account of Jesus' "bloody sweat" is a secondary incursion into his Gospel. Given the fact that the verses are lacking from the earliest and best Greek witnesses and that their key terms occur nowhere else in Luke's two-volume work, there should be increasing certitude concerning which way the corruption went.

And yet the case against the verses can be made even stronger. Not only are they theologically intrusive in Luke's Gospel, but, as Plunkett and I maintained earlier, they are literarily intrusive as well. The argument over the structure of the passage cannot in itself carry the day in this debate, and was never meant to. But neither can it be ignored. Precisely the two verses that prove to be so problematic on other grounds are intrusive in an otherwise clear literary structure. Luke's account has been carefully modeled as a chiasmus, a structure that, despite the exorbitant claims of some scholars, is a relatively rare phenomenon within the pages of the New Testament.[49] This means that when a clear instance of its use does occur, one must do something with it—either deny its presence or its significance, or admit that an author has employed a literary device in order to contribute to his overall purpose. In this case, the chiasmus is nearly impossible to overlook. Jesus (a) tells his disciples to "pray lest you enter into temptation" (v. 40). He then (b) leaves them (v. 41a) and (c) kneels to pray (v. 41b). The center of the pericope is (d) Jesus' prayer itself, a prayer bracketed by his two requests that God's will be done (v 42). Jesus then (c[1]) rises from prayer (v. 45a), (b[1]) returns to his disciples (v. 45b), and (a[1]) finding them asleep, once again addresses them in the same words, telling them to "pray lest you enter into temptation" (vv. 45c–46).

The passage then is structured as follows.

(a) And when he came to the place, he said to them "Pray lest you enter into temptation."
   (b) And he went away from them, about a stone's throw,
      (c) and bending his knees, he began to pray,

         (d) saying, Father, if it be your will, remove this cup from me, except not my will but yours be done.

      (c[1]) And rising up from prayer,
   (b[1]) he came to his disciples and found them sleeping;
(a[1]) and he said to them, "Why do you sleep? Arise and pray, lest you enter into temptation.

What is significant here is not simply that one can discover some kind of structure for the passage. That is always possible, as I will have occasion to note in a later discussion.[50] What is striking is that this particular structure functions so clearly as an interpretive key to the point of the passage. The pericope is bracketed by the two injunctions to the disciples to pray so as to avoid entering into temptation. Prayer, of course, has long been recognized as a Lukan theme;[51] here it comes into special prominence. For at the very center of the pericope is Jesus' own prayer, a prayer that expresses his desire, bracketed by his greater desire that the Father's will be done (vv. 41c–42).

As the center of the chiastic structure, this prayer supplies the passage's point of focus and, correspondingly, its hermeneutical key. This is a lesson on the importance of prayer in the face of temptation. The disciples, despite Jesus' repeated injunction to pray, fall asleep instead. Immediately the crowd comes to arrest Jesus. And what happens? The disciples, who have failed to pray, *do* "enter into temptation"; they flee the scene, leaving Jesus to face his fate alone. Moreover, their chief representative, Peter, will soon deny all knowledge of his Lord. What about Jesus, the one who *has* prayed before the coming of his trial? When the crowds arrive he calmly submits to his Father's will, yielding himself up to the martyrdom that has been prepared for him.

Luke's passion narrative, as was recognized by Dibelius long ago, is a story of Jesus' martyrdom, a martyrdom that functions, as do many others, to set an example of how to remain faithful unto death.[52] Luke's martyrology shows that only prayer can prepare one to die, as it provides the strength that is needed to embrace one's destiny and not fly in the face of it. Jesus, unlike his disciples, prays before his time of trial, and through his prayer finds the strength he needs to confront his fate.[53]

What happens now when the disputed verses are injected into the pericope? On the literary level, the chiasmus that focuses the passage on Jesus' prayer is absolutely destroyed. Now the center of the passage, and hence its focus, shifts to Jesus' agony, an agony so terrible as to require a supernatural visitant for strength to bear it. As we have seen, this is precisely the image of Jesus that Luke has otherwise removed from his traditions. It is significant that in this longer version of the story Jesus' prayer does *not* effect the calm assurance that he exudes throughout the rest of the account; indeed, it is *after* he prays "yet more fervently" that his sweat takes on the appearance of great drops of blood falling to the ground. The point is not simply that a nice literary structure has been lost, although that in itself should give us pause in light of the clear care Luke has taken to redact his Markan source here.[54] Even more important, however, is the way in which the characteristically Lukan themes are now shifted to the background, indeed, virtually removed from the picture. No longer do we see Jesus calmed by his assurance of his Father's will, braced to meet his fate with equanimity and dignity. We instead see a non-Lukan Jesus, one in deep and heartrending agony and in need of miraculous intervention.

As has happened so many times in the course of our discussions, the arguments against these verses must be seen as working together in tandem. In this case, the verses that are lacking from our oldest and best manuscripts and that happen to contain a number of hapax legomena also violate (theologically) Luke's understanding of Jesus on the way to his cross and disrupt (literarily) a passage that Luke has carefully crafted to convey his characteristic message. The account of Jesus' "bloody sweat" did not belong to the original text of the Third Gospel.

Whence, then, did it come? This is where transcriptional probabilities must be taken into account. Such probabilities cannot be overlooked,[55] even if they do not prove decisive in and of themselves: as I have repeatedly argued, rarely does any one argument decide a textual issue. With respect to these particular verses, we can almost certainly eliminate the possibility that scribes effected the change "by accident." The passage is too long and too weighty to have been interpolated (or for that matter, deleted) by oversight. Much more fruitful is a consideration of the theological attractiveness of the verses for early Christian scribes. There have been scholars, of course, who have argued that scribes found them theologically objectionable and so omitted them, leading to the shorter text of the generally superior Alexandrian witnesses. Certainly, given the scribal proclivities already outlined, the view is not to be rejected on *a priori* grounds.[56] The merits, however, have to be weighed in each individual case. In the present instance, one needs to ask whether scribes were *ever* particularly reticent when it came to describing the real and tangible sufferings of Christ. Quite to the contrary, the focus on Jesus' real passion occupies a central place in early Christian reflections on the Gospels—at least in the orthodox circles that have produced the surviving literature. This then raises just the opposite possibility—that the verses were interpolated into the Gospel precisely because they portray so well a human Jesus, one who agonizes over his coming fate to the point of needing supernatural succor, an agony so deep as to cause him to sweat great drops as if of blood.

Although this was not at all the portrayal of Jesus facing his passion in the Gospel according to Luke, it *was* the view embraced widely throughout early Christendom, at least as far back as the traditions behind the Gospel according to Mark and on up into the middle ages.[57] It is particularly worth observing, in this connection, how the verses in question were used in the sources that first attest them, sources that, as I indicated at the outset, date precisely to the period of our concern. They can be found in three writers of the second century: Justin, Irenaeus, and Hippolytus. Remarkably, in all three cases the verses are cited to the same end, to counter any notion that Jesus was not a real flesh and blood human being. Thus, Justin observes that "his sweat fell down like drops of blood while He was praying," and claims that this shows "that the Father wished His Son really to undergo such sufferings for our sakes," so that we "may not say that He, being the Son of God, did not feel what was happening to Him and inflicted on Him" (*Dial.*, 103). So too, Irenaeus, in an attack on the docetic aspects of the Ptolemaean Christology, argued that if Jesus were not really a man of flesh, he would not "have sweated great drops of blood," for this is a token "of the flesh which had been derived from the earth" (*Adv. Haer.* III, 22, 2).[58] Somewhat later, and in a somewhat different vein, Hippolytus uses the passage to show the Patripassianist Noetus[59] that Jesus "did not refuse conditions proper to him as a man" in that, as a human, he hungers, thirsts, sleeps, and "in an agony sweats blood, and is strengthened by an angel" (*Adv. Noetum*, 18).

The conclusion should now be clear. We do not need to *hypothesize* the usefulness of these verses for an anti-docetic polemic; we *know* that the verses were put to precisely this use during the period of our concern. Second-century heresiologists used Jesus' "bloody sweat" to attack Christians who denied his real humanity. Given the other problems that the verses have posed, there can be little remaining doubt concerning their status. The story of Jesus praying in yet greater agony, being strengthened by an angel from heaven, and sweating great drops as if of blood, did not originate with the author of the Gospel of Luke. It was inserted into the Third Gospel some time in the early second century (prior to Justin) as part of the anti-docetic polemic of the orthodox Christian church.[60]

Other Examples

Having discussed this one textual problem at some length, I can now consider other variant readings that also highlight the real suffering and death of Jesus. I begin with an interesting corruption attested in one of the earliest papyri. Prior to the discover of 𝔭[66], the witnesses to the Fourth Gospel were virtually invariant in their account of Jesus' penultimate words: "Jesus, knowing that everything was already finished ($\tau\epsilon\tau\acute{\epsilon}\lambda\epsilon\sigma\tau\alpha\iota$), in order that the Scripture might be fulfilled ($\mathring{\iota}\nu\alpha\ \tau\epsilon\lambda\epsilon\iota\omega\theta\mathring{\eta}\ \mathring{\eta}\ \gamma\rho\alpha\phi\acute{\eta}$), said, 'I am thirsty' " (19:28). The third-century papyrus, however, omits the $\mathring{\iota}\nu\alpha$ clause. In this witness, when Jesus says he is thirsty, it is no longer "in order to fulfill the Scripture."

What is one to make of this omission? It does not appear to have been made accidentally. 𝔭[66] is notorious for leaving out single letters and particles and other small words, but is not particularly prone to omissions of entire phrases or clauses.[61] Nor could an accident be attributed to homoeoteleuton or homoeoarcton. If, then, we grant the possibility of a deliberate modification, we might be tempted to conjecture a relatively innocent motive: a scribe may not have understood how Jesus could say he thirsted "in order to *fulfill* the Scripture" (19:28b) immediately after the author has claimed that everything had "already" been *fulfilled* (19:28a).[62] At the same time, no other scribe appears to have considered this a problem; yet more puzzling, the same scribe was apparently not disturbed by Jesus' final words on the cross, words that should have seemed equally irregular: "When therefore he had received the vinegar, Jesus said, "It is finished" (or "fulfilled" [$\tau\epsilon\tau\acute{\epsilon}\lambda\epsilon\sigma\tau\alpha\iota$], same word as v. 28a).

How then can we account for this singular omission? We would be remiss in this case to overlook the theological possibilities of the corruption. When Jesus says he is thirsty "in order to fulfill Scripture" (the original text), it might well appear to a reader that he was in fact *not* thirsty, but said that he was simply because he was required to do so by the Scriptures. To be sure, by eliminating the $\mathring{\iota}\nu\alpha$ clause the scribe has not at all compromised the interpretation of the event as fulfilling Scripture. But he has made it look less like Jesus was saying that he thirsted simply because he was supposed to. Now Jesus really *is* thirsty in the throes of death. This is a real, human, suffering Jesus, the Jesus that proto-orthodox Christians set forth in opposition to various docetic heresies.

Moving to the passion narrative of the First Gospel one finds a better attested reading that is of equal interest. Prior to Matthew's statement that

Jesus "gave up his spirit" (27:50), several early witnesses insert a tradition otherwise known from the Gospel of John: "and another, taking a spear, pierced his side, and water and blood came out" (MSS ℵ B C L syr^{pal. mss}pc). The strong attestation of the verse in such high-quality manuscripts of the Alexandrian tradition, along with its support in the Palestinian Syriac, shows that the variant dates back to the period of our concern. But few scholars regard the reading as original. On the one hand, it appears suspect on internal grounds; λόγχη and νύσσω occur only in this tradition in the New Testament, whether here or in John, whereas the term πλευρά occurs three other times in John's passion narrative, but never elsewhere in Matthew. Transcriptional arguments prove yet more decisive: one can understand why scribes might insert such a familiar tradition into Matthew's account,[63] but why would they omit it? And why would they do so in Matthew but not in John? As Metzger notes, if scribes considered it to be a problem that the spear thrust occurred after Jesus' death in the Fourth Gospel but prior to it here, they (or at least one of them) would have been more likely to transpose the episode to follow Matthew 27:50 than to delete it altogether. Because the vast bulk of the tradition attests the shorter text, it is very difficult, all things considered, to regard the longer text as original.

Why, though, was the verse inserted into the Gospel of Matthew? We should not be misled into thinking that the change represents a "simple" harmonization. Here again there is the matter of disparate sequence: surely a scribe who wanted to make Matthew's account conform more closely with John's would have situated the spear thrust *after* Jesus' death. But what would motivate a scribe to insert the tradition *before* his death? In answering the question, we cannot afford to overlook how the tradition helped orthodox Christians in their struggles against docetic Christologies. Irenaeus refers twice to the water and blood that issued from Jesus' pierced side in order to show that Jesus was a real flesh and blood human being who in his passion experienced real pain and suffering. Moreover, on both occasions he directs his remarks against docetists, once against the Ptolemaeans and once against Marcion.[64] Interestingly enough, precisely the tradition of Jesus' pierced side became a point of contention between the orthodox and their docetic opponents, as evidenced even in docetic sources such as the *Acts of John*: "You heard that I was pierced, yet I was not wounded . . . that blood flowed from me, yet it did not flow; and in a word, that what they say of me, I did not endure, but what they do not say, those things I did suffer" (*Acts of John*, 101).

The point should be clear that orthodox Christians found the Johannine tradition of Jesus' pierced side and the subsequent issuance of water and blood to be of some use in their debates with docetists. Moreover, when the tradition occurs *before* Jesus death (as in Matthew) rather than *after* it (as in John), it suggests that Jesus really did suffer and shed blood while living, that his was a real body that bled, that his was a real and a tangible death. In short, the change was not merely a harmonization but an orthodox corruption.

Two other textual corruptions of Matthew's Gospel that occur outside of the passion narrative itself may also be attributed to orthodox scribes who sought to highlight and clarify the necessity of Jesus' suffering. In neither instance can the more patently orthodox reading make a viable claim to authenticity. The Byzantine tradition of Matthew 20:22, 23 presents a harmonization to the Markan parallel, in which Jesus asks James and John not only whether they are able to drink his "cup" but also whether they can endure his "baptism" (MSS C W 0197 Byz OL syr[p. h] bo[pt], cf. Mark 10:38–39). This could, of course, represent a "pure" harmonization; but as we have seen, it is rather unusual for scribes to harmonize the most familiar of the Gospels, Matthew, to the one least frequently read and copied, Mark. This might lead one to suspect some other reason for the change. Although there may be slim evidence for claiming that a proto-orthodox Christology "motivated" the alteration in this instance, there are reasons for situating it in an orthodox milieu. Here I should observe that the terminology of "baptism" traditionally proved useful for orthodox Christians who wanted to portray the completeness of Christ's passion—his was a baptism of blood.[65] The presence of the motif in the parallel passage, then, may well have provided scribes with just the rationale they needed to emphasize Jesus' passion yet more strongly in a passage that already intimated it. In this limited sense, the change may be understood as an orthodox corruption.

Of somewhat greater interest is the transposition of clauses firmly embedded in the Western text of Jesus' famous proclamation concerning the Baptist in Matthew 17:12–13. In its more widely attested and certainly original form, the text reads:

> "But I say to you that Elijah has come already, and they did not know him, but they did to him as many things as they desired. Thus also the Son of Man is about to suffer at their hands." Then the disciples realized that he was speaking to them about John the Baptist.

The problem with this text, if it is to be construed a problem, is that it could well be interpreted as saying that the disciples realized that Jesus' words about the suffering Son of Man were spoken about John the Baptist. Given the proclivity of orthodox Christians to emphasize the sufferings of *Christ,* it is not surprising to find that the archetype of the Western tradition transposed the final two sentences, so that what is now verse 13 came to be read as a parenthetic comment by the author, after which verse 12b resumed with the concluding statement of Jesus.[66] Now the text reads:

> "But I say to you that Elijah has come already, and they did not know him, but they did to him as many things as they desired." (Then the disciples realized that he was speaking to them about John the Baptist.) "Thus also the Son of Man is about to suffer at their hands."

Here, as in so many cases of this kind, the point is not that an orthodox scribe thought that by changing the text he would destroy the confidence of a docetic opponent; it is instead that the context within which such debates were being carried out, in which certain Christians came to value more and more the real, tangible suffering of their Lord, led certain scribes to change their texts of Scripture to emphasize just those doctrines that helped to define "orthodox" Christianity over against other systems of belief.[67]

The Christ Whose Body and Blood Brought Salvation

The anti-docetic corruptions we have considered so far have stressed that Christ experienced real pain and suffering in his passion. This christological doctrine had its soteriological corollary in the belief that when Christ died at the cross he shed real blood, and that it was this shed blood that brought redemption. The constant reassertion of these notions in our second- and third-century sources suggests that proto-orthodox Christians took the opposing position quite seriously, the docetic view that denied both the reality of Christ's shed blood and, naturally, its salvific necessity.[68] A clear statement of the orthodox position appears in Irenaeus's strongly worded polemic:

> But vain in every respect are they who despise the entire dispensation of God, and disallow the salvation of the flesh . . . maintaining that it is not capable of incorruption. But if this indeed do not attain salvation, then neither did the Lord redeem us with His blood, nor is the cup of the Eucharist the communion of his blood, nor the bread which we break the communion of His body. For blood can only come from veins and flesh, and whatsoever else makes up the substance of man, such as the Word of God was actually made. By His own blood he redeemed us, as also His apostle declares, "In whom we have redemption, through his blood, even the remission of sins" (*Adv. Haer.* V, 2, 2).[69]

As can be seen by Irenaeus's appeal to Colossians 1:14, orthodox Christians found their doctrine of the salvific efficacy of Christ's blood already embedded within the words of Scripture.[70] Orthodox scribes worked to make this emphasis yet more plain, as they occasionally imported the doctrine into passages that originally lacked it. The impact that this scribal activity made on the text of Scripture can still be seen at a number of points in our surviving manuscripts. Nowhere was the impact more jarring than in the textual history of Luke's narrative of the Last Supper (22:19–20), a passage that— as I will argue—originally said nothing about the atoning effect of Christ's body and blood. To be sure, not all scholars agree with this assessment. Indeed, since the publication of Westcott and Hort's *New Testament in the Original Greek,* no textual problem of Luke's entire two-volume work has generated more critical debate—or, one might add, occasioned more scholarly confusion. In light of the exegetical and historical significance of the passage, we do well to subject its various complexities to an extended examination.[71]

Luke 22:19–20

Documentary Considerations

The New Testament manuscripts present Luke 22:19–21 in six different forms of text, four of which can be readily dismissed as altogether lacking adequate documentary support and internal claims to authenticity.[72] Of the two remaining forms, one is conveniently labeled the "shorter text" because it lacks verses 19b–20, reading (19a, 21): "And taking bread, giving thanks, he broke it and gave it to them, saying, 'This is my body. But behold, the hand of the one who betrays me is with me on the table.' " The longer text includes the familiar material (italicized) between these two sentences (vv. 19b-20): "And taking bread, giving thanks, he broke it and gave it to them, saying, 'This is my body *that is given for you. Do this in my remembrance.' And the cup likewise after supper, saying, 'This cup is the new covenant in my blood that is poured out for you.* But behold, the hand of the one who betrays me is with me on the table.' "

The shorter text is one of Westcott and Hort's famous "Western non-interpolations." As the ill-famed designation suggests, it is a text preserved only in Western witnesses (D a d ff[2] i l) that has (for Westcott and Hort) all the earmarks of originality, despite the attestation of a longer form in all other manuscripts, including those Westcott and Hort labeled—with equal disingenuousness—"Neutral."[73] The sparse support for the shorter reading has naturally led most other commentators and textual specialists to reject it virtually out of hand. As I will argue more fully in the Excursus, however, to move too quickly in this direction would be a mistake, for Westcott and Hort did not depart from their beloved Neutral witnesses without compelling reasons.[74] With respect to the present text, their reasons were rooted in intrinsic and transcriptional probabilities, about which I will be speaking momentarily. But here, as with all the Western non-interpolations, Westcott and Hort also found *documentary* reasons for thinking the Western tradition original, even though they understood it normally to be corrupt. This is because the shorter reading, which appears to be original on internal grounds, represents the opposite *pattern* of corruption evidenced elsewhere in its supporting documents. The "Western" text is almost invariably expansionistic, as opposed to the normally succinct attestations of its Alexandrian counterparts (including Westcott and Hort's "Neutral" text). When Western witnesses, then, support an uncharacteristically shorter text in the face of an Alexandrian expansion, the reading in question must be given the most serious consideration. Westcott and Hort's decision to accept several such readings as original (not all of them, as a case must be made for each on the grounds of intrinsic and transcriptional probabilities) is commonly disparaged as tendentious. In point of fact, it is the least tendentious aspect of their entire system: these few readings virtually proved their cherished notions about a "Neutral" tradition mistaken.[75]

The upshot is that the nearly unconscious tendency to discount readings found "in only a few" witnesses must be laid aside when dealing with this kind of manuscript alignment, in which a shorter reading finds its chief support within the Western tradition. In such cases, both readings, the shorter and the longer, must have been available to scribes of the second century. The external evidence, however, can go back no earlier; it cannot, that is, determine the reading of the autograph. The investigation, then, must be moved to the realm of internal evidence. And here, in fact, is where a compelling case can be made for the originality of the shorter reading of Luke 22:19–20. The bottom line will be an argument from transcriptional probability: unlike the more commonly attested reading, there is no plausible explanation for the existence of the Western text if it is not original. Before drawing this line, however, we must first attend to the question of which reading is more intrinsically suited to Luke's two-volume work.

Intrinsic Probabilities: Vocabulary, Style, and Theology

It has sometimes been argued that the main difficulty with the longer text is its non-Lukan vocabulary and style.[76] This is probably overstating the case, even though the concatenation of non-Lukan features should certainly give us pause.[77] What is even more striking, however, is that precisely the non-Lukan features of the longer text comprise its key elements: the phrase ὑπὲρ ὑμῶν ("for you") occurs *twice* in this passage, but nowhere else in all of Luke-Acts,[78] the word for "remembrance," ἀνάμνησιν, occurs only here in Luke-Acts,[79] and never elsewhere does Luke speak of the "new covenant," let alone the new covenant "in my blood." Were the Gospel of Luke our only base of comparison for this distinctive vocabulary, the evidence might not be so telling; but given the ample opportunity afforded the author to refer back to the momentous event of the Last Supper in his second volume, the absence of any subsequent allusions to these significant words and phrases must be seen as more than a little discomforting for proponents of the longer text.[80]

Even more important than the mere absence of this vocabulary from the rest of Luke-Acts is the matter of its ideational content. It is surely significant that the understanding of Jesus' death expressed by these words and phrases is otherwise absent from Luke's two-volume work. When Jesus says in Luke 22:19b–20 that his body is given "for you" (ὑπὲρ ὑμῶν) and that his blood is shed "for you" (ὑπὲρ ὑμῶν), he is stating what Luke says nowhere else in his long narrative. Neither in his Gospel nor in Acts does he portray Jesus' death as an atonement for sins.[81] Even more significantly, Luke has actually gone out of his way to *eliminate* just such a theology from the narrative he inherited from his predecessor, Mark. This is a key factor in recognizing the secondary character of the longer text, a factor that has been surprisingly underplayed by most previous studies of the problem.

The data are by now familiar and here I will simply mention those that are particularly germane to the textual problem. Never in his two volumes does Luke say that Jesus died "for your sins" or "for you." Significantly, when he summarizes the significant features of the "Christ event" in the speeches of Acts, he portrays the death of Jesus with remarkable consistency not as an atoning sacrifice, but as a miscarriage of justice that God reversed by vindicating Jesus at the resurrection (Acts 2:22–36; 3:12–16; 4:8–12; 7:51–56; 13:26–41). The only apparent exception—and I will later argue that it is in fact only apparent—is the difficult text of Acts 20:28. Before turning our attention to the exceptional, however, we do well to stress the invariable. In none of these speeches is Jesus said to die "for" anyone, a surprising fact, given the number of opportunities Luke had to introduce the notion. In one passage in particular one might expect some reference, however distant, to Jesus' atoning death, only to find the expectation altogether frustrated. In Acts 8, Luke portrays the Ethiopian eunuch reading the text of Scripture used most widely by early Christians to explain Jesus' death as a vicarious atonement: Isaiah 53. Somewhat remarkably, however, when Luke cites the passage, he includes not a word about the Servant of the Lord being "wounded for our transgressions" (Isa 53:5), being "bruised for our iniquities" (53:5), or making himself "an offering for sin" (53:10). Luke has instead crafted his quotation to affirm his own view of Jesus' passion: he died as an innocent victim who was then vindicated (Acts 8:32–33). Particularly telling is Luke's decision to stop just short of the final statement of the Isaian text he quotes, a statement that does in fact intimate the vicarious nature of the Servant's suffering: he was "stricken for the transgression of my people" (53:8).[82] It should not be overlooked, in this connection, that Luke's only other allusion to the Song of the Suffering Servant also supports his view that Jesus was unjustly killed but then glorified. In Acts 3:13, Peter states that the God of Israel "glorified his servant" Jesus (Isa 52:13), but says nothing about Jesus' atoning sacrifice.

It is particularly important to stress that Luke has not simply overlooked or avoided making such references; he has gone out of his way to *eliminate* notions of atonement from the one source we are virtually certain he had before him, the Gospel of Mark. Mark makes two poignant references to the salvific significance of Jesus' death and Luke changes them both. The first and most obvious comes in the famous words of Jesus in Mark 10:45: "For the Son of Man came not to be served but to serve, and to give his life a ransom for many." If Luke found this theology acceptable, it is virtually impossible to explain why he omitted the verse altogether.[83]

The other reference is more subtle, but nonetheless forms a kind of linchpin for Mark's theology of the cross. It has to do with the events surrounding the moment of Jesus' death, and to recognize the significance of Luke's portrayal of the event one has to understand how it was presented in his source. As has already been observed, Mark records that Jesus' death is immediately followed by two signs that demonstrate its meaning: the Temple curtain is ripped in half and the Roman centurion confesses him to be "the Son of God" (15:38–39).[84] The tearing of the curtain has been subject to two major interpretations over the years, depending on whether it was the outer or inner curtain of the Temple that was torn.[85] Both interpretations are plausible within a Marcan context, the first probably indicating a divine judgment against the Temple, the second a not unrelated notion that God now comes to humans (from the Holy of Holies behind the curtain) no longer through temple sacrifice but through the death of Jesus.[86] The latter interpretation is perhaps to be preferred, because (a) the only other use of the verb σχίζω in Mark occurs at the baptism (1:10), where again the idea of a divine advent occurs (the heavens rip and the Spirit descends), and (b) the second event of 15:38–39—the centurion's confession—indicates a moment of salvation rather than, purely, of judgment. If this interpretation is correct, then Mark uses the ripping of the curtain to indicate that in the death of Jesus God has made himself available to human beings, who correspondingly now have direct access to him. And the confession of the centurion represents the first (and only) instance of a person in Mark's Gospel fully recognizing who Jesus is: he is the Son of God who had to die, whose death was not alien to his divine sonship but was instead constitutive of it.[87] In short, the ripping of the curtain and the confession of the centurion reveal Mark's understanding of Jesus' death as an atoning sacrifice (in it God makes himself available to humanity, cf. 10:45) and as the key to salvation (by the profession of faith in the Son of God who died).

Luke's account of Jesus' death is in no small measure dependent upon Mark's.[88] Here there also is a tearing of the temple curtain and a confession of the centurion. It is all the more striking that both events are modified so as to transform their significance. The tearing of the curtain in the Temple no longer results from Jesus' death, because in Luke it occurs *before* Jesus dies (23:45). What the event might mean to Luke has been debated, but because it is now combined with the eerie darkness that has come over the land,[89] it appears to represent a cosmic sign that accompanies the hour of darkness ("this is your hour and the power of darkness," 11:43). It may, then, represent the judgment of God upon his people who have rejected his gift of "light to those who sit in darkness and the shadow of death" (1:79), a judgment that falls in particular on the religious institution that his people have perverted to their own ends (Luke 19:45–46).[90] In Luke's account the ripping of the Temple curtain does not show that Jesus' death has opened up the path to God;[91] it now symbolizes God's judgment upon his own people who prefer to dwell in darkness.[92]

Luke also has changed the confession of the centurion. No longer does it indicate a profession of faith in the Son of God who has died ("Truly this man was the Son of God," Mark 15:39); it now coincides with Luke's own understanding of Jesus' death: "Truly this man was innocent" (δίκαιος, Luke 23:47).[93] The death of Jesus in Luke-Acts is not a death that effects an atoning sacrifice. It is the death of a righteous martyr who has suffered from miscarried justice, whose innocence is vindicated by God at the resurrection.[94] What matters chiefly for our purpose is not the theological adequacy of such a view, but rather the consistency with which Luke has set it forth; he was able to shift the focus away from the atoning significance of Jesus' death only by modifying the one account of that death which we are certain he had received. What has this to do with our textual problem? As I will stress momentarily, only one of our two textual variants, the shorter reading, coincides with the Lukan understanding of Jesus' death; the other attests precisely the theology that Luke has otherwise taken pains to suppress.

Before returning to this text-critical issue, however, I must first deal with Acts 20:28, the one passage that is frequently treated as an exception to Luke's understanding of the death of Jesus. In fact, the passage is an exception only in appearance. For even here the notion of atonement does not emerge from the text but has to be imported into it. In his farewell address to the Ephesian elders, the Apostle Paul urges them to "pastor the church of God, which he obtained through the blood of his Own" (τοῦ αἵματος τοῦ ἰδίου). The phrasing is enigmatic and, as we have already seen, has led to several interesting textual modifications.[95] Despite its ambiguity ("His own blood"? "The blood of his unique [Son]"?) the phrase almost certainly refers to Jesus, whose blood God used to acquire an *ekklesia*.[96] But even here, I must point out, the text does not speak of Jesus' self-giving act as an atoning sacrifice for sin, but of God's use of Jesus' blood to acquire (NB, not "redeem") the church. And so, strictly speaking the thrust of the allusion is not soteriological; the foci are God's prerogatives over the church, which he obtained through blood and the elders' corresponding need to exercise appropriate supervision over it. Only by inference can one find a word concerning the expiatory benefits of Christ's death; even here there is no word of atonement, no claim that Christ died "for your sake."

But what does it mean to say that God obtained the church through Christ's blood? The problem interpreters have typically had with the verse is that they have seen in it a remnant of Pauline soteriology, and have concluded from this either that Luke *did* accept the notion of an atoning sacrifice or that he unwittingly reproduced an undigested fragment of tradition.[97] In fact, neither conclusion is necessary, since the verse makes perfectly good sense if one suspends any previous knowledge of (or commitment to) Pauline thought and allows it to draw its meaning from its Lukan context. On only one other occasion does Luke mention the "blood" of Jesus, and this should be the first place to turn in trying to understand the reference in 20:28. In Acts 5:28 the Jewish leaders in Jerusalem accuse the apostles of working to make them the culprits for "the blood of this man." When Peter hears their accusation, he launches into one of his patented speeches, proclaiming that even though "You killed [Jesus] by hanging him on the tree. God raised him from the dead, exalting him to his right hand as Ruler and Savior." He then ties Jesus' reversal of fortune to a typically Lukan notion of soteriology. God exalted the unjustly executed Jesus so that he could give "repentance and forgiveness of sins to Israel" (5:31). In light of 5:28, what does Luke mean in 20:28 that "God obtains the church through blood"? The blood of Jesus produces the church because it brings the cognizance of guilt that leads to repentance.[98]

I should point out that this understanding of Jesus' blood is perfectly consistent with Luke's soteriology elsewhere in his two-volume work, in which repentance and forgiveness of sins are the perennial keynotes. The constant refrain of the speeches of Acts is: "You killed Jesus, but God raised him from the dead." In each instance the claim represents an appeal to repentance, which brings forgiveness of sins.[99] Failure to repent, on the other hand, results in judgment.

Moreover, this construal is consistent with the other references to "blood" throughout Luke-Acts. While the word can certainly refer neutrally to such things as the blood of menstruation or of edible beasts (Luke 8:43–44; Acts 15:20, 29; 21:25) or to cosmic signs of the eschaton (Acts 2:19–20), it most frequently refers to the unjust and violent suffering of the people of God— especially of prophets and martyrs (Luke 11:50; 13:1; Acts 22:20). Strikingly, Luke sees Jesus himself as, above all, a prophet and martyr.[100] Somewhat ironically, the term "blood" can also symbolize the fate of those who refuse to repent when they encounter the apostolic preaching of Jesus (18:6). It is worth noting that the term is used in just this way within the immediate context of 20:28; Paul states his relief at being guiltless of "the blood" of the Ephesian elders—meaning that he fulfilled his obligation to preach to them his message of salvation, a message that can save them from the coming judgment.[101] Only if his hearers repent when confronted with Jesus' blood will they be saved from spilling their own.

This contextual understanding of Acts 20:28 shows that, at least for Luke, the tradition that God obtained the church through Jesus' blood—if it is a tradition—has nothing to do with the Pauline notion of atonement. One can only conclude that interpreters have read such a notion into the text because their knowledge of Paul (and of later developments) naturally leads them to see atonement wherever they see blood. Acts 20:28 neither requires nor intimates such a construal, however, so that it is not at all the exception to an otherwise consistent Lukan soteriology. Even this text makes good sense within the narrative of Luke, and the sense it makes is not related to the idea of vicarious suffering.

The result is that in no case does Luke understand Jesus' death as an atonement for sins. As I have already said, this is not at all to disparage Luke's own Christology or his theology of the cross. It is simply to say that he understands the death of Jesus differently from both the predecessor of his Gospel (Mark) and the hero of his Acts (Paul).

How does this consistent reconstrual of the salvific importance of Jesus' death affect our query into the original text of Luke 22:19–20? Only one of the two readings conforms with the theology of Luke otherwise, and specifically with his demonstrable handling of his Marcan source. The verses of the longer reading stress the atoning significance of Jesus' death for his disciples. How can they be original when they emphasize precisely what Luke has gone out of his way to *deemphasize* throughout the rest of his two-volume narrative? How could Luke have blatantly eliminated from Mark's account any notion of Jesus' death as an atoning sacrifice (Mark 10:45; 15:39) only to assert such a notion here in yet stronger terms? The conclusion appears unavoidable: either Luke constructed his narrative with blinding inconsistency or he penned the shorter form of the text, known to us from the Western tradition.

Intrinsic Probabilities: The Structure of the Passage

Before turning to the arguments of transcription that, in my judgment, serve to cinch the argument, it is neccessary to consider one other matter of intrinsic probability: the competing virtues of the passage's structure as presented in the two forms of the text. It is here that advocates of the longer text feel confident in the superiority of their claims. Most frequently it simply is noted that without the addition of verses 19b-20 the text appears to end abruptly, so abruptly that it is difficult to imagine a Christian author not supplementing the account with additional material. As Earle Ellis puts it, the reader naturally expects to find a word about the cup after the word about the bread.[102]

One certainly does expect to find such a word, which is exactly what makes this argument so suspect. As with most arguments of this kind, the expectation of a reader can cut both ways. Readers who are thoroughly conversant with the eucharistic liturgy feel that something is "missing" when Jesus' words over the bread are not followed by his passing of the cup. Of course, this is not only the case for modern critics who assume that Luke could not have ended the passage with such abruptness but also for ancient scribes who were equally accustomed to the traditions of Jesus' Last Supper. How this proves decisive for the *longer* text of Luke 22, however, is more than a little perplexing. What would be more natural for scribes conversant with what "really happened" at Jesus' last meal than to supplement Luke's version with the words drawn from a tradition with which they were otherwise familiar?

Interestingly, this "other tradition" (i.e., vv. 19b-20 in the longer text) is not only anomalous within Luke's Gospel itself, it also has very few connections with Luke's source, the Gospel of Mark. Instead, as has been frequently noted, the additional words practically mirror the familiar account of the institution preserved in Paul's first letter to the Corinthians.[103] The fact that the words of the longer text of Luke are not *precisely* those of Paul should not be used, as it sometimes is, to argue that they could not have been added secondarily to the text of the Gospel. No one need think that a scribe referred to his manuscript of 1 Corinthians to check the accuracy of his interpolation into Luke. Instead, the addition has all the marks of a familiar narrative based on, or at least parallel to, Paul's account of Jesus' Last Supper.

The question of whether the shorter text of Luke's account is too truncated to be considered original has been treated with greater sophistication by J. H. Petzer in his recent study of the literary structure of the passage.[104] Petzer notes that when one considers the broader context of verses 15–20, the longer text preserves a number of literary parallelisms that speak in its favor as original. According to Petzer, the passage evidences a bipartite parallel structure, each part of which comprises two "signs" and their "explanations": verses 15–18 record a first "sign" (eating) and its "explanation" (it will be fulfilled in the Kingdom of God), then a second "sign" (drinking) and its comparable "explanation" (it too will be fulfilled in the Kingdom). Corresponding to this is the text of verses 19–20 in its longer form, in which two "signs" (the bread, v. 19a; the cup, v. 20) receive appropriate explanations ("This is my body . . ."; "This cup is the new covenant in my blood"). The passage can then be structured as follows:

(A)	(a) τὸ πάσχα φαγεῖν	sign:	eating (bread)	(15, 16a)
	(b) τῇ βασιλείᾳ	explanation:	Kingdom	(16b)
(B)	(a') τὸ ποτήριον, πίω	sign:	drinking (cup)	(17, 18a)
	(b') ἡ βασιλεία	explanation:	Kingdom	(18b)
(A')	(a") ἄρτον	sign:	bread	(19a)
	(b") τὸ σῶμά μου	explanation:	body	(19b)
(B')	(a⁺) ποτήριον	sign:	cup	(20a)
	(b⁺) τὸ αἷμά μου	explanation:	blood	(20b)

For Petzer this structure demonstrates that the longer text is original, because removing verses 19b-20 destroys the bipartite parallelism:

> The structure of the passage is thus very much inclined in favour of the long reading. This conclusion is not reached because of the mere fact that there is *a* structure in the passage. It is surely possible to identify *a* structure in almost any given New Testament passage. It is rather the nature of the structure which is convincing. Luke used a parallelism, a structure very well known to the authors of both the Old and New Testaments. Had any other structure, not as commonly used as the parallelism, been identified, the argument would have been much weaker.[105]

Petzer is certainly right that one can find a structure wherever one looks; structural analyses are often as fascinating for what they reveal about the creativity of the critic as for what they reveal about the text. But to claim that the structure he uncovers is compelling *because* it is common is really rather hard to evaluate.[106] At any rate, I might observe that if we simply accept Petzer's own categories of sign and explanation but modify his structure by removing the words of the longer text, we have not simply eliminated the bipartite parallelism; we have also uncovered a chiasmus (A – B – A), a structure that is vying with parallelism for most favored status among New Testament exegetes who look for such things.[107]

The suggestion of a chiasmus in this case, however, is probably a dead end, in part because (as we shall see) Petzer's categories do *not* work very well for the passage, and in part because verse 19a has to be considered in relation to its broader context, specifically verses 21–22. In fact, there are clear reasons for seeing verse 19a as the beginning of the *following* pericope, rather than the conclusion of the preceding. And, interestingly enough, it is *this* pericope (vv. 19a, 21–22) that is shaped through a parallelism comparable to what one finds in verses 15–18. Here again one may simply be finding a structure wherever one looks, but in this instance there are specific linguistic indicators of the structure, indicators that are missed when verse 19a is isolated from the verses that follow.

To set the structure of verses 19a–22 in its broader linguistic context, we do well to consider Petzer's analysis of verses 15–18. He appears to be right in claiming that these verses form a self-contained unit in which Jesus first expresses his desire to eat the passover with his disciples, describing his action in terms of the Kingdom of God, and then distributes the cup, again speaking of the Kingdom. The structure is suggested in part by the author's use of the phrase λέγω γὰρ ὑμῖν to introduce the words about the kingdom in both verses 16 and 18. But is the category of explanation really the most suitable for understanding these words? Are the disciples to distribute the cup *because* Jesus will drink no more wine until the kingdom comes? No, these words instead indicate a *contrast* between Jesus' eating and drinking with his disciples at this meal and his eating and drinking in the future Kingdom (note that he speaks only of himself in the "explanations"). Or to put the matter differently, the contrast is between Jesus sharing food and drink with the faithful in the present, and his own eating and drinking in the eschatological future.[108]

What would lead one to take verse 19a as the opening of the following pericope (vv. 19a-22, without vv. 19b-20)? In brief, doing so reveals a formally similar parallelism: Jesus makes a statement and then a contrast. But now the contrast does not involve his participation in the future Kingdom as it implicitly relates to the disciples who share his fellowship; it is instead a contrast between Jesus' ignominious fate on earth and the one follower who is responsible for delivering him over to it. As was the case with the earlier pericope, here the linguistic indicator of the structure appears in the repetition of a key transitional term at the beginning of each contrast. Whereas the contrasts of verses 16 and 18 were introduced with the words λέγω γὰρ ὑμῖν, here they are indicated by πλήν, one of Luke's favorite conjunctions.[109] Furthermore, Jesus' opening statement in each part concerns his coming fate, and in each case the contrast is made to the one who betrays him (παρα-δίδωμι both times):

(A) And taking bread, giving thanks, he broke it and gave it to them, saying, This is my body (v. 19a)

  (B) But (πλήν) behold, the hand of the one who betrays (τοῦ παραδιδόντος) me is with me on the table (v. 21)

(A¹) For (ὅτι, continuation!) the Son of Man goes as it was ordained for him (v. 22a);

  (B¹) But (πλήν) woe to that man through whom he is betrayed (παραδι-´δοται) (v. 22b)

This structure, as indicated, is able to account for the repetitions of πλήν and παραδίδωμι in the passage, something left out of account in Petzer's analysis, and serves better to highlight the contrasting character of the two pericopes (vv. 15–18, 19–22) when considered together.[110] In the first, Jesus discusses his fate in light of the coming Kingdom of God, a fate associated with his faithful followers who partake of this meal with him (perhaps suggesting that they too will share his vindication as they continue to break bread with him; see, e.g., Luke 24:35); in the second, he focuses on his approaching martyrdom, in which his body will be broken because of the betrayal of an unfaithful follower, whose destiny is not the joys of the eschatological kingdom but the sufferings of the eschatological woes.

The plausibility of this structure is only heightened by the circumstance that it avoids the words and theology of the longer text that are found nowhere else in Luke-Acts.

It also avoids the problem of having to explain how the text came to be changed in the course of its transmission, a problem that proves insurmountable for all advocates of the longer text. Petzer's explanation of the omission is as typical as it is illuminating: "A scribe must have omitted these disputed words in order to avoid the difficult cup-bread-cup sequence so that Luke's account of the institution of the Lord's Supper could be harmonized with the other institution narratives."[111] A remarkable comment, this, for precisely here is the problem: the shorter text neither solves the problem of the sequence of the narrative nor effects a harmonization with the other three New Testament accounts of the institution. The order of cup-bread occurs in none of the other passages, and the closest verbal parallels with any of them occur only in the *longer* text's similarities to 1 Corinthians 11. The shorter text is by no means a harmonization to any of the other accounts. How can one explain an omission if the longer text is original?

Transcriptional Probabilities

In point of fact, no one has been able to provide a convincing explanation for how the shorter text came into existence if the longer text is original. One of the standard explanations is that a scribe who either could not understand or did not appreciate the appearance of two cups in Luke's narrative eliminated one of them to make the account coincide better with all the others. The explanation has proved popular because it has all the appearance of plausibility. But it is only an appearance; over a century ago Hort showed why the theory does not work and no one has been able to refute his arguments.[112] If a scribe was concerned with harmonizing the account to its parallels, why did he eliminate the *second* cup instead of the first? It is the first that is problematic, because it is distributed before the giving of the bread; and it is the second that is familiar, because the words of institution parallel so closely those of Paul in 1 Corinthians. Still more damaging, this explanation cannot at all account for the omission of verse 19b, where the cup is not yet mentioned. Why did the alleged scribe, concerned to eliminate the second cup, take away with it the words of institution over the bread? Did he just happen to excise the words and theology that otherwise appear intrusive in Luke's Gospel but reflect the words of institution known from Paul? Whatever the motivation for the change, it was not simply to eliminate the mention of a second cup or to harmonize the account with the others.

The frustration scholars have had in explaining the shorter text is particularly evident in a theory that for all its popularity represents little more than a counsel in despair. Advocated originally by Jeremias,[113] the theory claims that scribes abbreviated the text to keep the sacred words of institution from becoming a part of the public domain, lest they be used by nonbelievers for insidious magical purposes. In Jeremias's hands this theory of the so-called *disciplina arcani* provided a panacea for all kinds of problems in the Gospels: it explained why, for example, Mark refused to reveal the words Jesus spoke to Satan in the wilderness during the days of his temptation in Mark 1:12–13 and why he ended his Gospel at 16:8 without disclosing the parting words of Jesus to his disciples. Apart from these curiosities, one must ask how well the theory resolves the textual problem of Luke 22:19–20. Whom exactly did these second-century scribes, fearful of the misuse of the text, envisage as the users of their gospels? Were they planning to sell their manuscripts at the local book mart? If the words of institution were problematic, why did the scribes in question not eliminate them in their entirety? Why, that is, did they leave verse 19a intact? And, still more perplexing, why was the *same* motivation not operative in the transmission histories of Matthew, Mark, and 1 Corinthians, where the texts are liable to precisely the same abuse but nonetheless survived the penknives of the second-century scribes unscathed?[114] Even most proponents of the longer text have failed to be convinced.

This leaves us, however, with our query concerning the origin of the shorter text if the longer one is original. Virtually the only explanation that might account for it is that verses 19b–20 dropped out by accident. Unfortunately, this proves to be as problematic as the theory that the text was cut on purpose. For it would be remarkable indeed for thirty-two words to drop out of a text for no apparent reason (such as homoeoteleuton). Is it an accident that these thirty-two words just happen to supply precisely what is missing otherwise in the account, a notion that Jesus' body and blood would be given on behalf of his disciples? Is it an accident that this theological construal, found in this passage only in the disputed thirty-two words, is otherwise alien to Luke's entire two-volume work? Is it an accident that these words, and only these words, parallel the words found in 1 Corinthians? An intriguing accident indeed!

In short, it is well-nigh impossible to explain the shorter text of Luke 22:19–20 if the longer text is original. But it is not at all difficult to account for an *interpolation* of the disputed words into Luke's brief account of Jesus' last supper with his disciples.[115] As we have seen, Luke's two-volume work avoids all mention of Jesus giving his body and shedding his blood *for* his followers (ὑπὲρ ὑμῶν); Luke eliminated or changed the Marcan references to Jesus' atoning sacrifice; he chose not to quote Isaiah 53 to depict Jesus' death as an atonement for sins, even though he quoted the passage otherwise; he referred back to Jesus' death in the book of Acts simply as if it were a miscarriage of justice that God set right in raising Jesus from the dead. To be sure, this author's account of Jesus' confrontation with death proved useful for proto-orthodox Christians of the second century who themselves emphasized the necessity of martyrdom and the need to emulate the tranquility of

Jesus in the face of it.[116] But it was not at all useful when they wanted to stress, in direct opposition to certain groups of docetic opponents, that Christ experienced a real passion in which his body was broken and his blood was shed for the sins of the world.

It is no accident that Tertullian refers to Christ's consecration of the wine as his blood to disparage Marcion's view that he was merely a phantom (*Treatise on the Soul,* 17), and on another occasion cites the entire institution narrative as known from 1 Corinthians 11 and the longer text of Luke to the same end:

> [Jesus] declared plainly enough what He meant by the bread, when He called the bread His own body. He likewise, when mentioning the cup and making the new testament to be sealed "in His blood," affirms the reality of His body. For no blood can belong to a body which is not a body of flesh. Thus from the evidence of the flesh, we get a proof of the body, and a proof of the flesh from the evidence of the blood (*Adv. Marc.* IV, 40).

In using the text in this way, Tertullian allied himself with other proto-orthodox authors of the second century. Somewhat earlier Irenaeus too had refuted Marcion by asking how his docetic Christology could be reconciled with Jesus' insistence that the bread represented his body and the cup his blood (*Adv. Haer.* IV, 33, 2). Yet more significantly, Irenaeus attacked other unnamed docetists for refusing to see that Christ's shed blood alone is what brings human redemption, and that for this blood to be efficacious it had to be real: real blood shed to bring real salvation, Christ's real flesh given to redeem our human flesh (*Adv. Haer.* V, 2, 2).

It is precisely the emphasis on Jesus' giving of his own flesh and blood for the salvation of believers, as represented in the physical elements of the bread broken "for you" and the cup given "for you," that made the longer text of Luke 22:19–20 so attractive to the proto-orthodox heresiologists of the second century. And it is the same theological concern that can account for the genesis of the corruption in the first place. Whereas Luke's account served well to portray his own understanding of Jesus' last meal and death, it did not prove as serviceable for later Christians who wanted to emphasize the atoning merits of that death, a death that involved the real shedding of real blood for the sins of the world. And so the text was modified by means of a partial assimilation to the familiar institution narrative reflected in Paul's letter to the Corinthians. In changing the text in this way, these scribes were part of a much larger phenomenon that has left its abiding mark throughout the manuscript record of the New Testament.

Other Examples

We are now in a position to consider more briefly other variant readings that similarly stress the salvific significance of Jesus' broken body and shed blood.

I begin with the modifications of a parallel account, the narrative of Jesus' Last Supper found in Paul's first letter to the Corinthians (11:23–24). In Paul's version of the story, Jesus breaks bread and says, "This is my body that is for you (τοῦτό μού ἐστιν τὸ σῶμα τὸ ὑπὲρ ὑμῶν). Do this in my remembrance." Just as some scribes felt that the saying of Luke 22:19a ended all too abruptly, others considered Jesus' first sentence here ("This is my body that is for you") to be lacking as well. Consequently, over the course of its transmission, the statement came to be amplified through the addition of a participle, normally taken from a parallel passage (διδόμενον)[117] or from the immediate context (κλώμενον, cf. ἔκλασεν, v. 24a).[118] The latter addition, however, is not merely an inadvertent completion of the thought. Not only does it occur in a number of scribal corrections, showing that it was made conscientiously rather than accidentally, it also provides a more vivid statement that Christ's (real) body was broken like the bread of the Eucharist, an emphasis particularly germane for the proto-orthodox insistence on the physical nature of Jesus' passion. Still more clear is the theological implication of the singular reading preserved in codex Bezae. Here Jesus is recorded as saying, "This is my body that is *broken in pieces* for you" (τὸ σῶμα τὸ ὑπὲρ ὑμῶν θρυπτόμενον). In this instance the participle has been drawn neither from the context nor from a parallel passage; the word θρύπτω occurs nowhere else in the manuscript tradition of the New Testament. Moreover, the addition does not serve merely to round out Jesus' words concerning his coming fate; it instead provides a graphic emphasis on the reality of Jesus' passion.[119]

Other textual variants focus less on Jesus' body than on his blood. Rather than making a full list, I will simply consider an interesting example in the scribal modification of Colossians 1:14.[120] In a phrase that closely parallels Ephesians 1:7, Colossians speaks of Christ, "in whom we have redemption, the forgiveness of sins" (ἐν ᾧ ἔχομεν τὴν ἀπολύτρωσιν, τὴν ἄφεσιν τῶν ἁμαρτιῶν). The differences from the text in Ephesians are slight but significant: the latter refers to "transgressions" (παραπτωμάτων) rather than to "sins" and makes the important additional statement that "redemption" comes "through his blood" (διὰ τοῦ αἵματος αὐτοῦ). It is perhaps not surprising to find that scribes have occasionally interpolated this addition into Colossians as well,[121] and one might suspect that in doing so they have either intentionally or subconsciously effected a harmonization. But again one must ask what kind of scribe would have done so and for whom the emphasis on Christ's blood for redemption would have been so important. Significantly, Irenaeus appears to have the longer text already in the second century, if we can trust the Latin translation of his magnum opus. There he quotes the passage, using the distinctively Colossian form of "sins" and proceeding several sentences later to introduce a quotation of Ephesians by referring to "The Blessed Paul in his Letter to the Ephesians," as if he were citing the epistle for the first time in his argument (*Adv. Haer.* V, 2, 3). It would appear that the modification of Colossians had transpired already by the mid-second century, and it is perhaps of no small significance that Irenaeus cites the modified text explicitly against those who deny the salvation of the flesh, reasoning that if the flesh were not to be saved, there would have been no purpose in Christ actually shedding his blood (V, 2, 2).

A number of textual corruptions scattered throughout the tradition lay a comparable stress on the salvific necessity of Christ's suffering and death by interpolating such stock phrases as "for us," "for the sins of the world," or "for the forgiveness of sins" into passages that originally lacked them. In many instances these interpolations are brought over from parallel accounts. Returning for the moment to the institution narratives, one finds two such corruptions in the Gospel according to Mark. When Jesus says "This is my body," in 14:22, it is not surprising to find that one Old Latin manuscript has "completed" the thought: "This is my body, which is broken *(confringitur)* for many for the remission of sins."[122] Nor is one taken aback two verses later to find the same witness, this time in better company, adding the phrase "for the forgiveness of sins" to Jesus' words over the cup: "This is my blood of the covenant poured out for many" (W f^{13} a).

Although John lacks a narrative of the institution, a comparable change occurs early in his Gospel where some scribes, beginning at least in the third century, assimilated the statement of the Baptist in 1:36 to what they had already copied in 1:29, so that now the text doubly emphasizes that this Lamb of God "takes away the sins of the world" (𝔭^{66} C [W^s] 892 1241 pc). Not altogether dissimilar is the scribal change of Paul's familiar statement that "Christ our paschal lamb has been sacrificed" (1 Cor 5:7). An early corruption that proved influential for Christian liturgy adds ὑπὲρ ἡμῶν, so that now Christ is said to be the paschal lamb sacrificed "for us" (א^2 C^3 Ψ Byz syr sah bo^{ms}). So, too, in 1 Peter 4:1, where Christ is said to have "suffered in the flesh," a vast array of witnesses among the Greek manuscripts, versions, and patristic sources, in a variety of ways, have inserted the same phrase to the same end, in order to show that Christ's sufferings were "for us."[123]

Christ, Raised Bodily from the Dead

The anti-docetic variants considered to this point have all related to the orthodox notion that Christ really did suffer and die in the body and that this bodily suffering and death were essential for the salvation of the world. I now shift my attention to textual corruptions that emphasize the necessary corollary (necessary, that is, for the orthodox), that the Christ who died in the body was also raised in the body. The importance of Jesus' bodily resurrection is stressed throughout the writings of the early heresiologists.[124] In his attack on Marcion, Irenaeus ironically asks: "What body was it that those who buried him consigned to the tomb? And what was that which rose again from the dead?" (*Adv. Haer.* IV, 33, 2). Tertullian expresses the logic of the orthodox view:

> Now if [Christ's] death be denied, because of the denial of His flesh, there will be no certainty of His resurrection. For He rose not, for the very same

reason that He died not, even because He possessed not the reality of the flesh, to which as death accrues, so does resurrection likewise. Similarly, if Christ's resurrection be nullified, ours also is destroyed (*Adv. Marc.* III, 8).[125]

The representatives of proto-orthodoxy could appeal, of course, to writings of the New Testament to support their claim that Christ was raised in the body. Not many passages, however, discuss the matter directly, and most that do are notoriously vague with respect to the precise nature of Christ's existence after his resurrection. Was it his own physical body that was resuscitated and made immortal, or did he live on in a numinous state? A number of heretical Christians, to the consternation of their proto-orthodox antagonists, assumed the latter.[126] In response, the early heresiologists urged not only that Christ's body was real while he lived, but also that it continued to be real after he came back from the dead.[127] It is not my intention to evaluate the exegetical strengths of these two positions. For the present purpose, it is enough to note that the ambiguity of the biblical teachings about the physicality of Jesus' resurrected body can help explain why proto-orthodox scribes may have wanted to insert support for their views into significant passages. Some of the most disputed corruptions of this kind happen to occur in the final chapter of the Gospel according to Luke, in a series of modifications found almost exclusively outside of the so-called Western tradition. I begin my discussion by looking at one of the thorniest and most debated texts, the account of Peter's visit to the tomb in Luke 24:12.

Luke 24:12

Luke 24:9–11 tells the familiar story of the women returning from Jesus' empty tomb to report to the eleven disciples what they had seen. The disciples find their story ridiculous (λῆρος) and refuse to believe them. This brief account is supplemented in the vast majority of witnesses with the addendum of verse 12: "But Peter, rising up, ran to the tomb; and stooping down he saw the linen cloths alone, and he returned home marvelling at what had happened."[128] The verse is lacking only in key elements of the Western tradition (D a b d e l r¹)[129] and represents another of Westcott and Hort's "Western non-interpolations" (cf. Luke 22:19b–20), a short Western text that, in their judgment, preserves the original reading, despite the attestation of a longer form in all other witnesses. As is the case with all such "non-interpolations," the complexities of the textual data do not permit a simple judgment to be based on the external evidence; despite the paucity of its attestation, the shorter Western reading almost certainly derives from a period no later than the second century.[130] Moreover, intrinsic and transcriptional probabilities speak so strongly in its favor that its claim to represent the original form of the passage cannot be easily laid aside.

Most recent scholars have laid it aside nonetheless, dismissing the arguments in its favor more or less out of hand.[131] In the discussion that follows, I will try to show why this emerging consensus is wrong. The presence of the verse in a wide range of textual witnesses actually represents an orthodox corruption.

I begin by examining the arguments typically adduced in favor of the longer text, arguments based not only on its superior external attestation but even more on its intrinsic suitability. Most of the recent literature affirms Adolf von Harnack's judgment that the verse represents "a sentence in good Lukan style." [132] The most compelling spokesperson has been Joachim Jeremias, who cites three features of the verse as "characteristically Lukan": the pleonastic use of ἀναστάς, the term θαυμάζειν, and the phrase τὸ γεγονός. The argument has proved influential, with few critics recognizing the force of the countervailing evidence. In point of fact, however, not only are these "characteristic" features problematic, but the verse also contains an extraordinary number of decidedly non-Lukan elements. Just from the perspective of language and style, not to speak yet of the broader literary context and the problems of transcription, it is difficult to believe that Luke penned this brief narrative of Peter's visit to the tomb.

It is certainly true that pleonastic ἀναστάς, deprived, that is, of its literal meaning, is frequent in Luke, occurring there some thirteen times. [133] At the same time, this usage is not at all *unique* to Luke, as it occurs elsewhere in the Gospel traditions—some five times, for instance, in the much shorter Gospel of Mark. Yet more significantly, the usage in Luke 24:12 is absolutely *atypical,* because, as has sometimes been noted, this is the only time in all of Luke-Acts that a pleonastic ἀναστάς follows rather than precedes its subject. [134] Although this anomaly cannot be used by itself to indicate that Luke could not have authored the verse, it should at least put us on guard concerning claims that the style is "characteristically" Lukan. What now of Jeremias's other data? Not much can be made of his appeal to θαυμάζειν as "characteristically Lukan." The θαυμα- word group is, to be sure, common in Luke, where it occurs twelve times. But it occurs throughout the other Gospels as well, some nine times in Matthew alone. A better case can be made for τὸ γεγονός, which Luke uses four times outside the present verse, although it should be noted that in one of these four instances he has borrowed the term from his source, the Gospel According to Mark (Luke 9:35, Mark 5:14). At the very least, then, these observations relativize the claim that the verse is "characteristically" Lukan, if by that we mean "distinctively" Lukan: of the data normally used to establish the claim, one is anomalous and the others to some degree are the common stock of the New Testament writings.

One could, of course, argue that the *concatenation* of such features creates a kind of Lukan flavor. Even this conclusion loses much of its force, however, when one considers the contrary evidence. For the verse contains an inordinate number of *non*-Lukan features as well. One glaring instance struck even Jeremias, forcing him to compromise his claim that the verse bore Luke's clear imprint. This is the use of the historic present βλέπει, a usage that stands at odds with Lukan style virtually everywhere else. How rare is the historic present in Luke? Of its ninty-three occurrences in the Markan material that Luke reproduced, he changed ninty-two.[135] For Jeremias, the historic present in 24:12 meant that the verse was not *exactly* Lukan in style: Luke must have inherited the verse from his tradition, seriously editing parts of it (implementing his characteristic style), but leaving other parts unedited (those that are uncharacteristic).

Other key features of the text are completely alien to Luke. Three words or phrases of this solitary verse occur nowhere else throughout his entire two-volume work: παρακύψας, τὰ ὀθόνια, and ἀπῆλθεν πρὸς ἑαυτόν. It would be quite a stretch to argue, as is sometimes done, that these words cannot count against the Lukan authorship of the verse because they are "required by the nature of the material."[136] There are alternative words and idioms for each of them and Luke was perfectly free to make use of whatever vocabulary he chose (especially if he edited the tradition in accordance with his characteristic style). It is surely of some significance that Luke does in fact refer to some of this "material" elsewhere—specifically, the material of Jesus' burial shroud—and that when he does so he uses one of these alternative terms (σινδών, in 23:53). An interesting result is that in the disputed verse the resurrected Jesus has vacated *not* the kind of garment in which he was buried (σινδών) but a kind that Luke has never mentioned (τὰ ὀθόνια).

What all investigators of this verse have noticed, of course, is how closely it parallels the much longer story of the Fourth Gospel, where Peter and the Beloved Disciple race to the tomb to find it empty (John 20:3–10). It is particularly striking, in this connection, that precisely those words that are otherwise alien to Luke-Acts (along with the historic present) are attested in the Johannine story, with John 20:5 providing a particularly close parallel: καὶ παρακύψας βλέπει κείμενα τὰ ὀθόνια. Among other things, as I will emphasize in a moment, this means that the text that is problematic in terms of Lukan style is also more closely harmonized with a parallel account; here again intrinsic and transcriptional probabilities work in tandem to favor one of the two readings. Moreover, it is worth observing that if the nature of the material constrained Luke to use the unusual words and phrases of the verse only here, it did not at all affect John in the same way: the disputed terms occur elsewhere in his account.[137]

In sum, the intrinsic probabilities appear to work *against* the longer form of the passage. If Luke did edit this verse from his source, molding it according to his own characteristic style, he did so in a remarkably haphazard way, leaving a syntactical construction that he eliminated virtually everywhere else (the historic present), failing to reverse the sequence of the pleonastic participle with the subject in accordance with his consistent style, using a word for Jesus' burial clothes that does not correspond to the word he used just a few verses earlier, and employing two other terms that occur nowhere else in his entire two-volume *magnum opus*. All this in a single verse.

When one turns from intrinsic to transcriptional probabilities, there can be little question as to which of our readings is to be preferred. The words of the longer reading are closely paralleled in another Gospel text; yet more importantly, it is nearly impossible to explain their absence from an early stream of the tradition here, if in fact they were original. What is at stake is not simply the character and quality of the witnesses that lack the verse; it is even more a question of how one *accounts* for their omission. The one thing proponents of the verse have never been able to explain is why the Western scribe(s) might have deleted it.[138] Were the words dropped by accident? There are no orthographic grounds for thinking so, no homoeoteleuton or homoeoarcton, for example, that could explain it. And it is scarcely possible that the Western scribe(s) simply overlooked a story of such significance and length (over twenty words). An omission, then, would almost certainly have been made deliberately.

Is it possible that the verse was deleted because of its slight discrepancies with the Johannine parallel or with its own literary context? In the Fourth Gospel Peter does not run alone to the tomb but is accompanied by the Beloved Disciple; and later in Luke's own story, the two disciples on the road to Emmaus acknowledge that "some of our number" (not an individual, Peter) had gone to corroborate the women's tale of the empty tomb. Since both stories portray a plurality of apostolic witnesses at the tomb, whereas this account speaks only of Peter, could alert scribes have eliminated the problem simply by removing the verse?[139]

This too seems an unlikely scenario. If a scribe were to find a discrepancy with verse 12 when he copied verse 24, he would more likely have changed verse 24 (the one he copied second), for example, by making it say that "one" of us or "Peter" verified the women's story. Even if a scribe were to change verse 12, it would surely have been simpler for him to add someone else's name to the text (to explain "some of our number") than to erase the story altogether. When do scribes ever *obliterate* their sacred traditions when they can so easily "correct" them?[140] The same might be said if the discrepancy with John were really the issue: modifying the text in light of the parallel might make sense—but eliminating it?

It is worth observing that some scholars who accept the Western text here, that is, who agree that verse 12 is a corruption, have thought that it was added precisely in order to provide an antecedent for the claim made in verse 24—namely, to allow Luke to narrate the apostolic verification of the women's tale that he claims has transpired. In my judgment, this explanation of the textual problem, although right with regard to the corruption, is wrong with regard to its motivation, for it creates more problems than it solves. Surely a scribe concerned to explain the "backward glance" of verse 24 would have "some" apostles examine the tomb, rather than Peter alone (cf. the Fourth Gospel). Indeed, this is another major sticking point, even for those who think that verse 12 is original. How could Luke have used verse 12 to set up the backward glance of verse 24, when the latter verse claims that several persons have done what in fact only one has?

We are left with a text that is permeated with non-Lukan features, that resembles an account of the Fourth Gospel, that stands at odds with its literary context, and that is absent from an an early stream of the tradition in a way that can scarcely be explained if it originally formed part of the Lukan narrative.

If we were to accept the secondary character of the verse, yet acknowledge that it was not inserted to explain the statement of verse 24, how else might we account for its interpolation? Even those who accept the verse as original recognize its two salient points: Jesus was bodily raised from the dead and this was fully recognized at the outset by Peter, the chief of the disciples. To be sure, the women had earlier beheld an empty tomb and were told by "two men" that Jesus had been raised. But this may indeed have been a "silly tale" of hysterical women; it was, in any case, understood this way by the disciples themselves (Luke 24:11), who might understandably press for a clarification of the report. Who were these two men that they could be trusted with such an important revelation?[141] And what does it mean to say that Jesus was "raised"? Just such issues proved important to the orthodox understanding of the resurrection in the second and third centuries, in no small measure because proto-orthodox Christians insisted that Christ experienced a particular mode of resurrection (the body that died was itself revived; i.e., the resurrection was not "spiritual" but "physical") and claimed that the leaders of the early (orthodox) Christian movement, especially Peter, were the first to embrace such a view.[142] Our verse supports both notions. Peter, patriarch of the orthodox, enters the tomb and finds indisputable proof that his Lord has indeed been raised in the body, the concrete physical evidence that the women had not seen: the linen burial clothes are still in the tomb.

It is probably no accident that this evidence of Jesus' bodily resurrection is given where it is. Without these revelatory linens, Luke's subsequent tales of the resurrected Jesus can appear more than a little ambiguous, susceptible to a patently unorthodox interpretation by those who did not recognize that the Jesus who appeared to his disciples after his resurrection did so precisely in the body that had died. For Luke's resurrected Jesus seems to have powers even beyond those manifest while he was living: he can now change appearances at will (cf. the account of the road to Emmaus, 24:13–32) and appear out of thin air in the midst of a crowd (24:36). Does this not indicate that Jesus' resurrected body was numinous or spiritual rather than physical? It is a sensible conclusion, one that the disciples themselves draw ("thinking they beheld a spirit," v. 37), until Jesus shows them his hands and feet and eats some of their fish. We can observe that Peter is evidently among this group of the incredulous, a circumstance more than a little curious if 24:12 were original. Once this earlier verse has been inserted into the account, Peter at least (patriarch of the orthodox!) has already beheld the truth: Jesus was raised in body, precisely the body that had bled and died and been buried. This is the distinctively orthodox understanding of the resurrection, as attested by Origen: "The church alone, in distinction from all the heresies that deny the resurrection, confesses the resurrection of the dead body. . . . For if his body had not become a corpse, capable of being wrapped in a gravecloth . . . and being laid in a tomb—these are things that cannot be done to a spiritual body" (Origen, *Dial. Heracl.* 132–33).[143]

To sum up: Luke 24:12 does not fit well into its context, it contains a remarkable number of non-Lukan features that do, however, occur in a parallel account of the Fourth Gospel, and its absence from an early stream of the tradition can scarcely be explained if it were original. But it does stress the orthodox notion that the real body of Jesus that was buried was the real body that was raised, and that this has always been the correct understanding of the faithful, beginning with Peter, head of the apostles. The verse appears, then, to have been inserted by an orthodox scribe as a hermeneutical lens through which the stories of Jesus' post-resurrection appearances in the rest of Luke's account could be read. The insertion was made early in the second century, and came then to infiltrate a sizable portion of the textual tradition of the Third Gospel.

Other Examples among the "Western Non-Interpolations"

I can now turn to other "heightenings" of the orthodox view of Jesus' resurrection that occur within the same Lukan context among the same textual witnesses. Contrary to widespread opinion, there is no reason to take all the so-called Western non-interpolations en masse, as if they all stand or fall together. As I will point out in the Excursus, not even Hort did this, even though he has occasionally been faulted, somehow, for refusing to do so. Instead, each variant must be considered on its own merits and without prejudicing the issue by claiming that readings found "only" among Western witnesses cannot possibly be original.[144]

All the same, it is striking that a pattern appears to be emerging among the so-called non-interpolations considered to this point (Matt 27:49; Luke 22:19–20; 24:12): the corruption in each case represents an early *interpolation* (outside of the Western tradition) that works against a docetic form of Christology. To my knowledge, the specifically anti-docetic character of these corruptions, as a group, has never been fully recognized.[145] Remarkably, the trend appears to continue in the variants I will now consider. This can be done in relatively brief fashion as the terms of the discussion have already been set.

I have suggested that the traditions of Luke's resurrection narrative proved significant for orthodox Christians who emphasized Christ's real bodily existence.[146] This significance is evidenced in the close parallels found in the writings of Ignatius, who says in his letter to the Smyrneans: "For I myself know and believe that even after his resurrection he was in the flesh. And when he came to those around Peter he said to them: 'Take, handle me and see that I am not a disembodied spirit' (οὐκ εἰμὶ δαιμόνιον ἀσώματον). And immediately they touched him and believed" (Ign. *Smyrn.* 3, 2). The literary relationship of this passage to Luke 24:39–40 has long intrigued scholars, but has proved difficult to resolve.[147] On the one hand, Jesus' second injunction is the same in both texts: "Handle me and see" (ψηλαφήσατέ με καὶ ἴδετε).[148] But the introduction to this exhortation differs, as does the conclusion that the disciples are to draw from having obeyed it.[149] Yet more significantly, Ignatius identifies this as an incident that happened when Jesus appeared to those "around Peter." As has been seen, Peter is not explicitly mentioned in the Lukan account.

These considerations make it appear that Ignatius is not directly quoting Luke, but is referring to an incident that was independently known to them both.[150] What matters for our purpose is the meaning that Ignatius draws from the event: he uses it to show the physical character of Jesus' body after his resurrection. To this extent he agrees with a whole range of proto-orthodox Christians, including Hippolytus of Rome, who conflates Luke's account with the story of doubting Thomas (John 20:26–29) to establish that Jesus' resurrection was in the body: "For He, having risen, and being desirous to show that that same (body) had been raised which had also died, when his disciples were in doubt, called Thomas to Him, and said, "Reach here; handle me, and see: for a spirit does not have bone and flesh, as you see that I have.' "[151]

In light of this orthodox emphasis, what is one to make of the textual variations evidenced among the witnesses to Luke's account? Of particular interest is the fact that codex Bezae and a number of Old Latin and Syriac witnesses do not include Luke 24:40: "Having said this, he showed them his hands and feet." Here again (cf. Luke 24:12) the verse in question finds a parallel in the Johannine account: "and having said this, he showed them his hands and side" (John 20:20).[152] There is little doubt that the addition of verse 40 makes the Lukan text assert yet more strongly the physicality of Jesus' resurrected body. Not that most interpreters would doubt the point, even without the verse, given verse 39 ("Handle [me] and see . . ."). With verse 40, however, Jesus not only urges his disciples to touch him, but actually presents his hands and feet for their inspection. That this kind of heightened emphasis could prove serviceable for the orthodox proponents of Jesus' real physical resurrection is evidenced by Tertullian's ironical query of Marcion, "Why, moreover, does He offer his hands and His feet for their examination—limbs which consist of bones—if he had no bones?" (*Adv. Marc.* IV, 43).[153]

One is left with the question of how to account for both forms of the text. Here I can ask a telling transcriptional question: Which is more likely, that a scribe took over a tradition known from the Fourth Gospel and, *mutatis mutandi,* brought it into the Gospel of Luke where it could strengthen the orthodox interpretation of the text, or that a scribe excised the passage? It is in fact extremely difficult to explain an excision, as becomes clear when one sees the explanations that are sometimes given. The verse would scarcely have been deleted as redundant after verse 39.[154] When did scribes omit passages that emphasized their cherished beliefs? Nor would the apparent incongruence with John 20:20 ("feet" instead of "side") have caused an omission, but at most a simple harmonization.[155] Jeremias strains all credulity when he argues that the verse was omitted because it contradicts John 20:17 ("Do not touch me, for I have not yet ascended to my Father"). Within John itself Jesus shows his body and urges others to touch it! Why then, on this score, were John 20:20 and 27 not omitted in the tradition as well?

There is no good reason to think that the account of Luke 24:40 was excised. But given the orthodox insistence that Jesus was raised and appeared to his disciples in a real physical body, there are solid grounds, so to speak, for seeing the verse as an interpolation.

Three other so-called Western non-interpolations appear to demonstrate the same kind of scribal proclivity seen so far, although in less clear-cut fashion. In Luke 24:3 the women are said to come to the tomb of Jesus only to find the stone rolled away. "And entering in they did not find the body of the Lord Jesus." The Syriac tradition and several later Greek manuscripts (including the Alexandrian MS 1241) state only that the women did not find the "body of Jesus" (i.e., they omit κυρίου); more significantly, the entire phrase "of the Lord Jesus" is lacking from the "Western" text as found in codex Bezae and most of the Old Latin witnesses. Is the phrase original to Luke?

It is worth observing that its occurrence here is anomalous: in no other verse of any of the four Gospels does an evangelist speak of "the Lord Jesus" (except for the long ending of Mark 16:19——another scribal addition!). The phrase *is* used, however, by Luke in the book of Acts, where it occurs rather commonly as an expression of belief in the resurrected Jesus.[156] In Luke 24:3, however, it is not used as an expression of belief, for the women have yet to learn from the heavenly witnesses that Jesus has been raised. The wording of the disputed phrase, then, appears to run counter to established Lukan usage.

It does not, however, run counter to the proto-orthodox understanding of the resurrection (witness Mark 16:19), leaving us again with a shorter text that can scarcely be explained if it is not original. Why would a scribe have deleted these words? On the other hand, it is easy to see why one might have wanted to insert them, namely, as a testimony to the orthodox belief that the "body of the Lord Jesus" that was placed in the tomb was also the body that left it.

A comparable heightening of emphasis appears to have been at work in the transmission of Luke 24:6. In the preceding verse the "two men" have asked the terrified women why they are "seeking the living among the dead." In the Western tradition they continue by exhorting the women to "remember how he spoke to you while yet in Galilee, saying that the Son of man must be turned over to the hands of sinful people, and be crucified, and on the third day be raised again" (v. 6). Outside the Western tradition, however, the heavenly visitants preface their exhortation with an unequivocal statement of Jesus' resurrection: "He is not here, but has been raised." Once again the sentence is absent from codex Bezae and most of the Old Latin witnesses, and again one must ask what might have compelled a scribe to delete it. It surely was not seen as redundant: it is the first clear word that the angels have spoken of Jesus' resurrection from the dead. And scribes were not at all inclined, as we have seen, to eliminate from their texts precisely those emphases that they were most eager to find in them. Some scholars have argued that the backward glance of verse 23 ("and they had a vision of angels, who said that he was alive") demonstrates that the angels must have originally proclaimed Jesus' resurrection, as in the majority text of verse 6.[157] But verse

23 has very little to do with the disputed text because its summary of the angelic message states that Jesus "lives," not that he has "been raised," suggesting that it alludes to the question of verse 5 ("Why do you seek the *living* among the dead") rather than the disputed statement of verse 6.[158]

One is left with few internal grounds on which to decide the issue, but a telling transcriptional point: whereas there appears to be no good reason for any scribe of any time to have deleted the statement from an account that originally had it, there *was* a reason to insert it: the interpolation explicates the orthodox notion that Jesus' body, which was no longer in the tomb, had been raised from the dead.

A similar motivation may lie behind the corruption of verse 36. This is the story of Jesus' sudden appearance in the midst of the disciples, who in their fear mistake him for a "spirit" or a "ghost."[159] Outside of the Western tradition, one finds a somewhat lengthier account of the scene; in most witnesses Jesus speaks to his disciples immediately upon his arrival: "And he said to them, 'Peace be to you.'" Only then do they fear the phantasmal presence. In other witnesses, Jesus attempts to calm his disciples by making it yet clearer that it is he; in these witnesses he announces upon his arrival, "Peace be to you. It is I [ἐγώ εἰμί], do not be afraid." The disciples ignore his injunction and become afraid nonetheless.

Which of these three forms of text is original? The longest has the weakest claims to authenticity, given its relatively scattered attestation[160] and its obvious transcriptional appeal. Most critics have seen it as a gloss drawn from John 6:20.[161] But why was it made? It clearly functions to identify the resurrected Jesus with the one whom the disciples knew to have been crucified ("It is I"), and so may be accounted for as a scribal attempt to emphasize that identification. Given the versional support for the reading and its presence in two of the secondary Alexandrian manuscripts (579 1241), it may well date back to the period of our concern.

What now of the two other readings? Here again the non-Western witnesses present a text that mirrors a verse from the Fourth Gospel,[162] a text that is difficult to explain as an original component of the Gospel of Luke. On the one hand, it appears intrusive in its context. Without it (i.e., in the Western tradition), one can well understand why the disciples are terrified: they think they see an apparition, who to this point has remained speechless. Less understandable is their fear in the more common text, where Jesus speaks peace immediately upon appearing among them. To be sure, even in this longer text Jesus' subsequent conversation shows that he is not to be perceived as a "spirit," but as one who has "flesh and bones" (v. 39). The disciples then have erred in their initial judgment. It is less easy, though, to see *why* they have erred; in the Western tradition, at least, they appear justified in thinking they see an apparition because Jesus materializes without word or warning in their midst.

Orthodox Christians, of course, used this resurrection appearance to show that the disciples were mistaken in thinking that Jesus' post-resurrection existence was phantasmal. Tertullian appealed specifically to the passage to show that Jesus should have been recognized by his followers as having the same body he had while yet living (*Adv. Marc.* IV, 53). In light of the orthodox understanding of Jesus' resurrection, attested, so it was claimed, by this passage as a whole, it should be fairly obvious why a scribe may have interpolated the half-verse in question from the familiar tradition of John 20:19. It clarifies at the outset the disciples' foolish mistake. After his resurrection Jesus was no spirit; the Jesus who had been laid in a tomb was the one who had risen from the dead. Here again, then, while one can posit no plausible reason for an omission of these words, one can see a clear reason for their insertion. The harmonizing interpolation functions as an anti-docetic corruption.

What we have seen in the preceding deliberations is that a number of the readings that Hort isolated as Western non-interpolations evidence a theological *Tendenz*.[163] Or to put the matter more accurately, the non-Western *interpolations* evidence this *Tendenz*; for in these cases, the "Western" text evidences no scribal tendency at all, but simply attests the original text that came to be corrupted in another stream of the tradition early on in the history of its transmission. Moreover, these secondary corruptions of which the Western tradition is innocent all work in the same direction: each functions to counter the docetic Christologies that can be dated to the time of their creation, the early to mid-second century.[164]

Other Examples

The preceding discussion is not meant to suggest that the Western tradition itself was isolated from these controversies, or that Western witnesses escaped the anti-docetic biases of orthodox scribes as a *rule*. Quite to the contrary, we have already seen precisely this kind of corruption embodied in significant variations of the Western text (see Luke 22:43–44). Nor has the Western tradition survived unscathed even within the resurrection narrative of Luke. As an interesting example drawn from the textual problem just discussed, codex Bezae stands alone against all other witnesses of Luke 24:37 in saying that the disciples feared that they beheld a "ghost" (or "phantasm," φάντασμα) rather than a "spirit." Lacking the support of any versional evidence, this reading has far less claim to being original, and can be accounted for by its more vivid character; just as the disciples were at fault for considering Jesus a phantasm after his resurrection, so too did the docetists err in subscribing to this false belief. Tertullian explicitly quotes the Lukan narrative (Luke 24:39) to repudiate heretics who understand Jesus to have been a phantom after his resurrection (Latin "phantasma," *de carne Christi* 5). The disciples, at least, were willing to accept correction.[165]

Somewhat earlier in Luke's narrative Western witnesses again evidence the anti-docetic tendencies of early scribes. In chapter 23 Luke describes the burial of Jesus, observing that Joseph of Arimathea placed him in a rock-hewn tomb "where no one had ever yet been laid" (23:53). Not unexpectedly, some witnesses supplement the account with the words found in the parallel passages of Matthew and Mark: "and he rolled a great stone before the door of the tomb" (U f^{13} 700 bo al). Codex Bezae and several other witnesses go yet further in providing an interesting, if apocryphal, detail: "and having placed him [there] he positioned before the tomb a stone that scarcely twenty people could roll" (D [0124] c [sa]). The exaggerated emphasis on the enormity of the stone serves to magnify the sheer physical power needed to bring Jesus forth from the tomb. Given this emphasis on the physicality of Jesus' triumph over death, it is perhaps best to see this detail too as a kind of anti-docetic flourish supplied by an imaginative orthodox scribe.

One should not think that this kind of anti-docetic emphasis, whether Western or non-Western, is restricted to the final chapters of Luke. Similar modifications were made in the texts of other Gospels as well. There is little reason to doubt, for example, that the shortest text of Matthew 28:3 is correct in reporting the angel's words to the women at the tomb: "Come, see the place where he was laid" (so ℵ B Θ 33 892* e syr^c cop). Given what has been discussed so far, however, it is not surprising to find scribes throughout the tradition explaining in greater detail what most readers will have taken for granted. In a large array of witnesses the angel speaks of the place "where the Lord [rather than simply "he"] was laid" (A C D L W 0148 f$^{1.13}$ Byz OL al); one witness of the sixth century reads "where Jesus was laid" (Φ), and one other significant but late witness provides precisely the anti-docetic stress on Jesus' body that one might expect: "Come see where the body of the Lord (τὸ σῶμα τοῦ κυρίου) was laid" (MS 1424).

A different kind of anti-docetic corruption appears near the conclusion of the Fourth Gospel. The famous words of John 20:30 assure the reader that "Jesus did many other signs in the presence of his disciples that are not written in this book." The verse has generated some considerable debate among modern scholars; it is widely thought to have been drawn from the conclusion of the "Signs Source," the pre-Johannine narrative of Jesus' miracles that provided much of the material for chapters 1–11. If the verse did conclude such a document, it has been violently removed from its original context in order to serve as the conclusion of the entire Gospel here (prior, that is, to the appendage of ch. 21).[166] Part of the debate over the verse in its present context focuses on whether Jesus' appearance to Thomas itself constitutes a "sign" and whether the "other signs" to which the author refers were signs effected while Jesus was living and "revealed his glory" (2:11; i.e., whether they were the signs recounted in the "Signs Source") or whether they were signs he did after his resurrection to demonstrate its physical reality (cf., e.g., Acts 1:3). The latter explanation has a kind of anti-docetic appeal to it, making it no surprise to find it secured in the textual tradition of the verse by at least one fifth-century scribe, who can almost certainly be assumed to have reproduced an older tradition. In the words of manuscript e of the Gospels, Jesus did many other signs "after he had been raised from the dead." Some two verses later several other scribes proceed to complete the statement that "Jesus manifested himself again to the disciples" by adding the words "after having been raised from the dead" (Γ f^{13} 1241 1424 al), thereby reasserting the proto-orthodox emphasis on Jesus' resurrection "from the dead."

EXCURSUS: WESTERN NON-INTERPOLATIONS

In my discussion to this point I have dealt with a number of the so-called Western non-interpolations, treating them as discrete textual issues rather than addressing the theoretical problems that they pose as a group.[167] These problems will not go away, however, and I cannot simply refuse to address them; for if the non-interpolations are ruled out of court en masse, as they sometimes are, my case for the anti-docetic character of the longer readings, the "non-Western interpolations," is obviously tarnished.[168] I have decided, therefore, to devote a separate excursus to the theoretical problems that are involved in accepting the shorter Western readings as original.

My discussion at this stage is entirely theoretical; I take as a guiding principle the need to evaluate each of the readings in question on its own merits, not on the basis of its inclusion in a cluster of variants that scholars (in this case, Westcott and Hort) have artificially created. This distinction is sometimes lost in the literature, implicitly when commentators refuse to deal with the intrinsic and transcriptional issues peculiar to each of these readings (on the grounds that Westcott and Hort's views no longer hold sway)[169] and explicitly when scholars fault these nineteenth-century critics for failing to include other variant readings in their group, when these also represent shorter texts attested only among Western witnesses.[170] This explicit demurrer has sometimes been advanced with considerable rhetorical force, as if Westcott and Hort were either willful or ignorant in leaving vital data out of the equation, data which, if figured in, would demonstrate that shorter Western readings cannot make any claim to being original. For all the mileage their opponents have derived from the argument, it nonetheless turns out to be a straw man; anyone who has actually read Westcott and Hort knows that they did not overlook these other data at all, but carefully incorporated them into their theory.

The theory in brief is that *on some rare occasions* "Western" textual witnesses have preserved the original text against all other witnesses. These instances, for Westcott and Hort, are texts in which the Western reading is shorter than its alternative, a circumstance that is immediately striking in itself, given the general propensity of this tradition to *expand* the text so as to help clarify its meaning. Westcott and Hort did acknowledge that in such instances the Western witnesses might be culpable of reproducing accidental or intentional omissions. But given the expansionistic tendencies of these witnesses in general, they felt justified in harboring some initial doubts. Moreover—and this is the key point—they did not at all reject out of hand the non-Western readings in these instances simply because they were longer; they explored the intrinsic and transcriptional probabilities in each case to determine whether the words in question were better construed as interpolations or deletions.

In the end they argued for three kinds of shorter Western readings (in the Gospels): six were deemed, on internal grounds, altogether unlikely to represent the original text (Matt 4:15, 25; 13:33; 23:26; Mark 10:2; Luke 24:9), twelve others were considered as possibly, but not probably, original readings (Matt 9:34; 21:44; Mark 2:22; 14:39; Luke 5:39; 10:41f; 12:19, 21, 39; 22:62; John 3:32; 4:9); nine others were regarded as probably original (thus the "Western non-interpolations" into Matt 27:49; Luke 22:19b-20; 24:3, 6, 12, 36, 40, 51, and 52).[171]

In view of this careful delineation and the insistence that *each* of the variant readings be determined on internal grounds, it simply will not do to accuse Westcott and Hort of arbitrariness or inconsistency in their selection of nine readings with purely Western attestation while overlooking so many others. Their argument was that some such readings might be original but not all of them had to be. This stands in perfect harmony with the methods of criticism that are currently in vogue (whether termed "eclectic" or "local-genealogical"), methods advocated most strongly precisely by those who have detracted from Westcott and Hort on this score.[172] Westcott and Hort were right to consider each reading according to its own merits; it would be foolish to adopt or reject them all—or even just those that Westcott and Hort contended were original—en masse.

The other major argument leveled against the theory of Westcott and Hort's Western non-interpolations relates to manuscript discoveries made since their time, specifically, the discovery of the New Testament papyri, Greek textual witnesses that antedate Westcott and Hort's beloved codex Vaticanus by nearly a century and a half. In its simplest terms, the argument is that the attestation of the longer readings in question by such early and high-quality witnesses as $\mathfrak{p}^{75}$ removes any real doubt as to their originality; they are not only scattered throughout the tradition, but are now datable to the late second century in the best witnesses available.

For all its commonsensical appeal, it is curious that such an argument can carry any weight with anyone already conversant with Westcott and Hort's understanding of the history of the text. Their nomenclature does cloud the issue, but the conception behind it is at all events clear, and the discovery of the papyri has done nothing to alter its force (with respect to the issue at hand).[173] Hort, the actual author of the argument, maintained on the basis of the evidence then available to him that already by the second century there had emerged two strong kinds of textual tradition, one that later came to be embodied in the so-called Western witnesses, such as codex Bezae, and the other that he labeled Neutral (from which derived the Alexandrian), embodied especially in codex Vaticanus. The picture we now draw is murkier overall, and the integrity of the Western tradition is subject to some considerable doubt. But as we shall see, these are not really the vital issues here. According to Hort's model, one of these two traditions (the Neutral) preserved the original text of the New Testament in virtually every instance; the other represented a kind of wild and uncontrolled transcription of that text (meaning, among other things, that Hort himself recognized the murkiness of the second-century tradition). In many instances, of course, the Western witnesses also attested the original text, whenever they did not vary from the Neutral (which, after all, is true for most of the words of the New Testament). On other occasions, however—and these were extremely rare—the Western tradition stood alone in preserving the original text. These were cases in which the "other" stream of tradition had become corrupted by interpolations at an extremely early point in its history. It just so happened, by a kind of historical quirk, that the Western tradition had broken off as an independent stream of tradition before this infrequent exercise in interpolation had taken place, so that where it did occur the surviving Western witnesses coincidentally—purely coincidentally—preserve the original text, while all other forms of the tradition evidence contamination.[174]

Once the discussion is put in these terms (Hort's own terms), it becomes clear that the papyri have very little to do with his so-called Western non-interpolations and cannot be used as (additional) evidence against their originality. How can an early Alexandrian witness such as $\mathfrak{P}^{75}$, a predecessor of codex Vaticanus, prove Hort wrong? With the limited evidence available to him, Hort already *knew* that second- and third-century Alexandrian manuscripts of the highest quality must have contained the verses in question. Subsequent findings have simply shown that his intuitions were correct. The fact that we now have the manuscripts that he knew must have existed, and that these manuscripts say precisely what he said they would, can scarcely be taken as an argument against his claim that the corruption had crept into the text prior to the end of the second century.

Furthermore, one must not overlook the fact, which is obvious and therefore rather easily overlooked, that the papyri that are currently (and rightly) lauded as revolutionary all derive from Egypt and, by and large, attest to the status of the New Testament text there, *in Egypt*. Kurt Aland in particular has used these early witnesses to make sweeping claims about the status of the text in the early centuries. To be sure, we are no longer restricted to hypothetical reconstructions of what that text "must" have looked like, because we now have some direct evidence. But the direct evidence is *not* widespread, and we cannot afford to ignore its constricted provenance. In general terms Aland is certainly correct that the papyri by and large do not attest the kind of text found among the so-called Western witnesses (but see below). The problem, however, is that Hort argued that it was precisely in Alexandria that the Western text had made very little headway. Would Hort have expected Egyptian manuscripts of the second and third century to attest the type of text evidenced elsewhere throughout the Christian world? No, he claims quite to the contrary that they would not.[175] Does Aland have direct evidence for the textual traditions outside of Egypt, say in North Africa, Syria, Asia Minor, and Gaul, evidence that Hort did not have? Not in the papyri. Where then does that leave us? With second- and third-century witnesses, manuscripts that show that the early scribes were not overly scrupulous in their habits of transcription, which Hort already knew, and that codex Vaticanus represents a very ancient and vastly superior line of Alexandrian text, which Hort devoted his learned *Introduction* to proving. It is difficult to see how p[75] and its early allies can possibly be used against Hort, when the burden of his argument was to demonstrate that such a manuscript must have existed.

What now of the evidence that Hort did have to reconstruct the textual tradition of the second century outside of the Neutral (our Alexandrian) text? He indeed was too bold in claiming that the typical manuscript of the time probably looked more like codex Bezae than anything else.[176] Even today, however, with all the advances since Hort, no one can yet deny that the Greek witness codex Bezae, the Old Latin manuscripts, and (often) the Old Syriac tradition evidence wide-ranging agreements with one another and that these points of agreement can scarcely be explained except on the theory of their relative antiquity. It would be foolish to ignore this confluence of traditions as if it no longer means anything, now that we happen to have early *Alexandrian* papyri.[177] For certainly the New Testament textual tradition of the second century was not restricted to Egypt. To be sure, the agreements among these Western witnesses are not as statistically significant as those that obtain, for instance, between codex Vaticanus and p[75]; but neither should they be expected to be. We are now talking about witnesses separated not only by date but also by geography and language.

The so-called Western witnesses occasionally attest readings found neither among the witnesses of the Alexandrian text nor among any other witness. In almost every instance these variants appear clearly secondary: they are harmonizations, explanatory additions, or paraphrases. But what about instances in which a Western variant is shorter and more difficult, where in fact the text attested elsewhere does *not* fit in its broader literary context and *can* be explained as a harmonization or an explanatory addition? Such Western readings cannot be discounted without further ado. They are, after all, evidenced in witnesses of the fourth and fifth century in Greek, Latin, and Syriac, so that if they did not originate in the autographs, they must have been generated in quite early times, at least by the end of the second century. Moreover, it should not be too quickly forgotten, as Hort's detractors appear to do, that several of the papyri discovered subsequent to Hort's investigations, despite their Egyptian provenance, *do* derive from just such a Western stream of tradition. Even though these witnesses are so lamentably fragmentary, they provide clear evidence that entire manuscripts of this sort were produced and used in the period.[178] That none may have survived to attest this or that textual variant with which we may be concerned is a mere accident of history.

In short, the case for or against the so-called Western non-interpolations, and, indeed, for all the shorter readings of the Western tradition, cannot be made simply on the basis of the paucity of their documentary support. These readings must be judged on other grounds. We are therefore justified in turning to internal evidence, that is, to arguments based on a consideration of intrinsic and transcriptional probabilities.

Christ: Ascended in Body

I have expended some considerable effort in seeing how the anti-docetic emphasis on the real and salvific suffering of Christ, and on his bodily existence both before and after his death, came to affect the transmission of the New Testament text. Two corollaries of these notions played a much slighter role in the debates of the second and third centuries, and correspondingly on the transcription of the sacred texts over which, to some degree, these debates were waged. Nonetheless I must observe that for the orthodox, Jesus' resurrection did not end his story. After he was raised from the dead, Christ ascended bodily into heaven to sit at the right hand of God, whence he will come, bodily, to judge the living and the dead. For proto-orthodox heresiologists such as Tertullian, these convictions were part and parcel of the *regula fidei* that was believed unquestioningly by all Christians, but not by heretics intent on wreaking havoc by disputing the doctrines established by Christ.[179]

Luke 24:51–52

How did the proto-orthodox doctrines of Jesus' bodily ascension and return in judgment affect the text of Scripture? I begin by considering a problem that proves particularly difficult to adjudicate, the last of the so-called Western non-interpolations. The final verses of Luke's Gospel record Jesus' departure from his disciples: "And it happened that while he was blessing them, he was removed from them and was taken up into heaven. And they, worshipping him, returned into Jerusalem with great joy" (Luke 24:51–52). Two of the key phrases of this climactic scene, however, are lacking in significant Western witnesses: "and he was taken up into heaven" (v. 51) from manuscripts D a b d e ff² l (syrˢ) geo¹ᐟ along with (interestingly enough) codex Sinaiticus, and "worshipping him" (v. 52) from D a b d e ff² l and syrˢ. Without these disputed phrases we have a very different conclusion to Luke's Gospel. Now Jesus simply leaves his disciples (without ascending into heaven) and they do not worship him when he does.

The textual problem is complicated by the circumstance that the author of the Third Gospel begins his sequel in the book of Acts by narrating (again?) Jesus' ascent into heaven (Acts 1:1–11). As critics have long recognized, the two versions of the event are not at all easy to reconcile. On the one hand, it will appear odd to those not intimately familiar with the geography of Judea that the Gospel has Jesus ascend from the town of Bethany (Luke 24:50), whereas in Acts he does so from the Mount of Olives just outside of Jerusalem (Acts 1:12). The contradiction is more imaginary then real, however, as Bethany is located on the slopes of the Mount.[180] More serious is the chronological discrepancy; in the Gospel Jesus ascends on the day of his resurrection (if the verses in question are original), whereas the book of Acts explicitly states that he did so forty days later (1:3). Yet more puzzling, Luke begins his second volume—immediately prior to recounting the event—by claiming that his former book had *already* narrated "the things Jesus began to do and teach until the day when, having through the Holy Spirit commanded the disciples whom he had chosen, he was taken up" (ἀνελήμφθη, 1:2).

Hence the internal complications of our textual problem. Did a scribe who recognized the contradiction with the chronology of Acts 1:3 delete the reference to Jesus' ascension in Luke 24:51, thereby creating the Western form of the text? Or did a scribe who knew of Luke's backward glance in Acts 1:2 try to make sense of it by providing a point of reference at the end of the Gospel? Or is there some other option? Given the comprehensive analyses of the problem that are already available,[181] I will restrict myself here to making a few observations that contribute to a new solution, one that I advance somewhat tentatively in view of the complexities of the data: the longer text of Luke 24:51 may best be understood as an interpolation made not to resolve a contradiction but to emphasize Jesus' bodily ascension against docetic Christologies that denied it.

Given my earlier discussions of the theoretical viability of Western non-interpolations, I do not need to delve at length into the external merits of both readings.[182] I should note, however, that in this particular instance (24:51, but not 24:52) codex Bezae is aligned with one of the earliest and best representatives of the Alexandrian text, codex Sinaiticus. Although in other portions of the New Testament, Sinaiticus is a close ally of Bezae, here at the end of Luke it does not appear to be;[183] as a result, in this case we have stronger attestation of a shorter Western reading than for any other considered so far. This variant tradition, at least, enjoyed a place in the text of early Alexandria, the majority of Alexandrian manuscripts notwithstanding.

More germane to our discussion of the shorter reading are the various intrinsic and transcriptional probabilities that speak in its favor. I begin by noting a peculiarity in the wording of the longer text: the term used for Jesus' "ascension," ἀναφέρω, occurs only here in all of Luke-Acts. Its anomalous character is heightened by several additional considerations. The only time Luke reproduces a story in which Mark uses the word, he changes it (Mark 9:2; cf. Matt 17:2, Luke 9:28). Moreover, on the other occasions that Luke explicitly describes the ascension he uses different terms: πορεύομαι (Acts 1:10, 11), or compounds of λαμβάνω in the passive (Acts 1:2, 22). The one exception is Acts 1:9, where ἐπήρθη is used, although even this is immediately followed by νεφέλη ὑπέλαβεν αὐτόν. These data cannot be pushed too hard, but they should certainly give us pause, especially when the references in Acts that appear to look "back" to the account of the ascension in the Gospel do not in fact say that Jesus was "borne up" (ἀνηνέχθη) but that he was "taken up" (ἀνελήμφθη; 1:2, 22).[184]

At the same time, we need to ask whether this common construal of Acts 1:2 and 22 as "backward glances" to the end of Luke is either necessary or correct.[185] It is remarkable that this exegetical question has rarely been addressed, for it is central to the textual issue: [186] if the author of Acts *does* mean to mention his earlier narration of Jesus' ascent, then for all of its problems, the longer text of Luke 24:51 must surely be original. Luke would scarcely claim to have narrated an event about which he has said not a word. But here I must take a contrary stand and point out that Luke does *not* actually say that he has previously narrated an account of Jesus' ascension. He states only that he has told of the things Jesus began to do and teach "until the day" (ἄχρι ἧς ἡμέρας) he was "taken up." Neither the preposition (ἄχρι) nor the content of the verse as a whole requires that the *terminus* itself has been previously narrated, but only that the events leading up to it have been. Given the fact that Luke explicitly states that this terminal event transpired forty days after Jesus' resurrection, it would be more than a little odd for him to have placed the event forty days earlier. [187] It would be even more odd to think that he would admit to having done so. That is to say, the common understanding of Acts 1:2 as a backward glance to the ascension described in Luke 24:51 generates a flat-out contradiction between the Gospel and Acts, and even worse, a contradiction within the narrative of Acts itself, a contradiction between its second and third verses! [188]

This contradiction occurs, of course, *only* if Acts 1:2 is taken to refer back to an account of Jesus' ascension in Luke. If it is not to be taken this way, then Luke does not contradict himself on the one hand and, more importantly for our purpose here, he has not yet described Jesus' ascent into heaven on the other. [189]

What now of transcriptional probabilities? Is it conceivable that a scribe who read Acts 1:2 the way most modern commentators do realized that Luke "must have" already narrated an ascension account, and so inserted one? To be sure, this would argue for the shorter text, which I prefer for other reasons; but it is not altogether satisfying as an explanation of our textual data. On the one hand, a scribe intent on reconciling the two accounts can scarcely be expected to create precisely the contradiction that makes the longer text problematic in the first place. On the other hand, this way of explaining the relationship between Luke and Acts assumes that scribes shared the modern perception of their unity, a perception rooted in the circumstance that they were both penned by the same author. This assumption has very little basis in fact. It is certainly true that early Christians knew that Luke had written both volumes. [190] But that meant something quite different for ancient Christians than it does for modern critics. For ancient Christians, the human authors of the New Testament were important to the extent that they guaranteed an apostolic tradition that could be traced back to Jesus' earliest followers (in this case, from Luke back to his traveling companion, the Apostle Paul). But the ultimate author of Scripture was the Holy Spirit, so that the circumstance that one man wrote two books did not provide any particular hermeneutical key to its interpretation (unlike in modernist modes of exegesis). In other words, a supposed contradiction between Luke and Acts was no more severe than one between Mark and Acts, for all were equally rooted in divine authority. That Luke and Acts were not read together by the ancients as they normally are today is demonstrated by their canonical histories; their separation within the biblical canon was never seen to be a violation of their literary character. What this means is that scribes were probably not inclined to turn the page, so to speak, from Luke 24 to Acts 1, and upon finding that the author refers back to his previous account decide to provide the necessary reference themselves.

At the same time, and for the same reasons, it is equally unlikely that a scribe who recognized the contradiction in sequence with Acts 1 would remove it by deleting the reference to Jesus' ascension in Luke 24. This is the most frequent solution to the textual problem, namely, to call it a "harmonizing omission." [191] In point of fact, quite apart from the question of the authorial unity of Luke and Acts, there is almost no evidence to suggest that scribes typically, if ever, harmonized texts of the New Testament by excising their contradictions, despite the popularity of the charge in modern treatments. [192]

The other solution commonly advanced to account for the discrepant traditions of Luke 24:51 is to appeal to the possibility of an accidental omission occasioned by homoeoarcton. Interestingly, the letters NKAI begin both the phrase in question and the one that follows, so that theoretically a scribe may well have copied the first and, when his eye returned to his exemplar, mistakenly picked up on the second, inadvertently leaving out the disputed words. This solution is as intriguing as it is common, but it does not appear to work for several reasons. For one thing, the same accidental error would have to have been made independently by the ancestors of both codex Bezae (and its Western allies) and codex Sinaiticus, unless it be thought that here, unlike the rest of Luke 24, these traditions happen to go back to the same corrupted exemplar. But even worse, it hardly seems accidental that the omission comprises a complete sense unit, that the sense unit is absolutely vital to the interpretation of the passage as a whole, and that, perhaps most tellingly of all, each of the witnesses that attests the shorter text of verse 52 (a text that cannot be explained on such grounds) also attests the shorter text here. This is to say, it does not appear accidental that the witnesses which say nothing of the disciples having worshipped Jesus are also the ones that say nothing of his having ascended into heaven.

None of these difficulties is insurmountable, of course, and in this particular instance one must be acutely aware of the need to argue on the basis of probabilities rather than certainties. All the same, the cumulative case against the clause in question appears to be mounting. Its key word occurs nowhere else in all of Luke-Acts and is demonstrably not the word the author uses when referring to the ascension; the author does not think the ascension occurred when the longer text says it did; the account is lacking in a significant portion of the textual tradition, and its exclusion cannot readily be explained either as a harmonizing omission or as an accidental exclusion. Is there some other way to account for the textual data?

In a thorough treatment of the ascension accounts in the Western text of Luke-Acts, Eldon Jay Epp recognized that in relation to other streams of tradition, the Western witnesses tended to minimize the physical nature of the event.[193] The *Tendenz* is not evidenced with any kind of rigorous consistency, but various Western witnesses nonetheless appear to attenuate the Lukan notion of an observable ascension into heaven. On the basis of the data he collected, Epp hypothesized an original Western version of Luke 24:51 and Acts 1:1–11, 22, in which all references to Jesus' actual ascent were eliminated. The Western non-interpolation in 24:51, then, is instead a tendentious Western omission.

Epp's study is in some ways a model analysis, attentive to detail yet concerned to relate the data to a larger picture. My reservations have to do with whether the picture is drawn quite large enough. To begin with, we should probably ask whether speaking of "the original Western text" (i.e., an archetype that can theoretically be reconstructed) is the best way to envisage the history of the tradition. This is by no means a minor point, as it affects our entire approach to the data. The search for an "original" Western text is in fact a blind alley that historically has caused more confusion than clarity;[194] there is no reason to posit an imaginary manuscript of the early second century to explain this tradition. Even in the text at hand, the fact that Epp can isolate a clear "trend" and yet not find it consistently attested, either among the witnesses or even within a single one, should be taken to suggest that he has uncovered a Western *tendency* rather than the testimony of a solitary Western *archetype*. Much the same can be said about the physiognomy of the Western tradition as a whole, where one readily detects trends but rarely a statistically significant level of agreement even among witnesses that attest them. What we appear to have, then, is a Western *Tendenz* pure and simple, an established pattern of transcription evidenced among a number of witnesses that are loosely related to one another.

Once one has identified the tendency, however, one still has to explain it. This is where, in my opinion, Epp's study pulls up short; for one is left wondering *why* a scribe or group of scribes might be inclined to eliminate any reference to Jesus' actual ascent. Without some kind of sociohistorical explanation for the phenomenon, the data in and of themselves lose their force as evidence for the priority of one form of the text over another. Epp himself recognizes the problem, as he acknowledges the possibility—one that he admittedly sees as remote—that in fact the Western tradition may preserve the original text in these instances.[195]

In my judgment, the Western text *is* original in Luke 24:51, and this in itself may contribute to our understanding of the *Tendenz* attested elsewhere throughout the tradition. Whereas it is difficult to see why Western scribes might have wanted to minimize the physical aspects of Jesus' ascension, there are clear and certain reasons for thinking that other scribes wanted to heighten them. This doctrine was, to be sure, not the most frequently used weapon of the orthodox arsenal, but it nonetheless *could* be used, and on occasion *was* used precisely in the proto-orthodox confrontation with docetic Christologies. Against the Marcionites Irenaeus stressed that Jesus' physical ascension—along with the rest of his entire life—represented a literal fulfillment of

Old Testament prophecy (*Adv. Haer.* IV, 34, 3). And against certain Gnostics he argued that Jesus' bodily ascension reveals the nature of the general resurrection: it is to be a literal event, not a "spiritual" (i.e., docetic) one, meaning, among other things, that the Gnostics themselves had not yet experienced it (*Adv. Haer.* V, 31, 11–12). So too for Tertullian, Jesus' bodily ascension and present status as the one who sits at the right hand of God demonstrates that eternal life will come to believers bodily (*de resur. carn.*, 51).

Given the non-Lukan phrasing of the verse, its apparent discrepancy with Luke's own chronology for the event, and its nearly inexplicable absence from an early stream of tradition, it is perhaps best to see the longer text of Luke 24:51 as a secondary addition made in the second century precisely in order to elevate, so to speak, the orthodox emphasis on the bodily ascension of Jesus. The spiritualizing "tendency" that Epp has isolated among Western witnesses in *other* parts of the tradition (not Luke 24:51–52, as these are original) is therefore *not* to be seen as an attempt to eliminate the objectifiable and empirical aspects of the ascension per se. It is better construed as a move to conform the characterization of the event in Acts with the conceptualizations found elsewhere throughout early Christianity (e.g., in the ending of each of the Gospels, including the Gospel according to Luke), in which Jesus does not physically "leave" earth but simply "departs" from his disciples.[196]

Other Examples

That scribes were concerned to emphasize, to some degree, the ascension of Christ into heaven is demonstrated in other, less disputed, corruptions. Two familiar examples occur in the final chapter of the Gospel According to Mark. In Mark 16:4 the Old Latin manuscript Bobiensis (OL k) gives an actual description of Jesus' physical resurrection and exaltation to heaven, which are apparently understood as comprising a single event: "But suddenly at the third hour of the day there was darkness over the whole circle of the earth, and angels descended from the heavens, and as he [the Lord] was rising in the glory of the living God, at the same time they ascended with him; and immediately it was light."[197] Unlike the *Gospel of Peter*, which also narrates the actual events of the resurrection, here one finds a report of Jesus' literal ascent into heaven whence his accompanying angels have come.[198] The manuscript itself derives from the late fourth century, although this particular gloss appears to have originated during the earlier period, when an emphasis on Jesus' physical ascent was particularly germane. So too the longer ending of the Gospel according to Mark, which by common consent forms no part of the original text, attests the actual ascent of Jesus into heaven: "Then the Lord Jesus, after speaking to them, was taken up into heaven and sat at the right hand of God" (Mark 16:19). Here there can be no doubt concerning the dating of the tradition: it is attested in the main by sources as early as Irenaeus. What we have in these traditions, then, are corruptions that emphasize the physical character of Jesus' ascent, useful material for proto-orthodox Christians bent on opposing docetic forms of Christology.

Christ's Return in Judgment

Just as the orthodox belief in Jesus' physical ascent into heaven played a role in the transmission of the texts of Scripture, so too did its corollary, the belief that Jesus was to return bodily from heaven in judgment. This doctrine can be found scattered throughout the writings of the second- and third-century heresiologists, most of whom adopted Justin Martyr's idea that two separate advents of Christ, one in humility and one in glory, had been predicted by the Old Testament prophets.[199] For these representatives of proto-orthodoxy, in contradistinction to heretics like Marcion, the predictions of humility and exaltation referred to one and the same Messiah. Jesus had suffered in the body while on earth, and would return from heaven in the same body to bring in his kingdom and to wreak vengeance on those who rejected his message.[200] For the orthodox, of course, heretics were particularly liable.

The orthodox doctrine of Jesus' physical return in glory made some slight impact on the text of the New Testament. In particular, passages that might otherwise appear to speak but tentatively of this glorious event were occasionally modified so as to eliminate any uncertainty. A clear example occurs in 1 John 2:28, which originally read, "And now, children, remain in him, in order that if he should appear ($\H{\iota}\nu\alpha$ $\H{\epsilon}\grave{\alpha}\nu$ $\phi\alpha\nu\epsilon\rho\omega\theta\hat{\eta}$) we might have boldness and not be put to shame by him in his coming." Interestingly enough, the $\H{\iota}\nu\alpha$ clause is frequently changed in the manuscript tradition, so that the author no longer equivocates on the matter of Christ's return but states with bold assurance: ". . . in order that *when* he appears" ($\H{\iota}\nu\alpha$ $\H{o}\tau\alpha\nu$ $\phi\alpha\nu\epsilon\rho\omega\theta\hat{\eta}$).[201]

Elsewhere one finds textual interpolations that emphasize Christ's physical return in judgment. A clear example occurs in the final scene of the book of Acts, where the Apostle Paul is left under house arrest, "preaching the Kingdom of God and teaching the things concerning the Lord Jesus Christ ($\tau\grave{\alpha}$ $\pi\epsilon\rho\grave{\iota}$ $\tau o\hat{v}$ $\kappa v\rho\acute{\iota}o v$ '$I\eta\sigma o\hat{v}$ $X\rho\iota\sigma\tau o\hat{v}$) with all boldness, unhindered" (Acts 28:31). Of the various changes attested for the verse,[202] the one most interesting for my purpose is found in the Old Latin manuscript p, along with several manuscripts of the Latin Vulgate and the Harclean Syriac. Here the content of Paul's teaching about Christ is explicated more clearly in the message that "this is Jesus, the Son of God, through whom the whole world is about to be judged."[203]

The same orthodox emphasis affected the New Testament text elsewhere in far more subtle ways. In particular, we should consider the familiar story of Luke 23, where Jesus engages in conversation with one of the criminals who is crucified with him. After proclaiming that Jesus has done nothing to deserve his fate, the criminal asks: "Jesus, remember me when you come into your kingdom" (v. 42, $\mu\nu\acute{\eta}\sigma\theta\eta\tau\acute{\iota}$ $\mu o v$ $\H{o}\tau\alpha\nu$ $\H{\epsilon}\lambda\theta\eta\varsigma$ $\epsilon\grave{\iota}\varsigma$ $\tau\grave{\eta}\nu$ $\beta\alpha\sigma\iota\lambda\epsilon\acute{\iota}\alpha\nu$ $\sigma o v$). This, at least, is the form of his request as it occurs in the best of our Alexandrian witnesses, $\mathfrak{p}^{75}$ and B (also L OL vg al). The majority of witnesses, however, evidence a slight modification: the preposition εἰς is changed to ἐν, so that now the criminal requests, "Remember me when you come *in* your kingdom" (א A C K W Δ Θ Π Ψ f¹. ¹³ 565 700 892 Byz Origen al). Which of these readings is to be preferred, and why was it changed?

Here is a case in which the general superiority of the primary Alexandrian tradition coincides with both intrinsic and transcriptional probabilities. It has been widely recognized by scholars since Conzelmann that Luke went to some lengths to de-emphasize the futuristic components of Jesus' teaching about the Kingdom of God.[204] As a standard example that relates to the problem here, Luke changed Mark's claim that "Some of those standing here will not taste death until they see the Kingdom of God having come in power" (Mark 9:1) by eliminating the final participial clause (9:27). Indeed, for Luke the disciples *do* see the Kingdom of God, but not its having come in power. In the mission of the seventy, the kingdom of God has "come near" (10:9, 11); in Jesus' own mission, it is said to have "arrived" (11:20) and thus already to be "in your midst" (17:21). Even in Luke, though, these experiences of the kingdom are proleptic of the final denouement in which the kingdom is to come in a decisive act of history at the end of the age (Luke 21:7–32). The tragic experiences of the world prior to that coming of the kingdom are mirrored in the experiences of Luke's Jesus, whose own tragedy comes in his martyrdom. Moreover, just as the world experiences a proleptic vision of God's kingdom (in Jesus' ministry) prior to the eschatological woes that will finally usher it in, so too Jesus experiences and manifests this kingdom before suffering and "entering into his glory" (24:26).

Jesus' reply to the criminal on the cross makes some sense given this context; asked to remember him when he "enters into his kingdom," Jesus speaks of what will happen momentarily: "Today you will be with me in paradise" (23:43). Luke then relates this question and answer not to some future eschatological event in which Jesus will manifest his glory by bringing the kingdom to this earth in power, but to the truly imminent event in which Jesus will enter into that glorious reign of God upon the completion of his task.

Given this understanding of Lukan theology, which variant reading appears more appropriate? There can be little doubt on this score that the text of 𝔭⁷⁵ and B are superior on all counts. Here Jesus is asked to remember the criminal upon his imminent entrance "into" his glorious kingdom.

What of the variant? By the change of a preposition the question now refers not to Jesus' destiny at death but to his glorious return in power, when he brings in the kingdom of God: "Remember me when you come in (or with) your kingdom." What we have here is a heightening of an emphasis that Luke has otherwise minimized, the physical return of Jesus in glory. As we have seen, the change, slight as it may be, does not synchronize particularly well with the Lukan context whether defined narrowly ("Today"!) or broadly ("it *was* necessary for the Christ to suffer and enter into his glory," 24:26); but it does harmonize perfectly well with the orthodox emphasis seen throughout the New Testament textual tradition, the emphasis on the real, tangible return of Christ. Because the variant is attested already by Origen, this is clearly a text that was modified during the period of the docetic controversies. That we are not misguided in taking this as the context within which the variant was created is confirmed by one other reading attested for the passage, this one preserved in codex Bezae alone. There the criminal on the cross requests of Jesus, "Remember me in the day of your coming" (ἐν τῇ ἡμέρᾳ τῆς ἐλεύσεως σου).

Christ, The Real Man of Flesh and Blood

In my considerations of anti-docetic corruptions of Scripture, I have concentrated on textual variants that stress Christ's real bodily passion, resurrection, ascension, and return. A good deal of the orthodox polemic, however, dealt directly with what we might call the "metaphysical" issue, the question of the materiality of Christ's existence. As opposed to the docetists, who claimed that Christ was a phantom, a man in appearance only, the orthodox insisted on his humanity, urging that he was a real man of real flesh and blood. It comes as no surprise to find a number of textual corruptions that serve to advance this orthodox Christology, either by emphasizing the fleshly nature of Christ's existence or by stressing the orthodox claim that he was in fact "a man."

We have already seen that the letter of 1 John is directed against the beliefs of a group of secessionists who claimed that Christ only appeared to be human. The letter's emphasis on the idea that Jesus had real flesh and shed real blood is occasionally heightened by orthodox scribes who found this view amenable to their own theology and sought to bring it yet more clearly to the fore. A striking example occurs in the Latin tradition of 1 John 5:20. When the author says that "We know that the Son of God has come," several manuscripts of the Vulgate add "and [that he] was clothed with flesh for our sake, and suffered, and arose from the dead. And he took us to himself." [205] This longer text has no Greek attestation; but because it appears in two different forms already in the fourth century, [206] Adolf von Harnack argued for a Greek original that read something like the following: καὶ ἐσαρκοποιήθη (or ἐσαρκώθη) δι᾽ ἡμᾶς καὶ ἔπαθεν καὶ ἀναστὰς ἐκ νεκρῶν προσ εδέξατο (or προσελάβετο) ἡμᾶς. Moreover, von Harnack dated its formulation to the controversies of the late second or early third centuries, when an emphasis that Christ took on flesh and suffered enjoyed a certain prominence. [207] Soon thereafter it would have been interpolated into texts of 1 John as a fitting addition to a document already perceived as anti-docetic.

A comparable motivation may help to explain the interpolation found some verses earlier in 1 John 5:9, which speaks of God who "has borne witness concerning his son." In the fuller text that appears in several of our witnesses, the author speaks of ". . . his son whom [God] sent as a savior upon earth. And the son bore witness on earth by fulfilling the Scriptures; and we bear witness because we have seen him, and we proclaim to you that you may believe for this reason." [208] Among the orthodox emphases in evidence here are the connection between Christ and the Old Testament Scriptures, a connection we will consider in more detail later, and the stress on his having been "seen" as a basis for faith, a stress that coincides well with original features of 1 John, such as the prologue (1:1–4). Rather than inserting a doctrine foreign to the text, then, this interpolation appears to magnify an anti-docetic emphasis that the orthodox could claim was already present and available for use.

Something similar can perhaps be said of a variant that occurs outside the Johannine corpus, in the book of Hebrews. To be sure, the text of Hebrews 2:14 as it stands can be taken as anti-docetic: "Since the children have shared blood and flesh, even he [i.e., Christ] likewise partook of the same things" (καὶ αὐτὸς παραπλησίως μετέσχεν τῶν αὐτῶν). But this understanding appears to be heightened by the addition of παθημάτων in some of the Western witnesses (D* b [t]), so that now the text speaks of Christ partaking "of the same sufferings" or, perhaps, of his enduring "the same experiences" as other humans. In this case, in fact, we should probably *not* construe the variant as an attempt to elevate the reality of Christ's suffering on the cross. For in the immediate context, blood and flesh are said to characterize human existence itself as a kind of limitation, a kind of suffering. Christ, then, participated fully in this human existence, he "partook of the same sufferings" that everyone must endure as flesh and blood creatures of this world. The emphasis, then, falls more on Christ's full humanity than on his passion per se.

A final example of a variant generated by such polemical concerns is the widely attested addition to Ephesians 5:30. The variant is intriguing in part because of its context: the passage as a whole is parenetic rather than christological. Nonetheless, in the midst of his discussion of marital relations, the author draws an analogy for a husband's treatment of his wife from Christ's treatment of the church. A husband should love his wife as his own body, in imitation of Christ, "for no one hates his own flesh, but feeds and nourishes it, just as Christ does for the Church, for we are members of his body" (vv. 29–30). The author then cites Genesis 2:24 to support his argument: "For this reason, a man will leave his father and mother and cleave to his wife, and the two shall become one flesh." There can be little doubt that this scriptural citation was to some degree responsible for the modification of verse 30 ("we are members of his body") in the vast majority of manuscripts, some of which can be dated all the way back into the second century. In these witnesses the text affirms that "we are members of his body, of his flesh and of his bones." The addition, of course, echoes Genesis 2:23: "The man said, 'This at last is flesh of my flesh and bone of my bones.' "[209] But the change could scarcely have been made *simply* because Genesis 2:24 is quoted subsequently. It should not be overlooked, in this connection, that with the addition the church is said not only to be the body of Christ, but also to consist of his own flesh and bones. Does this not suggest something of Christ's own body, that it comprised flesh and bones?

At first sight this kind of connection between the *varia lectio* and a proto-orthodox christology may appear farfetched; but it receives a striking confirmation in the earliest witness to the longer text, the second-century Irenaeus, who cites the verse precisely to oppose a phantasmal kind of Christology:

> . . . even as the blessed Paul declares in his Epistle to the Ephesians, that 'we are members of His body, of His flesh, of His bones.' He does not speak these words of some spiritual and invisible person, for a spirit has not bones nor flesh; but [he refers to] that dispensation [by which the Lord became] an actual man, consisting of flesh, and nerves, and bones (*Adv. Haer.* V, 2, 3).

Here, in conjunction with the text of Luke 24:39, which we have already discussed, Irenaeus uses the words of the apostle—or rather, the words of the apostle's early interpolator—to the anti-docetic ends that we have come to expect of such corruptions. It is thus no stretch to think that the corruption itself, which to be sure may have been suggested by the Genesis citation, was generated out of just such a context.

In addition to these textual corruptions that stress Christ's possession of real flesh, bones, and blood, a number of others emphasize that Christ was in fact "a man." As I observed at an earlier stage of this study, variants of this kind are particularly enigmatic in that while they support the orthodox position against the docetists, they could theoretically also work *against* the orthodox, if they were pressed by adoptionists (who could, to be sure, use them against the docetists as well). Here we should recall the data discussed in Chapter 2. There we found several anti-adoptionistic readings that stressed that Jesus was not *only* a man, but none that denied he was a man at all. A similar phenomenon occurs here as well. Anti-docetic variants stress that Jesus *was* a man but do not necessarily indicate that he was *only* that. If these readings can be taken in this "heretical" way, it is simply due to historical realities: orthodox Christianity, with its highly paradoxical Christology, had to defend itself on two (and more!) fronts at once. Against docetists it had to maintain that Jesus was a real human being and against adoptionists that he was far more than that, since he was also God. It is this kind of paradoxical emphasis that led some orthodox scribes to corrupt texts that could be taken to say that Jesus was "just" a man, while other scribes (or perhaps even the same ones) corrupted other texts to emphasize that in fact he *was* a man.[210]

As few of the textual variants in question can make any serious claim to being original, I will simply consider some of the representative cases. One that has already been mentioned is the singular reading of codex Vaticanus concerning Pilate's presentation of Jesus to the Jewish leadership in John 19:5. Whereas in the vast majority of manuscripts the text reads "Behold the man" (ἰδοὺ ὁ ἄνθρωπος), Vaticanus drops the article. Now Pilate exhibits Jesus, recently beaten and mockingly arrayed in purple, as a mere mortal: "Behold, a human being."[211] The change, slight though it be, serves both to emphasize Jesus' real humanity and, perhaps, to provide an additional sense of pathos to an already moving scene.

On other occasions scribes have simply interpolated references to Jesus' "humanness" into passages that otherwise say nothing directly about it. In

John 7:46, the servants of the high priests and Pharisees return to inform their leaders about Jesus: "No man has ever spoken thus" (οὐδέποτε ἐλάλησεν οὕτως ἄνθρωπος). As it stands, the text is ambiguous with respect to its conceptualization of Jesus: does it mean that among all humans, he is the best teacher, or that his teachings are not those of a mortal? The ambiguity is relieved by the change attested in a vast array of witnesses as early as the third-century manuscript 𝔓[66]. Here the servants state that "No man has ever spoken as this man speaks" (οὐδέποτε οὕτως ἄνθρωπος ἐλάλησεν ὡς οὗτος λάλει ὁ ἄνθρωπος).[212] A comparable change is occasionally attested in manuscripts of the First Gospel, in the equally ambiguous query of the disciples after Jesus calms the sea: "What sort is this one (ποταπός ἐστιν οὗτος) that even the winds and the sea obey him?" (Matt 8:27). Rather than allow the conclusion that "whatever he is," he is clearly not human, several witnesses make a slight but patently orthodox change by adding the words ὁ ἄνθρωπος, so that now the one who has the power over nature is still clearly a man: "What sort of man is this . . ." (W Theodoret pc).

This kind of explicit designation of Jesus as a man occurs in some texts outside of the Gospels as well. In his typological comparison of Adam with Christ in Romans 5:19, Paul contrasts the "disobedience of the one man" (τῆς παρακοῆς τοῦ ἑνὸς ἀνθρώπου) with the "obedience of the one" (τῆς ὑπακοῆς τοῦ ἑνός). Clearly an ellipsis is to be read, so that in the second instance as well he is referring to "one man," as in fact he makes explicit some four verses earlier when he speaks of "the one man Jesus Christ" (τοῦ ἑνὸς ἀνθρώπου Ἰησοῦ Χριστοῦ, v. 14). The passage proved important to heresiologists such as Irenaeus, who used it to show that just as Adam was a flesh and blood human being, despite his remarkable "birth," so too was Jesus (*Adv. Haer.* III, 18, 7). And so it is perhaps something more than a stylistic change when scribes have made the point more explicit by supplying the word ἀνθρώπου to the text.[213]

Christ: Born Human

For the orthodox, Jesus' real humanity was guaranteed by the fact that he was actually born, the miraculous circumstances surrounding that birth notwithstanding. This made the matter of Jesus' nativity a major bone of contention between orthodox Christians and their docetic opponents. Marcion, as we have seen, denied Jesus' birth and infancy altogether. In response, Irenaeus could ask, "Why did He acknowledge Himself to be the Son of man, if He had not gone through that birth which belongs to a human being?" (*Adv. Haer.* IV, 33, 2). The question is echoed by Tertullian, who cites a number of passages that mention Jesus' "mother and brothers" and asks why, on general principles, it is harder to believe "that flesh in the Divine Being should rather be unborn than untrue?" (*Adv. Marc.* III, 11).

In light of this orthodox stand, it is not surprising to find the birth of Christ brought into greater prominence in texts used by the early polemicists. I can cite two instances. In both cases one could argue that the similarity of the words in question led to an accidental corruption. But it should not be overlooked that both passages proved instrumental in the orthodox insistence on Jesus' real birth, making the changes look suspiciously useful for the conflict. In Galatians 4:4, Paul says that God "sent forth his Son, come from a woman, come under the law" (γενόμενον ἐκ γυναικός, γενόμενον ὑπὸ νό μον). The verse was used by the orthodox to oppose the Gnostic claim that Christ came through Mary "as water through a pipe," taking nothing of its conduit into itself; for here the apostle states that Christ was "made *from* a woman" (so Irenaeus, *Adv. Haer.* III, 22, 1, and Tertullian, *de carne Christi*, 20). Irenaeus also uses the text against docetists to show that Christ was actually a man, in that he came from a woman (*Adv. Haer.* V, 21, 1). It should strike us as odd that Tertullian never quotes the verse against Marcion,[214] despite his lengthy demonstration that Christ was actually "born." This can scarcely be attributed to oversight, and so is more likely due to the circumstance that the generally received Latin text of the verse does not speak of Christ's birth per se, but of his "having been made" (*factum ex muliere*).

Given its relevance to just such controversies, it is no surprise to see that the verse was changed on occasion, and in precisely the direction one might expect: in several Old Latin manuscripts the text reads: misit deus filium suum, natum ex muliere ("God sent his Son, born of a woman"), a reading that would have proved useful to Tertullian had he known it. Nor is it surprising to find the same change appear in several Greek witnesses as well, where it is much easier to make, involving the substitution of γεννώμενον for γενόμενον (K f¹ and a number of later minuscules).

A similar corruption occurs in Romans 1:3-4, a passage I have already discussed in a different connection.[215] Here Paul speaks of Christ as God's Son "who came from the seed of David according to the flesh" (τοῦ γενομένου ἐκ σπέρματος Δαυὶδ κατὰ σάρκα). The heresiologists of the second and third centuries also found this text useful for showing that Christ was a real man who was born into the world. Tertullian, for example, claims that since Christ is related to David (his seed) because of his flesh, he must have taken flesh from Mary (*de carne Christi* 22; cf. Irenaeus, *Adv. Haer.* III, 22, 1). Given the orthodox assumption that "having come from the seed of David" must refer to Jesus' own birth—an event not actually described by Paul— one is not taken aback to find the text of Romans 1:3 changed as early as the second century, as attested by the citations of Origen, and periodically throughout the history of its transmission (61* syr^pal, Byz^mss OL^mss acc to Aug). As was the case with Galatians 4:4, the change was a matter of the substitution of a word in the versions and of a few simple letters in Greek (from γενόμενον to γεννώμενον), so that now the text speaks not of Christ "coming from the seed of David" but of his "being born of the seed of David."

Jesus, the Christ of the Old Testament God

We have seen that one of the major points of controversy between orthodox Christians and Marcion concerned the status of the Hebrew Scriptures and

Christ's relationship to them. Many of the Gnostics rejected the Old Testament as well, in that for them, the God it describes is not the true or ultimate God. For Marcion, the Old Testament God was indeed the God who called Israel and gave it his law. He was also the God who created the world (as described within that law) and promised a Messiah to redeem it, a Savior who has not, however, yet arrived. But this God was unrelated to the God of Jesus Christ, the Stranger-God of love and redemption who sent Christ into the world in order to buy humans back from the just but harsh God of the Jews. For Marcion, as for the Gnostics, Christ did not come from the Creator but from another God.

Orthodox Christians made quite a point of saying just the opposite, that there is only one God, that this God created the world, chose Israel, gave them the Scriptures, and sent his Son for redemption in fulfillment of the promises found within them. As we have grown to expect, this orthodox emphasis played some role in the transmission of the New Testament. Here again it was not simply a matter of orthodox scribes importing alien doctrines into their sacred texts. From their vantage point, at least, the New Testament itself showed that the God of the Jewish Scriptures and the God of Jesus Christ are one and the same, and that this God sent Christ as predicted by the prophets of old. But as we have seen repeatedly, the fact that their sacred texts could be read as already supporting an orthodox understanding did not at all prevent scribes either from securing their view more firmly in texts that might appear to equivocate or from introducing it into texts that originally said not a word about it. Here we can consider several interesting examples.

Orthodox Christians must surely have been puzzled when they read Jesus' claims in the Fourth Gospel: "I am the door of the sheep. All who came before me are thieves and robbers" ($\pi \acute{\alpha} \nu \tau \epsilon \varsigma$ ὅσοι ἦλθον πρὸ ἐμοῦ κλέπται εἰσὶν καὶ λῃσταί; 10:7–8). Were *all* of Jesus' predecessors entirely wicked? Is this not a rather harsh indictment, for example, of the righteous followers of God whose lives are presented in the pages of the Old Testament? We know from the testimony of Hippolytus that certain Gnostics understood the passage in precisely this way.[216] The possibility of this construal is no doubt what led to several textual modifications. It is difficult otherwise to explain the omission of $\pi \acute{\alpha} \nu \tau \epsilon \varsigma$ in one strain of the Western tradition (D d). With the omission, Jesus' claim is not so severe; now at least he does not castigate *all* of his predecessors. So too with the omission of πρὸ ἐμοῦ attested in earlier and more diverse witnesses (p[45vid. 75] ℵ* Δ 28 892 2148 Byz[pt] OL vg syr[s. p. h. pal] cop[sa. ach2] al).[217] Jesus' saying is now more elusive,[218] but the alteration has a salubrious effect as well. In Bruce Metzger's words, the change works "to lessen the possibility of taking the passage as a blanket condemnation of all Old Testament worthies."[219]

A somewhat different motivation appears to lie behind the modification of Romans 9:5. Using a string of relative clauses, Paul enumerates the prerogatives of "his compatriots according to the flesh," whom he identifies as "Israelites, of whom is the adoption and the glory and the covenants and the giving of the law and the service and the promises, of whom are the fathers and from whom is the Christ according to the flesh" (ὧν οἱ πατέρες καὶ ἐξ ὧν ὁ Χριστὸς τὸ κατὰ σάρκα). On one level, of course, not even Marcion could deny that Christ came "from the Israelites," in that he lived and worked among them, even though he was the representative of the God who was a Stranger to this people and its history. The orthodox, however, could and did use the passage to argue Christ's essential connection with Israel and consequently with its God (thus Irenaeus, *Adv. Haer.* III, 16, 3). This connection is solidified in several textual witnesses (F G f g and several patristic sources) whose text can be dated back into the period of our concern by the citations of Hippolytus (*Adv. Noet.* 2, 5). In these witnesses, the conjunction καί is simply omitted, so that now the text speaks of the "Israelites . . . of whom are the fathers from whom (i.e., from the Jewish patriarchs) is the Christ. . . ." Now Christ's lineage is more unequivocally traced back to the Jewish ancestors.

We can conclude these deliberations by mentioning one other text that again, without any assistance from the scribes, appears to forge a close connection between Christ and the Old Testament patriarchs. In Galatians 3:16, Paul refers to the promise made to Abraham's "seed" (not "seeds," emphasizes Paul), "who is Christ" (ὅς ἐστιν Χριστός). It does not appear accidental that the two principal witnesses for the earlier corruption of Romans 9:5 also attest a similar change here. In both F and G the relative pronoun is changed from the nominative to the genitive, so that rather than referring to the seed, it evidently refers directly to Abraham, "of whom is the Christ." In any event, the textual tradition of the next verse preserves a change that appears to achieve the same end; notably, the change is attested again in the same two witnesses, although this time, to be sure, in somewhat better company. In Galatians 3:17, where Paul speaks of the (Abrahamic) covenant that was "ratified by God," several scribes have made the connection of Christ to Israel's covenant more explicit by adding the words εἰς Χριστόν: "the covenant ratified by God unto Christ" (D F G I Byz OL Syr al).

Summary and Conclusions

Orthodox Christians of the second and third centuries opposed a number of individuals and groups who espoused docetic views of Christ. Of the various representatives of these views, we are best informed about the secessionists confronted by the author of 1 John, the unnamed opponents of Ignatius in Asia Minor, several groups of Gnostics attacked by a range of heresiologists, and, above all, Marcion of Pontus, the most infamous and influential dissident of the period.

Although the docetic Christologies embraced by these various individuals and groups were not identical in every respect, they all denied that Christ was a real flesh and blood human being, a man who experienced pain and suffering, who actually shed blood and died, who was raised bodily from the dead and exalted to heaven. Some of these Christologies denied any kind of birth to Christ; they all denied a birth in which he received his body from a human mother. Many of the representatives of these views rejected the creation of the world as the act of an evil or inferior deity; most of them denied any real connection between this God, the God of the Old Testament, and Jesus Christ.[220]

The orthodox opposition to these views was not only read out of the texts of Scripture, it was also read into them—commonly in the process of interpretation, and occasionally in the process of transmission. Of the textual corruptions that resulted, some of the most interesting occur in texts that speak of the physical reality of Christ's passion (e.g., Luke 22:43–44; John 19:28; Matt 20:22, 23; 27:49; Mark 9:12) or of its salvific necessity and redemptive effect (e.g., Luke 22:19–20; 1 Cor 11:23; Col 1:14; Mark 14:22, 24; 1 Cor 15:50). They occur no less frequently in narratives of Jesus' resurrection, passages that showed the orthodox that Jesus was actually raised in the body, making his postresurrection existence physical rather than numinous. In particular, this emphasis came to affect a group of texts that Westcott and Hort labeled Western non-interpolations. These texts are perhaps better construed as "non-Western interpolations," for in them the Western tradition stands alone in withstanding the anti-docetic tendencies of early scribes (e.g., Luke 24:3, 6, 12, 36, 39–40). The Western tradition itself, however, was by no means immune to such changes (cf. Luke 23:53; 24:37), which in any case were not restricted to the narratives of the Third Gospel (cf. Matt 28:3; John 20:30).

The orthodox belief in Jesus' bodily ascension into heaven made an analogous impact on New Testament texts (Luke 24:51–52, Mark 16:4; 19), as did the notion that he would return in judgment (1 John 2:28; Acts 20:31; Luke 23:42). Moreover, several orthodox modifications speak directly to the physical dimension of Christ's existence (1 John 5:9, 20; Heb 2:14; Eph 5:30) or stress that he was "a man" (John 19:5; 7:46; Matt 8:27) or emphasize his real physical birth (Gal 4:4; Rom 1:3). Finally, proto-orthodox scribes occasionally modified their texts in order to link Christ more closely with the Old Testament and the God of Israel (John 10:8; Rom 9:5; Gal 5:16, 17).[221]

In all of these textual modifications, great or small, we can detect the anonymous workings of proto-orthodox scribes, unnamed Christians who were very much involved in the conflicts and struggles of their day. Despite the slight attention afforded these combatants in modern scholarship, the alterations they made in the text of the New Testament prove to be significant, not only in revealing the orthodox Christology in its early stages, but also in showing how this Christology came to be cemented in the evolving Christian tradition and thereby endowed with canonical authority.

Notes

1. Like the adoptionists, docetists argued that their views were original to the faith. As we shall see, Marcion, in particular, made this claim an essential component of his program.

2. The most exhaustive study to date remains an unpublished dissertation by Peter Weigandt, "Der Doketismus im Urchristentum und in der theologischen Entwicklung des zweiten Jahrhunderts." Other general studies have pursued both the descriptive task and the quest for appropriate definition. See especially, J. G. Davies, "The Origins of Docetism"; Jürgen Denker, *Die theologiegeschichtliche Stellung des Petrusevangeliums;* Karl Wolfgang Tröger, "Doketistische Christologie in Nag-Hammadi-Texten"; Michael Slusser, "Docetism: A Historical Definition"; Edwin M. Yamauchi, "The Crucifixion and Docetic Christology"; Norbert Brox, " 'Doketismus'—eine Problemanzeige"; and McGuckin, "The Changing Forms of Jesus." A good deal of discussion can also be found in the literature on the Johannine secessionists, the opponents of Ignatius, the apocryphal Acts, and, especially, Marcion. On the latter, see note 22.

3. See the debate summarized up to 1961 in Weigandt, "Der Doketismus im Urchristentum." A recent advocate of this position is Slusser, "Docetism." See further, note 17.

4. The fathers themselves do not always make this distinction. Nonetheless, it can be found in important contexts (e.g., Irenaeus, *Adv. Haer.* III, 18, 5–6), and for us to fail to make it simply muddles the picture. Scholars who refuse to acknowledge the difference between these two views fail to recognize the "hybrid" quality of the Christologies discussed already in Chapter 3 (note 17; see also note 17 in this chapter).

5. Hippolytus does discuss a group that he labels the "Doketae," even though he acknowledges, along with his fellow heresiologists, other heretical groups that share a docetic Christology. See *Ref.* 8. 1–4 (the Doketae); 10. 15 (succinctly, on Marcion).

6. See, for example, note 24.

7. Chapter 3, pp. 130–34.

8. The following have been among the most significant contributors to the consensus (with respect either to the Fourth Gospel, the Epistles, or both): Wayne Meeks, "The Man from Heaven in Johannine Sectarianism"; J. Louis Martyn, *History and Theology in the Fourth Gospel;* id., *The Gospel of John in Christian History;* Raymond E. Brown, *The Community of the Beloved Disciple;* id., *Gospel According to John;* id., *Epistles of John;* D. Moody Smith, *Johannine Christianity.* The effect of this consensus is evident in the detailed studies of the literature that constantly appear; see, for example, Alois Stimpfle, *Blinde sehen: Die Eschatologie im traditionsgeschichtlichen Prozeß.*

9. On Käsemann, see note 74, Chapter 3. For a recent disavowal of this view, see Marianne Meye Thompson, *The Humanity of Jesus in the Fourth Gospel,* nicely reviewed by Martinus C. de Boer, "Review of M. M. Thompson"; a less compelling case is made by Panackel, ΙΔΟΥ Ο ΑΝΘΡΩΠΟΣ; see my "Review of C. Panackel." The exalted Christology of the Fourth Gospel is evident, for example, in the statements that bracket the narrative (1:1–18 and 20:28) and in the words of Jesus recorded in 8:58; 10:30; 14:6–9—logia not to be found on the lips of the Synoptic Jesus.

10. For example, *The Epistles of John,* 69–103.

11. Against Brown, who construes the Christology of the secessionists differently. See Chapter 3, pp. 132–34, especially notes 53 and 66.

12. See the discussion in Chapter 3, pp. 132–33. For a lucid sketch of the relevant issues, see, above all, Schoedel, *Ignatius of Antioch;* of the growing literature on important related issues (the authorship of the Ignatian letters, the nature of the heresies he attacks, his own place in the history of early Christianity), see especially Caroline P. Hammond Bammel, "Ignatian Problems." Bammel's work is particularly

useful for its critical evaluation of two revisionist sketches, J. Rius-Camps, *The Four Authentic Letters of Ignatius, the Martyr,* and Robert Joly, *Le dossier d'Ignace d'Antioche.*

13. See pp. 132–33.

14. Unfortunately, we are also unable to determine whether the heterodox Christians of Smyrna and Tralles developed their views under conditions comparable to those of the Johannine secessionists (i.e., because of social ostracism from a dominant religious group) or whether there were other factors at work.

15. Some scholars have been far too lax in labeling certain documents of the period docetic simply on the basis of their miraculous portrayals of Jesus. Yamauchi, for example, cites the tradition of Jesus as *Wunderkind* in the Infancy Gospel of Thomas as evidence of docetism, overlooking the fact that Jesus as *Wundermann* in the canonical Gospels runs into precisely the same problem. Furthermore, he agrees with other exegetes that in Luke's resurrection narrative Jesus eats fish (and a honeycomb) not because he needs to, but to show that he is not a phantom; he then argues, however, that the statement in the *Acts of Peter* that Jesus "ate and drank for our sakes, though he was himself without hunger of thirst" (chap. 20), represents docetism! See further note 21.

16. Or at least "proto-Gnostic." See note 12. The term *gnostikos* is not attested in Christian sources for another half century; see Smith, "History of the Term Gnostikos."

17. A particularly instructive example of such a "hybrid" Christology appears in the group about whom Irenaeus appears to be best informed, the Ptolemaeans, an offshoot of the Valentinians. Unlike other Gnostics whom Irenaeus attacks for a purely separationist Christology—for example, the unnamed group I have already discussed (*Adv. Haer.* I, 30, 12–14)—the Ptolemaeans maintained that even though Christ was a man who was born into the world, he did not have an actual human body; whereas all other humans have a "hylic" or "material" body that is doomed to annihilation, Christ arrived in the world with a "psychic" body that came "through" Mary but took nothing "of" her (I, 7, 2). Christ's birth was like water that flows through a pipe and takes nothing of the conduit with it. Subsequently, the spiritual Savior came from the Pleroma into the psychic Christ at his baptism and departed from him prior to his crucifixion, leaving Christ to die alone on the cross (a separationist view). But even this suffering in some senses was only apparent (since even Christ's earthly body was made by a "special dispensation" of the Demiurge, i.e., it was not really human), and represented an imitation of events of the Pleroma, where the Aeon "Stauros" (the "cross") was "stretched out" as a protective boundary for the other aeons (I, 7, 2).

One might be tempted to see in this Ptolemaean view a movement away from an earlier and separationist Christology towards a docetism that represents a more consistent delineation of the Gnostic notions of the inferiority of the material world. In fact, it appears that the move went in just the opposite direction, away from a pure docetism towards a separationist Christology. At the very least, one can say that the Gnostics who allegedly embraced docetic views were typically portrayed by the orthodox heresiologists as the progenitors of the later separationists. Here, as elsewhere, of course, Irenaeus's views were simply adopted by his successors.

18. On the differences between Irenaeus and Hippolytus on Basilides' views, see Chapter 3, note 10.

19. In addition to Irenaeus, and dependent upon him, see Ps-Tertullian, *Adv. Haer.* 1 and Epiphanius, *Pan.* 24, 3, 1.

20. See Hans Gebhard Bethge, "Zweiter Logos des großen Seth," and Koschorke, *Die Polemik der Gnostiker,* 44–48.

21. The notion that Jesus could change forms occurs repeatedly in texts that are generally adjudged Gnostic. The most notable example is the apocryphal *Acts of John,* (known, e.g., to Eusebius, *Hist. Eccl.* III, 25, 6), in which Jesus appears to be a child to the Apostle James but a young man to John; when they approach him, he looks like a bald man to John but a stripling to James. John then recalls that Jesus never blinked, that his body did not always yield to the touch, and that he did not leave footprints when he walked (*Acts of John,* 88–93). Here it should be stressed, however, that the idea of Jesus changing forms is not in and of itself "heretical"; as we have seen, it is found within the writings of proto-orthodox authors as well (on Clement and Origen see note 35, Chapter 1; even in the anti-docetic *Epistula Apostolorum,* Christ can be everything at once [chap. 13], and ubiquitous even when in the body [chap. 17]). The proto-orthodox adoption of such views should come as no surprise, given the New Testament witness to Jesus' miraculous activities both before and after his resurrection (e.g., while living, his transfiguration [Mark 9:2–8 par.] and walking on water [Mark 6:45–52 par.]; after his resurrection, his sudden appearance inside locked rooms [John 20:19] and his ability to assume unfamiliar appearances [Luke 22:13–27]). The difference between the orthodox and docetic notions is nonetheless clear; for orthodox Christians, Jesus' body was real, a body that was born into the world, that felt hunger and thirst, that experienced pain, that shed blood, and that actually died on the cross. Jesus—despite his remarkable abilities—was a real man, not a phantom. See further McGuckin, "Changing Forms of Jesus."

22. The most significant study remains von Harnack, *Marcion: Das Evangelium vom fremden Gott,* the main text of which (though not the valuable appendices) is available now in the English translation of Steely and Bierma. (Unless otherwise indicated, references will be to this translation.) Other standard monographs include E. C. Blackman, *Marcion and His Influence,* and John Knox, *Marcion and the New Testament.* The revisionist study of R. Joseph Hoffmann, *Marcion: On the Restitution of Christianity,* has not been well received. See especially the critical assessments of Caroline P. Hammond Bammel, in "Review of R. J. Hoffmann," and Gerhard May, "Ein neues Markionbild?" Recent studies that have proved useful for various aspects of the present study include the following: Barbara Aland, "Marcion"; David Balás, "Marcion Revisited"; Karlmann Beyschlag, "Marcion von Sinope"; Robert M. Grant, "Marcion and the Critical Method"; Stephen G. Wilson, "Marcion and the Jews"; and Peter Lampe, *Die stadtrömischen Christen in den ersten beiden Jahrhunderten,* 203–19.

23. See von Harnack, whose Marcion is for all practical purposes the founder of Catholicism: "[B]y means of his organizational and theological conceptions and by his activity Marcion gave the decisive impetus towards the creation of the old catholic church and provided the pattern for it. Moreover, he deserves the credit for having first grasped and actualized the idea of a canonical collection of Christian writings. Finally, he was the first one in the church after Paul to make soteriology the center of doctrine, while the church's apologists contemporary with him were grounding Christian doctrine in cosmology" (p.132).

24. Like the earlier Johannine Christians, Marcion also experienced ostracism from a larger religious community, was expelled, and then developed his own church. But his theological views appear to have been formulated while he was still very much *within* the larger community, and not upon his separation from it; and this community was, after all, Christian, not Jewish. Moreover, there is no convincing evidence that Marcion had any contact with or knowledge of the community that produced the Johannine writings.

25. Note 37.

26. See Tertullian's magnum opus in five books, the *Adversus Marcionem*. Epiphanius deals with Marcion and his followers in the *Panarion*, Book 42. For a brief statement of many of Marcion's doctrines that proved most offensive to the heresiologists, see Irenaeus, *Adv. Haer.* I. 27, 2–3. Rather than overloading the following sketch with footnotes, I simply refer the reader to the standard overviews of von Harnack, Blackman, and Knox, and the recent sketch by Lampe, all cited in note 22.

27. Hence the enigmatic charge by the orthodox heresiologists (e.g., Epiphanius, *Pan.* 42, 1) that Marcion was expelled for "seducing a virgin," that is, the church.

28. For an assessment of the amount and its significance, see Lampe, *Die stadtrömischen Christen,* 207–09.

29. And others; see Hoffmann, *Marcion,* 33, and Lampe, *Die stadtrömischen Christen,* 213, for references. Theodoret and Eznik de Kolb give firsthand accounts of thriving Marcionite communities in Syria and Armenia as late as the fifth century.

30. Thus Tertullian: "The separation of Law and Gospel is the primary and principal exploit of Marcion. His disciples cannot deny this, which stands at the head of their document, that document by which they are inducted into and confirmed in this heresy. For such are Marcion's *Antitheses,* or Contrary Oppositions, which are designed to show the conflict and disagreement of the Gospel and the Law, so that from the diversity of principles between those two documents they may argue further for a diversity of gods" (*Adv. Marc.* I. 19; translation by E. Evans, *Tertullian's Adversus Marcionem*).

31. Thus Tertullian: "In the fifteenth year of Tiberius Casesar Christ Jesus vouchsafed to glide down from heaven, a salutary spirit" (*Adv. Marc.* I. 19; translation by Evans); so too Hippolytus, in one of the few pieces of information he actually gives about Marcion in his refutation (*Ref.* 7, 20)

32. Nonetheless, for Marcion, Christ did "shed blood" and "die" in some sense; this was apparently the Stranger-God's arrangement to purchase humankind away from the Creator God, who required such an expiation as the price for human sin. This redemption then was to be received by faith; see von Harnack, *Marcion,* 87–89.

33. Above, pp. 19–20.

34. The assumption of Blackman (*Marcion and His Influence,* 43) and others that Marcion chose Luke because of the traditional identification of its author as the traveling companion of Paul is weakened by the circumstance that Marcion apparently never *identified* the Gospel as "Luke," but simply called it "the Gospel." It may be that Luke was more adaptable to Marcion's purposes, as (on the surface) less "Jewish" in its orientation than Matthew and John, or it may be that it was simply the Gospel that was known in Marcion's home church when he was growing up, before the four-Gospel canon had become standard. This final option, urged by von Harnack (*Marcion,* 29), strikes me as the least unsatisfactory. On the physiognomy of this Gospel, that is, whether it was comparable to the Luke that became canonized, see David Salter Williams, "Reconsidering Marcion's Gospel."

35. That Marcion was not altogether consistent in eliminating such passages is clear both from Tertullian's incredulity (as he concludes that Marcion must have left some things in so as not to appear tendentious! [*Adv. Marc.* IV, 43]) and Epiphanius's systematic collection of texts of Marcion's own Bible that contradict his theology (*Pan.* 42. 11–16). For recent studies of Marcion's text, see D. Williams, "Reconsidering," and John J. Clabeaux, *A Lost Edition of the Letters of Paul.*

36. *Prescription,* 38.

37. It matters little to my discussion as to whether one should classify Marcion as a Gnostic. This is an old debate that nonetheless continues to spark lively interest.

For my part, Marcion's system appears to differ so radically from what is essential to Gnosticism that it is difficult to see them as closely linked. To be sure, Marcion separates the Old Testament God from the God of Jesus, but he has only two gods, not a multitude. Correspondingly, there is no elaborate mythology in his system, no complex explanations either of a theogonic or a cosmogonic nature, and no account of a cosmic catastrophe that led to the entrapment of elements of the divine. Indeed, the Gnostic anthropology is far removed from his thought: he has no conception of an imprisoned divine spark that needs to be liberated. Quite to the contrary, for Marcion, humans belong body and soul to the Creator, until Christ effects their redemption. And this redemption is not through a revelation of knowledge but through faith in Christ's death; *gnosis* plays no role in this system! Moreover, although while both Marcion and the Gnostics see the discrepancies between the Old Testament and their systems, their resolutions of this problem are poles apart: the Gnostics self-consciously allegorize difficult passages, whereas Marcion vehemently opposes anything but a literal hermeneutic, insisting that literal contradictions to his system represent contaminations that are not to be explained away. For further discussion of these much debated issues, see especially Aland, "Marcion," 428ff.

38. This aspect of the proto-orthodox Christology is attested *in extenso* throughout our period. It can be found at the outset in Ignatius's terse but emphatic defamation of those "who say that he only appeared to have suffered." Such persons themselves, commented Ignatius, "are but an appearance" (Ign. *Smyrn.* 2. 1). For him, "Jesus Christ . . . truly was persecuted under Pontius Pilate, truly was crucified and died . . . and truly was raised from the dead" (Ign. *Trall.* 9. 1–2). Earlier still, of course, one finds a comparable position advanced by the author of the Johannine epistles. See pp. 132–33. The most lavish expression of this view comes in the writings of Tertullian: "The Son of God was crucified; I am not ashamed because others must needs be ashamed of it. And the Son of God died; it is by all means to be believed because it is absurd. And he was buried, and rose again; the fact is certain because it is impossible. But how will all this be true in Him if He was not Himself true—if He really had not in Himself that which might be crucified, might die, might be buried, and might rise again? I mean this flesh suffused with blood, built up with bones, interwoven with nerves, entwined with veins, a flesh which knew how to be born, and how to die, human without doubt, as born of a human being. It will therefore be mortal in Christ, because Christ is man and the son of man" (*de carne Christi*, 5).

39. See Bart D. Ehrman and Mark A. Plunkett, "The Angel and the Agony." The argument we advanced in this article was directed in no small measure against the broad consensus that had been built on the influential studies of von Harnack, "Probleme im Texte der Leidensgeschichte Jesu," and Lyder Brun, "Engel und Blutschweiss." While we were conducting our research another important contribution appeared, which again argued for the authenticity of the passage: Jean Duplacy, "La préhistoire du texte en Luc 22:43–44." To my knowledge, only one serious challenge to our conclusions has appeared, Jerome Neyrey, *The Passion According to Luke*, 55–57. In what follows, I will try to show why Neyrey's position strikes me as unconvincing.

40. "Probleme im Texte der Leidensgeschichte Jesu," 88. ὤφθη occurs thirteen times in Luke and Acts, once in Matthew, once in Mark; the entire phrase ὤφθη δὲ αὐτῷ ἄγγελος occurs elsewhere only in Luke 1:11; ἐνισχύειν occurs in Acts 9:19, nowhere else in the New Testament; ἐκτενέστερον προσεύχεσθαι is paralleled only in Acts 12:5 (cf. 26:7).

41. For example, even though Luke often speaks of angels, they never occur in the Gospel outside of the birth and resurrection narratives. Moreover, nowhere else does Luke use the phrase ἄγγελος ἀπ' οὐρανοῦ, and nowhere else does an angel remain silent.

42. For example, both ἐκτενῶς (ἐν ἐκτενείᾳ) and γίνεσθαι ἐν. This highlights the problem so typical in studies like von Harnack's—the restriction of stylistic and vocabulary statistics to the canonical texts, as if these have some kind of special status in determining patterns of usage. See Brun, "Engel und Blutschweiss," 266–71.

43. For a fuller treatment and a consideration of other arguments similarly attempted in previous studies, including Brun's own tour de force, see Ehrman and Plunkett, "The Angel and the Agony," 408–12.

44. It is remarkable that Neyrey read the argument that Plunkett and I advanced in "The Angel and the Agony" as exclusively transcriptional, as if our only concern was to see which reading scribes would have preferred. To be sure, this transcriptional question cannot be ignored; Neyrey himself does so at his own expense. But the bulk of our argument focused precisely on the non-Lukan character of the theology of the verses and their literarily intrusive nature, the latter of which Neyrey simply overlooks.

45. See the discussion on pp. 200–201.

46. A passage I take to be original, as I hope to show in a forthcoming publication. For a brief overview (and contrary opinion), see Fitzmyer, *Gospel According to Luke*, II. 1503–04, and the literature he cites there.

47. On the textual problem of verse 42, see pp. 233–35.

48. Neyrey offers a defense of the Lukan character of these verses, arguing that they are consistent with Luke's notion of Jesus' passion as an athletic contest (ἀγωνία) from which Jesus emerges victorious. The disputed verses, then, portray Jesus as overcoming his Satanic foe through strength, not weakness. Neyrey has done a commendable service in collecting the various ἀγωνία texts in Stoic and other Greco-Roman documents, but how one can read the present passage in this way puzzles me. A key element of the ἀγωνία motif is "courage," which is never mentioned here. Moreover, these verses do anything *but* portray Jesus as "strong": were he strong he would scarcely need the support of an angel from heaven. Nor does the angel supply Jesus with the strength he lacks; it is only *after* it appears that Jesus begins to sweat great "drops as if of blood." The angel may, then, provide succor to a soul in distress, but it scarcely effects a triumph. It cannot be replied that the angelic appearance is a typical Lukan motif because in the one other instance in which one would expect an angel to appear in order to strengthen Jesus, the temptation narrative, Luke has in fact *omitted* the reference to angelic help found in his Markan source (Luke 4:13; cf. Mark 1:13)! And so Neyrey is right to see that Luke is intent on portraying Jesus as strong and in control, but he fails to see that precisely these verses compromise such a portrayal. Finally, it is important to insist that any consideration of the intrinsic merit of the verses *not* be conducted in isolation of all the other issues (e.g., literary structure, transcription, etc.) that relate to a textual problem of this complexity. Neyrey's analysis is regrettably lacking in this regard. See further, note 55.

49. Contra, for example, N. W. Lund, *Chiasmus in the New Testament*.

50. See pp. 204–07.

51. προσεύχομαι occurs nineteen times in Luke, sixteen in Acts; in relation to Jesus, see especially Luke 3:21; 5:16; 9:18; 11:1.

52. See the discussion of pp. 201–02.

53. Not through some supernatural intervention such as a ministering angel, an

intervention that Luke elsewhere removes from his traditions about Jesus (i.e., in the temptation narrative; see note 48).

54. For a complete redactional analysis of the passage, see Marion L. Soards, *The Passion According to Luke.*

55. As they are in fact by Neyrey, *The Passion According to Luke.* If one does think these verses are original, their omission in such early and high-quality witnesses must be given a plausible explanation.

56. See Ehrman and Plunkett, "The Angel and the Agony," 403–07.

57. This is not to say that early Christians generally thought that Jesus lost all self-control in his passion. Along with the Gospel of Luke, for example, the Fourth Gospel also portrays Jesus as directing his own destiny. The point, however, is that early Christians did not shy away from Jesus' real agony in the face of his death, especially proto-orthodox Christians (who produced our manuscripts) for whom Jesus' real suffering became a central tenet of the faith.

58. On the confluence of docetic and separationist features of this Christology, see note 17.

59. For textual corruptions generated out of the context of this particular debate, see the discussion of pp. 262–69. That this particular variant proved useful in such a context but was not generated in it is demonstrated by its occurrence already in the "Memoirs of the Apostles" known to Justin in mid-century, prior to the propagation of the views of the Patripassianists.

60. It makes sense that these verses were inserted into Luke's Gospel in particular, given precisely what I have already shown: without them, Luke's portrayal of Jesus as calm and collected does not coincide with what one expects of a man who is about to be nailed to a cross. It should be further noted that part of the textual difficulty with the verses results from the fact that f^{13} relocates the story by placing it in Matthew's Gospel (following 26:39). This too shows the instability of the tradition and suggests that it represents a "floating" narrative that has been inserted in different Gospels for similar reasons.

61. Colwell, *Studies in Methodology*, 115–18.

62. It might also be, as Joel Marcus has suggested to me, that a scribe who did not understand *which* Scripture was said to be fulfilled excised the statement altogether. The problem with this view is that early Christians rarely had trouble finding Old Testament passages to support their christological interpretations. In the present case, Psalms 22 and 68 both come to mind as possible points of reference. See further, Brown, *Gospel According to John,* II. 928–30.

63. In view of the slight variations from the Johannine tradition, Metzger suggests an interpolation made simply from memory. See his *Textual Commentary,* 71.

64. Against the Ptolemaeans: If Jesus had not taken a human body from Mary, blood and water would not have come from his side when it was pierced (*Adv. Haer.* III, 22, 2); against Marcion: "And how, again, supposing that he was not flesh, but was a man merely in appearance, could he have been crucified, and could blood and water have issued from his pierced side?" (*Adv. Haer.* IV, 33, 2)

65. See the words of Tertullian: "We have indeed, likewise, a second font (itself withal one with the former) of blood, to wit; concerning which the Lord said, 'I have to be baptized with a baptism,' when He had been baptized already. For He had come 'by means of water and blood,' just as John has written; that He might be baptized by the water, glorified by the blood, to make us in like manner, called by water, chosen by blood. These two baptisms He sent out from the wound in His pierced side, in order that they who believed in His blood might be bathed with the water;

they who had been bathed in the water might likewise drink the blood" (*de Bapt.* 16).

66. It is not that John did not suffer, but proto-orthodox Christians were naturally more interested in emphasizing that Christ did. The change was probably not made in reaction to the followers of John the Baptist, who may have seen him in messianic terms, as this controversy was very much a thing of the past when our discrepant manuscripts were produced.

67. This understanding of the way orthodox scribes may have worked can explain other textual problems as well. It may be only coincidental that the interesting variant of Mark 9:12 also occurs in a context of Jesus' discussion of John as Elijah and of the need of the Son of Man to suffer. Be that as it may, it is worth observing that some witnesses have changed Jesus' question, "And how [καὶ πῶς] is it written about the Son of Man that he should suffer many things?" In the modified text, Jesus' words are construed as a statement, "Just as [καθώς] it is written about the Son of Man that he should suffer many things" (MSS A K M Δ Π). To be sure, there are grounds for suspecting that this is a simple scribal blunder occasioned by orthography (καιπως / καθως). All the same, the alteration emphasizes precisely the vital issue of Jesus' suffering; he now *declares* that it comes in fulfillment of Scripture, rather than *questioning* how this could be so. One cannot help suspecting, therefore, that the orthodox inclination to stress the suffering of Jesus contributed to the corruption of the text.

A similar conclusion may be drawn concerning Acts 13:29, in which are described the events of Jesus' death and burial. Among its additions to the text, codex Bezae specifies that Jesus' opponents asked Pilate to have him "crucified," a word otherwise absent from the account. The change may simply reflect the orthodox proclivity toward emphasizing Christ's real death (by crucifixion). On another tendency also at work here and throughout the distinctively Bezan materials, see Epp, *Theological Tendency of Codex Bezae*, 41–51.

68. As we have seen, Marcion's views on this score were somewhat exceptional. See p. 186.

69. For an earlier statement, compare the words of Ignatius, "For he suffered all these things on our account, that we might be saved. And he truly suffered . . . not as some unbelievers say, that he merely appeared to suffer" (Ign. *Smyrn.* 2, 1). For Ignatius, apart from the blood of Christ, there can be no salvation: "Let no one be led astray: whether heavenly beings, the glory of angels, or rulers visible or invisible— if they fail to believe in the blood of Christ, they will have to face judgment" (Ign. *Smyrn.* 6, 1).

70. Although, interestingly enough, the reference to "blood" in Irenaeus's text of Colossians is itself nothing but an orthodox corruption! See the discussion of pp. 210–11.

71. I have drawn the following discussion, slightly revised, from my article "The Cup, the Bread, and the Salvific Effect of Jesus' Death in Luke-Acts." Among the more important discussions of the problem, in addition to the works cited in note 73, are the following: H. Schürmann, "Lk 22, 19b–20 als ursprüngliche Textüberlieferung"; Martin Rese, "Zur Problematik von Kurz- und Langtext in Luk xxii.17ff"; J. H. Petzer, "Luke 22:19b–20 and the Structure of the Passage"; id., "Style and Text in the Lucan Narrative of the Institution of the Lord's Supper"; Fitzmyer, *Gospel According to Luke*, 1386–95; and E. Earle Ellis, *The Gospel of Luke*, 254–56.

72. See the convenient chart and discussion in Metzger, *Textual Commentary*, 173–77. Three of the four readings are each attested by only one form of the Syriac,

the fourth by two Old Latin manuscripts (b e). All four are readily understood as deriving from one or the other of the two remaining forms; all four circumvent one of the major stumbling blocks of the text by reversing the sequence of cup and bread.

73. See Westcott and Hort, *The New Testament in the Original Greek* II. 175–77, and the general discussion of Metzger, *Textual Commentary*, 191–93. Among those who call the entire theory of Western non-interpolations into question are Joachim Jeremias, *The Eucharistic Words of Jesus*, 84–106; Kurt Aland, "Die Bedeutung des P75 für den Text des Neuen Testaments"; and dependent upon these two, Klijn Snodgrass, "Western Non-Interpolations." See further the Excursus pp. 223–27.

74. Pp. 223–27.

75. In anticipation of my fuller discussion in the Excursus (pp. 223–27), I should also point out that Westcott and Hort's dependence on the text of codex Vaticanus was not based on sheer prejudice in favor of the oldest manuscript, as it is sometimes misunderstood to be; nor did they blindly follow the Neutral text without regard for other considerations. The text of Vaticanus was judged superior by a careful analysis of the *internal* quality of its readings; whenever clear textual decisions could be reached on the basis of intrinsic and transcriptional probabilities, Vaticanus was seen to attest the original text. For Westcott and Hort, this suggested that in ambiguous cases its text was also likely to be correct. As a whole, then, their system was not built simply on "external" or "documentary" evidence but on a thorough assessment of the internal quality of textual variations and their supporting witnesses.

76. Most recently by Joel Green, "The Death of Jesus, God's Servant," 4.

77. In addition to the stylistic features I cite here, see the list in Green, "The Death of Jesus," 4. On the difficulties of basing a text-critical judgment solely on such stylistic features, however, see Petzer, "Style and Text."

78. Nor do the closely related phrases ἀντὶ ὑμῶν or ὑπὲρ πολλῶν.

79. Nor, interestingly, does Luke preserve either of Mark's two uses of the verbal form ἀναμιμνήσκω, omitting Mark 11:21 altogether for other reasons, and changing the word in Mark 14:72 to ὑπομιμνήσκω (22:61).

80. Schürmann ("Lk 22,19b–20") is followed by Ellis (*Gospel of Luke*) in arguing that backward glances to the longer text in the subsequent narrative demonstrate its presence in the original form of the text. But none of the proposed examples proves at all convincing: there is no reason to think that the πλὴν ἰδού of verse 21 refers back to ὑπὲρ ὑμῶν, or that "this cup" of verse 42 alludes to "the cup" of verse 20 (why not v. 17!), or that the verbal form διατίθεμαι in verse 28 requires the establishment of the διαθήκη in verse 20.

81. Scholars traditionally have pointed to Luke 22:19–20 and Acts 20:28 as the only two exceptions to the rule. I will deal with the latter momentarily. In addition to the commentaries, see Richard Zehnle, "The Salvific Character of Jesus' Death in Lucan Soteriology"; Augustin George, "Le sens de la mort Jésus pour Luc"; and the consensus that is reflected now in the collection of essays edited by Sylva, *Reimaging*, especially Green, "The Death of Jesus,"; Earl Richard, "Jesus' Passion and Death in Acts"; and, above all, John T. Carroll, "Luke's Crucifixion Scene."

82. Whether or not Luke "borrowed" the story from the tradition, the point is that as it is presented in his Gospel, there is not a word about the Servant of the Lord suffering as an atoning sacrifice.

83. Joel Marcus has suggested to me that instead of deleting Mark 10:45, Luke has placed in its stead his characteristic understanding of Jesus: "But I am among you as one who serves" (22:27). See further Soards, *The Passion According to Luke*, 30–31.

84. See p. 190.

85. In addition to the commentaries, see, for example, Frank J. Matera, *Passion Narratives and Gospel Theologies*, 47, and the literature that he cites. Most recently Ulansey ("The Heavenly Veil Torn") has argued that Mark refers to the outer curtain, because on it was drawn a likeness of the cosmos (Josephus, *Jewish Wars* 5. 5. 4) that would then correspond symbolically to "the heavens" of Mark 1:10. This is probably supposing too much of Mark's implied readers, however (i.e., that they would catch the allusion that most subsequent interpreters have missed), readers who otherwise do not evidence particular knowledge of Palestinian Judaism (cf. 7:1–3!).

86. Or it may be that the emphasis is to be reversed, that with the ripping of the curtain humans now have access to God in his holy place.

87. Throughout Mark's Gospel Jesus is portrayed as the Son of God who must suffer and die, but who is universally misunderstood. His family thinks he has gone mad (3:21), the Jewish leadership thinks he is inspired by the Devil (3:22), his towns-people think that he is simply the local carpenter (6:1–6), and his own disciples are never able to understand either who he is or what he means (6:52, 8:1–14). When they do begin to understand, they do so only partially at best (8:27–38). When Jesus tells them he must go to Jerusalem to die, they object (8:31–32); when he describes his coming rejection by those in power, they argue among themselves concerning who is the greatest (9:30–37; cf. 10:33–45). At the end of the Gospel he is betrayed by one of his disciples, denied by another, and deserted by all the rest. He is crucified a lonely, forsaken man, crying out in his despair, "My God, my God, why have you forsaken me?" before breathing his last (15:34–37). Only then, in his death, does his identity become known (15:39).

88. The source questions are particularly difficult here. In addition to the commentaries, see especially Franz Georg Untergaβmair, *Kreuzweg und Kreuzigung Jesu*, 97–101.

89. Luke has added an explanation to Mark's terse notation "there was darkness over the whole earth until the ninth hour," by indicating that it was because the sun had failed (τοῦ ἡλίου ἐκλιπόντος). On the textual problem and meaning of the phrase, see, for example, Fitzmyer, *Gospel According to Luke*, 1517–18.

90. In addition to the commentaries, see the diverging opinion of Dennis Sylva, "The Temple Curtain and Jesus' Death in the Gospel of Luke," and the more popular treatment of Donald Senior, *The Passion of Jesus in the Gospel of Luke*.

91. Or (depending on the slant one chooses to put upon it) that it has effected a revelation of God's grace to his people.

92. An alternative explanation has recently been set forth by Susan Garrett, *The Demise of the Devil*, that the darkness indicates the temporary victory of Satan. This interpretation equally distances Luke's construal of the event from Mark's.

93. For a strong case that the text should be rendered "Truly this man was righteous," see Robert J. Karris, "Luke 23:47 and the Lucan View of Jesus' Death." In my judgment, J. Carroll ("Luke's Crucifixion Scene," 116–18 and notes) is more likely correct that one should not press too far the difference between "righteous" and "innocent" because if Jesus is one, he is also the other.

94. See especially Carroll, "Luke's Crucifixion Scene," 116–20.

95. See p. 88 and p. 264.

96. *Contra* Waldemar Schmeichel, "Does Luke Make a Soteriological Statement in Acts 20:28?", who argues that τοῦ ἰδίου refers to Paul, who establishes the church by his self-giving ministry and eventual death. For Luke, however, the church was "obtained" well before Paul's ministry and sacrifice!

97. In addition to the commentaries, see the recent study of Lars Aejmelaeus, *Die Rezeption der Paulusbriefe in der Miletrede,* 132–42, who goes yet further to claim an actual literary dependence of 20:28 on 1 Thessalonians 5:9–10 and Ephesians 1:7. This is part of Aejmelaeus' larger thesis that Pauline allusions in Acts are invariably due to Luke's knowledge of the Pauline letters.

98. See Carroll, "Luke's Crucifixion Scene," for the Lukan emphasis on guilt and repentance. Even the disciples, who evidently were not among those who called for Jesus' death at his trial, had to repent in light of his blood to become members of his church; their unwillingness to die with him in the Gospel is then reversed after his death in the book of Acts.

99. See, for example, Luke 24:47; Acts 2:38; 3:19; 5:31; 8:22; 17:30; 11:18; 20:21; 26:20.

100. See Carroll, "Luke's Crucifixion Scene," 113–20, and the literature he cites there.

101. Interestingly, he also predicts that "fierce wolves" will be set loose upon the congregation who will not "spare the flock" (i.e., who will bring them to a violent end) unless the elders protect them (20:29). Blood is spilled when one does not repent and believe in the one God has vindicated.

102. *Gospel of Luke,* 254–55.

103. Where again Jesus refers to τὸ σῶμα τὸ ὑπὲρ ὑμῶν, to "doing this in my remembrance" (τοῦτο ποιεῖτε εἰς τὴν ἐμὴν ἀνάμνησιν), to his taking "likewise the cup after supper" (ὡσαύτως καὶ τὸ ποτήριον μετὰ τὸ δειπνῆσαι), and to his pronouncing that "this cup is the new covenant in my blood" (τοῦτο τὸ ποτήριον ἡ καινὴ διαθήκη [ἐστὶν] ἐν τῷ αἵματί μου).

104. "Luke 22:19b–20."

105. "Luke 22:19b–20," 251 (emphasis his).

106. If parallelism is half again as common as some other structure in the New Testament, will this argument for the original text be half again as valid?

107. There are other problems with Petzer's structure. For example, it requires the phrase τὸ πάσχα φαγεῖν to be understood as a reference to eating "bread," (as in v. 19), when in fact it appears simply to mean "to celebrate the Passover."

108. The γάρ, then, does not function causally but to express continuation or connection. See BAGD, 151.

109. Mark uses it once; Luke, in the Gospel alone, uses it fifteen times.

110. It should be noted that the sequence in which the followers are mentioned is reversed: the faithful who partake with him in his final meal are mentioned in the first element of each member of the first pericope (vv. 15, 17); the unfaithful one who betrays him is both times named second in the pericope that follows (vv. 21, 22b).

111. "Luke 22:19b–20," 252.

112. Westcott and Hort, *New Testament in the Original Greek,* I. Appendix, "Notes on Selected Readings," 63–64.

113. *Eucharistic Words,* 87–106.

114. Jeremias's solution to these problems was to say that a particular scribe was asked by a particular pagan for a copy of Luke's Gospel, which he produced, leaving out the words in question (19b–20). But he retained verse 19a as a hint to Christian insiders of what happened next at the meal. It is a creative solution, but is nonetheless entirely implausible. Where is the evidence of such an unlikely sequence of events (How many pagans asked scribes for copies of Scripture? What scribes were fearful of the magical abuse of their texts? If the text was for a pagan, why was the hint of verse 19a left in? and so on.)? Furthermore, Jeremias can still not explain why

similar motivations played no role in the transmission of other New Testament passages that reflect Christian liturgical passages, let alone the other narratives of institution.

115. On the character of the Lukan redaction, in which he changes Mark's understanding of the meal as the institution of the Lord's Supper to depict it instead as Jesus' last Passover meal with his disciples, see Rese, "Zur Problematik."

116. See the discussion of Luke 22:43–44 above. On different views of martyrdom in the period, see especially Elaine Pagels, "Gnostic and Orthodox Views of Christ's Passion."

117. In Coptic witnesses; compare the longer text of Luke.

118. In a wide range of Greek, Latin, and Syriac witnesses, including ℵᶜ Cᶜ Dᶜ OL syrᵖ· ʰ and virtually the entire Byzantine tradition.

119. That the text originally lacked any participle is demonstrated by the attestation of the shortest and most difficult reading in the earliest and best manuscripts of the Alexandrian tradition (𝔭⁴⁶ ℵ* A B C* 33 1739* Origen pc).

120. Another example occurs in Hebrews 10:10, a passage that could well be taken as anti-docetic with either reading. Nonetheless, one finds the "blood" of Christ stressed here in a variant attested in two otherwise unrelated witnesses: both D and E (along with d and e) substitute αἵματος for σώματος, so that "sanctification" is said to come from Christ's offering his "blood" rather than his "body." This is a case where one might suspect a simple confusion of letters; but here again one must ask what kind of scribe with what kind of theology would be likely to make such an error. The question can be asked as well of a variant that is but poorly attested among several Byzantine manuscripts of Acts 10:43, where forgiveness of sins is no longer said to come through the "name" (ὀνόματος) of Jesus but through his "blood" (αἵματος, MSS 36 453). Whether or not the variant antedates its first extant occurrence in the twelfth century is immaterial to my overarching point, that orthodox Christians, beginning at least with the docetic controversies of the second century, began focusing on the salvific importance of the real blood of Christ to such an extent that they naturally "read" such things in (and into) texts that originally said not a word about them.

121. For example, in manuscripts 614 630 2464, the Harclean Syriac, and Cassiodorus.

122. Old Latin a. The manuscript dates from the fourth century, although it may be preserving an older tradition.

123. Here again the shortest text is attested by the earliest and best manuscripts (𝔭⁷² B C Ψ OL copˢᵃ), and is almost certainly original.

124. See, for example, Elaine Pagels, "Visions, Appearances, and Apostolic Authority," and, on a more popular level, id., *Gnostic Gospels*, 3–32.

125. See also, for example, Origen's *Dial. Heracl.* 132–34.

126. See, for example, Irenaeus, *Adv. Haer.* I, 30, 13; Tertullian, *de carne Christi,* 5. This heretical teaching relates, as has been seen previously, to the notion that the afterlife of those who have been saved will be spiritual rather than physical. For a proto-orthodox refutation, see Tertullian, *de resur. carne.*

127. For example, Tertullian, *de carne Christi,* especially Chap. 5.

128. The witnesses that attest the verse are not themselves invariant, although their differences have little bearing on our present discussion. κείμενα is attested by the bulk of the manuscripts, but not by such high quality and early witnesses as 𝔭⁷⁵ ℵ B W 0124 syrˢ· ᶜ cop; μόνα is omitted by ℵ* A K 063 al.

129. Franz Neirynck has convincingly shown that Marcion, the Diatesseron, and

the Palestinian Syriac cannot be cited in support of the Western text here, despite their appearance in most of the apparatuses. See his "Lc xxiv 12: Les témoins du texte occidental."

130. The "certainty" in this case is provided by the confluence of a relatively early Greek witness with a number of Old Latin manuscripts. See further the excursus on Western non-interpolations (pp. 223–27).

131. In addition to the standard commentaries, which generally reproduce the conventional grounds of rejection (if any at all), see the following important studies: J. Jeremias, *Eucharistic Words,* 145–52; K. Aland, "Die Bedeutung des P^75"; Snodgrass, "Western Non-Interpolations"; George E. Rice, "Western Non-Interpolations: A Defense of the Apostolate"; F. P. G. Curtis, "Luke xxiv.12 and John xx.3–10"; P. Benoirt, "Marie-Madeleine et les disciples au tombeau selon Joh 20,1–18"; John Muddiman, "A Note on Reading Luke xxiv.12"; Franz Neirynck, "The Uncorrected Historical Present in Lk. xxiv.12"; id., "Lk. xxiv.12."

132. *Marcion,* 247* (German edition).

133. It is frequent in Acts as well, although adding up statistics from both books, while useful for determining Luke's own "style," is deceptive when trying to compare that style with those attested in much shorter books (Luke-Acts together comprise well over a fourth of the entire New Testament).

134. So already Kirsopp Lake, *The Historical Evidence for the Resurrection of Jesus Christ,* 95.

135. It is true that Luke uses the historic present in several passages that he did not take over from Mark (also traditional?); nearly all of these, however, involve verbs of "saying" (λέγει seven times, φημί once, out of a total of eleven).

136. For example, Jeremias, *Eucharistic Words,* 150.

137. As noted by Jeremias: ὀθόνιον in 19:40; 20:5, 6, 7; παρακύπτειν in 20:5, 11. Otherwise, the precise significance of the Johannine parallel is much debated. In view of the growing consensus that neither Luke nor John had access to the other's work *per se,* most of the recent scholars who subscribe to the originality of Luke 24:12 have argued for its presence in a common source, which both authors have redacted for their own purposes.

138. As acknowledged, for example, by Snodgrass, "Western Non-Interpolations," 373. It is worth noting that many of the supporters of the verse have not even tried to explain the Western "omission." Compare Jeremias, *Eucharistic Words,* 149–51; K. Aland "Die Bedeutung des P^75" 168.

139. As, for example, Muddiman claims was done by a "logic-chopping" Western scribe, in an article that serves the modifier well ("A Note on Reading Luke xxiv. 12").

140. On the infeasibility of the contrived category of "harmonizing omissions," see note 192.

141. Of course, the astute reader knows; see 9:30 and Acts 1:10.

142. See especially Pagels, "Visions, Appearances, and Apostolic Authority," and *Gnostic Gospels,* 3–32.

143. Translation by John E. L. Oulton and Henry Chadwick, *Alexandrian Christianity (Library of Christian Classics* II; Philadelphia: Westminster, 1954).

144. See pp. 223–27.

145. So far as I know, the only scholar who comes close to broaching the subject is Mikeal Parsons, "A Christological Tendency in P^75," who sees these readings as changes that the scribe of p^75 himself created in order "to accent an already exalted Christology," in opposition to Gnostic Christologies of early third-century Egypt (p.

476; see also his book, *The Departure of Jesus in Luke-Acts*, 29–52). Parsons is certainly to be commended for moving along the right track, and I do not want to detract from the merits of his work by my criticisms. At the same time, his article lacks precision in identifying both the *nature* of this "exalted" Christology and its appropriateness for attacking "the heretical tendencies of Gnosticism" (p. 475). These non-Western interpolations do not appear to counter Gnostic Christologies in general (which, in any case, are anything but monolithic) but specific docetic tendencies in particular, tendencies that are sporadically attested in Gnosticism but are attested more frequently elsewhere (e.g., Marcion). Moreover, the Christologies countered by these changes are themselves about as exalted as they come (Christ is no longer human). This is not a case of scribes fighting fire with fire; the interpolations *oppose* a high Christology. Finally, I doubt seriously whether we can think in terms of a solitary surviving manuscript as the actual *source* of corruption for virtually the entire manuscript tradition of the Greek New Testament. 𝔭⁷⁵ was one of hundreds (thousands?) of manuscripts of its age. It survives *purely* by accident. Are we to think that it just happens to be the smoking gun?

146. It should be noted that Tertullian directly quotes Luke 24:39 against Marcion to demonstrate the point (*de carne Christi* 5; cf. the use of 24:40 in *Adv. Marc.* IV, 43, discussed below).

147. See the clear discussion of Schoedel, *Ignatius of Antioch*, 225–27, and the literature he cites there.

148. On the use of the pronoun in the Lukan text, see note 153.

149. The introduction in Ignatius is "Take," in Luke, "Behold my hands and my feet, that it is I." The inference to be drawn in Ignatius is that Jesus is not a "disembodied spirit," in Luke "that [or because] a spirit does not have flesh and bones as you see that I have."

150. Thus Schoedel, *Ignatius of Antioch*, 227.

151. Fragment III (letter to an unnamed queen); in ANF, V. 240, slightly altered. See also Tertullian, *de carne Christi*, 5.

152. Except, of course, that in the Lukan version Jesus shows his feet rather than his side. The change is not surprising: Luke records no spear thrust, as both he and his scribes know full well.

153. A similar kind of strengthening of the point can be seen in the addition of the pronoun με to non-Western witnesses in verse 39. Now the disciples are instructed by Jesus to "handle *me* and see."

154. *Contra* K. Aland, "Die Bedeutung des P⁷⁵," 169.

155. *Contra* Snodgrass, "Western Non-Interpolations," 373.

156. See for example, F. W. Farrar, *The Gospel According to Luke*, 358; Snodgrass, "Western Non-Interpolations," 375.

157. Snodgrass, "Western Non-Interpolations," 375.

158. Other scholars have argued that the antithetical character ("not . . . but") of the statement indicates that it is original because this kind of phraseology is lacking in the Matthean and Markan parallels (e.g., Jeremias, *Eucharistic Words*, 149). There is no reason, however, to think that a scribe wanting to insert the phrase would be bound to follow either of the other Synoptic accounts verbatim: these accounts are not aligned perfectly even with each other.

159. φάντασμα occurs only in codex Bezae, as I will have occasion to mention below. All other witnesses read πνεῦμα.

160. P (W 579) 1241 vg syrᵖ˙ ʰ boᵖᵗ.

161. So Metzger, *Textual Commentary*, 186.

162. Luke 24:36: "and he said to them, 'Peace be to you' "; compare John 20:19 "And he said to them, 'Peace be to you.' "

163. The two Western non-interpolations I have not yet discussed (Luke 24:51, 52), move along related lines, as I shall show on pp. 227–32.

164. As I have already indicated, some of the theoretical problems involved in accepting the Western text as original in these cases have been taken up in the Excursus, pp. 223–27.

165. The word πνεῦμα was not changed in verse 39, perhaps because there the word functions clearly as a synonymn of φάντασμα and works better in the contrast with σάρξ.

166. The influential opinion of Bultmann, *The Gospel of John,* 697–99.

167. I will discuss the anti-docetic character of the remaining instances (Luke 24:51, 52) on pp. 227–32. For another attempt to resuscitate these issues, see Parsons, "A Christological Tendency in 𝔭⁷⁵."

168. Though not altogether so: if the longer text is to be construed as original in these passages, one might explore the usefulness of these texts for the docetic controversies, and speculate concerning the reasons for their deletion from the Western tradition.

169. This appears to be the position, for example, of Fitzmyer, *Gospel According to Luke,* 1.130–31, who sees the material gain of the papyri since Westcott and Hort's day as sufficient reason to overturn their theories. On this see further below, pp. 224–27.

170. As is done, for example, by K. Aland, "Die Bedeutung des 𝔭⁷⁵," compare Metzger, *Textual Commentary,* 192.

171. Hort was quite candid that he delivered this judgment strictly on the basis of intrinsic and transcriptional probabilities. The shorter readings found within the Western witnesses in these cases could not be plausibly explained apart from the theory of their originality. This should not be construed as inconsistent with Hort's theory concerning the vast superiority of the Neutral text, however, as this superiority was itself ultimately established on precisely such grounds.

172. Metzger, *Textual Commentary, passim;* B. Aland and K. Aland, *Text of the New Testament,* in which their eloquent defense of the "local-genealogical method" amounts to an *apologia* for the method of considering the "genealogy" of each textual variant on the basis of its own merits. Despite their protestations (p. 34), this is simply eclecticism under a different name.

173. That is, the feasibility of original readings being preserved only in "Western" witnesses. Compare Westcott and Hort, *New Testament in the Original Greek,* I. 176–77.

174. See note 171.

175. *New Testament in the Original Greek,* I. 126–30.

176. *New Testament in the Original Greek,* I. 148–49.

177. As K. Aland appears to do, "Die Bedeutung des 𝔭⁷⁵," 171–72. For an insightful and sober evaluation of the significance of the papyri generally, see now Epp, "The Significance of the Papyri."

178. This is especially true where the Western text is most distinct from the other forms of tradition, that is, in the book of Acts. The papyri belonging to the group include 𝔭²⁹, ³⁸, ⁴⁸.

179. *Prescription of Heretics,* 13. As my graduate student from Duke University, John Brogan, has pointed out to me, the doctrine of Jesus' bodily ascension played a surprisingly scant role in the debates with heretics, particularly with Marcion. Tertul-

lian, for example, scarcely mentions it throughout his entire five-book refutation, where otherwise he bars no holds and slights no texts. Interestingly enough, it occurs not at all where one would expect to find it, at the end of Tertullian's exposition of the Gospel of Luke in Book IV. In this book Tertullian works through the Third Gospel passage by passage in order to refute Marcion from his own text and to malign the excisions he has made. It is somewhat curious, then, that he ends the exposition with the narrative of Jesus' resurrection, saying not a word concerning his ascension. This lacuna is difficult to explain apart from the conclusion that neither Marcion nor Tertullian had the first variant I will be examining in their Gospel text ("And he was taken up into heaven," Luke 24:51), a conclusion that makes additional sense when one considers the Western character of the shorter text.

180. See Fitzmyer, *Gospel According to Luke* 2. 1248, 1589–90.

181. See esp. Eldon J. Epp, "The Ascension in the Textual Tradition of Luke-Acts," and the literature he cites there. For a summary of the issues surrounding the comparable textual problem in Acts 1:2, see Metzger, *Textual Commentary*, 273–77, and Parsons, *Departure of Jesus*, 124–34.

182. See the Excursus.

183. As it supports none of the other distinctively Bezan readings (e.g., the Western non-interpolations). Its alignments here, then, contrast with its text in the opening chapters of John. See Fee, "Codex Sinaiticus in the Gospel of John."

184. With regard to intrinsic probabilities, one argument that is frequently put forth in favor of the longer text strikes me as particularly weak (see Jeremias, *Eucharistic Words* 151; Marshall, *Commentary on Luke,* 909), namely, that because the sentences in 24:50 on the one hand and 24:52f on the other both comprise two coordinate clauses (i.e., two clauses joined with καί), one should expect the same kind of sentence in the intervening verse 51. No one who advances this argument, so far as I am aware, ever tells us *why* we should expect three sentences in a row like this—the argument is never set in the context of any discussion of Lukan style (or Greek composition generally). Does Luke *normally* string three such sentences together? Yet more to the point, even a cursory glance at the passage shows that we are not at all dealing here with a carefully crafted unit whose structure serves to unpack its meaning (contrast, e.g., 22:39–46). None of the five unquestioned clauses uses the same syntactical structure; the entire unit simply comprises five (or six) clauses strung with καί. The loose character of the construction is easily demonstrated by considering the second clause of each undisputed pair of coordinates (vv. 50, 53). The second clause of verse 50 begins with a subordinate participle (ἐπάρας), followed by an object (τὰς χεῖρας), and picked up by the main verb (εὐλόγησεν) with its object (αὐτούς); in verse 53 the coordinate clause begins with the main verb (ἦσαν) followed by two prepositional phrases (διὰ παντός, ἐν τῷ ἱερῷ). If the final words are original, the clause ends with a subordinate participial clause (εὐλογοῦντες). Where is the craft in this? I should point out that in the second sentence (i.e., v. 51), with or without the words in question, there is no participle at all. This is not a highly structured passage. Why should one suppose that Luke created a triumvirate of such loosely constructed pairs of coordinate clauses?

185. Of course, 1:22 can be taken to refer to the event described in 1:9–11 rather than the one described in Luke 24:51.

186. The issue was seriously considered by Wilhelm Michaelis, *Das Neue Testament verdeutscht und erläufert*, II. 7, whose views were rejected out of hand, more recently, by Haenchen, *Acts of the Apostles,* 138. Most major commentators do not address the problem (e.g., F. F. Bruce, *The Acts of the Apostles,* 66).

187. For common explanations of why he did so, based on the assumption that he *has* done so, see Parsons, *Departure of Jesus,* 189–99. See further note 188.

188. The common explanation is that Luke intended to narrate two ascensions, not because he believed Jesus actually ascended twice, but in order to provide both a fitting end to Jesus' earthly ministry (the account in the Gospel) and a fitting beginning to that of the church (the account in Acts). It is an expedient solution, with all the force of a virtue born of necessity. The real question is whether there *is* any necessity. Who has decided, for example, that a physical ascent into heaven is "fitting" for *either* event? Certainly no other writer from the first century appears to have thought so; Luke is the only surviving author who narrates the incident.

189. The frequent objection that only the ascension can make sense of Luke 24:52b, that the disciples returned to Jerusalem with great joy (see, e.g., K. Aland, "Die Bedeutung des $\mathfrak{p}^{75}$," 170), is particularly puzzling. Were the disciples in Matthew and John not elated that their Lord had been raised from the dead?

190. As acknowledged, for example, in the Muratorian canon and patristic writers beginning with Irenaeus (*Adv. Haer.* III, 14, 1).

191. Cited as one of the two major possibilities, for example, by Jeremias, *Eucharistic Words,* 151; Snodgrass, "Western Non-Interpolations," 375; and Metzger, *Textual Commentary,* 189–90.

192. For example, Jeremias, throughout his treatment of Western non-interpolations. To check my claim, one need simply look at texts that appear to present glaring discrepancies and see whether omissions have occurred to reconcile them. There are no "omissions" made to square Jesus' command for Mary not to touch him in John 20:17 with his command for Thomas to do so ten verses later; no omissions to square Paul's claim that he did not confer with the apostles in Jerusalem after his conversion (Gal 1:16–17) with Luke's claim that he did just that (Acts 9:26–30); no omissions to square the various accounts in Acts of what happened to Paul on the road to Damascus, that is, whether his companions were knocked to the ground or left standing (9:7; 26:14), whether they heard the voice but saw nothing or saw the light but heard no voice (Acts 9:7; 22:9); no omissions even in the "ascension" passages currently under review (in witnesses that attest them both), for example, to square the apparent discrepancy in geography over whether the ascent was from just beyond the city walls on the Mount of Olives or from the town of Bethany. In point of fact, when scribes do note differences between passages and work to resolve them, this is almost always done by addition or transformation, not omission. One thinks of the variant forms of the Lord's Prayer in Matthew and Luke, in which the textual tradition shows a consistent augmentation of the latter account to make it conform with the fuller version of the former, with the reverse process occurring almost never. And so the contradictions and textual discrepancies that have so motivated modern scholarship functioned much differently in ancient Christianity, although even there one cannot speak in terms of a monolithic approach. One way such discrepancies appear not to have functioned, however, was as a motivation to harmonize the text through omissions.

193. "The Ascension in the Textual Tradition of Luke-Acts."

194. In his more recent study, "The Significance of the Papyri," Epp takes a more useful approach, speaking of textual "trajectories" from the early period on, rather than "originals" of the sundry text types.

195. As his study did not involve establishing the original text, but rather was compelled to assume it, he did not mount an argument either way.

196. Thus, for example, Western scribes may have changed Acts 1:2 to avoid

making it appear that Luke was referring *back* to an event that he was about to relate in verses 9–11.

197. Following the textual emendations and translation of Metzger, *Textual Commentary*, 121–22.

198. Metzger, *Textual Commentary*, 122. To be sure, in the *Gospel of Peter*, the heads of the angels "reached to heaven," while the head of Jesus "overpassed the heavens." This is no allusion to the ascension per se, however, but an indication of the exalted majesty of the angelic beings and the yet more exalted majesty of Christ, through the stock technique of using extraordinary height to indicate divine stature. See Denker, *Die theologiegeschichtliche Stellung des Petrusevangeliums*, 96–102.

199. *Dial.* 32; 52; 110.

200. This doctrine could be read with some ingenuity into all sorts of passages of Scripture. In his castigation of Marcion's docetic Christology, for instance, Tertullian proffers an interpretation of the two goats used on the Day of Atonement, as described in Leviticus 16: "They were of like size, and very similar in appearance, owing to the Lord's identity of aspect; because He is not to come in any other form, having to be recognised by those by whom He was also wounded and pierced" (*Adv. Marc.* III, 7).

201. Uncials K L and most of the Byzantine tradition.

202. Others involve the omission of Χριστοῦ (ℵ* al), the change of "concerning the Lord Jesus" to "concerning the Kingdom of Jesus" and "boldness" to "salvation" (p⁷⁴).

203. ὅτι οὗτός ἐστιν Ἰησοῦς ὁ υἱὸς τοῦ θεοῦ, δι' οὗ μέλλει ὅλος ὁ κόσμος κρίνεσθαι. OL p also omits τὰ περὶ τοῦ κυρίου Ἰησοῦ Χριστοῦ. On other variations among the witnesses, see Donatien de Bruyne, "Le dernier verset des Actes, une variante inconnue."

204. A major contention of his groundbreaking work, *The Theology of Saint Luke*. See now John T. Carroll, *Response to the End of History*, whose correctives to Conzelmann's position I find persuasive. For a history of research, see his discussion on pp. 1–30.

205. *et carnem induit nostri causa et passus est et resurrexit a mortuis adsumpsit nos*.

206. In addition to Pseudo-Augustine and the Old Latin d (eighth century?), both of which attest the traditional form (except *quoniam* for *quia* in d), Hilary of Poitiers cites the text with *quod* for *quia*, *concarnatus est propter nos* for *carnem induit nostri causea*, and *resurgens de mortuis* for *resurrexit a mortuis*. See von Harnack, "Zur Textkritik und Christologie der Schriften des Johannes," I. 149–51.

207. Because of the phrase δι' ἡμᾶς von Harnack sees it as having originated within a creedal formula; the exclusion of any mention of Jesus' "death" (i.e., the movement directly from suffering to resurrection) strikes him as Roman.

208. *quem misit salvatorem super terram, et filius testimonium perhibuit in terra scripturas perficiens, et nos testimonium perhibemus quoniam vidimus eum et adnuntiamus vobis ut creadatis et ideo* (Vgᵐˢˢ armᵐˢˢ [derived from the Latin], and the eighth-century Beatus of Libana).

209. Most critics judge this longer reading to be almost certainly secondary. Despite its widespread support among the manuscripts (ℵ² D F G Ψ Byz OL) it is lacking in a number of widely distributed witnesses, including those that are normally adjudged superior for the Pauline epistles (p⁴⁶ ℵ* A B 33 81 1739* 1881 copˢᵃ ᵇᵒ al). Moreover, while there are scant internal grounds for considering it original, there are plausible arguments for its having been interpolated into the text.

210. See the discussion in Chapter 6, Conclusion.

211. See the discussion of p. 94.

212. The addition is expressed in a variety of ways among the numerous witnesses that preserve it. None of these variants is germane to the discussion here.

213. As early as Irenaeus himself. Also, manuscripts D F G.

214. He does cite Galatians 4:4a in *Adv. Marc.* V, 5 and 8, but not the words in question ("come from a woman").

215. See pp. 71–72.

216. *Ref.* 6, 30. Hippolytus is speaking here of the Valentinians, which shows among other things that the variant could just as easily be seen as an "anti-separationist" corruption. The particular view Hippolytus mentions, however, is more commonly associated with Marcion.

217. The longer text is attested in $\mathfrak{p}^{66}$ ℵ' A B D K L W Π Ψ f[13] 33 700 Byz[pt] bo, Clement, Origen, and a range of other witnesses. This superior attestation, the ambiguity of the shorter text, and the ready explanation of an omission combine to suggest that the phrase is original.

218. If Jesus is not referring to those who came "before him," what might he mean by "all those who came"?

219. *Textual Commentary,* 230.

220. I am not construing the rejection of creation or of the Old Testament God as necessarily docetic, but as inferences that were often drawn by docetists from other aspects of their systems of belief. As I have shown, other kinds of Gnostics shared similar views.

221. See note 220. These final changes could conceivably have been directed against other kinds of heretics (e.g., Gnostics) as well.

5

Anti-Patripassianist Corruptions of Scripture

I will devote a relatively brief discussion to "Patripassianism"—sometimes known as "modalism"—because the controversy was relatively limited in scope and generated far fewer textual corruptions than the adoptionistic, separationist, and docetic heresies we have considered so far. The reasons for this sparsity are not difficult to discern, as we shall see momentarily. Before turning to the textual issue, however, we must examine the positions taken by the Patripassianists and see why they proved so objectionable to some of the representatives of proto-orthodoxy.[1]

Patripassianism and Its Orthodox Opposition

Because the Patripassianists centered their theology around the notion of God's absolute unity, orthodox heresiologists sometimes likened them to the Roman adoptionists, the followers of Theodotus the Cobbler.[2] As we have seen, the adoptionists maintained their "monarchian" views by denying that Christ was himself God. The Patripassianists attained the same theological end by espousing the opposite christological claim; for them, Christ was God the Father himself, come down to earth in human flesh.

At first sight this may appear closely related to docetism, the view that because Christ was fully God, he was not really human. And in fact one prominent docetist, the arch-heretic Marcion, was sometimes accused of affirming "modalistic" views, of maintaining that Christ was simply one "mode" of existence for the Father.[3] Nonetheless, the similarities are more apparent than real. Marcion himself was patently ditheistic, and most other docetists (e.g., certain Christian Gnostics) maintained that because Christ was God, he did not really suffer, shed blood, and die.[4] This, however, was precisely the claim made by the Patripassianists: "The Father Himself came down into the Virgin, was Himself born of her, Himself suffered, indeed was Himself Jesus Christ."[5] Hence the pejorative label: "Patri-passianist," "one who believes the Father suffered."[6]

As it is presented by the orthodox opponents, the logic of the Patripas-

262

sianist system appears quite simple.[7] Scripture repeatedly affirms that there is only one God (e.g., Isa 44:6; 45:18). If Christ is God, then he must be that One. For Patripassianists, to understand Christ as something other than the incarnation of God Himself is to revert to ditheism.[8] The first outspoken proponent of the view was Noetus, a Smyrnean whose ideas were propagated in Rome at the end of the second century by two disciples named Epigonus and Cleomenes. The Noetian Christology enjoyed a warm reception among leaders of the Roman church. According to Hippolytus, both Zephyrinus and Callistus, bishops at the end of the second century and the beginning of the third, joined the majority of Roman Christians in embracing the heresy. This provoked a violent reaction from Hippolytus, who not only polemicized against these views,[9] but also set himself up in opposition to Callistus as history's first anti-pope.

Hippolytus claimed that Callistus excommunicated a certain Sabellius in order to throw the scent off his own heretical leanings. As the first to be excommunicated on such grounds, Sabellius's notoriety far outpaced his actual historical significance: although he is virtually unknown otherwise, the Patripassianist heresy itself commonly goes under his name (Sabellianism). Another obscure figure in the controversy is Praxeas, the alleged opponent of Tertullian who is not mentioned elsewhere in the ancient sources.[10] Because Tertullian treated him as a leading proponent of this heresy and claimed that he was responsible for its spread in Rome, some modern scholars have considered the name a cipher ("evil-*doer*") for either Epigonus or Callistus himself.[11]

As I have mentioned, these controversies appear not to have made a major impact on the text of the New Testament. The reasons are not difficult to find. On the one hand, this is a "heresy" that sprang up among the ranks of the orthodox themselves. That is to say, both sides of this conflict—the so-called Patripassianists and their opponents—agreed that Christ was one being not two, and that he was both human and divine. They both subscribed, that is, to orthodox christological affirmations. Given the paradoxical nature of these affirmations, the problem was (and continued to be) knowing how to reconcile them with one another. The Patripassianists devised one way of understanding the orthodox mystery, and their views found widespread popular support.[12] Tertullian speaks forthrightly of the "majority of believers" who have difficulty accepting the notion that the "one only God" is to be understood as a trinity within his "economy" (*Adv. Prax.* 3). Moreover, as I have already mentioned, even the Roman leadership at the highest echelons found such views entirely palatable,[13] whereas opponents (especially Hippolytus) were, for the time being, seriously marginalized.

Indeed, it was only in rejecting the modalist option that thinkers like Hippolytus and Tertullian began to formulate the orthodox idea of the trinity in a serious way.[14] In response to their modalistic opponents, both heresiologists insisted that God is distinctively three in expression even though one in essence: in Tertullian's formulation, he is three in degree, not condition;

in form, not substance; in aspect, not power. As Hippolytus puts it, "with respect to the power, God is one; but with respect to the economy (οἰκον-ομίαν), the manifestation (ἐπίδειξις) is triple (τριχής)" (*Ref.* 8, 2).

The key point for my discussion is that the modalist view was not widely seen to be a problem during the second and early third centuries. Most Christians, including most Christian leaders, had not begun to make the fine distinctions between God and his Son that came to characterize the christological debates soon thereafter. When these distinctions *did* gain in importance for orthodoxy at large, in the early third century, the textual tradition of the New Testament, as we have seen, had already begun to solidify. That is to say, it was only during the latter half of the period under our consideration that we would *expect* to find evidence of anti-Patripassianist corruptions of Scripture, as it was only then that the position was beginning to appear heretical; but this was precisely the time when orthodox corruptions were on the wane, as scribes began to guard their traditions more closely and to introduce deliberate changes in them with far less frequency.

Nonetheless, there are several instances of scribal corruptions that appear to have been generated in opposition to a Patripassianist Christology, and these demand our attention at this stage. Few of the variant readings I will discuss can make any real claim to being original, allowing me to keep these deliberations relatively brief.

Anti-Patripassianist Corruptions of Scripture

I have already discussed one variant reading of some relevance to our present concerns. Some scribes of Acts 20:28 modified the phrase "the church of God, which he purchased with his own blood" to read "the church of the Lord, which he purchased with his own blood."[15] Given the controversy I have just outlined, the change makes some considerable sense: scribes opposed to the idea that God the Father himself shed his blood would have wanted to clear up any ambiguity. It was the "Lord" (Jesus) who purchased the church with his blood, not God (the Father). With respect to the date of the variant, the confluence of Greek, Coptic, Syriac, and Latin witnesses in its support is difficult to explain, apart from a third-century provenance.

Other variants, some of them quite interesting, work to distinguish God the Father from the divine Christ (without necessarily implying a difference in "substance").[16] We know from Hippolytus that Noetus appealed to John 14:9 in support of his view that Christ was God himself: "Whoever has seen me has seen the Father" (*Ref.* 7, 4; cf. Tertullian, *Adv. Prax.* 20). For the modalist, the verse is to be taken quite "literally": seeing Christ *is* seeing the Father. Hippolytus disposes of this interpretation by providing an exegesis of the entire context (*Ref.* 7, 5–7), in which, he claims, the Father and Son are clearly differentiated. Scribes roughly contemporaneous with Hippolytus achieved a similar result by taking a different tack, that is, by altering the text. Thus, one of our third-century papyri, along with several other witnesses, inserts an adverbial καί after the main verb, so that now Christ replies to Philip: "Whoever has seen me, has seen the Father *also*" (ἑώρακεν καὶ τὸν πατέρα). The text now reflects the orthodox view: Christ and God are two persons, and Christ reveals the Father.

The need to differentiate Christ from God is also evident in the interesting variant at Hebrews 1:8, one of the few New Testament passages that appears to designate Christ as "God." The author quotes Psalm 44:7 as a declaration of God to (πρός) Christ: "Your throne O God is forever and ever; and the righteous scepter is the scepter of your kingdom." Interpretive problems abound in the passage, in part because the nominative ὁ θεός, normally construed as a vocative ("O God"), could also be taken as a predicate. In that case, the introductory clause would be rendered, "Your throne is God forever and ever, . . ." Understood in this way, the text no longer calls Christ "God."

For a variety of contextual reasons, however, the majority of scholars prefer to understand the nominative as a vocative.[17] Recognizing the exegetical issue, however, makes the textual problem at the end of the verse all the more interesting. For the second person pronoun σοῦ ("your" kingdom) has been changed to the third person αὐτοῦ in some of the best Alexandrian witnesses from the third-century on (p[46] א B). With this reading, the kingdom is said not to be Christ's but God's. The change affects the interpretation of the first element of the dystich as well; now it must be *God's* throne that is "forever and ever." In other words, the textual change at the end of the verse naturally leads one to understand the earlier nominative ὁ θεός as a predicate rather than a vocative, so that now the verse reads "God is your throne forever and ever; the righteous scepter is the scepter of his kingdom."

Most scholars reject the Alexandrian reading because it does not fit as well into the context.[18] Why, though, was the change made in the first place? It dates to the period of our concern and appears to resolve a problematic feature of the verse. Christ is no longer identified as the one God (ὁ θεός) himself, but is in some sense (in the economy!) made subordinate to him: "God [himself] is your throne."[19]

There are, of course, other New Testament passages that have traditionally been understood to designate Christ explicitly as God.[20] It is interesting to observe that the same manuscripts that evidence corruption in Hebrew 1:8 do so in John 1:18 as well, one of these other passages. In this instance, however, the change is much better attested.[21] Moreover, as I observed in my earlier discussion of the verse, we are now dealing not with a corruption of the original text but with a corruption of a corruption.

In Chapter 2 I argued that the prologue of the Fourth Gospel ended by referring to Christ as "the unique Son (ὁ μονογενὴς υἱός) who is in the bosom of the Father"; the text widely preferred by textual critics today (ὁ μονογενὴς θεός, "the unique God") represents a modification that arose during the adoptionist controversies. The issue to be addressed now concerns the absence of the article in a number of the witnesses that otherwise evidence the corruption. Here I can press home the point I made earlier: the original form of the corruption appears to have had the article.[22] Why would a subsequent scribe decide to delete it? The change makes sense in light of our present discussion: the article may well have been deleted by a scribe early in the third century because of its Patripassianist implications.[23] In the earliest form of corruption, Christ is directly identified as "the one and only God" (ὁ μονογενὴς θεός) himself; with the change the identification is less exalted: he is uniquely God, but less explicitly "the" one and only God.[24]

Another passage that can be taken to suggest that Christ is "God" himself (i.e., ὁ θεός, with the article) occurs near the end of the Fourth Gospel, and here again one should not be surprised to find scribes modifying the text. Upon seeing the resurrected Jesus, Thomas exclaims, "My Lord and my God" (ὁ θεός μου). The passage has caused interpreters problems over the years; Theodore of Mopsuestia argued that the words were not addressed directly to Jesus but were uttered in praise of God the Father.[25] Modern commentators have also found the phrasing problematic, because unlike the statement of 1:1, where the Word is θεός (without the article), here Jesus is expressly entitled ὁ θεός. How can one avoid drawing from this designation the conclusion that he is the one and only "God"? Several scribes of the early church adroitly handled the matter in what can be construed as an anti-Patripassianist corruption: the predecessor of codex Bezae and other Gospel manuscripts simply omitted the article. Jesus is divine, but he is not the one "God" himself.

The same motivation appears to have been at work in passages in which Jesus is not explicitly referred to as God, but in which the inference, for the orthodox, was nonetheless quite strong. In Mark 2:7 the Pharisees object to Jesus' pronouncement that the sins of the paralytic are forgiven. In their view, only the One God (εἷς ὁ θεός) can forgive sins. For orthodox interpreters, of course, Jesus was himself divine, and so was perfectly able to forgive sins. But at the same time, he was not "the one" God.[26] And so it comes as no surprise to find one of our earlier manuscripts, codex Bezae again, modifying the text to allow for the orthodox construal. In this case the change has been made simply by omitting the emphatic εἷς. Now, by implication, Christ is still divine (*contra* the adoptionists), yet he is not the embodiment of the Father himself.

A similar kind of variation may be found in manuscripts of Mark 12:26, where Jesus refers to the words of God spoken to Moses from the burning bush: "I am the God (ὁ θεός) of Abraham, the God (ὁ θεός) of Isaac, and the God (ὁ θεός) of Jacob."[27] Orthodox Christians often interpreted the passage as referring to the pre-incarnate Christ who spoke to Moses; indeed, for them, all of God's "manifestations" on earth come through Christ the Son (Tertullian, *Adv. Prax.* 16). Small wonder, then, that some manuscripts allow for the orthodox view that Christ as divine could appear and speak to the faithful of old, without himself, however, being "the" one God. This they have done by eliminating the articles in the passage, so that the divine voice identifies himself as θεός but not ὁ θεός.[28]

Somewhat different in nature is the change attested in manuscripts of 2 Peter 1:1, which speaks of "the righteousness of our God and [our?] Savior

Jesus Christ" (τοῦ θεοῦ ἡμῶν καὶ σωτῆρος Ἰησοῦ Χριστοῦ). Because the article is not repeated before Ἰησοῦ, it would be natural to understand both "our God" and "Savior" in reference to Jesus (our "God and Savior"). In view of the orthodox insistence that God and Jesus are to be differentiated, however, it is worth observing a reading preserved among Greek, Latin, Coptic, and Syriac witnesses, which change "God" to "Lord," so that now the text speaks unambiguously of "our Lord and Savior Jesus Christ" (τοῦ κυρίου ἡμῶν καὶ σωτῆρος Ἰησοῦ Χριστοῦ).[29] A similar problem occurs in the next verse, which speaks of "the knowledge of God and our Lord Jesus" (τοῦ θεοῦ καὶ Ἰησοῦ τοῦ κυρίου ἡμῶν), again without repeating the article. In this case, as we have seen in an earlier context, at least one early scribe made the identification explicit by deleting the καί, so that Jesus *is* said to be "God," perhaps in response to adoptionistic Christologies that claimed he was not. But given the later problems raised by the Patripassianists, it is also no surprise to find scribes taking an opposite course of action as well. Some manuscripts simply omit the problematic phrase and speak now of "the knowledge of our Lord."[30]

An analogous situation occurs in the textual tradition of Colossians 2:2. Critics are relatively certain that the reading attested in the early Alexandrian manuscripts p[46] and B is to be seen as original: the author speaks here of the knowledge τοῦ μυστηρίου τοῦ θεοῦ χριστοῦ.[31] But it is difficult to know how to construe the syntax of the phrase; does it mean the "mystery of the Christ of God"? Or the "mystery of God, namely Christ"? Or "the mystery of the God Christ" (i.e. of God, who is Christ)? Not only the ambiguity, but also, I would argue, the Patripassianist potential of the phrase is what led to the plethora of changes in the tradition. Some fourteen variations are attested, virtually all of them eliminating the possibility of understanding the verse as equating Christ with God (ὁ θεός) [the Father] himself.[32] Thus, we have manuscripts that speak of "the mystery of God," or "the mystery of Christ," or "the mystery of God which (neuter, referring to mystery) is Christ," or "the mystery of God the Father of Christ," etc.

A comparable motivation may well lie behind the textual variant found in Alexandrian manuscripts of 1 John 5:10. In the first part of the verse the author speaks of "the one who believes in the Son of God," in antithetical parallel to "the one who does not believe God" (ὁ μὴ πιστεύων τῷ θεῷ). Perhaps to avoid the equation that the parallel may imply, that is, between the "Son of God" and God himself (ὁ θεός), several manuscripts have exchanged *nomina sacra* in the second line of the parallelism, τῷ υἱῷ for τῷ θεῷ, so that now both elements of the verse speak of belief in the Son of God.[33] A similar concern may explain the change of Acts 16:34 in some manuscripts. In this passage the Philippian jailer is urged to believe in "the Lord Jesus" (v. 31); he complies by "believing in God" (πεπιστευκὼς τῷ θεῷ). Greek, Latin, and Coptic witnesses have changed the final statement so as to eliminate the identification of Jesus as ὁ θεός himself: now the jailer comes to believe "in the Lord."[34]

Something comparable may lie behind changes of Luke's Gospel in passages where it is ambiguous as to whether references to ὁ θεός may in fact be taken to designate Jesus. After Jesus raises the widow's son at Nain (Luke 7:11–15) the crowds begin to proclaim that "God (ὁ θεός) has visited his people." A number of textual witnesses make the expected modification: it is "the Lord" (ὁ κύριος) who has visited his people.[35] So too, in the following chapter, where Jesus enjoins the man he has just healed to "declare what God has done for you," several witnesses have modified the injunction to have the man "declare what the Lord has done for you" (8:39; C* 2643 b syr^c); in another witness, Jesus gives the interesting exhortation to "declare what Jesus has done for you" (MS 213).[36]

In addition to scribal alterations that serve to prevent an absolute identification of Christ with God the Father, there are others that work to "subordinate" him to God within the divine economy. These variants are also to be construed as the remnants of proto-orthodoxy, even though the explicit claim that Christ was not fully equal with God would at a later date be condemned as heretical.[37] To be sure, even for the proto-orthodox, Christ was in one sense *equal* with God (although not *identical* with him). But this involved an equality of substance, not of function within the divine economy; with respect to the latter, the Father was, to use the words of the Fourth Gospel, "greater" than Christ. Not so for the Patripassianists, who saw Christ as God himself. Certain changes within the New Testament manuscript tradition work to dissociate the text from such a view by clarifying the relationship between Christ and God.

An interesting example occurs in the well-known Christ hymn of Philippians 2:6–11, in which, at his exaltation, Christ is said to be awarded "the name that is above every name." But "the" name above all others is surely that of God the Father himself, a name that, in the orthodox understanding of the hymn, Christ was *not* given when made "Lord" over all creation. And so we find in witnesses as early as the Alexandrian fathers Clement and Origen, along with a number of Western and Byzantine manuscripts, the change that clarifies Christ's exaltation. By eliminating the article these witnesses state that Christ was given "*a* name" that is above all others.[38] Although not to be identified as the Father, Christ is made Lord of all else.[39]

The priority of God the Father over Christ is also held up in an early modification of Ephesians 4:15, where the author speaks of "growing up in every way into him who is the head, Christ," (αὐξήσωμεν εἰς αὐτὸν τὰ πάντα, ὅς ἐστιν ἡ κεφαλή, Χριστός). Elsewhere in the New Testament Christ is spoken of as the "head" of the church (Eph 1:22; 5:23; Col 1:18) or of a "man/husband" (1 Cor 11:3a) or of every "rule and authority" (Col 2:10). For orthodox Christians, however, it was important to affirm the teaching of 1 Corinthians 11:3b as well, that Christ was not the absolute head over all things, because over him stood God, the "head" of all. Without a qualifier, Ephesians 4:15 is too readily construed as giving Christ the position that belongs to God the Father alone (he is "the" head), so that it comes as no surprise to find our earliest manuscript of the letter, penned already in the third century, modifying the statement to eliminate the possible misconstrual.

In $\mathfrak{p}^{46}$ Christians are said to "grow up in every way into him who is the *head of Christ*" (i.e., God; ἡ κεφαλὴ τοῦ Χριστοῦ).[40] Other variants achieve a similar end, eliminating the absolute character of Christ's "headship" simply by deleting the article before κεφαλή.[41]

The issue of God's priority over Christ may also be responsible for the changes attested in the next chapter of Ephesians, where the author speaks of "the inheritance in the Kingdom of Christ and God" (βασιλείᾳ τοῦ Χριστοῦ καὶ Θεοῦ, v. 5). The wording of this unusual phrase may itself have led scribes, at least as early as the early third century, to change it to the standard "Kingdom of God" ($\mathfrak{p}^{46,}$ Tertullian), or to the sequence more to be expected, the "Kingdom of God and of Christ" (F G al). But the move to familiarize the phrase does not account for other changes attested somewhat later in the tradition (changes that themselves may derive from earlier sources); for example, "the Kingdom of the Christ of God" (1739* eth Theodoret), "the Kingdom of Christ" (38* 90), or "the kingdom of the Son of God" (1836). Furthermore, one should not overlook what all of these changes, even those that bring the phrase into conformity with the more familiar phrasing of the Synoptics, provide for the orthodox scribe. In the text that is almost certainly original ("the Kingdom of Christ and God"), Christ appears to be given a certain kind of priority over God himself. This problem is resolved by all of the changes, whether attested early or late. It may be, then, that the orthodox need to present Christ as subordinate within the divine economy is what led to the change.[42]

Many of the modifications I have discussed in this chapter are susceptible of other explanations; some, for example, may appear at first glance to represent unconscious harmonizations of passages to their parallels or improvements of their grammar or sense. But in no case can we overlook how these changes may have functioned theologically as well. To be sure, changes of this kind do not appear as frequently as the others we have considered. Nonetheless, the Patripassianist controversy of the early third century occasionally led scribes to corrupt the text of Scripture in view of their proto-orthodox conviction that although Christ was divine, he was also distinct from and, within the divine economy, subordinate to, God the Father.

Notes

1. Not to all, as we shall see. A masterful survey of the literary materials can still be found in von Harnack, *History of Dogma* III. 51–118. For a re-evaluation of the evidence, see M. Slusser, "The Scope of Patripassianism."

2. For example, Hippolytus, *Ref.* 9, 12; 10, 27; *Adv. Noet.* 3, 1. For the same reason, Tertullian (*Adv. Prax.* 31) likens the Patripassianists to the Jews, who similarly reject the Son of God in order to affirm the unity of God.

3. See Blackman, *Marcion*, 98–99, and the more nuanced statement of von Harnack, *History of Dogma* III. 53–54, note 3.

4. See pp. 181–87.

5. Tertullian, *Adv. Prax.* 1; compare Hippolytus, *Adv. Noet.* 1: "[Noetus] said

that Christ was the Father Himself, and that the Father Himself was born, and suffered, and died."

6. Slusser, "Scope of Patripassianism," insists that modalism is a more generic heresy, with Patripassianism one form of it. He observes that only rarely are modalistic monarchians accused of saying that the Father actually suffered, and urges therefore that the term Patripassianism be applied only to those whom we know for certain made the claim. I have chosen in my treatment, however, to use the terms interchangeably, both because it is difficult to see how anyone who thought that Christ was the Father could avoid drawing the conclusion that the Father suffered and died (unless, of course, they were docetists, which none of the persons in question appears to have been), and more importantly because the proto-orthodox sources themselves labeled representatives of the broader heresy as Patripassianists—rightly or wrongly—and it is with the orthodox *perception* of heresy that I am concerned in this study.

7. Although, interestingly, both Hippolytus and Tertullian are forced to admit that their opponents have a much more nuanced view than their own caricatures allow (*Ref.* 9. 7; *Adv. Prax.* 29). As I have indicated before, however, we need only be concerned with the *perception* of heresy for the present study, as it was their perceptions that led orthodox scribes to modify their texts. For a discussion of the real philosophical complexities of the modalist theology, see von Harnack, *History of Dogma*, III. 51–73.

8. The charge leveled by Popes Zephyrinus and Callistus against their orthodox detractor, Hippolytus (Hippolytus, *Ref.* 9.6, 8).

9. His *Adversus Noetum* attacks the heresy head on; moreover, Koschorke (*Hippolyt's Ketzerbekampfung*) has plausibly argued that Hippolytus's entire *Refutation of All Heresies* was designed to discredit Callistus personally.

10. The only exception: Ps-Tertullian, *Adv. Omn. Haer.* 8, 4.

11. See Timothy Barnes, *Tertullian: A Historical and Literary Study*, 278–79, and the literature he cites there.

12. Against Slusser ("The Scope of Patripassianism"), who claims that the views were embraced by a narrow band of Christians. This judgment is more or less forced upon him, again, because he chooses (for methodological reasons) to restrict the term Patripassianist to those who actually are *known* to have said, "The Father suffered" (see note 6). The modalistic view in general, however, as Slusser admits, was much more widespread, and it is this broader view that I am concerned with here.

13. In addition to Hippolytus's statements about Zephyrinus and Callistus, we have the enigmatic statement of Ps-Tertullian, *Adv. Omn. Haer.*: "*Praxeas quidem haeresim introduxit quam Victorinus corroborare curavit,*" sometimes taken to mean that Pope Victor was also inclined in this direction. See the arguments of von Harnack, *History of Dogma* III. 60, note 3.

14. See von Harnack, *History of Dogma*, III. 70.

15. Manuscripts $\mathfrak{p}^{74}$ A C* D E Ψ 33 1739 gig p cop syr[h mg] Iren[lat] Lcf.

16. To use Tertullian's categories: God and Christ are two in number but one in substance. See pp. 263–64.

17. See most recently Attridge, *Epistle to the Hebrews*, 58–59, and the literature he cites there.

18. See Metzger, *Textual Commentary,* 662–63 for the issues involved. Cf. also Attridge, *Epistle to the Hebrews,* 58–59.

19. Of course, the orthodox could use the verse even as it stands against the Patripassianists, by noting that in the text God the Father addresses God the Son, and presumably was not simply talking to himself. See, for example, Tertullian, *Adv. Prax.,*

who refers explicitly, however, to the text of the Psalm rather than to its quotation in the book of Hebrews. Nonetheless, the point is that at least one scribe evidences a similar concern but took a different route to implement it, by requiring the modification of the address of Christ as "the [one and only] God."

20. For a judicious survey, see Brown, *Jesus: God and Man*, 1–38.

21. $\mathfrak{p}^{66}$ ℵ* B C* L syr Irenaeus Origen.

22. See p. 80. It is to be noted that this form of the text is attested by the best early witness, $\mathfrak{p}^{75}$. Moreover, it would have been the easiest to create out of the original text, simply by changing θεός to υἱός, the change of a single letter (since these would have been abbreviated as *nomina sacra*: ΘΣ / ΥΣ), without deleting the article.

23. With $\mathfrak{p}^{66}$ and Origen, the third-century date is secure.

24. It cannot be replied that because the text even with the article differentiates between the Father and the Son who dwells in his bosom, orthodox scribes would not have felt impelled to make the change. We know that the Fourth Gospel was a real battleground between Patripassianists and the orthodox: the followers of Noetus appealed specifically to this Gospel to support their notion that Christ *was* God the Father, the only God (cf., e.g., Hippolytus, *Ref.* 6 and 7).

25. See Brown, *Gospel According to John*, 1026.

26. Compare the orthodox insistence of Origen in the *Dialogue with Heraclides* [122–29] that Jesus and the Father are both God, so that there are in a sense "two Gods," even though they are absolutely united in power. He is divine, but not God the Father.

27. Although the final two occurences of the article may not be original. Given their omission in manuscripts B D and W, the NA²⁶ places them in brackets. Only in B, however, is the article given before the first θεός. In this manuscript, then, all three references to "God" are definite (the final two drawing on the article of the first), so that whether the archetype of D and W attested one article or three, the omission(s) functions to render the entire phrase indefinite.

28. For example, manuscripts D W. See note 27. The cautionary note I have sounded throughout this study applies in the present case as well: given the fragmentary nature of our surviving evidence and the tendency of later scribes to preserve, rather than create, corruptions, we should not be surprised to find this kind of modification occurring only sporadically throughout the tradition. The same kind of change appears not to have affected the parallel passages of Matthew and Luke.

29. ℵ Ψ pc vg^mss syr^ph sa.

30. Manuscripts P Ψ 1852 2464 pc. On the problem of conflicting tendencies, the tension, that is, between anti-adoptionist and anti-Patripassianist corruptions, see the discussion of pp. 87–88.

31. See the discussion in Bruce M. Metzger, *The Text of the New Testament*, 236–38.

32. Conveniently listed in Metzger, *Text of the New Testament*, 236–37.

33. Manuscripts A 81 322 323 623 1241 1739 2464 vg syr^h mg al.

34. Manuscripts 51 61 326 441 460 618 d Lect sa.

35. Thus f¹ and the Old Latin witnesses aur c l.

36. As I noted in an earlier discussion, part of the intrigue of this passage involves the subsequent narrative. In the original text, after enjoined to declare what "God" had done for him, the man went about proclaiming what "Jesus" had done for him. Confronted with the problem that the text could be taken then to identify Jesus as the one God himself, several textual witnesses (047 343 716) have simply deleted this final statement altogether. Other manuscripts (f¹ 579 cop pc) resolve the

same problem by substituting θεός for Ἰησοῦς in the final phrase: now the man does not relate what "Jesus" has done for him after being enjoined to tell what "God" had.

37. Subordinationism came to be seen as a heresy only in the later christological developments of the fourth century. During the first three centuries, most of the proto-orthodox, while acknowledging that Christ was fully divine, nonetheless affirmed that within the "economy" he was subordinate to God the Father, whose will he did. See von Harnack, *History of Dogma*, III. 70, who argues that the christological theses of Tertullian and his theological allies were completely dependent on their opposition to the modalists. This opposition reveals itself, above all, in their strict subordination of the Son to the Father, for by positing such a relationship within the Godhead could they repel the charge, made by their opponents, of teaching that there were two Gods.

38. Manuscripts D F G Ψ Byz.

39. The proto-orthodox understanding of the relationship of the Lord Christ to God the Father may also lie behind simple changes introduced into the New Testament quotations of Psalm 110:1a. This psalm was a favorite of the early Christians, who saw in it a prophecy of Christ's exaltation to lordship. (See especially David M. Hay, *Glory at the Right Hand: Psalm 110 in Early Christianity* [SBLMS 18; Nashville: Abingdon, 1973].) In the Synoptic triple tradition, Jesus himself quotes the text to make a christological point (Matt 22:44; Mark 12:36; Luke 20:42), whereas his apostle, Peter, uses it to a different end on the day of Pentecost in Acts 2:34. On all four occasions the quotation is the same: "[The] Lord said to my lord, sit at my right hand . . ." (εἶπεν κύριος τῷ κυρίῳ μου· κάθου ἐκ δεξιῶν μου). In none of the Synoptic accounts, and possibly not in the original text of Acts, is the article used with the first occurrence of κύριος, despite the fact that the context indicates that this is God himself speaking to the κύριος (of David). Possibly in order to clarify the relationship of the two κύριοι, that is, in order to solidify the point orthodox interpreters would draw from the context, numerous scribes from early times supplied the article in each case (e.g., in Matt 22:44, MSS L W Θ f¹·¹³ Byz; in Mark 12:36, א L W Θ Ψ f¹·¹³ Byz; in Luke 20:42, א L W R Θ Ψ f¹·¹³ Byz; in Acts, 𝔓⁷⁴ אᶜ A Bᶜ C E Ψ Byz). Now it is clearly *the* Lord, God himself, who is instructing the Lord Christ concerning what he is to do.

40. Taking the genitive as possessive rather than epexegetical.

41. Manuscripts D* F G. Other variants omit the article before Χριστός, a change that does not affect the theological character of the passage.

42. One might suspect a similar motivation behind variants that stress the orthodox view that Jesus was actually God's *Son*, a view that only became an issue when challenged by the Patripassianists. The emphasis on Jesus' sonship is indirectly attested in changes that speak of God as Jesus' own father. In many cases, these variants represent harmonizations either with other verses in the context or with parallel passages, showing that what we have here are heightenings of emphases that the orthodox could already find within their texts. Thus, perhaps, Matthew 18:14 (change "your" father to "my" father, as in v. 10); 24:36 (add μου, to read "my" father); 26:39 and 42 (if the shorter readings attested in the papyri are taken as original); Rev. 2:7 (add μου, so that Christ refers to "my" God); and a number of Johannine passages in which the word πατήρ is added to references that speak of "the one who sent me" (e.g., 6:38–39; 7:16; 16:5). Because such changes occur with relatively frequency in both directions (especially in the text of the Fourth Gospel), probably noth-

ing can be definitively stated concerning an orthodox *Tendenz*. But in the one passage in which Jesus actually claims a unity with God, it is worth observing that the text is sometimes changed to allow a notion of some kind of subordination: "I and *my* Father are one" (10:30; MSS W Δ e syr[s, p] cop pc). Even here, however, we may simply be dealing with a harmonization to verse 29a.

6

Conclusion:
The Orthodox Corruptors of Scripture

The wide-ranging diversity of early Christianity, with its variegated social structures, practices, and beliefs, was matched only by the diversity of the individuals who comprised it. Among them were the unnamed transmitters of their texts, scribes who themselves, no doubt, constituted no monolith. We unfortunately do not know who these persons were and are scarcely informed about their level of education, class, rank, or social status, either within the Christian community or without.[1] They are nameless, faceless, transcribers of texts, texts that became, and in their minds probably already were, the sacred Christian Scriptures. Our knowledge of who these persons were and what they stood for, what they hoped and feared and cherished, can be discerned only from what they chose to reproduce and from the distinctive features of their final products. To understand the scribes, we can only study their transcriptions.

This has been one of the goals of the present study, to learn something more about the early transcribers of the New Testament and the social world within which they worked. My focus, of course, has been narrowly defined by a set of debates that occupied Christians of the second and third centuries—or at least the educated elite who left us our sources: the theological controversies over the nature of Christ, his humanity, his divinity, and his unity. As we have seen, these debates cannot be construed as *purely* theological, as if they bore no relation to sociopolitical realities. In no small measure, debates over doctrine are debates over power, and deciding what is "correct" to believe means deciding who can wield that power. At the same time, the debates *were* carried out, and to some extent resolved, on the ideational plane. Here, as in most cases of social conflict, an entire nexus of social, economic, political, cultural, historical, and ideological factors were at work, and reducing the debates to just one set of factors skews the perspective. For practical purposes, however (i.e., to produce a manageable study), I have focused my attention on one component of these debates and worked to see some of its wider implications. My overarching concern has been to determine how the debates over Christology affected the transcriptions of the sacred texts over which, in part, they were waged.

I can now restate my general conclusions and assess their significance. I will not, however, provide a blow-by-blow summary of the analysis itself. Each of the previous chapters ends by recapitulating the data that are discussed and the specific inferences that can be drawn as a consequence. Different scholars, of course, will evaluate some of these data differently, and not everyone will be convinced by the argument at every point. I nonetheless take my overarching thesis to be established: proto-orthodox scribes of the second and third centuries occasionally modified their texts of Scripture in order to make them coincide more closely with the christological views embraced by the party that would seal its victory at Nicea and Chalcedon.

These views developed in response to aberrations from different quarters, as proto-orthodox Christians engaged in a series of conflicts with competing views—or better, with competing groups that held contrary views. In the eyes of the proto-orthodox, these outsiders typically urged one christological extreme to the exclusion of another.[2] Some "heretics," like the Ebionites and the Theodotians, claimed that Christ was a "mere man" and therefore not at all divine; in response, the proto-orthodox insisted that he was God. Others, like Marcion and the opponents of Ignatius, claimed that Christ was completely God and was thus human in appearance only; the proto-orthodox responded that he was a real man of flesh and blood. Yet others, like the Valentinian Gnostics, maintained that Jesus Christ was two beings, the man Jesus and the divine Christ; the proto-orthodox argued to the contrary that he was a unified person, "one and the same." The proto-orthodox Christology, then, emerged as a direct response to these alternative perspectives and was distinguished by the paradoxes of its pedigree: Jesus Christ was both God and man, one indivisible being, eternal yet born of the virgin Mary, an immortal who died for the sins of the world.[3]

While these christological issues were under debate, before any one group had established itself as dominant and before the proto-orthodox party had refined its christological views with the nuance that would obtain in the fourth century, the books of the emerging Christian Scriptures were circulating in manuscript form. The texts of these books were by no means inviolable; to the contrary, they were altered with relative ease and alarming frequency. Most of the changes were accidental, the result of scribal ineptitude, carelessness, or fatigue. Others were intentional, and reflect the controversial milieux within which they were produced.

To be sure, it is impossible to establish an argument on scribal intentions; the scribes are no longer available for questioning, and even if they were, their intentions might well lie beyond our reach (and theoretically, even beyond theirs). All the same, it is possible to evaluate the fruit of their labors—by determining, that is, how the text appeared before they copied it and seeing how it had been altered once it left their hands. By establishing the earliest form of the text we can construct a functional taxonomy of its subsequent modifications: some serve to improve the grammar of a text, others to eliminate discrepancies, still others to effect harmonizations. And others change the text's meaning, or to put a different slant on it, "improve" its theology. It is not only thinkable that scribes *would* make such changes, it is manifest that they did. Scribes altered their sacred texts to make them "say" what they were already known to "mean."

This is the thesis of the study, and I take it to be demonstrated. What, in conclusion, can we say about its significance?

The question mark of significance has long bedeviled analyses of this kind. For the past century many textual scholars have stood beneath the mesmerizing gaze of the mighty Hort, who judged that apart from Marcion, scribes did not effect theological changes in their copies of Scripture. Naturally, other scholars have dutifully demurred, and produced interesting if scattered examples of just this disputed phenomenon. But apart from the investigation[4] of a solitary manuscript—a critical and ground-breaking study[4]—and isolated analyses of random samples, no full-length investigations have been forthcoming.[5] Nor is the reason hard to find: even those who have recognized the phenomenon have underplayed its scope.[6]

If significance were to be measured simply by numbers, then the data I have amassed may not appear significant to "the big picture"—depending, that is, on what that big picture might be. But significance cannot simply be quantified; it is pointless, for example, to calculate the number of words of the New Testament affected by such variations or to determine the percentage of known corruptions that are theologically related.[7] When one gauges significance in this way, by far the most "consequential" variations are orthographic. But beyond their sheer quantity, what do such divergences *signify*, except that people in antiquity could spell no better than people today?[8] The importance of theologically oriented variations, on the other hand, far outweighs their actual numerical count.[9]

We can begin by reflecting on their implications for exegesis and the rise of Christian doctrine. The textual problems we have examined affect the interpretation of many of the familiar and historically significant passages of the New Testament: the birth narratives of Matthew and Luke, the prologue of the Fourth Gospel, the baptismal accounts of the Synoptics, the passion narratives, and other familiar passages in Acts, Paul, Hebrews, and the Catholic epistles. In some instances, the interpretations of these passages—and the books within which they are found—hinge on the textual decision;[10] in virtually every case, the variant readings demonstrate how the passages *were* understood by scribes who "read" their interpretations not only out of the text but actually into it, as they modified the words in accordance with what they were taken to mean.[11]

It might also be observed that a number of these textual problems affect broader issues that have occupied New Testament scholars for the better part of our century. The following list is suggestive rather than exhaustive: Do the preliterary creedal and hymnic fragments cited by the New Testament authors preserve an adoptionistic Christology? Conversely, do they portray Jesus, already in the 30s or 40s C. E., as divine? How does Mark entitle his Gospel? How does he understand Jesus' baptism at the beginning of his narrative, or the cry of dereliction near the end? Does Luke have a doctrine of atonement? Does he envisage a "passionless Passion"? Just how "high" is the Christology of the Fourth Gospel? Why did the secessionists leave the Johannine community? Is Jesus ever actually called God in the New Testament?

In sum, the passages I have examined and the nature of the issues they raise provide a kind of innate significance to the study—innate, that is, for scholars interested in issues pertaining to the interpretation of the New Testament and the development of Christian doctrine. What can be said, though, about the significance of my particular conclusions?

We can first consider the broader implications of the study for New Testament textual research. Textual critics have long imposed a set of unnecessary restrictions on the parameters of their discourse, blinders that prevent fruitful dialogue with scholars in other fields and, as a consequence, skew the results of their labors. To engage in a study of the text requires a much greater awareness of the sociohistorical context of scribes than is normally envisaged. It is simply not enough to think in terms of manuscripts as conveyors of data; manuscripts were produced by scribes and scribes were human beings who had anxieties, fears, concerns, desires, hatreds, and ideas— in other words, scribes worked in a context, and prior to the invention of moveable type, these contexts had a significant effect on how the texts were produced.

Moreover, this study has reinforced the notion that theologically motivated changes of the text are to be anticipated particularly during the early centuries of transmission, when both the text and the theology of early Christianity were in a state of flux, prior to the development of a recognized creed and an authoritative and (theoretically) inviolable canon of Scripture. It should be emphasized, however, that the instability of the text in the early centuries is equaled by the instability of the scribes, who did not effect the changes that one might expect with any kind of rigor or consistency. We have detected such inconsistencies in texts that are changed at random throughout the tradition. It is equally evident in texts that might be *expected* to have been altered, but that apparently escaped the pens of the early scribes unscathed.[12] Throughout the course of the study I have considered reasons for these kinds of inconsistency; I will not prolong these concluding remarks by repeating those discussions here.[13]

I should, however, reiterate two less prominent conclusions concerning scribal "trends." First, despite the irregularity of their changes, it appears that scribes were more likely to modify texts that could serve as proof texts for the opposition than those that had, in their original form, little bearing on the debates. This is to say, scribes were apparently more inclined to "correct" or "improve" a passage than to interpolate into it a notion that was previously wanting.[14] The reason for this relative (not absolute) frequency is not difficult to locate: passages with no obvious relation to the conflict are already easy to construe in orthodox ways. On the other hand, passages that appear, on the surface, to support an opposing opinion require more extraordinary measures. The second point is perhaps less expected, but nonetheless in equal evidence: scribes who made such alterations of difficult passages were, in many cases, sensitive to their literary context. Passages that appear problematic only in isolation are less likely to be changed than those that are problematic even in situ.[15]

A final point concerning the text-critical implications of this study deserves to be restated with all due force, particularly in light of its usefulness for future investigations. Theologically oriented changes coincide with, and in a sense highlight, the paradoxical nature of the proto-orthodox Christology itself. As I have just now stressed again, proto-orthodox Christians had to defend—at one and the same time—Christ's deity against adoptionists, his humanity against docetists, and his unity against separationists. This, and primarily this, I would argue, is why scribes modified the New Testament text in seemingly contrary directions: some textual changes work to *emphasize* aspects of Christ's human nature whereas others work to *de-emphasize* it; some work to *heighten* his divinity, whereas others work to *diminish* it. It was precisely the paradoxical character of the proto-orthodox Christology that produced such seemingly contradictory impulses: texts that appeared to compromise Christ's humanity were just as subject to alteration as texts that seemed to compromise his deity.[16]

Two final observations should be made about this conclusion. First, it in no way disparages the analysis itself, for the difficulty results directly and inevitably from the paradoxical nature of the orthodox Christology that happened to emerge as victorious. Second (an observation that perhaps requires special emphasis), even those changes that de-emphasize Christ's humanity do not preclude it altogether (i.e., they do not appear to be "docetic" changes), just as those that emphasize his humanity do not serve to absolutize it (i.e., they are not "adoptionistic"). So far as I have been able to judge, orthodox changes "mollify" the extremes (namely, that Christ is God but not man, or man but not God); rarely do they attack one extreme by embracing another.

Given the close ties of these text-critical conclusions to questions concerning the nature of nascent Christianity, what can we say about the significance of this study for the historian of the period?

The textual variants I have considered constitute hard data for a field of inquiry that is otherwise sparsely attested: the nature of the internecine conflicts of early Christianity, especially as these affected proto-orthodox Christians outside the ranks of the heresiologists.[17] The social location of these data, insofar as it can be surmised, is itself of some significance: it shows that the controversies transcended the rarified atmosphere of the Christian *literati*. The heresiologists who produced the better known sources—for example, Justin, Irenaeus, Tertullian, Clement of Alexandria, and Origen—clearly enjoyed a rhetorical education.[18] Even though scribes too were by and large among the literary elite (they could at least write, and had the leisure to do so), there is nothing to suggest that they were all, or even mostly, at its highest levels, that is, among the intelligentsia of the faith.[19] Given the quality of some of their transcriptions, and the enormous amounts of time they must have devoted to such menial labor, quite the reverse appears likely. This means, then, that the early christological controversies affected far more than the orthodox polemicists, whose reports might otherwise be taken to reflect simply the concerns of a handful of Christian intellectuals.

Significantly, these data also reveal that theology itself, the ideational content of the faith, played a significant role (even if not an absolute one) in these debates, the opinion of some scholars notwithstanding.[20] This theology, moreover, was a *biblical* theology, with the interpretation of Scripture standing at the heart of the conflicts, even when contestants disagreed concerning the scope of the canon and appropriate modes of exegesis.[21] These conclusions are significant not only for the church historian interested in the internal development of early Christianity, but also for for the historian of late antiquity concerned to identify distinctive aspects of this religion in its Greco-Roman context. For none of the pagan religions emphasized the importance either of "right" doctrine or of "authoritative" texts.[22] Proto-orthodox Christianity placed a high premium on both, even though this dual allegiance occasionally created the difficulties that generated the data we have investigated—when, that is, the authoritative texts did not appear to affirm, or to affirm strongly enough, the "right" doctrines. As a result, it is never easy, from the historian's perspective, to determine whether the text led Christians to embrace a doctrine or whether the doctrine led Christians to modify the text (either in their minds or on the page). In this religion, in particular, texts and beliefs coalesce into a messy symbiotic relationship, not always susceptible to the discrete conceptual categories of the historian.

What now can we say about the actual polemical function of the orthodox corruptions of Scripture? As I have mentioned throughout the course of the study, it appears that the modification of sacred texts must be construed as a secondary form of polemic, an offshoot of the theological controversies, not a primary mode of engagement with the adversaries themselves. It is scarcely conceivable that any scribe of any persuasion actually thought that by modifying his text of Scripture he would convert his opponents. It is (and was) well known that interested parties were widely suspected of "corrupting" the text under the guise of "correcting" it. We can be fairly certain, therefore, that variant texts favoring one point of view over another were rather easily dismissed as aberrations. If the scribes *did* intend their transcriptions to influence their readers—an "if" that is virtually swallowed up by our inability to fathom intentions—they more likely would have sought either to influence Christians who were vacillating between opposing camps or to edify those who already shared their own predilections but who welcomed the certitude that such alterations could provide. In fact, however, there is scarce need to posit any kind of ulterior motive for this kind of scribal activity. It is enough to recognize that when scribes modified their texts, they did so in light of what they already believed their Scriptures taught.

What, though, were scribes actually *doing* when they effected these modifications? This is the question I raised at the outset of the study, and it has lost none of its force in the intervening pages. The proposal I advanced there may now be restated with the benefit of the data accumulated in the interim. In no instance of scribal corruption that we have examined, even the most blatant among them, have we uncovered evidence to suggest that proto-orthodox scribes acted out of sheer malice or utter disregard for the constraints of the text— that is, that they strove to make the text say precisely what they knew it did not. Quite to the contrary, it appears that these scribes knew exactly what the text said, or at least they thought they knew (which for our purposes comes to the same thing), and that the changes they made functioned to make these certain meanings all the more certain.[23]

In *some* respects, then, the scribes who enacted their changes were no different from any reader who interprets a text. It is a striking fact of human experience that those who read texts rarely think that they are engaged in an act of "interpretation" per se. For most people, reading and understanding simply involve making sense of the words, seeing what they say, explaining their straightforward meaning; understanding a text (to simplify matters) involves putting it "in other words." Anyone who explains a text "in other words," however, has altered the words.

This is exactly what the scribes did: they occasionally altered the words of the text by putting them "in other words." To this extent, they were textual interpreters. At the same time, by *physically* altering the words, they did something quite different from other exegetes, and this difference is by no means to be minimized. Whereas all readers change a text when they construe it in their minds, the scribes actually changed the text on the page. As a result, they created a new text, a new concatenation of words over which future interpreters would dispute, no longer having access to the words of the original text, the words produced by the author. It is only from this historical perspective that these scribal activities can be said to constitute a *unique* hermeneutical enterprise. Correspondingly, only from the distance afforded by our own temporality, as readers who are ourselves situated in time and space, can we evaluate the causes and recognize the effects of these kinds of scribal modifications, and so designate them "the orthodox corruptions of Scripture."

Notes

1. We cannot write a proper prosopography, and our questions concerning their identity are met only with wide stretches of silence in our surviving sources. Did scribes enjoy a high status within their own Christian communities? Within the world at large? What kind of occupations did they have? They were almost certainly better educated than most—they could at least write, and presumably read, both of which required no little training. And they appear to have had the leisure to do so. But did second- and third-century scribes generally, or ever, enjoy a rhetorical education? Were any of them actually paid for their labors? Were non-Christian copyists ever employed to copy the Christian sacred texts? Is it conceivable that wealthy Christians might have had their texts copied by their own (non-Christian or uninterested) slaves? If so, what does this say about different kinds of corruptions that one finds more frequently in some manuscripts than in others (e.g., the relative frequency of harmonizations to the immediate context as compared to parallel passages; or of harmonizations to par-

allel passages in the New Testament as compared to the Old)? What does it tell us about ideological corruptions? Moreover, how might the social histories of particular communities, for example, Jerusalem, or Antioch, or Alexandria, or Rome (to pick the ones we are best informed about) have affected the ways local scribes copied their texts? Questions like these have rarely been asked—which is not surprising, given the dearth of evidence—but advances in the social sciences and the study of the social history of early Christianity at least make it thinkable that they *can* be asked, and desirable that they should. I hope to undertake an assessment of just these kinds of issues in a future monograph. See further the insightful study of C. H. Roberts, *Manuscript, Society, and Belief.* For a discussion of the broader issues pertaining to literacy in late antiquity (i.e., not just among early Christian scribes) see William V. Harris, *Ancient Literacy,* especially 175–337.

2. This is not to say, of course, that they failed to recognize the confluence of views in a number of groups. On such hybrid Christologies, see note 17 in Chapter 3 and note 17 in Chapter 4.

3. See the statement of the Definition of Chalcedon, cited in note 3 in Chapter 1.

4. Epp, *Theological Tendency of Codex Bezae.* Epp's study of the text of codex Bezae in Acts was extended, with less spectacular results, into the Gospel of Luke by George E. Rice "The Alteration of Luke's Tradition by the Textual Variants in Codex Bezae," and into the Gospel of Matthew by Michael W. Holmes, "Early Editorial Activity and the Text of Codex Bezae in Matthew."

5. Devoted, that is, to this particular issue from the point of view adopted here. For earlier efforts that moved in a similar direction, and others that are significant in and of themselves, see note 94 in Chapter 1.

6. As is implicit, for example, in the comment tendered by a textual scholar who, having learned of my research for this book, opined that it would be "a very slim volume indeed."

7. A convicted felon could as well reason that of the five billion people in the world, he has robbed only twelve. Scholars who try to quantify significance in this way have tended to do so for ahistorical reasons, most typically to assure their readers both of the noble intentions of scribes and of the reliability of the textual tradition. A clear-headed challenge to such attempts can be found already in such earlier studies as K. W. Clark, "Textual Criticism and Doctrine." See also the other works cited in note 94 in Chapter 1.

8. Orthographic changes *do* assist us, of course, in determining how Greek was pronounced at certain periods, as the regular confusions of certain letters and diphthongs (i.e., "itacisms") demonstrate beyond reasonable doubt that they must have sounded alike.

9. For those who *are* interested in numbers, the variants I have examined in the course of my study are not difficult to calculate: in each of the main chapters, they number in the dozens (normally five or six dozens), not the thousands. Here again I should emphasize that the relative paucity of christological corruptions (relative, that is, in numerical terms) results in no small measure from the relative paucity of New Testament verses that relate to Christology.

10. For example, just from the Gospels consider my discussions of Luke 3:22; 22:19–20 (and the other "Western non-interpolations"); 22:43–44; Mark 1:1; 15:34; John 1:18, 34.

11. Naturally, the same data relate to the basic doctrinal concerns of early Christians—theologians and, presumably, laypersons alike: Was Jesus the Messiah pre-

dicted in the Old Testament? Was Joseph his father? Was Jesus born as a human? Was he really tempted? Was he able to sin? Was he adopted to be the Son of God at his baptism? At his resurrection? Or was he himself God? Was Jesus Christ one person or two persons? Did he have a physical body after his resurrection? And many others. The ways scribes answered these questions affected the way they transcribed their texts. And the way they transcribed their texts has affected, to some degree, the way modern exegetes and theologians have answered these questions.

12. With an emphasis on "apparently." To take a clear example, Hebrews 3:2 describes Christ as faithful "to the one *who made him*," a statement surely puzzling to those who subscribed to the eternal generation of the Son. To the best of my knowledge, however, in none of our surviving witnesses has the text experienced corruption. On a similar situation in the book of Acts, see p. 71.

13. See for example pp. 56–58, 68, Chapter 2, note 185, and Chapter 5, note 28.

14. I do not mean this judgment to be quantified in the sense that if one were to add up the corruptions we have discussed, there would be more corrections than interpolations. Rather, what I mean is that a *substantial proportion* of the "questionable" passages have been changed (outstanding examples: Mark 1:10, 15:34; Luke 3:22, 24:12; John 1:34; the references to Joseph as Jesus' "father"; Heb 2:9; for exceptions, see note 12), whereas by no stretch of the imagination have most other passages. Moreover, many of the problematic passages have been changed so widely as virtually to remove the original reading from the tradition after our period.

15. See, for example, pp. 56–58 especially note 67, and pp. 68 and 71.

16. The interesting result is that some of the anti-adoptionistic corruptions I have set forth here could conceivably be construed in docetic or Patripassianist terms by those inclined in that direction at the outset, just as many of the anti-docetic corruptions were no doubt palatable for adoptionists. At the same time, I should re-emphasize that this circumstance cannot easily be attributed to the work of docetic or adoptionistic scribes, as I will note again below. To some degree, of course, the different *kinds* of changes may simply have resulted from the individuality of the scribes, who, under their own unique circumstances, may have felt inclined to emphasize one component of Christology over another. It strikes me as equally likely, however (and here we simply have no evidence to lead us in one direction or the other), that the same scribe may have seen different kinds of problems in different texts and made the requisite changes depending on his perceptions and moods at the moment of transcription.

17. Other aspects of the topic have found new life, of course, with the discoveries at Nag Hammadi, as scholars now have a fuller picture from one (or better, some) of the other combatants. See especially note 8 in Chapter 3.

18. For Justin, Tertullian, Clement of Alexandria, and Origen, the point is fairly obvious; for Irenaeus, see Robert M. Grant, "Irenaeus and Hellenistic Culture," and more recently, William Schoedel, "Theological Method in Irenaeus."

19. See note 1.

20. See note 24 in Chapter 1.

21. See, for example, Brox, *Offenbarung, Gnosis, und gnostischen Mythos,* 39–45.

22. Nor did Judaism, prior to the codification of the Mishnah, circa 200 C.E. Even afterwards, doctrine itself played only a minimal role in the development of the religion, and as a consequence, the sacred texts, although construed in a sense as inviolable, functioned differently from the way they did in Christianity. For an accessible overview, see Shaye Cohen, *From the Maccabees to the Mishnah,* 60–103, 174–213.

23. It is striking in this connection that when the orthodox author of the Little Labyrinth accused the Theodotian scribes of corrupting their texts, he observed that they believed they were actually "correcting" them. The case is patently the same with Marcion as well, the most renowned proponent of surgical criticism. There is no reason to think that the scribes of the orthodox persuasion understood their own activities any differently. See my article, "Theodotians as Corruptors of Scripture."

Bibliography of
Secondary Works Cited

Aejmelaeus, Lars. *Die Rezeption der Paulusbriefe in der Miletrede (Apg 20:18–35)*. Helsinki: Suomalainen Tiedeakatemia, 1987.

Aland, Barbara. "Die Münsteraner Arbeit am Text des Neuen Testaments und ihr Beitrag für die frühe Überlieferung des 2. Jahrhunderts: Eine methodologische Betrachtung," in *Gospel Traditions in the Second Century: Origins, Recensions, Text, and Transmission*, ed. William L. Petersen. South Bend, Ind.: Notre Dame University Press, 1989; 55–70.

———. "Die Rezeption des neutestamentlichen Textes in den ersten Jahrhunderten," in *The New Testament in Early Christianity*, ed. Jean-Marie Sevrin. Leuven: University Press, 1989; 1–38.

———. "Gnosis und Kirchenväter: Ihre Auseinandersetzung um die Interpretation des Evangeliums," in *Gnosis: Festchrift für Hans Jonas*, ed. B. Aland. Göttingen: Vandenhoeck & Ruprecht, 1978; 158–215.

———. "Marcion: Versuch einer neuen Interpretation," *ZTK* 70 (1973) 420–47.

Aland, Barbara and Aland, Kurt. *The Text of the New Testament: An Introduction to the Critical Editions and to the Theory and Practice of Modern Textual Criticism*, 2nd ed., revised and enlarged, tr. Erroll F. Rhodes. Grand Rapids, Mich. : Eerdmans, 1989.

Aland, Kurt. "Die Bedeutung des P^{75} für den Text des Neuen Testaments: Ein Beitrag zur Frage des 'Western non-interpolations,' " in *Studien zur Überlieferung des Neuen Testaments und seines Textes*, ed. K. Aland. Berlin: Walter de Gruyter, 1967; 155–72.

Allison, Dale and Davies, W. D. *A Critical and Exegetical Commentary on the Gospel According to Matthew*, vol. 1. ICC; Edinburgh: T & T Clark, 1988.

Altendorf, Hans-Dietrich. "Zum Stichwort: Rechtgläubigkeit und Ketzerei im ältesten Christentum," *ZKG* 80 (1969) 61–74.

Attridge, Harold W. *The Epistle to the Hebrews. Hermeneia*; Philadelphia: Fortress, 1989.

Balás, David. "Marcion Revisited: A 'Post-Harnack' Perspective," in *Texts and Testaments: Critical Essays on the Bible and Early Church Fathers*, ed. W. Eugene March. San Antonio, Tex.: Trinity University, 1980; 95–108.

Bammel, Caroline P. Hammond. "Ignatian Problems," *JTS* n.s. 33 (1982) 62–97.

———."Review of R. J. Hoffmann, *Marcion*," *JTS* n.s. 39 (1988) 227–32.

Bardy, Gustav. "Cerinthe," *RB* 30 (1921) 344–73.

————. *Paul de Samosate: étude historique,* 2nd ed. Spicilegium Sacrum Lovaniense, Études et Documents, 4; Louvain: Spicilegium Sacrum Lovaniense, 1929.

Barnes, Timothy D. "Pre-Decian *Acta Martyrum,*" *JTS* 19 (1968) 510–14, reprinted in *Early Christianity and the Roman Empire* (London: Variorum Reprints, 1984).

————. *Tertullian: A Historical and Literary Study.* Oxford: Clarendon, 1971.

Barth, Markus. *Ephesians.* AB 34A; Garden City, N.Y.: Doubleday, 1974.

Bauer, Walter. *Das Leben Jesu im Zeitalter der neutestamentlichen Apocryphen.* Tübingen: J. C. B. Mohr (Paul Siebeck), 1907; reprinted Darmstadt, 1967.

————. *Rechtglaübigkeit und Ketzerei im ältesten Christentum.* BHT, 10; Tübingen: J. C. B. Mohr (Paul Siebeck), 1934; English translation of second edition (1964, ed. by Georg Strecker), *Orthodoxy and Heresy in Earliest Christianity,* tr. Robert Kraft et al., ed. Robert Kraft and Gerhard Krodel. Philadelphia: Fortress, 1971.

Bellinzoni, Arthur J. *The Sayings of Jesus in the Writings of Justin Martyr.* Leiden: Brill, 1967.

Benko, Stephen. "The Libertine Gnostic Sect of the Phibionites," *VC* 21 (1967) 103–19.

Benoit, A. *Saint Irénée, Introduction à l'étude de sa théologie.* Paris: Presses Universitaires de France, 1960.

Benoit, P. "Marie-Madeleine et les disciples au tombeau selon Joh 20,1–18," in *Judentum, Urchristentum, Kirche: Festschrift für Joachim Jeremias,* ed. Walther Eltester. Berlin: Töpelmann, 1960; 141–52.

Bethge, Hans Gebhard. "Zweiter Logos des großen Seth," *TLZ* 100 (1975) 98–110.

Bettenson, Henry. *Documents of the Christian Church,* 2nd ed. London: Oxford University Press, 1963.

Betz, Hans Dieter. "Orthodoxy and Heresy in Primitive Christianity," *Int* 19 (1965) 299–311.

Beyschlag, Karlmann. "Marcion von Sinope," in *Alte Kirche 1,* ed. Martin Greschat. *Gestalten der Kirchengeschichte*; Stuttgart: W. Kohlhammer, 1984; 69–81.

Blackman, E. C. *Marcion and His Influence.* London: S.P.C.K., 1948.

Blank, Josef. "Zum Problem 'Häresie und Orthodoxie' im Urchristentum," in *Zur Geschichte des Urchristentums,* ed. Josef Blank et al. Freiburg: Herder, 1979; 142–60.

Blevins, James L. *The Messianic Secret in Markan Research, 1901–1976.* Washington D.C.: University Press of America, 1981.

Bludau, A. *Die Schriftfälschungen der Häretiker: Ein Beitrag zer Textkritik der Bibel.* NTabh, 11; Münster: Aschendorf, 1925.

Boismard, M.-É. *St. John's Prologue.* London: Aquin, 1957.

Bovon, François. "The Synoptic Gospels and the Non-Canonical Acts of the Apostles," *HTR* 81 (1988) 19–36.

Brown, Raymond E. *The Birth of the Messiah: A Commentary on the Infancy Narratives in Matthew and Luke.* Garden City, N.Y.: Doubleday & Co., 1977.

————. *The Community of the Beloved Disciple.* Paramus, N.J.: Paulist, 1979.

————. *The Epistles of John.* AB 30; Garden City, N.Y.: Doubleday & Co., 1982.

————. *The Gospel According to John.* AB 29–29A; Garden City, N.Y.: Doubleday, 1966.

————. "The *Gospel of Peter* and Canonical Authority," *NTS* 33 (1987) 321–43.

————. *Jesus: God and Man.* Milwaukee: Bruce Publishing Co., 1967.

Brox, Norbert. *Die falsche Verfasserangaben: Zur Erklärung der frühchristlichen Pseudepigraphie.* SBS 79; Stuttgart: KBW, 1975.

———. " 'Doketismus'—eine Problemanzeige," *ZKG* 95 (1984) 301–14.

———. "Häresie," in *Reallexikon für Antike und Christentum: Sachwörterbuch zur Auseinandersetzung des Christentums mit der antiken Welt,* eds. Theodor Klauser et al. Stuttgart: Anton Kiersemann, 1986; 13.248–97.

———. *Offenbarung, Gnosis, und gnostischen Mythos bei Irenäus von Lyon. Salzburger patristische Studien* 1; Salzburg and Munich: Anton Pustet, 1966.

Bruce, F. F. *The Acts of the Apostles.* Grand Rapids, Mich.: Eerdmans, 1951.

———. *The Canon of Scripture.* Downers Grove, Ill: Intervarsity Press, 1988.

———. *The Epistle to the Hebrews. NICNT;* Grand Rapids, Mich.: Eerdmans, 1964.

Brun, Lyder, "Engel und Blutschweiss: Lc 22,43–44," *ZNW* 32 (1933) 265–76.

Büchsel, F. *Die Johannesbriefe.* Leipzig: A. Deichertsche, 1933.

Bultmann, Rudolf. *The Gospel of John,* tr. G. R. Beasley-Murray et al. Philadelphia: Westminster, 1971.

———. *The Johannine Epistles,* tr. R. Philip O'Hare et al. *Hermeneia*; Philadelphia: Fortress, 1973.

Burke, Gary T. "Walter Bauer and Celsus: The Shape of Late Second-Century Christianity," *SecCent* 4 (1984) 1–7.

Caird, G. B. "The Descent of the Messiah in Ephesians 4:7–11," in *SE* II, ed. F. L. Cross; TU 87; Berlin: Akademie Verlag, 1964; 535–45.

Campenhausen, Hans von. "Bearbeitungen und Interpolationen des Polykarpmartyriums," in *Sitzungsberichte der Heidelberger Akademie der Wissenschaften,* Abhandlungen 3. Heidelberg: Universitätverlag, 1957.

———. *The Formation of the Christian Bible,* tr. J. A. Baker. Philadelphia: Fortress, 1972.

———. *The Virgin Birth in the Theology of the Ancient Church,* tr. Frank Clarke. SHT 2; London: SCM, 1964.

Carroll, John T. "Luke's Crucifixion Scene," in *Reimaging the Death of the Lukan Jesus,* ed. Dennis Sylva. Frankfurt: Anton Hain, 1990; 108–24.

———. *Response to the End of History: Eschatology and Situation in Luke-Acts.* SBLDS 92; Atlanta: Scholars, 1988.

Chadwick, Henry. *Priscillian of Arila.* London: Oxford University Press, 1976.

Chadwick, Henry and Oulton, John E. L. *Alexandrian Christianity. Library of Christian Classics* II; Philadelphia: Westminster, 1954.

Charlesworth, James. *The New Testament Apocrypha and Pseudepigrapha: A Guide to Publications with Excursuses on Apocalypses.* Metuchen, N.J.: Scarecrow, 1987.

Chesnut, Glenn F. *The First Christian Histories: Eusebius, Socrates, Sozomen, Theodoret, and Evagrius,* 2nd rev. ed. Macon, Ga.: Mercer, 1986.

———. "Radicalism and Orthodoxy: The Unresolved Problem of the First Christian Histories," *ATR* 65 (1983) 292–305.

Clabeaux, John J. *A Lost Edition of the Letters of Paul: A Reassessment of the Text of the Pauline Corpus Attested by Marcion.* CBQMS 21; Washington, D.C.: Catholic Biblical Association of America, 1989.

Clark, Elizabeth. *The Origenist Controversy.* Princeton, N.J.: Princeton University Press, 1992.

Clark, Kenneth W. "Textual Criticism and Doctrine," in *Studia Paulina in honorem Johannes De Zwaan Septuagenarii.* Haarlem: De Erven F. Bohn, 1953; 52–65.

———. "The Theological Relevance of Textual Variation in Current Criticism of the Greek New Testament," *JBL* 85 (1966) 1–16.

Cohen, Shaye. *From the Maccabees to the Mishnah*. Philadelphia: Westminster, 1987.

Colwell, E. C. *Studies in Methodology in Textual Criticism of the New Testament*. NTTS 9; Grand Rapids, Mich.: Eerdmans, 1969.

Connolly, R. H. "Eusebius *Hist. Eccl.* V. 28," *JTS* (1948) 73–79.

Conybeare, F. C. "Three Doctrinal Modifications of the Text of the Gospels," *Hibbert Journal* 1 (1902–03) 96–113.

Conzelmann, Hans. *The Theology of Saint Luke*, tr. Geoffery Buswell. New York: Harper & Row, 1961.

Countryman, L. William. "Tertullian and the Regula Fidei," *SecCent* 2 (1982) 208–227.

Crossan, John Dominic. *The Cross that Spoke: The Origins of the Passion Narrative*. San Francisco: Harper & Row, 1988.

Crouzel, Henri. *Origen*, tr. A. S. Worrall. San Francisco: Harper & Row, 1989.

Curtis, F. P. G. "Luke xxiv.12 and John xx.3–10," *JTS* n.s. 22 (1971) 512–15.

Danielou, Jean. *The Theology of Jewish Christianity*, tr. John A. Baker. London: Darnton, Longman, and Todd, 1964.

Davies, J. G. "The Origins of Docetism," in *Studia Patristica* 6, ed F. L. Cross. TU, 81; Berlin: Akadamie Verlag, 1962; 13–35.

Davies, W. D. *Jewish and Pauline Studies*. Philadelphia: Fortress, 1984.

Dawson, David. *Allegorical Readers and Cultural Revision in Ancient Alexandria*. Berkeley: University of California Press, 1992.

de Boer, Martinus C. "Jesus the Baptizer: 1 John 5:5–8 and the Gospel of John," *JBL* 107 (1988) 87–106.

———. "Review of M. M. Thompson, *The Humanity of Jesus*," *CBQ* 52 (1990) 366–68.

de Bruyne, Donatien. "Le dernier verset des Actes, une variante inconnue," *RBén* 24 (1907) 403–04.

Dechow, Jon. *Dogma and Mysticism in Early Christianity: Epiphanius of Cyprus and the Legacy of Origen*. NAPSPMS 13; Macon, Ga.: Mercer, 1988.

Deichgräber, Reinhard. *Gotteshymnus und Christushymnus in der frühen Christenheit. Untersuchungen zu Form, Sprache und Stil der frühchristlichen Hymnen*. SUNT 5; Göttingen: Vandenhoeck & Ruprecht, 1967.

de Jonge, Marinus. *Christology in Context: The Earliest Christian Response to Jesus*. Philadelphia: Westminster, 1988.

Denker, Jürgen. *Die theologiegeschichtliche Stellung des Petrusevangeliums: Ein Beitrag zur Frühgeschichte des Doketismus*. Frankfurt: Peter Lang, 1975.

de Riedmatten, Henri. *Les Actes du procès de Paul de Samosate*. Fribourg: Éditions St. Paul, 1952.

Dibelius, Martin. "The Speeches of Acts and Ancient Historiography," *Studies in the Acts of the Apostles*, ed. Heinrich Greeven. London: SCM Press, 1956.

Dobschütz, Ernst von. *Eberhard Nestle's Einfuhrung in des griechische Neue Testament*, 4th Auf. Göttingen: Vandenhoeck & Ruprecht, 1923.

Drijvers, Han. *East of Antioch*. London: Variorum Reprints, 1984.

Dümmer, Jurgen. "Die Angaben über die Gnostische Literatur bei Epiphanius, Pan. Haer. 26," in *Koptologische Studien in der DDR*. Halle: Martin Luther Universität, 1965; 191–219.

Dunn, James D. G. *Christology in the Making: A New Testament Inquiry into the Origins of the Doctrine of the Incarnation*, 2nd ed. London: SCM Press, 1989.

———. "Jesus—Flesh and Spirit: An Exposition of Romans 1:3–4," *JTS* 24 (1973) 40–68.

—. *Unity and Diversity in the New Testament: An Inquiry into the Character of Earliest Christianity,* 2nd ed. London: SCM Press, 1990.

Duplacy, Jean. "La préhistoire du texte en Luc 22:43–44," in *New Testament Textual Criticism: Its Significance for Exegesis. Essays in Honour of Bruce M. Metzger,* ed. Eldon J. Epp and Gordon D. Fee. Oxford: Clarendon, 1981; 77–86.

Edwards, M. J. "Gnostics and Valentinians in the Church Fathers," *JTS* n.s. 70 (1989) 29–47.

Ehrman, Bart D. "The Cup, the Bread, and the Salvific Effect of Jesus' Death in Luke-Acts," *Society of Biblical Literature Seminar Papers.* Atlanta: Scholars Press, 1991; 576–91.

—. "1 John 4.3 and the Orthodox Corruption of Scripture," *ZNW* 79 (1988) 221–43.

—. "Methodological Developments in the Analysis and Classification of New Testament Documentary Evidence," *NovT* 29 (1987) 22–45.

—. "Review of C. Panackel, ΙΔΟΥ Ο ΑΝΘΡΩΠΟΣ," *CBQ* 52 (1990) 151.

—. "Review of S. Smalley, *1, 2, and 3 John*," *PSB* 7 (1986) 86–87.

—. "The Text of Mark in the Hands of the Orthodox," in *Biblical Hermeneutics in Historical Perspective,* ed. Mark Burrows and Paul Rorem. Philadelphia: Fortress, 1991; 19–31.

—. "The Theodotians as Corruptors of Scripture," in *Studia Patristica,* ed. E. Livingstone. Leuven: Peeters, forthcoming.

Ehrman, Bart D., Holmes, Michael W., and Fee, Gordon D. *The Text of the Fourth Gospel in the Writings of Origen.* Atlanta: Scholars Press, 1993.

Ehrman, Bart D. and Plunkett, Mark A. "The Angel and the Agony: The Textual Problem of Luke 22:43–44," *CBQ* 45 (1983) 401–16.

Elliott, J. K. "When Jesus was Apart from God: An Examination of Hebrews 2:9," *ExpTim* 83 (1972) 339–41.

Ellis, E. Earle. *The Gospel of Luke.* Century Bible; London: Marshall, Morgan, & Scott, 1974.

Elze, Martin. "Häresie und Einheit der Kirche im 2.Jahrhundert," *ZTK* 71 (1974) 389–409.

Epp, Eldon J. "The Ascension in the Textual Tradition of Luke-Acts," in *New Testament Textual Criticism: Its Significance for Exegesis. Essays in Honour of Bruce M. Metzger,* ed. Eldon J. Epp and Gordon D. Fee. Oxford: Clarendon, 1981; 131–45.

—. "The Significance of the Papyri for Determining the Nature of the New Testament Text in the Second Century: A Dynamic View of Textual Transmission," in *Gospel Traditions in the Second Century: Origins, Recensions, Text, and Transmission,* ed. William L. Petersen. South Bend, Ind.: Notre Dame University Press, 1989; 71–103.

—. *The Theological Tendency of Codex Bezae Cantabrigiensis in Acts.* SNTSMS 3; Cambridge: Cambridge University Press, 1966.

Epp, Eldon J. and Fee, Gordon D., eds. *New Testament Textual Criticism: Its Significance for Exegesis. Essays in Honour of Bruce M. Metzger.* Oxford: Clarendon, 1981.

Ernst, Joseph. *Das Evangelium nach Lukas.* RNT; Regensburg: Friederich Pustet, 1977.

Evans, E., trans. *Tertullian's Adversus Marcionem.* Oxford: Clarendon, 1972.

Farrar, F. W. *The Gospel According to Luke.* Cambridge: Cambridge University Press, 1981.

Fascher, Eric. *Textgeschichte als hermeneutisches Problem.* Halle: Max Niemeyer, 1953.

Fee, Gordon D. "Codex Sinaiticus in the Gospel of John: A Contribution to Methodology in Establishing Textual Relationships," *NTS* 15 (1968–69) 23–44.

———. *The First Epistle to the Corinthians.* NICNT; Grand Rapids, Mich.: Eerdmans, 1987.

Feneberg, Wolfgang. *Der Markusprolog: Studien zur Formbestimmung des Evangeliums.* Munich: Kosel, 1974.

Fennema, D. A. "John 1:18: 'God the Only Son,' " *NTS* 31 (1985) 124–35.

Feullet, A. "Le baptême de Jésus," *RB* 71 (1964) 333–34.

Fischer, Bonifatius. "Die Neue Testament in lateinischer Sprache," *Die alten Übersetzungen des Neuen Testaments, die Kirchenväterzitate und Lektionare,* ed. Kurt Aland. ANTF 5; Berlin: Walter de Gruyter, 1972; 1–92.

Fish, Stanley. *Doing What Comes Naturally: Change, Rhetoric, and the Practice of Theory in Literary and Legal Studies.* Durham, N.C.: Duke University Press, 1989.

———. *Is There a Text in This Class? The Authority of Interpretive Communities.* Cambridge, Mass.: Harvard University Press, 1980.

Fitzmyer, Joseph A. *The Gospel According to Luke.* AB 28–28A; Garden City, N.Y.: Doubleday, 1981/1985.

Foerster, Werner. *Gnosis: A Selection of Gnostic Texts,* tr. R. McL. Wilson. Oxford: Clarendon, 1972.

Froehlich, Karlfried. *Biblical Interpretation in the Early Church.* Philadelphia: Fortress, 1984.

Gamble, Harry. *The New Testament Canon: Its Making and Meaning.* Philadelphia: Fortress, 1985.

Garrett, Susan. *The Demise of the Devil.* Philadelphia: Fortress, 1989.

George, Augustin. "Jesus Fils de Dieu dans l'Évangile selon saint Luc," *RB* 72 (1965) 185–209; reprinted in *Études sur l'oeuvre de Luc.* Paris: Gabalda, 1978; 215–36.

———. "Le sens de la mort Jésus pour Luc," *RevBib* 80 (1973) 186–217.

Gero, Stephen. "With Walter Bauer on the Tigris: Encratite Orthodoxy and Libertine Heresy in Syro-Mesopotamian Christianity," in *Nag Hammadi, Gnosticism, and Early Christianity,* ed. Charles W. Hedrick and Robert Hodgson. Peabody, Mass.: Hendrickson, 1986; 287–307.

Globe, Alexander. "Some Doctrinal Variants in Matthew 1 and Luke 2, and the Authority of the Neutral Text," *CBQ* 42 (1980) 52–72.

———. "The Caesarean Omission of the Phrase 'Son of God' in Mark 1:1," *HTR* 75 (1982) 209–18.

Gnilka, Joachim. *Das Evangelium nach Markus.* Zürich: Benziger, 1978.

Goetchius, E. V. N. "Review of L. C. McGaughy, *Toward a Descriptive Analysis of EINAI," JBL* 95 (1976) 147–49.

Goltz, Eduard von der. *Eine textkritische Arbeit des zehnten bezw. sechsten Jahrhunderts.* Leipzig: Hinrichs, 1899.

Grant, F. C. "Where Form Criticism and Textual Criticism Overlap," *JBL* 59 (1940) 1–21.

Grant, Robert M. "Charges of Immorality Against Various Religious Groups in Antiquity," in *Studies in Gnosticism and Hellenistic Religions,* ed. R. van der Broek and M. J. Vermaseren. Leiden: Brill, 1981; 161–70.

———. *Eusebius as Church Historian.* Oxford: Clarendon, 1980.

———. "Gnostic Origins and the Basilidians of Irenaeus," *VC* 13 (1959) 121–25.

————. "Irenaeus and Hellenistic Culture," *HTR* 42 (1949) 41–51.

————. *Jesus After the Gospels: The Christ of the Second Century*. Louisville, Ky.: Westminster/John Knox, 1990.

————. "Marcion and the Critical Method," in *From Jesus to Paul: Studies in Honor of Francis Wright Beare*, ed. Peter Richardson and John C. Hurd. Waterloo, Canada: Wilfrid Laurier University, 1984; 207–15.

————. "The Use of the Early Fathers, From Irenaeus to John of Damascus," in *After the New Testament*. Philadelphia: Fortress, 1967; 20–34.

Grant, Robert M. and Tracy, David. *A Short History of the Interpretation of the Bible*, 2nd ed. Philadelphia: Fortress, 1983.

Green, Joel. "The Death of Jesus, God's Servant," in *Reimaging the Death of the Lukan Jesus*, ed. Dennis Sylva. Frankfurt: Anton Hain, 1990; 1–28.

Greer, Rowan. "The Dog and the Mushrooms: Irenaeus's View of the Valentinians Reassessed," in *The Rediscovery of Gnosticism*, ed. Bentley Layton. Leiden: Brill, 1980; I. 146–71.

Grundmann, Walter. *Das Evangelium nach Lukas*. THKNT III; Berlin: Evangelische Verlaganstalt, 1961.

Haenchen, Ernst. *The Acts of the Apostles: A Commentary*, rev. tr. R. McL. Wilson. Philadelphia: Westminster, 1971.

————. *Das Johannesevangelium*. Tübingen: J. C. B. Mohr (Paul Siebeck), 1980.

Hanson, R. P. C. *Allegory and Event: A Study of the Sources and Significance of Origen's Interpretation of Scripture*. Richmond, Va.: John Knox Press, 1959.

Harnack, Adolf von. "Die Reden Pauls von Samosata an Sabinus (Zenobia?) und seine Christologie." SPAW; Berlin, 1924; 130–51.

————. *History of Dogma*, tr. Neil Buchanan. New York: Dover, 1961.

————. *Marcion: Das Evangelium vom fremden Gott*, 2nd ed., Leipzig: J. C. Hinrichs, 1924; (partial) English translation by John E. Steely and Lyle D. Bierma, *Marcion: The Gospel of the Alien God*. Durham, N.C.: Labyrinth Press, 1990.

————. "Probleme im Texte der Leidengeschichte Jesu," in *Studien zur Geschichte des Neuen Testaments und der alten Kirche*, vol. I, *Zur neutestamentlichen Textkritik*. Berlin: Walter de Gruyter, 1931; 86–104.

————. "Zur Textkritik und Christologie der Schriften Johannes," *Studien zur Geschichte des Neuen Testaments und der alten Kirche*, vol I, *Zur neutestamentlichen Textkritik*. Berlin: Walter de Gruyter, 1931; 115–27.

————. "Zwei alte dogmatische Korrekturen im Hebräerbrief," in *Studien zur Geschichte des Neuen Testaments und der alten Kirche*, vol. I, *Zur neutestamentlichen Textkritik*. Berlin: Walter de Gruyter, 1931; 235–52.

Harrington, Daniel. "The Reception of Walter Bauer's *Orthodoxy and Heresy in Earliest Christianity* During the Last Decade," *HTR* 73 (1980) 289–98.

Harris, J. Rendel. "New Points of View in Textual Criticism," *Expositor*, 8th Ser., 7 (1914) 316–34.

————. *Side-Lights on New Testament Research*. London: Kingsgate Press, 1908.

————. "Was the Diatesseron Anti-Judaic?" *HTR* 18 (1925) 103–09.

Harris, William V. *Ancient Literacy*. Cambridge, Mass.: Harvard University Press, 1989.

Hay, David M. *Glory at the Right Hand: Psalm 110 in Early Christianity*. SBLMS 18; Nashville, Tenn.: Abingdon, 1973.

Head, Peter M. "A Text-Critical Study of Mark 1.1 'The Beginning of the Gospel of Jesus Christ,'" *NTS* 37 (1991) 621–29.

Hedrick, Charles W. and Hodgson, Robert, eds. *Nag Hammadi, Gnosticism, and Early Christianity*. Peabody, Mass.: Hendrickson, 1986.

Hennecke, Edgar. *Neutestamentliche Apokryphen in deutscher Übersetzung*, ed. W. Schneemelcher. 2 Bds. 6th Auf., Tübingen: J. C. B. Mohr (Paul Siebeck), 1991; English translation by R. McL. Wilson. *The New Testament Apocrypha*, vol. 1, 2nd ed. Louisville Ky.: Westminster/John Knox, 1991; vol. 2, Philadelphia: Westminster, 1963.

Henrichs, Albert. "Pagan Ritual and the Alleged Crimes of the Early Christians," in *Kyriakon: Festschrift Johannes Quasten*, ed. Patrick Granfield and Josef A. Jungmann. Münster: Aschendorff, 1970; 1. 18–35.

Heron, A. I. C. "The Interpretation of 1 Clement in Walter Bauer's *Rechtgläubigkeit und Ketzerei im ältesten Christentum*," *Ekklesiastikos Pharos* 55 (1973) 517–45.

Hilgenfeld, Adolf. *Die Ketzergeschichte des Urchristentums*. Hildesheim: Georg Olms, 1968; reprint of Leipzig, 1884.

Hoffmann, R. Joseph. *Marcion: On the Restitution of Christianity. An Essay on the Development of Radical Paulinist Theology in the Second Century*. Chico, Calif.: Scholars, 1984.

Hofius, Otfried. "Der in des Vaters Schoβ ist," *ZNW* 80 (1989) 163–71.

Holmes, Michael W. "Early Editorial Activity and the Text of Codex Bezae in Matthew." Unpublished Ph.D. dissertation, Princeton Theological Seminary, 1984.

Hort, F. J. A. *Two Dissertations*. London: Macmillan, 1876.

Hort, F. J. A. and Westcott, B. F. *The New Testament in the Original Greek*, 2 vols. New York: Harper and Brothers, 1882.

Howard, George. "The Gospel of the Ebionites," *ANRW* II, 25.5 (1988) 4034–53.

Howard, Wilbert F. "The Influence of Doctrine upon the Text of the New Testament," *The London Quarterly and Halborn Review* 166 (1941) 1–16.

Jenkins, C. "Origen on 1 Corinthians," *JTS* 10 (1909) 29–51.

Jeremias, Joachim. *The Eucharistic Words of Jesus*, tr. A. Ehrhardt. Oxford: Basil Blackwell, 1955.

———. "παῖς," *TDNT*, V. 687.

Johnson, Marshall D. *The Purpose of the Biblical Genealogies: With Special Reference to the Setting of the Genealogies of Jesus*. SNTSMS, 8; Cambridge: Cambridge University Press, 1969.

Joly, Robert. *Le dossier d'Ignace d'Antioche*. Bruxelles: Éditions de l'Université de Bruxelles, 1979.

Jonas, Hans. *The Gnostic Religion: The Message of the Alien God and the Beginnings of Christianity*, 2nd ed. Boston: Beacon, 1963.

Kaestli, Jean-Daniel and Wermelinger, Otto, eds. *Le canon de l'Ancien Testament. Sa formation et son histoire*. Geneva: Labor et Fides, 1984.

Karnetzki, Manfred. "Textgeschichte als Überlieferungsgeschichte," *ZNW* 47 (1956) 170–80.

Karris, Robert J. "Luke 23:47 and the Lucan View of Jesus' Death," in *Reimaging the Death of the Lukan Jesus*, ed. Dennis Sylva. Frankfurt: Anton Hain, 1990; 68–78.

Käsemann, Ernst. *Commentary on Romans*, tr. Geoffrey W. Bromiley. Grand Rapids, Mich.: Eerdmans, 1980.

———. *The Testament of Jesus: A Study of the Gospel of John in the Light of Chapter 17*, tr. Gerhard Krodel. Philadelphia: Fortress, 1968.

Kazmierski, Carl. *Jesus the Son of God: A Study of the Markan Tradition and Its Redaction by the Evangelist*. Würzburg: Echter, 1979.

Keck, Leander. "The Spirit and the Dove," *NTS* 17 (1970–72) 41–67.

Kilpatrick, George. "Atticism and the Text of the Greek New Testament," in *Neutestamentliche Aufsätze* (*Festschrift* for J. Schmid), ed. J. Blinzler et al. Regensburg, 1963; reprinted in *The Principles and Practice of New Testament Textual Criticism: Collected Essays of G. D. Kilpatrick*, ed. J. K. Elliott. Leuven: Leuven University Press, 1990; 19–24.

Kingsbury, Jack. *The Christology of Mark's Gospel*. Philadelphia: Fortress, 1983.

Klijn, A. F. J. "Das Hebraer- und Nazoraerevangelium," *ANRW*, II, 25.5 (1988) 3997–4033.

Klijn, A. F. J. and Reininck, G. J. *Patristic Evidence for Jewish-Christian Sects*. Leiden: Brill, 1973.

Kloppenberg, John S. *The Formation of Q*. Philadelphia: Fortress, 1987.

Knox, John. *Marcion and the New Testament. An Essay in the Early History of the Canon*. Chicago: Chicago University Press, 1942.

Koester, Helmut. *Ancient Christian Gospels: Their History and Development*. London / Philadelphia: SCM Press Ltd / Trinity Press International, 1990.

———. "Gnomai Diaphoroi: The Origin and Nature of Diversification in the History of Early Christianity," *Trajectories Through Early Christianity*, eds. H. Koester and James M. Robinson. Philadelphia: Fortress, 1971; 114–57.

———. "Häretiker im Urchristentum," in *RGG* (3rd ed., 1959) III.17–21.

———. *Synoptische Überlieferung bei den apostolischen Vätern*. TU, 65; Berlin: Akademie Verlag, 1957.

Koschorke, Klaus. *Hippolyt's Ketzerbekämpfung und Polemik gegen die Gnostiker. Ein tendenzkritische Untersuchung seiner "Refutatio omnium haeresium"*. Göttinger Orientforschungen, 4; Wiesbaden: Otto Harrassowitz, 1975.

———. *Die Polemik der Gnostiker gegen des kirchliche Christendum*. NHS 12; Leiden: Brill, 1978.

Kraft, Robert A. "In Search of 'Jewish Christianity' and Its 'Theology': Problems of Definition and Methodology," *RSR* 60 (1972) 81–92.

Kramer, Werner. *Christ, Lord, Son of God*. SBT 50; Naperville, Ill.: Alec R. Allenson, 1966.

Kraus, Hans-Joachim. *Psalms 1–59: A Commentary*, tr. Hilton C. Oswald. Minneapolis: Augsburg, 1988.

Lagrange, M. -J. *Évangile selon Saint Marc*, 9th ed. Paris: J. Gabalda, 1966.

Lake, Kirsopp. *Eusebius: The Ecclesiastical History*. LCL; London / New York: William Heinemann / G. P. Putnam's Sons, 1926; 1.ix–lvi.

———. *The Historical Evidence for the Resurrection of Jesus Christ*. New York: G. P. Putnam's Sons, 1907.

———. *The Influence of Textual Criticism on the Exegesis of the New Testament*. Oxford: Parker & Son, 1904.

———. *The Text of the New Testament*, 6th ed., rev. Silva New. London: Rivingtons, 1928.

Lampe, Peter. *Die stadtrömischen Christen in den ersten beiden Jahrhunderten: Untersuchungen zur Sozialgeschichte*, 2nd ed. WUNT² 18; Tübingen: J. C. B. Mohr (Paul Siebeck), 1989.

Lane, William. *The Gospel According to Mark*. IGNTC; Grand Rapids, Mich.: Eerdmans, 1974.

Layton, Bentley. *The Gnostic Scriptures.* Garden City, N.Y.: Doubleday, 1987.

———. ed. *The Rediscovery of Gnosticism.* Leiden: Brill, 1980; 1. 146–71.

Le Boulluec, Alain. "La Bible chez les marginaux de l'orthodoxie," in *Le monde grec ancien et la Bible,* ed. Claude Mondésert. Paris: Beauchesne, 1984; 153–70.

———. *Le notion d'hérésie dans la littérature grecque IIe-IIIe siècles.* Paris: Études Augustiniennes, 1985.

Linnemann, E. "Tradition und Interpretation in Röm 1:3f," *EvT* 31 (1971) 264–76.

Longenecker, Richard N. *The Christology of Early Jewish Christianity.* London: SCM Press, 1970.

Loofs, Fridriech. *Paulus von Samosata: Eine Untersuchung zur altkirchlichen Literatur und Dogmengeschichte.* Leipzig: J. C. Hinrichs, 1924.

Lövestam, Evald. *Son and Savior.* Lund: CWK Gleerup, 1961.

Lüdemann, Gerd. "Zur Geschichte des ältesten Christentums in Rom. I. Valentin und Marcion; II. Ptolemäus und Justin," *ZNW* 70 (1979) 86–114.

Lund, N. W. *Chiasmus in the New Testament.* Chapel Hill, N.C.: University of North Carolina, 1942.

Maddox, Robert. *The Purpose of Luke-Acts,* ed. John Riches. Edinburgh: T & T Clark, 1982.

Marcus, R. A. "The Problem of Self-Definition: From Sect to Church," in *Jewish and Christian Self-Definition,* ed. Ben Meyers and E. P. Sanders. Philadelphia: Fortress, 1980; I.1–16.

Marshall, I. Howard. *Commentary on Luke.* NICNT 3; Grand Rapids, Mich.: Eerdmans, 1978.

———. *The Epistles of John.* NICNT; Grand Rapids, Mich.: Eerdmans, 1978.

Martyn, J. Louis. *History and Theology in the Fourth Gospel,* 2nd ed. Nashville, Tenn.: Abingdon, 1979.

———. *The Gospel of John in Christian History.* New York: Paulist, 1978.

Matera, Frank J. *Passion Narratives and Gospel Theologies.* New York: Paulist, 1986.

———. *What Are They Saying About Mark?* New York: Paulist, 1987.

May, Gerhard. "Ein neues Markionbild?" *TRu* 51 (1986) 404–13.

McCant, Jerry. "The Gospel of Peter: Docetism Reconsidered," *NTS* 30 (1984) 258–73.

McCue, James. "Bauer's *Rechtgläubigkeit und Ketzerei im ältesten Christentum,*" in *Orthodoxy and Heterodoxy,* ed. Johann Baptist Metz and Edward Schillebeeckx. Edinburgh: T & T Clark, 1987; 28–35.

———. "Orthodoxy and Heresy: Walter Bauer and the Valentinians," *VC* 33 (1979) 118–30.

McGaughy, L. C. *Toward a Descriptive Analysis of EINAI as a Linking Verb in New Testament Greek.* SBLDS 6; Missoula, Mont.: Scholars, 1972.

McGuckin, John A. "The Changing Forms of Jesus," in *Origeniana Quarta. Innsbrucker theologische Studien,* 19; Innsbruck: Tyrolia, 1987; 215–22.

McReynolds, Paul R. "Establishing Text Families," in *The Critical Study of Sacred Texts,* ed. Wendy D. O'Flaherty. Berkeley, Calif.: Graduate Theological Union, 1979; 97–113.

———. "John 1:18 in Textual Variation and Translation," in *New Testament Textual Criticism: Its Significance for Exegesis. Essays in Honour of Bruce M. Metzger,* ed. Eldon J. Epp and Gordon D. Fee. Oxford: Clarendon, 1981; 105–18.

Meade, David. *Pseudepigrapha and Canon.* Tübingen: J. C. B. Mohr (Paul Siebeck), 1986.

Meeks, Wayne. "The Man from Heaven in Johannine Sectarianism," *JBL* 91 (1972) 44–72.

Menoud, P. H. "The Western Text and the Theology of Acts," *Studiorum Novi Testamenti Societas,* Bulletin 2 (1951) 19–32.

Metzger, Bruce M. *The Canon of the New Testament: Its Origin, Development, and Significance.* Oxford: Clarendon, 1987.

———. *The Early Versions of the New Testament: Their Origin, Transmission, and Limitations.* Oxford: Clarendon, 1977.

———. "Literary Forgeries and Canonical Pseudepigrapha," *JBL* 91 (1972) 3–24.

———. *Manuscripts of the Greek Bible: An Introduction to Palaeography.* New York: Oxford University Press, 1981.

———. "The Text of Matthew 1:16," in *Studies in New Testament and Early Christian Literature: Essays in Honor of Allen P. Wikgren,* ed. David E. Aune. Leiden: Brill, 1972; 16–24.

———. *The Text of the New Testament: Its Transmission, Corruption, and Restoration,* 3rd ed. New York: Oxford, 1991.

———. *A Textual Commentary on the Greek New Testament.* Stuttgart: United Bible Societies, 1971.

Metzger, Wolfgang. *Der Christushymnus 1. Timotheus 3,16: Fragment einer Homologie der paulinischen Gemeinden.* Arbeiten zur Theologie, 62; Stuttgart: Calwer, 1979.

Michaelis, Wilhelm. *Das Neue Testament verdeutscht und erläufert.* Leipzig, 1935.

Moody, Dale. "God's Only Son: The Translation of John 3:16 in the Revised Standard Version," *JBL* 72 (1953) 213–16.

Muddiman, John. "A Note on Reading Luke xxiv.12," *ETL* 48 (1972) 542–48.

Musurillo, H., ed. *The Acts of the Christian Martyrs.* Oxford: Clarendon, 1972.

Nautin, Pierre. *Origène: sa vie et son oeuvre.* Paris: Beauchesne, 1977.

Neirynck, Franz. "Lc xxiv 12: Les témoins du texte occidental," in *Miscellanea neotestamentica: Studia ad Novum Testamentum,* ed. T. Baarda et al. NovTSup 47–48; Leiden: Brill, 1978; 1. 45–60.

———. "The Uncorrected Historical Present in Lk. xxiv.12," *ETL* 48 (1972) 548–53.

Neufeld, Vernon. *The Earliest Christian Confessions.* Leiden: E. J. Brill, 1963.

Neuschäfer, Bernard. *Origenes als Philologe.* Schweizerische Beiträge zur Altertumswissenschaft; Basel: Friedrich Reinhardt, 1987.

Neyrey, Jerome. *The Passion According to Luke: A Redaction Study of Luke's Soteriology.* New York: Paulist, 1985.

Norris, Frederick W. "Asia Minor Before Ignatius: W. Bauer Reconsidered," in *Studia Evangelica 7,* ed. Elizabeth A. Livingstone; TU 126, Berlin: Akademie-Verlag, 1982; 365–77.

———. "Ignatius, Polycarp, and 1 Clement: Walter Bauer Reconsidered," *VC* 30 (1976) 23–44.

———. "Paul of Samosata: *Procurator Ducenarius,*" *JTS* n.s. 35 (1984) 50–70.

Osborn, Eric. "Reason and the Rule of Faith in the Second Century A.D." in *The Making of Orthodoxy: Essays in Honour of Henry Chadwick,* ed. Rowan Williams. Cambridge: Cambridge University Press, 1989; 40–61.

Osburn, Carroll D. "The Text of 1 Corinthians 10:9," in *New Testament Exegesis: Its Significance for Exegesis. Essays in Honour of Bruce M. Metzger,* ed. Gordon D. Fee and Eldon Jay Epp. Oxford: Clarendon, 1981; 201–12.

Pagels, Elaine. "Gnostic and Orthodox Views of Christ's Passion: Paradigms for the Christian's Response to Persecution?" in *Rediscovering Gnosticism,* ed. Bentley Layton. Leiden: Brill, 1980; I. 262–83.

————. *The Gnostic Gospels.* New York: Random, 1976.

————. *The Gnostic Paul: Gnostic Exegesis of the Pauline Letters.* Philadelphia: Fortress, 1975.

————. *The Johannine Gospel in Valentinian Exegesis: Heracleon's Commentary on John.* Nashville, Tenn.: Abingdon, 1973.

————. "Visions, Appearances, and Apostolic Authority: Gnostic and Orthodox Traditions," in *Gnosis: Festschrift für Hans Jonas,* ed. B. Aland. Göttingen: Vandenhoeck and Ruprecht, 1978; 415–30.

Painter, John. "The 'Opponents' in 1 John," *NTS* 32 (1986) 48–71.

Panackel, Charles. ΙΔΟΥ Ο ΑΝΘΡΩΠΟΣ: *An Exegetico-Theological Study of the Text in the Light of the Use of the Term* ΑΝΘΡΩΠΟΣ *Designating Jesus in the Fourth Gospel.* Analecta Gregoriana 251; Rome: Gregorian University, 1988.

Parsons, Mikeal. "A Christological Tendency in $\mathfrak{p}^{75}$," *JBL* 105 (1986) 463–79.

————. *The Departure of Jesus in Luke-Acts: The Ascension Narratives in Context.* JSNTSup 21; Sheffield: JSOT Press, 1987.

Pearson, Birger. "Anti-Heretical Warnings in Codex IX from Nag Hammadi," in *Essays on the Nag Hammadi Texts in Honour of Pahor Labib,* ed. M. Krause. NHS 6; Leiden: Brill, 1975; 145–54.

————. *Gnosticism, Judaism, and Egyptian Christianity.* Minneapolis: Fortress, 1990.

Pepin, Jean. *La tradition de l'allégorie: de Philon d'Alexandrie à Dante.* Paris: Études Augustiniennes, 1987.

————. *Myth et allégorie: Les origines grecques et les contestations Judéo-Chrétiennes.* Aubier: Montaigne, 1958.

Petersen, William. "Textual Evidence of Tatian's Dependence upon Justin's 'ΑΠΟΜ-ΝΗΜΟΝΕΥΜΑΤΑ," *NTS* 36 (1990) 512–34.

Petzer, J. H. "Luke 22:19b–20 and the Structure of the Passage," *NovTest* 3 (1984) 249–52.

————. "Style and Text in the Lucan Narrative of the Institution of the Lord's Supper," *NTS* 37 (1991) 113–29.

Piper, Otto. "1 John and the Primitive Church," *JBL* 66 (1947) 443–44.

Plooij, Daniel. "The Ascension in the 'Western' Textual Tradition," *Medeleelingen der Koninklijke Akademie van Wetenschappen, Afdeeling Letterkunde* 67 A, 2 (1929) 39–58.

Pollard, T. E. *Johannine Christology and the Early Church.* Cambridge: Cambridge University Press, 1970.

Pritz, Ray A. *Nazarene Jewish Christianity.* Jerusalem / Leiden: Magnes / Brill, 1988.

Rahlfs, Alfred. ("Mitteilungen") *TLZ* 40 (1915) 525.

Rese, Martin. "Zur Problematik von Kurz- und Langtext in Luk xxii.17ff," *NTS* 22 (1975) 15–31.

Rice, George E. "The Alteration of Luke's Tradition by the Textual Variants in Codex Bezae." Unpublished Ph.D. dissertation, Case Western Reserve University, 1974.

————. "Lk. 3:22–38 in Codex Bezae: The Messianic King," *AUSS* 17 (1979) 203–08.

————. "Western Non-Interpolations: A Defense of the Apostolate," in *Luke-Acts: New Perspectives from the SBL Seminar,* ed. Charles H. Talbert. New York: Crossroad, 1984; 1–16.

Richard, Earl. "Jesus' Passion and Death in Acts," in *Reimaging the Death of the Lukan Jesus,* ed. Dennis Sylva. Frankfurt: Anton Hain, 1990; 125–52.

Richards, William Larry. *The Classification of the Greek Manuscripts of the Johannine Epistles. SBLDS* 35; Missoula, Mont.: Scholars, 1977.

Richardson, Cyril. *Early Christian Fathers.* New York: Macmillan, 1970.

Riddle, Donald Wayne. "Textual Criticism as a Historical Discipline," *ATR* 18 (1936) 220–33.

Rius-Camps, J. *The Four Authentic Letters of Ignatius, the Martyr. Orientalia Christiana Analecta,* 213; Rome: Pontificium Institutum Orientalium Studiorum, 1979.

Roberts, C. H. *Manuscript, Society and Belief in Early Christian Egypt.* London: Oxford University Press, 1979.

Robinson, James M., ed. *The Nag Hammadi Library in English,* 3rd ed. San Francisco: Harper & Row, 1988.

Robinson, John A. T. "The Earliest Christology of All?" *JTS* 7 (1956) 177–89.

Robinson, Thomas. *The Bauer Thesis Examined: The Geography of Heresy in the Early Christian Church.* Lewiston, N.Y.: Edwin Mellen, 1989.

Royse, James A. "Scribal Habits in the Transmission of New Testament Texts," in *The Critical Study of Sacred Texts,* ed. Wendy D. O'Flaherty. Berkeley, Calif.: Graduate Theological Union, 1979; 139–61.

Rudolph, Kurt. *Gnosis: The Nature and History of Gnosticism,* tr. and ed. R. McL. Wilson. San Francisco: Harper & Row, 1983.

Sample, Robert L. "The Christology of the Council of Antioch (268 C.E.) Reconsidered," *CH* 48 (1979) 18–26.

Sanders, Jack. *The New Testament Christological Hymns.* Cambridge: Cambridge University Press, 1971.

Saunders, Ernest W. "Studies in Doctrinal Influences on the Byzantine Text of the Gospels," *JBL* 71 (1952) 85–92.

Schlier, H. "Zu Röm 1,3f," *Neues Testament und Geschichte (Festschrift* for Oscar Cullmann), ed. H. Baltersweiler and Bo Reicke. Zürich: Theologische Verlag, 1972; 207–18.

Schmeichel, Waldemar. "Does Luke Make a Soteriological Statement in Acts 20:28?" *SBLSP.* Chico, Calif.: Scholars, 1982; 501–14.

Schmid, Joseph. "Joh 1,3," *BZ* n.f. 1 (1957) 118–25.

Schmithals, Walter. *Das Evangelium nach Lukas.* Zürcher Bibelkommentare 3.1; Zürich: Theologischer Verlag, 1980.

————. *Der Römerbrief: Ein Kommentar.* Gütersloh: Gerd Mohn, 1988.

Schnackenburg, Rudolf. *Die Johannesbriefe.* HThK XIII²; Freiburg: Herder, 1963.

————. *The Gospel According to St. John,* tr. Kevin Smyth. New York: Herder and Herder, 1968.

Schoedel, William R. *Ignatius of Antioch: A Commentary on the Letters of Ignatius of Antioch. Hermeneia*; Philadelphia: Fortress, 1985.

————. "Theological Method in Irenaeus (*Adv. Haer.* 2. 25–28)," *JTS* n.s. 35 (1984) 31–49.

Schoeps, Hans Joiachim. *Jewish Christianity: Factional Disputes in the Early Church,* tr. Douglas R. A. Hare. Philadelphia: Fortress, 1969.

————. *Theologie und Geschichte des Judenchristentums.* Tübingen: J. C. B. Mohr (Paul Siebeck), 1949.

Scholer, David M. *Nag Hammadi Bibliography 1948–1969.* NHS 1; Leiden: Brill, 1971; updated annually as "Bibliographia Gnostica: Supplementum," *NovT.*

Schrenke, G. "ἐκλέγομαι," *TDNT* IV, 144–76.

Schürmann, H. "Lk 22, 19b–20 als ursprüngliche Textüberlieferung," *Bib* 32 (1951) 364–92; 522–41.

Schweizer, Eduard. "Concerning the Speeches in Acts," *Studies in Luke-Acts,* ed. Leander E. Keck and J. Louis Martyn. Fortress: Philadelphia, 1980.

———. "Röm. 1:3f und der Gegensatz von Fleisch und Geist vor und bei Paulus," *EvT* 15 (1955) 563–71.

Senior, Donald. *The Passion of Jesus in the Gospel of Luke.* Wilmington, Del.: Michael Glazier, 1989.

Sevrin, Jean-Marie, ed. *The New Testament in Early Christianity: La réception des écrits néotestamentaires dans le christianisme primitif.* BETL 86; Leuven: University Press, 1989.

Simon, Marcel. "From Greek Haeresis to Christian Heresy," in *Early Christian Literature and the Classical Intellectual Tradition: in Honorem Robert M. Grant,* ed. William R. Schoedel and Robert L. Wilken. Paris: Éditions Beauchesne, 1979; 101–16.

Slomp, Jan. "Are the Words 'Son of God' in Mark 1.1 Original?" *BT* 28 (1977) 143–50.

Slusser, Michael. "Docetism: A Historical Definition," *SecCent* 3 (1981) 163–72.

———. "The Scope of Patripassianism," in *Studia Patristica,* vol. 17; ed. Elizabeth A. Livingstone. Oxford: Pergamon Press, 1982; I.169–75.

Smalley, Stephen S. *1, 2, and 3 John. Word Biblical Commentary,* 51; Waco, Tex.: Word Books, 1984

Smith, D. Moody. *Johannine Christianity: Essays on its Setting, Sources, and Theology.* Columbia, S.C.: University of South Carolina, 1984.

Smith, Morton. "The History of the Term Gnostikos," in *The Rediscovery of Gnosticism,* ed. Bentley Layton. Leiden: Brill, 1981; II.796–807.

Snodgrass, Klijn. "Western Non-Interpolations," *JBL* 91 (1972) 369–79.

Soards, Marion L. *The Passion According to Luke: The Special Material of Luke 22.* JSNTSup 14; Sheffield: JSOT Press, 1987.

Soden, Hermann von. *Die Brief an die Kolosser, Epheser, Philemon.* HKNT 3; Freiburg: J.C.B. Mohr (Paul Siebeck), 1891.

Speyer, Wolfgang. *Die literarische Fälschung im heidnischen und christlichen Altertum. Ein Versuch ihrer Deutung.* HKAW 1, 2; Münich: Beck, 1971.

———. "Religiose Pseudepigraphie und literarische Fälschung im Altertum," *JAC* 8/ 9 (1965/66) 88–125.

———. "Zu den Vorwürfen der Heiden gegen die Christen," *Jahrbuch fur Antike und Christentum* 6 (1963) 129–35.

Stimpfle, Alois. *Blinde sehen: Die Eschatologie im traditionsgeschichtlichen Prozeß des Johannesevangeliums.* Berlin: Walter de Gruyter, 1990.

Streeter, B. F. *The Four Gospels: A Study of Origins,* 5th impression. London: Macmillan, 1936.

Suleiman, Susan R. and Crosman, Inge eds. *The Reader in the Text: Essays on Audience and Interpretation.* Princeton: N.J.: Princeton University Press, 1980.

Sylva, Dennis, ed. *Reimaging the Death of the Lukan Jesus. Theologie Bonner biblische Beiträge* 73; Frankfurt: Anton Hain, 1990.

———. "The Temple Curtain and Jesus' Death in the Gospel of Luke," *JBL* 105 (1986) 239–50.

Tate, J. "Plato and Allegorical Interpretation," *Classical Quarterly* 23 (1929) 142–54 and 24 (1930) 1–10.

Taylor, Joan E. "The Phenomenon of Early Jewish-Christianity: Reality or Scholarly Invention?" *VC* 44 (1990) 313–34.

Taylor, Vincent. *The Gospel According to St. Mark*. London: Macmillan & Co, 1953.

Telfer, W. "The Form of a Dove," *JTS* 29 (1928) 238–42.

Thiele, W. ed. *Vetus Latina*. Freiburg: Herder, 1956.

Thompkins, Jane, ed. *Reader-Response Criticism: From Formalism to Post-Structuralism*. Baltimore: Johns Hopkins University Press, 1980.

Thompson, Marianne Meye. *The Humanity of Jesus in the Fourth Gospel*. Philadelphia: Fortress, 1988.

Torjesen, Karen. *Hermeneutical Procedure and Theological Method in Origen's Exegesis*. Berlin: Walter de Gruyter, 1986.

Torrey, C. C. *Documents of the Primitive Church*. New York: Harper, 1941.

Trigg, Joseph W. *Origen: The Bible and Philosophy in the Third-Century Church*. Atlanta: John Knox, 1983.

Trites, Allison A. "The Transfiguration in the Theology of Luke: Some Redactional Links," in *The Glory of Christ in the New Testament: Studies in Christology, in Memory of George Bradford Caird*, ed. L. D. Hurst and N. T. Wright. Oxford: Clarendon, 1987; 71–81.

Tröger, Karl Wolfgang. "Doketistische Christologie in Nag-Hammadi-Texten: Ein Beitrag zum Doketismus in frühchristlicher Zeit," *Kairos* 19 (1977) 45–52.

Tuckett, C., ed. *The Messianic Secret*. Philadelphia: Fortress, 1983.

Turner, C. H. "A Textual Commentary on Mark 1," *JTS* 28 (1926–27) 145–58.

Turner, H. E. W. *The Pattern of Christian Truth: A Study in the Relations between Orthodoxy and Heresy in the Early Church*. London: A. R. Mowbray, 1954.

Turner, Nigel. *Grammar of New Testament Greek* (James Hope Moulton), vol. III, *Syntax*. Edinburgh: T & T Clark, 1963.

Ulansey, David. "The Heavenly Veil Torn: Mark's Cosmic *Inclusio*," *JBL* 110 (1991) 123–25.

Untergaßmair, Franz Georg. *Kreuzweg und Kreuzigung Jesu: ein Beitrag zur lukanischen Redaktionsgeschichte und zur Frage nach der lukanischen "Kreuzestheologie."* *Paderborner theologische Studien* 10; Paderborn: Ferdinand Schöningh, 1980.

Vaganay, Leon. *An Introduction to the Textual Criticism of the New Testament*, tr. B. V. Miller. London: Sands & Co., 1937; French original, 1934.

Vallée, Gérard. *A Study in Anti-Gnostic Polemics: Irenaeus, Hippolytus, and Epiphanius*. Studies in Christianity and Judaism 1; Waterloo, Ontario: Wilfred Laurier University, 1981.

van den Broek, R. "The Present State of Gnostic Studies," *VC* 37 (1983) 41–71.

van der Geest, J. E. L. *Le Christ et l'ancien testament chez Tertullian*. Nijmegen: Dekker & van de Vegt, 1972.

Visotzky, Burton L. "Overturning the Lamp," *Journal of Jewish Studies*, 38 (1987) 72–80.

———. "Prolegomenon to the Study of Jewish Christianities in Rabbinic Literature," *Association for Jewish Studies Review* 14 (1989) 47–70.

Vogels, Heinrich. *Handbuch der Textkritik des Neuen Testaments*, 2nd ed. Bonn: P. Hanstein, 1955.

Waszink, J. H. "Tertullian's Principles and Methods of Exegesis," in *Early Christian Literature and the Classical Intellectual Tradition: in Honorem Robert M. Grant*, ed. William R. Schoedel and Robert L. Wilken. Paris: Éditions Beauchesne, 1979; 17–31.

Watson, Francis. "Is John's Christology Adoptionistic?" in *The Glory of Christ in the New Testament: Studies in Christology, in Memory of George Bradford Caird,* ed. L. D. Hurst and N. T. Wright. Oxford: Clarendon, 1987; 113–24.

Weeden, Theodore. *Mark: Traditions in Conflict.* Philadelphia: Fortress, 1971.

Weigandt, Peter. "Der Doketismus im Urchristentum und in der theologischen Entwicklung des zweiten Jahrhunderts," 2 vols. Unpublished Ph.D. dissertation, Heidelberg, 1961.

Weiss, Johannes. *Das Urchristentum.* Göttingen: Vandenhoeck & Ruprecht, 1917.

Wengst, Klaus. *Christologische Formeln und Lieder des Urchristentums.* Gütersloh: Mohn, 1972.

———. *Häresie und Orthodoxie im Spiegel des ersten Johannesbrief.* Gütersloh: Mohn, 1976.

Wilckens, Ulrich. *Der Brief an der Römer.* EKKNT VI/1; Köln: Benzinger, 1978.

———. *Die Missionsrede der Apostelgeschichte.* WMANT 5; Neukirchen: Neukirchener Verlag, 1963.

Wiles, M. F. "Origen as Biblical Scholar," in *The Cambridge History of the Bible,* ed. P. R. Ackroyd and C. F. Evans. Cambridge: Cambridge University Press, 1970; 1. 454–89.

———. "Person or Personification? A Patristic Debate about Logos," in *The Glory of Christ in the New Testament: Studies in Christology, in Memory of George Bradford Caird,* ed. L. D. Hurst and N. T. Wright. Oxford: Clarendon, 1987; 281–89.

Wilken, Robert L. *The Christians as the Romans Saw Them.* New Haven, Conn.: Yale University Press, 1984.

———. "The Homeric Cento in Adversus Haereses I, 9, 4," *VC* 21 (1967) 25–33.

Williams, C. S. C. *Alterations to the Text of the Synoptic Gospels and Acts.* Oxford: Basil Blackwell, 1951.

Williams, David Salter. "Reconsidering Marcion's Gospel," *JBL* 108 (1989) 477–96.

Williams, Rowan, ed. *The Making of Orthodoxy: Essays in Honour of Henry Chadwick.* Cambridge: Cambridge University Press, 1989.

Williamson, G. A. *Eusebius: The History of the Church from Christ to Constantine,* rev. and ed. Andrew Louth. London: Penguin, 1989.

Wilson, Stephen G. "Marcion and the Jews," in *Anti-Judaism in Early Christianity,* vol. 2: *Separation and Polemic,* ed. Stephen G. Wilson. *Studies in Christianity and Judaism,* 2; Waterloo Canada: Wilfrid Laurier University, 1986; 45–58.

Wimsatt, W. K. *The Verbal Icon: Studies in the Meaning of Poetry.* Lexington: University of Kentucky Press, 1954.

Wisse, Frederik, "Die Sextus-Sprüche und das Probleme der gnostischen Ethik," in *Zum Hellenismus in der Schriften von Nag Hammadi,* eds. A. Böhlig and F. Wisse. Göttinger Orientforschung, VI. 2; Wiesbaden: Otto Harrasowitz, 1975; 55–86.

———. "The Epistle of Jude in the History of Heresiology," in *Essays on the Nag Hammadi Texts in Honour of Alexander Böhlig,* ed. Martin Krause. NHS III; Leiden: Brill, 1972; 133–43.

———. "The Nag Hammadi Library and the Heresiologists," *VC* 25 (1971) 205–23.

———. "The Nature and Purpose of Redactional Changes in Early Christian Texts: The Canonical Gospels," in *The Gospel Traditions in the Second Century:*

Origins, Recensions, Text, and Transmission, ed. William L. Petersen. South Bend, Ind.: Notre Dame University Press, 1989; 46–47.

———. "The Use of Early Christian Literature as Evidence for Inner Diversity and Conflict," in *Nag Hammadi, Gnosticism, and Early Christianity.* ed. Charles W. Hedrick and Robert Hodgson. Peabody, Mass.: Hendrickson, 1986; 177–90.

Wordsworth, J. and White, H. J. *Novum Testamentum Domini Nostri Jesu Christi Latine secundum editionem Sancti Heironymi.* Oxford: Clarendon, 1949.

Wright, Leon E. *Alterations of the Words of Jesus: As Quoted in the Literature of the Second Century.* Cambridge, Mass.: Harvard University Press, 1952.

Yamauchi, Edwin M. "The Crucifixion and Docetic Christology," *Concordia Theological Quarterly* 46 (1982) 1–20.

Zahn, Theodor. *Das Evangelium des Lucas.* Leipzig: A. Deichert, 1913.

———. *Das Evangelium des Matthäus,* 2nd ed. Leipzig: A. Deichert, 1905.

Zehnle, Richard. "The Salvific Character of Jesus' Death in Lucan Soteriology," *TS* 30 (1969) 420–44.

Zuntz, Günther. *The Text of the Epistles: A Disquisition upon the* Corpus Paulinum. Schweich Lectures, 1946; London: Oxford University, 1953.

Index of Scripture

303

Index of Modern Authors

Index of Subjects and Ancient Sources